Fictioning Namibia as a Space of Desire

Renzo Baas

Fictioning Namibia as a Space of Desire
An Excursion into the Literary Space of Namibia During Colonialism, Apartheid and the Liberation Struggle

Basler Afrika Bibliographien 2019

©2019 The author
©2019 Basler Afrika Bibliographien

Basler Afrika Bibliographien
Namibia Resource Centre & Southern Africa Library
Klosterberg 23
PO Box 2037
CH-4051 Basel
Switzerland
www.baslerafrika.ch

The Basler Afrika Bibliographien is part of the Carl Schlettwein Foundation.

All rights reserved.

Cover photo: The Unknown Soldier at Heroes' Acre; source: Namibian Tourism Board

ISBN 978-3-906927-08-4
ISSN 2296-6986

Contents

1. Introduction — 1
   - Producing Certain Spaces — 2
   - Literature on and about Namibia — 4
   - Literature List — 16
   - Terms and Conditions — 22
   - Looking Forward — 31

2. Social and Literary Space — 35
   - From Relative to Social Space — 41
   - The Social Space of Henri Lefebvre — 56
   - Social Space and Literary Space — 73

3. The Colonial Era: War, Toil, and Diamonds — 85
   - Introduction to the Texts — 93
   - Emptied Landscapes — 98
   - The Garden — 122
   - The *White* Female Colonialist — 136

4. The Apartheid Era: The Trust in Maps and Guns — 152
   - Introduction to the Texts — 161
   - Emptied Landscapes (?) — 170
   - Technologies of Conquest and Domination — 179
   - (De)Constructing the *White* Male Explorer — 188

5. The Namibian Moment: Learning to Sing — 196
   - Introduction to the Text — 197
   - Main Spaces of the Narrative — 201
   - Resistance and Disobedience — 218
   - The Resistance of One, the Resistance of Many — 235
   - Merging the Past, Present, and Future — 239

6. Conclusion — 247
   - Producing the 'Other' (and oneself) — 249
   - A Colonial Network of Spaces and Strategies — 256

The Metropole in Crisis	258
A Root of the Metropolitan Crisis	263
Monologic and Dialogic Narratives	266

Bibliography 271

Index 283

Acknowledgements

As any doctoral student can confirm, it is no easy task to start and finish a PhD. It takes time and preparation, additions and subtractions, new influences and ideas. It takes dedication, a will to finish. All of these things don't come by themselves, or overnight, or in the last sip of the midnight espresso. They come from the people you spend time with, the people you love, the people who decided – sometimes against their better judgement – to join you on your journey of late nights, late mornings, stressed meetings, and missed deadlines. Borrowed-and-never-returned books. Opened-and-shared wines. The great ideas that did not make it into the final version. The regrets thereof. The sweat on the day of submission. It's all worth it when the thesis becomes a book you can hold. When it becomes a way of saying thank you to everyone that helped along the way who made the book what it is.

To Henri and Karim Gunkel, who are my motivation, my inspiration, and my happiness. You make me want to change myself and the world for the better, to imagine, to dream. You make me realise how lucky and fortunate I am. I cannot imagine my life without you.

To Prof. Susan Arndt, who has been there to help me think, help me improve as a person, help me grow within this crazy world. You are an amazing scholar with so much to give and share. Know that there are countless people who appreciate how beautiful you are.

To Prof. Lindy Stiebel, for the guidance, the kindness, and for always backing me. Your encouraging words kept me going and got me out of numerous slumps.

To Dr. Dag Henrichsen, who has given me a new appreciation for my home country, who has continually shown me Namibia's complexities, and its beauty.

To BIGSAS who decided to take a chance on me by providing me with a full scholarship. Without your extraordinary financial, administrative, and intellectual support, this book would not have been possible. Thank you also to the BIGSAS community – PhD candidates, alumni, the administrative staff, the Senior Researchers – which is always warm and welcoming.

To my parents, Werner and Ingrid Baas, who have continually backed me in all my adventures and endeavours. You are the home I can always come back to.

To Hans and Ruth Brenner, as well as Michael Brenner and Melissa Schäfer, for being my family away from home. You made difficult winters manageable and you were a constant inspiration for my work and a positive influence on my world view.

To Philipp, Laura, Vincent, Carmen, René, Stefan, Lukas, Thorsten, and Matthias. Without you, Bayreuth would not have been what is was. You made it enjoyable and livable, a place I could also call 'home'.

To Petra Kerckhoff at the Basler Afrika Bibliographien, who has been the embodiment of patience and cooperation. I am grateful to you and the BAB for giving me the opportunity to publish my thesis with you.

To the Sam Cohen Library for the valuable resources and research material I could access and integrate into my book.

To the Namibian National Archives for your unlimited patience in locating all the maps, texts, and documents that I needed for my work.

To the University of KwaZulu Natal for offering me the Postdoctoral Fellowship, which gave me the time and space to finalise this book.

1 Introduction

Then-president of Namibia, Sam Nujoma, declared in his speech at the inauguration of Heroes' Acre in Windhoek in 2005: "we are writing the history of our country from our own perspective and through our own suffering and sacrifices. The time when colonisers distorted our history is now gone forever"[1]. This powerful assertion of writing one's own history is a strong reflection of postcolonial moments in which time and space are reconfigured to reflect local temporal and spatial regimes. These regimes, violently reshaped in order to serve European expansionist and imperialist ambitions, are being reactivated in a number of contexts. In Namibia, for example, this has taken the form of a national and symbolic cemetery. Included in the cemetery are a number of anti-colonial as well as anti-apartheid leaders and personalities taken from the larger Namibian societies of the Nama, the Herero, and the Owambo. Symbolic graves of elites such as the Nama *kaptein*[2] Hendrik Witbooi, Herero *omuhona*[3] Samuel Maharero, and the Kwanyama king, Mandume Ndemufayo, amongst others, are to be found within the bounds of the Acre. A larger-than-life statue of the "Unnamed Soldier"[4] involved in the liberation struggle and armed with gun and grenade stands watch over these historic Namibian personalities. The incorporation of non-elites also speaks to the involvement of 'ordinary' Namibians in the efforts for independence and self-rule, as the inclusion of Kakurukaze Mungunda exemplifies. Heroes' Acre thus amalgamates various communities, historical eras, and persons of different socio-cultural standing.

Heroes' Acre signifies a unified effort for self-governance, evident through the collection of a number of relevant personalities who each fought for this right. The sizable tract of land set aside for this monument outside of Windhoek is testament to the Namibian government's efforts to honour and maintain the memory of those who gave their lives in the pursuit of a life free from the terrors which foreign rule inflicted. The echoes of these sacrifices are palpable today still, when one considers the genocide committed against the Herero and Nama by the German colonial forces, one of the most defining moments in Namibian history and a moment that stretches from 1904 into the present. The Old

---

[1] This and all subsequent quotes are taken from "Statement By His Excellency President Sam Nujoma On The Occasion Of The Official Inauguration Of Heroes' Acre 26 August 2002"
[2] *Kaptein* is the term given to the leaders of Nama *kommandos* (the mounted military division of a 'nation'). The *kaptein* is responsible for administrative, judicial, and social issues for each 'nation' (subgroupings of the larger Nama society). The word is an Afrikaans expression meaning "captain".
[3] *Omuhona* is the Herero term for a traditional authority, meaning 'Big Man'.
[4] Although named as such, the statue bears a very strong resemblance to ex-President Dr Sam Nujoma.

Location shooting (1959) as well as the Cassinga massacre (1978) by the South African administration under the flag of apartheid are further traumas of which the graves are a painful reminder. President Nujoma's declaration, the graves, and their production of a national narrative of resistance powerfully link the independent Namibian state to its violent past.

Producing Certain Spaces

The reworking of this violent past through the combination of the speech and the monument opens up questions concerning the state production of space and the subsequent formation of a memory and hero cult. This is first noticeable when one looks at the location of Heroes' Acre. Situated outside of Windhoek, it lies centrally within Namibia. More importantly, it is incorporated within the limits of the city of Windhoek (Namibia's capital since its 'founding' by Curt von François in 1890[5]), but lies outside of its urban core. Windhoek's history points to its fluctuating status, as it was already a centre of commerce and contention before the arrival of the German colonial regime. It later lost some of its renown to other 'capitals' such as Hornkranz (Witbooi), Okahandja (traditional seat of the Herero elites), and Walvis Bay (as a centre of trade with the Cape Colony). It is now the largest urban centre in Namibia, centralising all branches of government (judicial, executive, and legislative) as well as finance and external political bodies (embassies and consulates). Windhoek therefore takes up a very important position in the trajectory of Namibian history: first as a space of power and of accumulation, then as a competing centre of authority, and finally as the ultimate pivot of Namibian power structures.

Windhoek's progression from a competing centre of commerce and accumulation to *the* Namibian centre of official power can be summed up by Henri Lefebvre's idea concerning the dialectical relationship between the city and the countryside:

> The city state thus establishes a fixed centre by coming to constitute a hub, a privileged focal point, surrounded by peripheral areas that bear its stamp. From this moment on, the vastness of pre-existing space appears to come under the thrall of a divine order. At the same time the town seems to gather in everything which surrounds it, including the natural and the divine, and the earth's evil and good forces. As image of the universe (*imago mundi*), urban space is reflected in the rural space that it possesses and indeed in a sense *contains*. Over and above its economic, religious and political content, therefore, this relationship already embodies an element of symbolism, of image-and-reflection: the town perceives itself in its double, in its repercussions or echo; in self-affirmation, from the height of its towers, its

---

[5] Jonker Afrikaner settled in what is now known as Windhoek in 1840, but this was destroyed after battles between Herero and the Orlam Nama. The space was later revitalised by the colonial administration and became its central locale of governance.

gates and its campaniles, it contemplates itself in the countryside that it has shaped – that is to say, in its *work*. (1974/1991:235, emphasis in original)

From this quotation it becomes clear that certain features define the city. The most recognisable of these appear to be the forces of *accumulation* and *concentration*. This in turn opens up the question: What can be said to be accumulated at Heroes' Acre? The most visible and prominent elements would be the symbolic graves of Namibian heroes and heroines. These should be considered as symbolic to a certain extent as the real graves of early heroes such as Witbooi and Maharero are situated in other locations[6]. Heroes' Acre accumulates the symbolic capital of these leaders without containing their physical bodies. The Acre accumulates signifiers with their respective referents to be found somewhere else, concentrating them within a space that is highly significant within the (post)colonial memorial landscape of Namibia. However, the inclusion of these symbolic graves into the Heroes' Acre space allows for a number of significant developments. The first of these would be the foundation of a new, independent Namibia, mirrored through the consolidation of a purely Namibian historic space. This monumental(ised) space is reclaimed through the connection between the soil and the history of the included heroes and heroines. On a superficial level this is achieved by concentrating achievements and sacrifices within the cemetery. Instead of erecting statues in the heroes' and heroines' honour, graves were chosen. They are now all linked to the soil, to the earth of a 'new' Namibia, separated and yet deeply connected to German South West Africa[7] and South West Africa[8]. In other words: elites involved in the brutal and historic wars of liberation are 'planted' in the ground, fertilising the soil for the production of a new future while always being deeply connected to the past.

On a secondary level, one can consider the Herero oral tradition of praise poetry (*omutandu* singular; *omitandu* plural), in which graves play a vital role in claims for land[9]. Following this logic, as well as the incorporation of Herero *ovahona* in this space, Heroes' Acre becomes a testament to an autochthonous, locally practised, rehabilitation of ancestral lands. This practice is cemented and augmented through the introduction of non-Herero graves, amplifying these claims on a national level. This claim is articulated by the

---

[6] Hendik Witbooi's body was hidden for a long time due to fears of the corpse being found by the colonial authorities, who might have exported it to Germany as they did with a number of Nama bodies. Samuel Maharero's body was first kept in exile in Botswana and then buried in Okahandja, the ancestral burial ground of Herero elites.

[7] From here on referred to as GSWA.

[8] From here on referred to as SWA.

[9] This powerful form of landscape production will be discussed briefly in the chapter dealing with colonialist literature and in more detail in the chapter on Namibian resistance.

state through its involvement in this project. What Heroes' Acre does is to concentrate previous hero cults within its space. The inclusion of these symbolic graves can be seen as a state-controlled memorial practice, a practice that is designed and supervised by the state apparatus. The decision to construct such a monument as well as who was to be included, who was to build it, and who may (and may not) be added shows strong governmental control and intervention. The partnership with North Korea's Mansudae Overseas Projects also limits local participation and puts it in the hands of a foreign organisation. The cemetery becomes an exercise in the reproduction of state power via the doubling of graves, the governing of memorial cults, and the fostering of new diplomatic relations. All of these factors are centralised within Heroes' Acre, a national(ist) monument focussing on the resistance to overbearing and alienating activities by occupying states, but also a monument that passes its shadow across the newly-established state.

Literature on and about Namibia

Nujoma's opening utterance connects a number of relevant tropes and terms that provide the backbone for this project, which uses literature as its main tool of inquiry. This begins with questions concerning how space can be 'claimed' as an expansionist strategy and how space can be 'reclaimed' as a resistant act. Although my thesis makes use of certain post-colonial terminology and theories, and although it begins with a strong post-colonial[10] moment, I am limiting the texts under discussion to the literature that emerged between 1884 and 1989. The reason for this is my interest in the production of 'foreign' space by European metropoles through the technology of literature. Namibia as a doubly occupied territory provides a unique arena in which to do a comparative as well as a discursive analysis. This is of course not to say that other territories have not suffered the same fate but the links to imperial Germany, apartheid South Africa, the United Nations, and its neighbouring states create a dense network of competing metropoles while simultaneously allowing a local (and later nationalised) form of resistance to become apparent. All of these aspects will be discussed through the interrogation of literary texts from certain moments in Namibia's long history as a contested territory.

The question of literary space will therefore be at the core of my thesis, while the discussion of 'real' space will be used as a supplementary resource. The aim is to connect seemingly opposing concepts in order to fully understand the process of 'fictioning'[11]

---

[10] The hyphenated version of 'postcolonialism' in this thesis refers to its temporal dimension, i.e. after being a colony. I will ignore concepts such as neo-colonialism deliberately as this is a development that is outside my time frame of analysis for Namibia.

[11] A term I have borrowed from O'Sullivan (2014) and one which will receive due attention at a later stage.

in reference to metropolitan desires, fantasies, and fears. While my basis is a European theory, steeped in a European spatial discourse, certain necessary and vital aspects of this perspective will be employed in order to create an understanding of colonial, apartheid, and near-independent Namibia. Beginning with a discussion of social space and the role of the subject in reproducing space, I will proceed to a discussion of the metropole's reproduction in the colony. Having initially been set up as a binary, I will expand upon the limiting understanding of the metropole as a specific *place* (as opposed to a *space*) of power and situate it within wider networks of power. The result is that it is not Berlin or Pretoria that reproduce themselves in the mythic *terra nullius* of the colony, but that it is Germany and South Africa that do so. This expansion dislocates power from a central space and creates an arena in which the entanglements and contestations between the imperial metropole and the occupied colony can fully unfold. The imperial and expansionist project becomes a project that is not couched within political desires, but becomes a project that permeates and influences public as well as personal desires. Individual *and* national imaginings of 'unclaimed' territories develop into the driving forces behind colonialism and apartheid territorialisation.

My mode of investigation will consist of an analysis of literary space[12] and how its fictional dimension is employed as a product of the occupying nations. Colonialism and apartheid are both projects that are reliant on a combination of *Realpolitik* and subjective/personal fantasies in producing knowledge. A focus on space[13] as an engine of development – for the 'nation' and the individual – appears to be a fitting tool. Furthermore, the interrogation of colonial/apartheid space and its production conversely emphasises how this process is resisted by space-producing practices that oppose metropolitan influence. Employing literary space as a liberating technology allows for a deeper appreciation of certain spatial regimes; spatial regimes that consist of networks but that are not reliant on capitalist, colonial, or commodified reproduction. Powerful strategies such as counter-discourses[14], appropriation, performativity, and reorganisation can be identified and placed within the larger framework of resistance against the imposition of European spatial imprints.

In essence, this project focuses on two European strategies of expansion. Firstly, I am interested in the question of the power of the imagination. How do narrators and

---

[12] Literary space is the space the narrative generates in order to: a) situate the characters and their actions, and b) to push the narrative forward.
[13] This does in no way mean that I see space in opposition to time, but rather I see this as a dialectic relationship.
[14] For more on this term see Ashcroft (2001), arguing that the term "is not a separate oppositional discourse but a tactic which operates from the fractures and contradictions of discourse itself" (102), further dedicating a subsection in the chapter "Resistance" to this term.

characters engage with a landscape and a not-as-yet-territory that is alien to them? What strategies and technologies are employed in order to make them comprehensible, controllable, hospitable, and organised? How does the metropole attempt to claim and occupy these spaces symbolically and discursively? And how does this reflect metropolitan desires, fantasies, and fears? Secondly, I want to look at how ideas of 'space', 'production[15]', and 'fictioning' create a dense web of dependence and mutual influence. What modes of (re)production do the texts make use of in respect to their space-forming and space-creating narratives? What constitutes these formed and created spaces? Who has access to these spaces and their production – and why? And finally, how deeply are these processes of production themselves products of imperial and expansionist fantasies?

To counter these Eurocentric questions and to create some equilibrium concerning my discussion of social space, I will concentrate on strategies and technologies that resist the European quest for spatial production. Even though I will make use of historic moments in my analysis of this resistance, these moments will be concentrated in the Namibian novel *Born of the Sun* (1988) by Joseph Diescho and not in the colonial and apartheid novels. This has two reasons. My aim is to compare the production of *literary* space in the chosen novels, meaning that I focus on how narrators and characters engage with, imagine, and inhabit this specific type of space. Because Black/Africanist[16] characters have marginal and negligible roles, and because their internal as well as imaginative processes are not revealed, I do not want to impose any interpretations upon the text. This may carry the danger of diminishing the resistant potential I plan to locate in the Namibian novel. The colonial and apartheid texts are constructed and produced in such a way as to limit or even silence the resistant potential of the Black/Africanist characters. This is why I will focus my efforts of locating resistant acts and ideas in the Namibian novel as it creates a narrative with which to contrast and compare the power of the production of literary space. Moreover, I intend to discuss the novel as a product in itself, i.e. as a form of resistant spatial production. This is because the fictioned spaces that colonial and apartheid narratives invented can be countered using the same technology, namely literature[17].

Literature's reproduction and exploitation of language (and itself being a product of language) and its undeniable involvement in subjugation are of extreme importance. Esaïe Djomo (2011) explains this link as follows:

---

[15] I would like to lean on Lefebvre's definition of 'product' in order to link it to my use of the term 'production': "a *product* can be reproduced exactly, and is in fact the result of repetitive acts and gestures" (emphasis in original, 1974/1991:70).

[16] This is a term that will receive due attention under a different section in this chapter.

[17] This is not to say that orature cannot do the same but considering literature's special place in the imperial project, different forms of dreaming and imagining seem like an appropriate response.

> Man kolonisiert indem man die fremde Welt (eigentlich die Welt des Fremden!) bezwingt. Symbolisch wie praktisch muss der Kolonist alles Fremde in deine Sprache übersetzen, um auf diese Weise das Gefühl des Fremdseins zu überwinden, so zum Beispiel durch umbenennen des Landes: Neu Caledonia, Neuseeland, Afrique Equitorial *française*, Deutsch-Südwestafrika, usf. Man führt seine eigene Sprache und Schule ein und negiert fremde Werte und Kultur." (emphasis in original, 216)

This link has a special significance when discussed within the context of German colonisation of GSWA. Commenting on the period in GSWA between 1885 and 1889/1900, Horst Drechsel ("Die Eroberung der Kolonien"[18]), defines this period as a "Fiktion einer deutschen Kolonie" (42), because "[m]an wollte Südwestafrika behalten und mußte es daher erst einmal wirklich erobern" (39). Colonialism, fiction, and violence are discursively linked, exemplifying literature's complicity within these processes.

The Metropole and the Periphery

In hindsight it is simple to place the label of 'metanarrative' upon German colonialism and the South African system of apartheid. The resultant worldwide webs of connections and power structures as well as the adverse effects on African populations (and current legacies) support this claim. And yet it seems that this would again reproduce the idea of *white* hegemony, positioning colonialism[19] and apartheid as the be-all and end-all of the violent historic encounter between Europe and Africa. From its overbearing formulation as the dominant discourse, it places the concentration of events from the European mainland onto the African continent. This separation puts the spotlight on Africa as an allegedly passive receiver without interrogating the European desire(s) to colonise. In effect, the implementation as well as mechanisms of colonialism have received wide academic discussion while the effects 'back home' are usually only of secondary consideration. This of course does not mean that colonialism (and apartheid) have not been theorised from an internal perspective, especially since this perspective has become more and more prominent through projects such as Postcolonial Studies and New Historicism. In many cases, however, historic approaches have taken precedence, with a strong emphasis on different political developments at the centre of these discussions, such as laws and their effects, racial policies and biopolitics, capitalist/industrialist developments, and medial output such as photography and postcards. However, it seems that the question of space,

---

[18] In Stoecker, Helmut (ed). *Drang nach Afrika*. (1991).
[19] Although he refers to colonialism in general, Carrigan's discussion in essence shows how I will work with the term and what I will focus on: "Colonialism has long been legitimized through celebratory narratives, emphasizing heroic voyages of discovery, exploration, and possession, with land and ocean territories either being considered 'empty' – and therefore ripe for settlement – or in need of 'cultivation' and 'improvement,' justifying external administration and control" (in Quayson 2016:84).

or fantasies and dreams of *white* space, have taken a back seat to these initial fields of inquiry. Colonialism and apartheid will therefore be interrogated and discussed from the perspective of literary space, as space is imagined and fantasised about in fictional texts.

When I write of colonialism, I am referring to German colonialism as it emerged from the Berlin Conference of 1884/1885. I am focussing on this specific moment as it is generally considered the most intense period of 'legitimised'[20] colonialism, with the notorious conference designing a blueprint in colonising procedures. This made sure that disputes over territories could be regulated from Europe without having to wage proxy wars on the African continent (although this was not always the case). This should, however, not be read as the date on which Germany was first involved in the occupation of foreign spaces. German involvement can be traced back to the transatlantic enslavement of African peoples, as well as the setting up of peripheral territories within Africa. A comparative superficial look at the empires of Britain and France, as well as their long history in conquering foreign territories shows Germany's rather limited and belated entry into colonial overseas expansion[21]. This may be due to its relatively recent status as a (developing) world power and its infant status as a unified nation[22], while the attractiveness of the colonial project appeared to be more present in the imaginary, symbolic realm than it did in the everyday political sphere[23]. Britain's position as colonisers before Germany's formal stepping into the sphere of conquest[24], with a number of colonialists showing deep admiration for Britain's empire and its running[25], also indicates a German inferiority complex. Germany of course did harbour colonial ambitions pre-1884[26], having miniature colonies

---

[20] 'Legitimised' in the sense that the involved European powers negotiated and designed the framework and parameters in which the African continent was to be 'cut up' and divided. This was deemed as a preventative measure to what can be considered as unorganised territorial acquisition, with officially demarcated borders guaranteeing imperial sovereignty. As a consequence, land usurpation was accelerated, as was imperial violence against local populations. Atrocities committed in the Belgian Congo were replicated and reproduced in a number of other colonial territories, in some instances resulting in genocides.

[21] This belated entry into colonial expansion would later have significant effects for the rest of Europe, with colonial strategies and rhetoric employed through Germany's eastward expansion in the middle 1930s and the resultant Second World War.

[22] It was only in 1871 that Germany became a unified state, previously existing as a number of individual, autonomous city-states and smaller kingdoms.

[23] The Herero and Nama genocide committed by the German colonial forces as well the atrocities committed by Carl Peters would impact upon this initial attitude towards the colonies.

[24] In many respects, a number of Germans saw in Britain the epitome of a colonising machine. This is reflected in Germans in GSWA wishing British administration of the territory, especially and during the Herero War. Characters in *Peter Moor* and *Heim Neuland*, for example, verbalise this wish.

[25] Frenssen was an admirer of British colonial policy. See for example Rolf Meyn," Abstecher in die Kolonialliteratur" in Dohnke & Stein (1997). Furthermore, some of his characters are shown to prefer British as opposed to German control over GSWA (1907:68).

[26] Possession of far-off territories already had a place in the German imaginary even before unification in

across the globe[27], but it was the official introduction of large-scale acquisition of foreign territory with the aim of claiming it as German soil that resulted in its imperial aspirations. This rapid progression from unified state to world power meant that Berlin would ultimately be attributed the label of metropole (although significantly smaller in size in surface area, population, and influence than its main competitors London and Paris). It is at this point that I would like to point out that the label of metropole as a centre of power should not only be attributed to the capital or hub of administrative and political power. The fact that the *Deutscher Kolonialverein* was founded in Frankfurt am Main (but later incorporated into the state-owned *Deutsche Kolonialgesellschaft für Südwestafrika*); that Adolf Lüderitz, born in Bremen and operating from a Lagos-based company, was the first to purchase land on a large-scale from a Namibian leader pre-1884; and that numerous colonialist authors, explorers, and missionaries came from all over Germany, means that power was not completely centralised in Berlin[28]. It follows from this that the concept of the metropole can be broadened to include all centres of colonial interests and be expanded to include the whole of Germany. In other words, the colonial project was largely regulated from Berlin but needed other centres. In this sense, when I speak of the metropole, I am equating it with the power network in Germany and not with Berlin. Berlin is only employed as a metonym for the state. What in essence is set up as a simple binary relationship can now become a dialectical relationship, with one term or concept (metropole) having an influence on the other (colony) and vice versa.

Moving from Binary to Dialectic

In *The Production of Space* (1974/1991), Lefebvre argued that the state has a perpetual need to produce the spaces it requires in order to achieve its ultimate goals: capitalist and market maintenance and expansion. He focussed on this assertion within the relationship between the city and the countryside (as was exemplified in relation to Windhoek's development over time). While the latter supplies the former with resources (in the form of raw materials, labourers, consumers, space), the former reproduces it in its mirror image. The city effectively consumes the countryside and recreates the city within the space

---

1871. See, for example, *Der Traum vom deutschen Orient* (Malte Fuhrmann, 2006), *Drang nach Afrika* (Stoecker, ed.), *Geschichte der deutschen Kolonisation* (Cornevin, 1974; Jenny (transl.), and *Die Außenpolitik in der Ära Bismarck* (Rose, 2013).

[27] According to Horst Gründer ("Imperialismus und deutscher Kolonialismus in Afrika"), Germany was already involved in the kidnapping and shipping of enslaved people, with Prussia possessing an outpost in Ghana (Groß-Friedrichsburg) as well as in St. Thomas in the Antilles (25) (in *Namibia-Deutschland: Eine geteilte Geschichte*, 2004).

[28] Add to this list further colonialist institutions such as military academies, colonial schools, trading companies, colonial exhibitions, publishers, and so forth, and it becomes clear that Berlin cannot be seen as the only centre of influence.

of the countryside. This may take a number of guises, from the symbolic (through media, through culture, values), to the physical (through architecture, through infrastructure), to the social (through hierarchies, through capital). An analogy can be drawn between Lefebvre's city as the state-metropole, and the colony as the occupied countryside. In both cases, the focus is on accumulation (of power, of resources, of people, of space) and reproduction (of power, of culture, of citizens, of space). The city-metropole consumes the countryside-colony and reshapes it in order to achieve its ultimate objectives.

I concede that it is impossible to achieve a one-to-one comparison for this analogy, especially due to the close proximity between city and countryside (where does one end and the other begin when its official and imagined 'borders' are both porous and artificial?). The metropole is extremely far removed from most of its colonies (a three month trip via ship between Germany and GSWA is testament to this). This is not the case for apartheid incorporation of SWA, as any official borders were merely adapted or ignored entirely. However, the structural and ideological dimensions of both occupying metropoles (resource procurement, laws and regulations, the infringement of indigenous rights and living spaces) push the two systems towards each other. The literature under investigation will to a certain degree seek to prove this, with the central ambitions of the city and the metropole relatively proximate. In both cases it is a hunger for resources (abstract and concrete) and the perpetual reproduction of the means of production serving as the weapons and machine of these processes. It is the involvement of the German state – through its various institutions – which created the conditions for colonial expansion from the coast of southern Africa into the interior, consuming everything in its path and churning out various products (fantasies, desires, resources, knowledge). The South African state would go on to incorporate similar strategies, ingesting even the regions in GSWA outside of the immediate sphere of colonial influence[29]. The relationship between the city-metropole and the countryside-colony is therefore at the heart of my investigation of how the fictioning of the available spaces – and those which have to be invented – are engaged in the creation of an alien and removed space in the service of the metropole.

Producing the Space of the Colony

The metropole's accumulation of knowledge from the colony is fed by a number of resources. The most well-known of these are reports, sketches/paintings/photographs, cul-

---

[29] Very little to nothing is said about northern GSWA and SWA in any of the chosen novels. This may be due to Germany's limited infiltration of the region (it was later cordoned off), and South Africa's inability to 'empty' it of signifiers (due to the large Black population and their undeniable interaction with their landscapes).

tural artefacts, as well as statistics[30]. The most powerful form of expansionist intelligence, however, stems from an age-old instrument of world-making, namely mapping. From its origins as a representational tool of the (unknown) world and built on assumptions and fantasies, the map became an indispensable weapon of control. The world was imagined to be so-and-so, with the edges marked with monsters and demons. Slowly, with more accurate data and more precise instruments of measurement, maps continuously became more detailed and expressive. However, the terror of blank spots had to be overcome in some way that was plausible and so previous images of dragons and mystical beings made way for 'real' objects such as elephants and people, although these did not necessarily always correspond with areas in question. The blank spots signified a lack of knowledge of these spaces, and therefore signified the boundaries of the knowable. For a science that prided itself on accuracy and truthfulness, this was a problematic occurrence. As was the case of maps of old, the imagination was used in order to overcome the blank spots on the map. Not only were speculations about rivers, mountains, and valleys incorporated into the making of maps (the most famous example being the far from accurate projection of the size of Australia and its assumed resources), but also people and animals that populated certain territories.

The map fused what was known (shapes, climate, flora) with that which was speculated about (cities, people, resources). Maps became instruments that signified both desire (comprehension, knowledge) and fear (ignorance, the unknown). In this sense, maps and literature share a number of similarities. Firstly, they attempt to make comprehensible what lies outside the spheres of direct knowledge production (thus the strong focus on the imagination). Secondly, they both position themselves as truth-producing products – maps being objective on the one hand, and literature relying on its inherent world-making energies. By tracing the outlines of territories, they become tangible (locatable on a map), organised (in reference to other territories and one's own position), comprehensible (by having a name, a shape), and finally, locatable (one can now say 'such-and-such is there/not there'). This relationship between the comprehensible and what is beyond comprehension is a strong link between the map as a source of data and organisation, and literature, which is reliant on such sources. The protagonist in *Robinson Crusoe*, for example, is unable to discern his location when washed up on a remote shore. Once he scales a mountaintop and realises he is on an island, he sketches its outline

---

[30] Examples include Charles John Anderson: *The Okavango River: a Narrative of Travel Exploration and Adventure* (1861) and *Notes of Travel in South West Africa* (1875); Carl Hugo Hahn, *Lüderitzland und sieben Begebemhieten* (1934); Theodor Leutwein, *Deutsch-Süd-West-Afrika mit einer Karte* (1898). The later established Odendaal Report (1964) can be seen the South African epitome of producing knowledge on SWA.

and locates his home base on the sketch. He is now able to at least pinpoint his location within his new, limited world, a world he controls via his map, his narrative, and his gun. Crusoe utilises the finite resources at hand in order to represent his 'new world'. This activity can be located along Nelson Goodman's contemplations on 'worldmaking', which "starts from worlds already on hand; the making is a remaking" (1978:6).

This is where literature can enter the conversation, since it is always a social product produced in a certain society and reflecting that society. Moments of extreme social and political shifts (the Industrial Revolution, the rise of fascist ideologies, imperial expansion and colonialism) have always been prophesied, problematized, and dissected by the tool of the literary imagination. Conversely, literature as a tool has also been utilised in order to justify and stimulate these processes. Said (1978;1993), Homi Bhabha (1993), McClintock (1995), Arndt (2004;2006), and Hashemi (2011), amongst others, have focussed on literature as a form of knowledge production and its application within the imperial and colonial contexts. So while literature has the potential and ability to reveal the paradox and ambiguous nature of these inhuman and privileging systems, it also has the power to present (racist) power at work and the ease with which it can be manipulated in order to achieve certain ends. The imperial dream of absolute spatial control can be identified within colonialist literature, especially fictions employing monologic[31] narrators who control the development of the plot. These narrators can therefore be said to control the narrative aspects that govern being, namely space and time.

Space and time are undoubtedly *the* fundamental pillars of being[32]. Control over these aspects constitute the authority to control being, and therefore controlling all aspects this would entail (subjectivity, agency, the quotidian). Space must therefore be looked at when thinking about being – whether in a fictional or real-world context, especially as the two forms of being inform each other. And because of literature's privileged position as an engine for influencing social dreaming, interrogating space can answer questions such as: Whose dreams and fantasies are reflected in the creation and manipulation of fictionalised space? Who has access to these dreams and fantasies, and who is marginalised? How does a literary space reflect/refute dominant discourses of power of the host[33] society? And finally, how does literary space offer alternatives to the status quo and the already-produced spaces of a society? Answering these questions can open up a broader

---

[31] The term 'monologic' will be discussed in more detail when discussing *Peter Moor, A Twist of Sand*, and "The Narrative of Jacobus Coetzee".
[32] Soja (1989) argues that matter is the third constitutive element to being; yet this is also reliant on the other two factors.
[33] "Host" in this sense refers to the society that predominantly produces (i.e. writes, publishes, and promotes) and consumes this literature.

understanding of space as a concept by feeding it with 'imaginary' space. I will briefly compare the composition of literary space to its artistic predecessor, landscape painting, in order to emphasise its complexity and constructedness.

While a painting should stand for itself, its literary equivalent is (in some cases) reliant on a number of mediators. "The Narrative of Jacobus Coetzee" might serve as a strong example of such a process, through which the original narrative is: a) translated and edited, then b) narrated from a fictionalised perspective, then c) retrospectively introduced, and d) reproduced as an official document. The various formats already create conflicting and/or assenting perspectives, allowing for different interpretations of a single landscape. The literary landscape may function as a palimpsest of translations of the same *space*. What, however, unifies the painted and the written product is its discursive dimension. The gazing eye, whether real or imaginary, constructs what the spectator/reader are able to see/read. Possession, control, and production are all at once unified through the constructor of the landscape. Yet, it is the literary landscape, maybe more than in any other format, which stretches the possibilities of the landscape because of its reliance on mediation and the participation of the reader. Although the description of a landscape may be fixed, the construction of this landscape within the reader's mind's eye is typically not similar to that of another reader. Experience, cultural background, vocabulary, and a host of other factors contribute to the creation of the artistic landscape. Although any format has the potential and the ability to create new spaces or manipulate existing spaces and places, literature has a long history in this regard. Apart from colonialist and apartheid literature, other genres have dreamed up spacesas their backgrounds, including fantasy and science-fiction, Gothic, Romantic, and postmodern literatures.

Although the landscape is one of the most universal and prominent spaces within the production of literary narratives, it is by no means the only one. Depending on the genre, certain spaces may be recycled, replicated, repeated, or reused. This has come to the attention of certain theorists, such as Mikhail Mikhailovich Bakhtin. He applied a term from physics, the chronotope[34], in order to discuss certain space-time configurations in novels. According to Arich-Gertz, Schimdt & Ziethen (2014), the chronotope "transformiert, und kondensiert dabei außerliterarische Wirklichkeit in raumzeitlichen Knotenpunkten, zu denen z.B. das Schloss im gotischen Roman oder der Salon in der Literatur des 19. Jahrhunderts gehören" (12–13). Bakhtin does, however, emphasise time over space, but his assertion still proves fruitful when we return to O'Sullivan's concept of

---

[34] Translated as "time-space". Initially a term coming from the field of physics, it was introduced by Bakhtin as a literary tool of analysis. For more, see "Forms of Time and of the Chronotope in the Novel" in *The Dialogic Imagination* (1981).

fictioning. Elements of the world-as-it-is are reflected in the novel, which again reflect the world-as-it-is at a certain period in time. This interplay is revealing for the literature under investigation as it opens up questions concerning the dissemination of knowledge on a number of pertinent subjects. Colonial and apartheid fantasies of the 'empty'/emptied landscape, the ahistorical relationship to the (foreign) soil, the right to land and resources, the spatial hierarchy of the different 'races', they are all reflective of a certain period and a certain tradition.

These fantasies are also responsible for producing certain ambitions, histories, and subjects that are connected to ideals and, more importantly, to a certain telos. The production of the 'empty' landscape, with its rhetoric and rationality of *terra nullius*, is infused with *white* potential and disavows previous claims to these so-called 'empty' spaces. The coloniser – by first possessing the landscape artistically – can claim the discursive landscape and start to infuse it with ideals imported from the metropole. An example would be the ideal of *whiteness* with its accumulation of positive markers such as cultivation, industry, progress, purity, and rationality. The colony becomes a space in which knowledge about the 'Other' is produced as much as knowledge about the Self is disseminated. The landscape is the laboratory and the characters become the test subjects with which to test the potential boundaries of metropolitan culture. The chronotope acts as a link between the 'real' (colonialist/apartheid ambitions, ethnographic evidence, geographic reproductions) and the fictitious (desires, fears, and imagination that result from and take place in the 'real'). The novel produces spaces filled with various degrees and methods of knowledge dissemination while simultaneously pointing to its truthfulness *and* its fictionality[35]. At the heart of this exercise is the production of colonial/apartheid spaces and colonialist/apartheid subjects.

Fictioning, Myth-creation, and World-Making

What the production of these discursive spaces reveals is the basis of imperial processes. The colonial era begins with a military seizure of the territory. The next steps are Germanisation (to 'make it German') of the territory and, finally, its defence against internal as well external threats (whether real or imagined). The apartheid era produces a landscape complicit with the apartheid system's base aspirations of creating an all-*white* space. It also reveals the complicated web of competing and conflicting histories and myths – all supporting an ideal *white* position within an idealised *Weltgeschichte*. At the core of these processes is the fictionalisation of these spaces, constructed predominantly out of desires

---

[35] *Peter Moor* and *Heim Neuland*, for example, have real events as their background yet their characters and their lives are fictions.

and fears. The narrated spaces thus create an environment in which these desires and fears become central, allowing for an interrogation into these narrated spaces. The fact that these spaces are recreations or representations of actual historic spaces further allows a different approach to how one can link the 'real'[36] to the fictional. Simon O'Sullivan's article "Art Practice as Fictioning (or, myth-science)" (2014) ascribes one of the outcomes of this practice as a

> collapsing of hitherto separate worlds – and the concomitant production of a 'new' landscape, a new platform for dreaming – is another definition of fictioning, especially when it is no longer clear where the fiction itself ends and so-called reality begins (or where reality ends and the fiction begins). Fictioning inserts itself into the real in this sense – into the world-as-it-is (indeed, it collapses the so-called real and the fictional), but in so doing, it necessarily changes our reality. This is fictioning as mythopoesis: the imaginative transformation of the world *through* fiction. (emphasis in original, 6–7)

O'Sullivan makes a number of relevant observations concerning literature, especially the collapse of the 'real' and the fictional. The term 'fictioning' becomes helpful when discussing 'real' spaces as they appear in fictional narratives. The spaces produced by Frenssen, Kraze, and Brockmann all have a 'real' dimension (the space/s of GSWA they employ as narrative settings undoubtedly exist/existed) but it is their fictionalisation of the territory that is the most significant aspect. The collapse of the 'real' and the fictional creates a new space in which desires, fears and, most importantly, dreams can find a home. More powerfully, the fictioning is essential as a discursive tool as it circumvents the need to continually point to a 'real' space in a fictional setting by combining both aspects. The flip side of this is that Frenssen et al are complicit in dreaming up a host of nightmares for the original populace of the imagined and imposed territory of GSWA. The fantasies of foreign land and territories meant that traditional networks and connections to ancestral lands were dissolved. Military, cultural, economic, and political terror against the local populations became the legacy of these *white* dreams. The collapse of the real and the fictitious into dreamworlds therefore had real consequences for the people of GSWA, not only the fictionalised characters of the narratives.

---

[36] The inverted commas only serve to point to the constructed nature of GSWA and its spatial production(s). Although GSWA did and does exist, it is more than just its borders and position on a map. Because of its violent ruptures concerning hegemony and acquisition, the inverted commas confirm a deeper reality concerning the territory, especially as a colonised and occupied space.

Literature List

The invention of these spaces, or the spaces to be occupied, are highly reflective of certain needs of the 'home nation', be they economic (access to new resources or markets), social (the adaptability or superiority of imperial cultures), or political (cementing hierarchies or the release of antagonistic class pressures). The places and landscapes created in narratives about the various historic forms of current-day Namibia (as a pre-colonial entity to GSWA to SWA, and finally Namibia) always carry with and reproduce certain European agendas. This becomes clear when looking at how, for example, the colony is imagined, fantasised about, and ultimately encountered. The alien space needs to be organised according to a European ideal. In order to organise this space certain aspects need to be 'emptied' so they can be claimed and reshaped. The colony becomes a resource for the metropole, allowing it to continually reproduce itself as well as adapting its strategies.

Colonialist Literature

My analysis begins with Gustav Frenssen's 1906 colonialist novel *Peter Moors Fahrt nach Südwest*[37], in which the landscape is a construct of the twin threat of the "bush" (the threatening landscape) and the "enemy" (the Herero). This strong association between the two opens up a war-torn and contested space in which the subjugation of one element of danger, in this case the rebellious Herero, would allow German appropriation of the other, namely the land and its accompanying resources. Peter Moor's continued focus on the terms "bush" and "enemy" are revealing of language's power of emphasis and evasion.

I want to briefly point to a number of things concerning the term "bush" and its use. Due to its high recurrence in the novel it must receive special attention. This is not only due to its over-use to produce a certain landscape, but also because it is a problematic colonial construction. Linking it to Anna Weicker and Ingrid Jakob's discussion[38] of the African jungle "als metaphorische Interpretationen des Waldes als undurchdringlicher, unbeherrschbarer, gefährlicher Raum (201), the "bush" as a generic term can also be translated in this vein. In order to keep it within the frame of Peter Moor's experience, I will consistently write it in quotation marks so as to lock it within that specific narrative. The repetition as well as quotes should serve to delimit its power as a sign, emphasising its use as a colonial term. This connects it to the other fear that Peter Moor experiences, namely the "enemy", another unspecific and generic term. As will become

---

[37] From here on referred to as *Peter Moor*.
[38] Taken from their contribution "Afrika" in Arndt, Susan & Nadja Ofuatey-Alazard. *Wie Rassismus aus Wörtern spricht*. (2011).

clear later, these two terms are powerful concepts when projected onto a non-European territory and have the potential to, a) 'empty' the space to be occupied, and b) legitimise this 'emptying'.

The protagonist produces a landscape in which he emphasises the spaces he encounters as singular, in other words: the foreign landscape is maintained as being foreign throughout the novel. He is disinterested in his surroundings, mirroring his disinterest for the society he is helping to violently annihilate. The strategy of not naming the Herero serves the purpose of distancing himself from the destructive violence committed by him and the other soldiers. The "enemy" is constructed as a placeholder, always implying danger to oneself while making a complete victory the only telos of the war. The twin threat is supported by the imagined emptiness of GSWA, where the signless and unreadable landscape is experienced through the lens of metropolitan signs and symbols. These signs and symbols assist Peter Moor in navigating his war experience while reproducing the imagined space of GSWA as propagated through travelogues, official reports, and soldier's accounts. This signlessness and emptiness as a metropolitan colonialist justification for the annihilation of the Herero[39] is based on the desire for sole control of spatial production. The literary technology of the 1907 version, in which Peter Moor's war exploits end in a published work, also reproduces the colonial technologies of knowledge production and dissemination.

Frieda Kraze's novel *Heim Neuland. Ein Roman von der Wasserkante und aus Deutsch-Südwest*[40] (1908) focuses on the potential of the land and its resources by placing the two main characters, who have the social status of landed gentry in Germany, in a pre-Herero genocide GSWA. This allows Kraze – as opposed to Peter Moor and the German military – to Germanise the foreign soil. The war against the Herero is remodelled as a war of self-preservation, i.e. in defence of German soil and livelihood as opposed to a war to gain control of a foreign space. In a temporal reversal, it is Frenssen's Peter Moor and the military who save and protect Kraze's Etta Wibrandt and Dirich Dierksen. At the time of publication of *Heim Neuland* the result of the war was already known[41], giving Kraze the freedom to place her characters within a territory that had been rid of its foreign and inherent dangers (i.e. Peter Moor's "bush" and the "enemy"). Where Peter Moor fails,

---

[39] Although the Nama waging war against the colonising forces predates the Herero rebellion, the events are briefly mentioned in passing. The sole focus of the novel is the war against the Herero army.
[40] From here on referred to as *Heim Neuland*.
[41] It would take another 60years, however, until the full repercussions of the war entered into debates concerning Germany's role in the destruction of the Herero. The German historian Horst Drechsler (1966) was the first to use the term *genocide* to describe the German military's actions against the Herero, an accusation that was only recently acknowledged by the German government. The consequences and next steps are, however, still unclear.

namely infusing lasting Germanness into the soil[42] and the landscape through labour and cultivation, the Dierksen couple succeeds. Their disavowal of Black labour, their desire to own land and the exclusive view of the landscape, and their constant need to reproduce their *whiteness* all point to the fantasy of keeping Black characters visible only to support their colonial ambitions. Black characters are designed and imagined only in opposition to the adventures and achievements of the *white* characters.[43]. Their mythological ties to the soil and the land are maintained even with the destruction of their farm Ettenhof and their subsequent escape to their native Germany. The return of the absconded German colonisers, granted by the military and subsequent political decimation of the Herero populace, is accompanied by an influx of further German nationals to the colony.

Clara Brockmann, having published her novel *Du heiliges Land! Roman aus den Diamantfeldern Südwestafrikas...*[44] (1914) under the pen name Marianne Westerlind, situates her characters within the context of increased German and international immigration to the colony. The background to Ingeborg Oberländer's, the female protagonist, arrival is the period of intense diamond mining activities in the south-western coast of GSWA. After Zacharias Lewala[45] found a diamond in the sand dunes outside the coastal town of Lüderitzbucht, a number of Europeans saw an opportunity to gain riches previously dreamt up in other colonialist narratives[46]. The diamond deposits placed GSWA, and its founding town of Lüderitzbucht, into the global commodity system, creating a space in which German possessions were threatened from the 'outside'. The German soil Etta and Dirich laboured to produce, came under threat due to greed, speculation, and the so-called diamond fever. These developments infer and mark developments in the understanding of GSWA as a German space, tracing its violent seizure to its consolidation in the international community – always with an imagined Germany and Europe at its centre and pushing Africanist characters to the periphery. The mining of diamonds – mostly by Black hands – is used as the backdrop to design an arena for 'pure' German love while

---

[42] There are brief instances where Peter Moor succeeds, but this is achieved only on a fleeting level, with his violence and participation in the war his only lasting impression. This is however extended as his narrative is published both in the 'real' as well as the fictional world.

[43] Yekani (2011) argues similarly when comparing Black and *white* masculinities, both of course categories of imagined difference themselves: "the status of Black masculinity is overwhelmingly to bodily capacities, never to intellect. Marginalised masculinity can be related exclusively to biology while hegemonic masculinity becomes a culturally elevated version of this biological masculinity" (48).

[44] From here on referred to as *Du heiliges Land!*.

[45] As is the case with a number of African contributions in the colonial context, Lewala's name is omitted from the novel's recounting of the discovery of the diamonds. Ingeborg's horse, the aptly named "Diamantenfinder", however, is accredited with being present during this event.

[46] A more than fitting example, Rider Haggard's *King Solomon's Mines* (1884), ends with the protagonists locating and stealing a large deposit of diamonds – the stones having been mined by local people many years ago.

tracing the demise of a number of characters who do not adhere to the strict regulations governing 'true' Germanness. The results are either social ostracisation (Oskar Vollmüller, Carola Oberländer, Dr. Shian) or elimination from the narrative through death (Hans Gothland, Adolf Oberländer). The reward for Ingeborg and Herbert Klinger's love is a return to Germany, and with it, the 'return' to a purely German society. In contrast to *Peter Moor* and *Heim Neuland*, a German society in a foreign space like the colony relies on the stringent reproduction of German virtues, not only the acquisition of a territory and the working of the 'uncultivated' soil. While the Germanness propagated by Frenssen and Kraze have immediate and material effects, Brockmann argues that Germanness is a constant struggle and process, one that is always reproduced in the struggle against the negative forces of vice and corruption.

Apartheid Literature

As Chapman (2003:129–133) observed in his genealogy of *white* South African literature from 1800 onwards, certain colonial strategies and tropes are observable. The result is, one can argue, that similar strategies employed during the writing of colonialist literature can be applied to apartheid literature dealing with the same space – but under noticeably different contexts and circumstances. With the German colonial era basically and officially[47] ended in 1919, it became possible to occupy the territory through a further imaginary. This imaginary can be said to have as its foundation one goal: the incorporation of the militarily occupied territory of SWA into the larger Union of South Africa. The aesthetic and poetic strategies employed in order to assist in this goal can be divided into two opposing streams of literary production. The farm novel and the novel of the colonial sojourner receive intensified attention during the post-1948 production of literature. Within the dehumanising system of apartheid, Afrikaner links to the soil and English adventure narratives take on a further powerful form in relation to the colonialist literature with similar motifs and themes. However, as is with all literary streams, it is very difficult (or near impossible) to neatly and cleanly separate various genres from one another.

Yet it is possible to point towards prominent mechanics of the production of literary space. The question is how far these spaces reflect and reproduce emerging apartheid desires and fantasies and to what extent the narrative is employed in the service of this racist and exclusionary system. The two novels under discussion reveal different accesses to the system and its reproductive imaginary and tropes, both relying on and reproducing spaces

---
[47] The 'phantom pain' of the lost colonies, the re-emergence of colonial discourse during the National Socialist era as well as the maintenance of the colonial school well after 1919 is indicative that the loss of the colonies was not fully accepted by segments of German society and polity.

which have generally been interpreted as being 'empty': the ocean and the desert. This is of course a mere superficial surface observation, but it is a powerful tool in which the focus of South African space is placed on the 'new' space to be incorporated – the neighbouring colony of (G)SWA.

Geoffrey Jenkins' *A Twist of Sand* (1959) moves away from the traditional interior settings of expansionist literature and places the narrative mainly on the waters off the coastline of SWA, alternatively referred to as Skeleton Coast and Kaokoveld. Not only is this landscape sparsely populated, but the absence of Black characters from the narrative is striking. Having been published after the most draconian apartheid laws, Jenkins reproduces the system's objective of removing African bodies from spaces of consequence. The fleeting addition of the coloured Captain Hendricks (who is described as having Malay descent) and the brief mention of the Kroo boy Jim (who will be killed off) are the only attempts to incorporate Black characters within the seascape. Not only are these characters not members of original Namibian societies, they come from the 'outside', so to speak[48]. Namibian characters are completely excluded from the main thread of the narrative. By choosing an environment to which the average Africanist character had little or no access except through serving under a *white* captain, Jenkins creates a narrative in which the exclusion of Namibian characters reproduces a European (in this case Afrikaner) hierarchical self-image. Not content with controlling the mainland and the mobility of undesired subjects, authority of the sea and its routes is incorporated.

The British protagonist Captain Peace, manoeuvring under the South African flag as Captain Macdonald, can be read as an archetypal representative of the apartheid dream: a producer and benefactor of a *whites*-only masculine space in which adventure and riches are (potentially) immeasurable. A lack of adventure and riches within the interior of the occupied territory is sidestepped. The undeniable presence of other *whites* (Germans in this case) negates the trope of an empty/emptied landscape[49]. Physical structures as well as artistic spatial (re)productions do not fully allow the South African fantasy of a *terra nul-*

---

[48] Hendricks, marked as a coloured character of Malay descent, points toward South Africa's history of colonial slavery, founded on indentured labourers from the Asian subcontinent (India, Malaysia). Jim is a member of the Kroo, a society originally based in Liberia, but involved as labourers on the ships passing the African west coast to GSWA and South Africa, for example. The Kroo are also mentioned in *Peter Moor* and *Heim Neuland*, signifying their strong link to, and presence in, the shipping routes between Europe and (southern) Africa.

[49] On a political level, it was impossible to deny any German (read: *white*) involvement within the former territory of GSWA (formation of a border state, bureaucratic machinery). On a visual/ perceptual level the influence of German infrastructure was undeniable (train system, towns/ cities, harbours, etc.). This was supplemented by artistic, official, and literary productions of the territory. The colonialist fantasy of an untouched and impressionable landscape was to a large extent nullified, necessitating the production of new 'empty/ emptied' spaces removed from those spaces already occupied via German involvement.

lius to unfold as German colonisers and colonialists had already mapped, photographed, and studied[50] the territory. Spaces produced by Black inhabitants on the other hand can be overwritten, as the 'unmapped' space of the Skeleton Coast illustrates. The sea thus offers a new space for desires and fears, far removed from those of the colonial period. Jenkins creates a space in which apartheid fantasies can still be realised, remote from any African involvement and interference.

This ideal is dealt with in a completely different way in "The Narrative of Jacobus Coetzee" (1974)[51] in which the Southern African landscape is saturated with European violence against the original inhabitants of the territories (in this case the derogatively called ~~Hottentot~~ and ~~Bushmen~~). Told from multiple perspectives and constructed as a layered narrative, the novella connects a number of generations and discursive practices. These are all concentrated in, and centred on, the (purported) first *white* explorer to cross the edges of the Cape Colony into the 'unknown' territory of the Great Nama[qua], Jacobus Coetsé[52]. The dialogic[53] reproduction of the narrative, consisting of an editor, a translator, an introduction (placed at the end), the narrative itself, as well as an official deposition, all contribute to a convolution of sources and voices. The linking of Coetzee himself to the original narrator, Jacobus Coetsé, as well as to the editor and writer of the introduction, Prof. S.J. Coetzee, creates a collage of history, with changes, deletions, additions, and translations contributing to the myth and demystification of a Dutch farmer and hobby elephant hunter's crossing of the Orange River. In this instance, the landscape – a keeper of history in its own right – is employed as a journeyman of the protagonist and becomes the witness and background to Jacobus Coetzee's (feverish) contemplations concerning *white* violence against Africanist subjects and its relevance within the philosophically generated *Weltgeschichte*. Here one is confronted with questions of history as a tool of myth-making and a product in the service of those in power. The landscape is constructed in a way that answers to European fantasies, its entire existence a result of the colonising mind willing it so and being produced in order to confirm desires (domination) and fears (insignificance). The landscape's production is firmly linked to

---

[50] Further examples of a negation of the apartheid fantasy of a South African 'empty space' would be the artistic reproduction of GSWA such as in the novels under discussion, landscape painting, German names of towns, etc.

[51] "The Narrative of Jacobus Coetzee" is the second novella of the larger work *Dusklands* (1974).

[52] To avoid confusion concerning the various "Coetzees", I will refer to each one as following: Coetzee: author of *Duskland*; J.M. Coetzee: 'author' and translator; S.J. Coetzee: editor; Jacobus Coetzee: fictional protagonist of the narrative; Jacobus Coetsé: historical figure and subject of the deposition.

[53] This is a term coined by M.M. Bakhtin and describes the phenomenon of a character being in a dialogue with other characters. This can also be applied to texts being in dialogue with each other (taken from "Discourse in the Novel" in *The Dialogic Imagination* (1981)).

the (re)production and assertion of *whiteness* as a constitutive factor in the creation and production of history.

Terms and Conditions

When talking and writing about violent systems such as colonialism and apartheid, it is easy to fall into the trap of perpetuation. Perpetuating discourses, gazes, myths, perspectives, positions, terms. One's own position plays into these perpetuations, or the lack of vocabulary and theoretical considerations. This becomes problematic when the aim is to unpack these terms, discourses, myths, gazes, perspectives, and positions. Other stumbling blocks are laziness (essentialism, universalism) or insensitivity (of developments, current discourses). It is therefore necessary to briefly give insight into and foreclose some of the mechanisms employed which will reflect this work's wish to positively contribute to discussions that deconstruct/theorise colonialism and apartheid without the pretence of 'speaking' for groups or individuals. Terms such as *white* and Black will be positioned as constructed, as socially designed categories and dislodged from their biologist origins[54]. This is again addressed when discussing Black characters and groups who have been named and defined by Europeans using derogatory terms such as 'H̶o̶t̶t̶e̶n̶t̶o̶t̶' and 'B̶u̶s̶h̶m̶a̶n̶'. Furthermore, this guise is extended to the characters themselves, who will be referred to as 'Africanist' as opposed to Africans. The suffix '-ist' is an allusion to the fictionally produced African figures and types who appear in the novels and who reflect the invented 'African' of the narratives[55].

One of the themes that needs to be addressed from the start is the literature chosen. Because the majority of novels chosen are by *white* authors (male and female) and focus almost exclusively on *white* characters and *white* dreams, a certain vocabulary and point of view need to be established. As mentioned previously, the cursive mode of referencing *whiteness* is based on the conviction that this category of definition is purely social and discursive and not reliant on any empirical evidence. In other words, the category of *whiteness* is a category that is socially constructed and has a long history of theorisation, paradigm changes, contestations, imaginings, and adaptations[56]. The use of the cursive aims to make this clear and to separate it from its position within the colour scheme, i.e.

---

[54] The 'fact of race' is propagated by conservative and right-wing intellectuals, but has been scientifically disproved on numerous occasions. The irony of the matter is that two people from the same 'race' are usually less related than two people from different 'races'.

[55] I use this term as proposed by Toni Morrison (1992) and in reference to Africanism (the designing of African characters in literature) and applied in a literary context in "Whiteness as a Literary Category of Analysis" (Arndt, 2009).

[56] See for example Arndt (2008).

the colour of objects. It is only when this colour enters the sphere of the symbolic that it will be stressed and its invented and 'unnatural' position made visible. Its binary, namely Black, will consistently be written with a capital letter. Not only does this serve as a separation between the racial construct and the naturally occurring colour, it also separates the written form from its antithesis. This last separation is important in order to emphasise *whiteness* as a visible construct while honouring the various changes and categories which Blackness has gone through and been theorised as. These categories include people of colour (PoCs) as discussed by Paul Gilroy, but also as created in the apartheid system of racist classification. Occasionally, I will make use of term of 'non-*white*' as a term referring to (mainly) Black characters, especially when discussing apartheid literature. This is in order to further emphasise the high focus on *whiteness* in respect to other groups within that system.

Furthermore, the aim is also to interrogate this official category by showing how arbitrary these definitions were and how they were changed according to caprice. Poor *whites* were occasionally defined as non-*white* as they did not represent the ideal image of 'proper *whites*' and were often marginalised and ostracised to a certain degree. Terms such as 'coloured' will be maintained throughout the text. Originally another apartheid category which referred to people who were neither *white*, nor Black, nor Indian, has been appropriated by those who were considered as coloured. This appropriation has seen the emergence and revaluation of various social spheres such as coloured culture, history, dialect (an offshoot of Afrikaans), and community. Although still a problematic term in terms of what it constitutes[57], it has largely lost its negative connotations that were prevalent during the apartheid era, however, only being partially acceptable in the South African (and to a certain extent Namibian) context.

Speaking and Writing the 'Other'

These markers are by no means the only ways in which to define or refer to various characters or people. History and literature make use of a number of ways in which to mention people, usually either by locating them in a trans-regional context (European, African) or nationally (German, British, South African, Namibian). It starts becoming problematic when those who have an established state (Germans, Bavarians) encounter those who do not work according to those classifications (Herero, Owambo). Here it is rather the cultural affiliation that is core, not the geographic location. For the first category this becomes a problematic classification as the cultural affiliation is further transposed onto

---

[57] Just like the categories of *white* and Black, coloured does not differentiate between language groups, ethnic belonging and historic processes. The main marker remains 'skin colour' but has become a term of self-identification and is considered as an acceptable term in South Africa and Namibia.

the national context. The main difference between these two categories is the imagined belonging to a much larger whole, one that is defined by abstract terms such as borders and a national culture. Although the Herero have an understanding of their 'nation'[58], as do the Nama[59] and Owambo[60], the concept is not as rigid as it is in the European case. Furthermore, many societies are not referred to according to their own terms, but according to terms that are easier to pronounce or have been imposed on them. Thus the terms '~~Bushman~~' and '~~Hottentot~~' have come to denote the Khoi and San as well as certain Nama and Damara. The term Damara has also been used erroneously or interchangeably when talking about the Herero. Because this thesis works with historic texts on one hand, and aims to avoid reproducing colonialist and apartheid discourses on the other, it becomes unavoidable to work with these racist and imperialist terms and concepts. However, instead of avoiding the use of these works, I will remain truthful to the original texts. As hard as this may seem when reading these terms, it does no justice to the novels if certain words are erased[61]. If words are erased, so are certain discourses around these words and any appropriations by those these words address as well[62].

What I propose is the taking up of a position concerning these terms when used outside of their original use (in the novels, in the colonial reports, etc.). While the references and quotations will remain intact and will not be manipulated, two strategies will be made use of to counter these terms. The first is the use of 'proper' terms in their place when discussing passages/quotes. Thus '~~Hottentot~~' will become Nama, or Khoi and San, depending on the context. The aim is to use terms based on self-determination. Other racist vocabulary, such as '~~verkafferung~~' will be scratched through in order to show their obsolete meaning and usage. Colonial and apartheid terms will appear in this thesis, but they will only remain in their context and not mentioned as a term that has a place in our contemporary society. They will be treated as that which they are – markers of a period and artefacts of the past.

This needs to be reflected when discussing the characters who are definitely marked as African(ist). Although external markers can be utilised and manipulated in order to (re)create certain assumptions and clichés about the characters described in the literature, one must always be aware that these are constructs. The Black types and figures referred to in the selected novels are superficial and have little space to unfold or develop and should

---

[58] The orally produced *ehi rOvaherero*.
[59] Reflected in names such as *Rooi Naasie / Red Nation* and Hendrik Witbooi's letters.
[60] Having kings/queens, and kingdoms.
[61] This is in reference to an academic working with this type of literature, and not within a public context in which these terms are generally not problematised.
[62] Examples of this include the appropriation of the N*word as used by Afro-Americans as well as the term Coloured as used in South Africa and Namibia.

therefore in no sense be treated as reflective of 'real' people. The term Africanist seems an appropriate method in pointing to this treatment, especially when discussing aggressive and violent literature that has colonisation and segregation at its core.

Expansion of the 'Metropole'
I have taken the liberty of appropriating certain terms associated with colonialism, apartheid, and imperialism. One of those buzzwords is the metropole, usually referencing the capital of the imperialist nation.

Although I am in general agreement with how this term has been used, it is my opinion that it can be further expanded upon in order to make stronger the relationship between the colonising nation (or the occupying nation in the case of South Africa) and the colonised or occupied territory. Not only because the metropole itself is reliant on other spaces which support and feed it (such as financial centres, judicial centres, harbours, etc.) but also because the relationship between the specific city and the huge colonial areas it configures cannot merely be seen as a relationship between two points. It is much more than that: the two spaces influence each other, however asymmetrical this influence may be. Rather, the relationship is a dense web of interconnections. By including the other centres and influences within the process of colonisation and apartheid, as well as taking away the capital's sole claim to authority, my aim is to question the larger network of power. This mirrors the colonised societies' power structures, as different centres of power were already established before the arrival of colonial forces. And even after this, power was spread out amongst different centres, from missionary influence, to ports, to border outposts, and traditional authorities. The term 'metropole' thus stands in place of Germany or South Africa, but not merely as geographic, border-based entities, but as abstract and symbolic spaces as well. I am interested in how the metropole *produces* spaces. Thus I want to place the metropole in a sphere separate from its geographic location – the capital – and expand it to reflect *national* interests. This allows a focus away from a single centre of power and creates a network of influences contributing to the understanding of a colonial space. The metropole now serves as an engine supplying the theoretical framework creating the *imagined* colony. The colony becomes the space that forms the foundation of my work: a space which functions on a symbolic, dreamt up level. My discussion rests upon ideas of the imagination, desires and fears of the 'home' nation, and fictionalisation of these 'new' spaces.

Contracting 'Spaces'

'Space' is a slippery term, not only because it works on two extreme poles of human existence (the subjective and the objective), but because of how it can be moulded to fit both categories at once. Following the introduction and the arguments put forward, it seems to have a number of qualities and attributes: it can be produced *and* reproduced. It is the focus of map-making as well as literature. It has a power relational and hierarchical dimension. It has both a material and fictional aspect. And it can be represented and imagined. This only proves that space has a fluid, if not highly complex, character, one which thinkers throughout time have attempted to tie down and place in some sort of box. To begin, I will firstly give a short genealogy of thinking around space. This serves to open up a significant relationship concerning space, namely its relation (or in early cases: non-relation) with the subjects inhabiting it.

The aim of this book is to dislocate space from its material base and look at its fictioned dimension. This means, in practical terms, to ground the theory in a framework focussing on how available space is manipulated in a real-world manner and then to transfer this to the sphere of the fictitious. As O'Sullivan and Goodman have shown, this step is possible – but the world-as-it-is needs to be located within the world-as-it-could-be. When interviewed by Airich-Gertz on his novel about the historical search for Timbuktu, for example, the Austrian author Stangl ends the answer to his literary belonging[63] with this question: "Warum sollen denn die Leute in den Romanen nicht fliegen können?" (Arich Gerz, Schmidt & Ziehen 2014:31). I mention this in order to refer to literature's privileged position in dealing with the world-as-it-is: by manipulating certain aspects of it. This is reflected in its dealing with space, in which it can expand and contract, make infinite or destroy – but it cannot divorce space from what it must always be: one of the two fundamental pillars of being. In the way I will be working with space, it is constitutive of the characters and their environments, it is not just a backdrop, but the plane on which everything must eventually unfold. And as is with the hierarchies in any society, so must its spaces be part of a hierarchy. Space takes centre stage in the analysis, and as Bakhtin's chronotope suggests, it can be used in order to zoom in on certain spatial constructions such as the landscape or the spaces of encounters.

I will trace European constructions of space from Gottfried Wilhelm Leibniz via Immanuel Kant, Martin Heidegger, Michel Foucault, and finally to Henri Lefebvre: European thinkers who have undeniably influenced Western understanding of space and its

---

[63] "'Das Mäandernde ist so etwas wie ein Prinzip'. Ein Gespräch mit Thomas Stangl über Raum und Räumlichkeit in *Der einzige* Ort" (24–32). In the interview he is asked whether he is comfortable with being classed as a postmodern writer, alongside Borges, Cortázar, and Pynchon.

qualities. The focus will be to trace the inclusion of the spatial subject within the theories of space. This exercise will not be a comprehensive analysis of what constitutes the concept of space, but merely what it can mean and what it can do. Or to put it in other words: where does space get its power (and conversely: who/what can space empower)? Space is thus not necessarily defined but rather used as a tool of analysis. Furthermore, the analysis of space will not pretend to be a final and complete theory on how space functions, rather the aim is to create a synthesis between Lefebvre's idea of social space and how it may be applied within a literary context. Because of space's social composition, it is impossible to divorce it from society. Lefebvre's conception of space will be linked to other thinkers of ((post)colonial) space such as Michel Foucault (1967/1984), Elahe Hashemi Yekani (2011), Anne McClintock (1995), and Ulrike Jureit (2012), amongst others, in order to establish space's hierarchical and social potential, while linking it to state power and focussing it on Lefebvre's idea of production and reproduction. The synthesis should thus allow for a general approach to the idea(s) of space and therefore create a platform on which to further interrogate the idea of literary space.

Producing the Colonialist Landscape

One space I have repeatedly focussed on thus far has been the landscape. As Tim Ingold (1993) rightly claims, this term is very slippery and difficult to pin down. He begins his discussion of landscape, by "explaining what the landscape is *not*. It is not 'land', it is not 'nature', and it is not 'space'" (153). He is correct in starting here and focussing on various (mis)conceptions concerning the term. Ingold dislocates landscape from its supposed elements (land, nature, and space) and places it in a sphere in which the abstract dominates. Like Lefebvre (113–116), he links landscape to human interaction and thus positions within it human agency and the ability to change its use (152). However, he deals with it in an anthropological and archaeological manner, ignoring the fact that landscaping in its original form was an artistic practice[64]. The etymology[65] of the word itself stems from the practice of painting stretches of *land* and of *nature* and placing these within a frame – and therefore artistically rendering a certain *space*. This representational and reproductive practice has a strong discursive dimension, with the contents of the frame first scrutinised by the painting eye and then organised via certain aesthetic judgements. Furthermore,

---

[64] 'Landscaping' as an artistic endeavour as used above is not the same as effecting a landscape, which involves a non-artistic manipulation and utilisation of a specific space.
[65] The German word for landscape (*Landschaft*) is a combination of the words *Land* (either land or countryside) and *schaft* (from *schaffen*, i.e. to make or create). There is thus a high degree of artificiality in the practice of landscape art, as the process itself is based on the act of creating something although that 'something' is already there in its physical form.

additions/renderings/omissions are decided upon before or during the process in order to represent a certain ideal. Another aspect for consideration is *where* the act of 'landscaping' takes place and *where* the finished product is placed[66].

Landscape art often takes place within a space that is considered natural (a stream, in front of a mountain range, a wide open space) where the eye has a clear view of the objects to be painted. In many cases the view is taken from an elevated position and is constructed around the organisational structure of background → centre → foreground. The idea of scale and dimension are the prominent categories for this level. Lighting plays a significant role, i.e. what is illuminated and what is left in the shadows. Finally, the mixture and interplay of the colours chosen complete the transformation from object-as-it-is to the finished article. One can therefore see that landscaping as an aesthetic practice is reliant on numerous steps and actions, all of which are decided upon and carried out by the painter-artist. The painting itself serves a function: that of possession. The artist 'possesses' the view, the gaze upon a fragment of the world. This view is recorded (however accurately), documenting this possession. An ultimate sign of this proprietorial attitude is to hang the painting in a space which is reflective of the possessive gaze. The introduction of value, whether trade or commodity, into the practice of landscape painting completes the cycle of nature as a raw material to a finished product for consumption.

Literary landscapes, contrary to Ingold's argument, contain a further set of elements. Firstly, they are described using words – not as a unified whole within a frame[67]. This has the effect that the landscape produced in a narrated work is sequential, created section by section, layer by layer. The author creates the landscape through a process requiring the reader to participate, not just via the stringing together of words and images that then create the landscape, but also through the imagination. Contrary to the painted landscape, the narrated landscape is not a finished product, but needs to be constantly 'remade' through the interplay between author, narrator, and reader. The aspect of landscape as a space is therefore applicable to this method of production as the landscape is not merely a visual, ocular experience, but takes in a prominent and dominant role within the further development of the narrative. While the painting is a moment, a still, an occasion in time made concrete, the narration of a landscape becomes the backdrop and the engine of the narrative[68]. A second difference between the painted landscape and its literary 'Other' is

---

[66] For an example of how to work with the imperial/ colonial landscape, see Mary Louise Pratt, *Imperial Eyes: Travel Writing and Transculturation.* (1991).
[67] One of the properties of a painting is undoubtedly its ability to govern the movement of the consuming eye. Various techniques have been devised to influence this movement, with the western practice of looking from right to left the most powerful basis. However, once the gazer is situated far enough from the painting as such, this action becomes unnecessary and the painting is taken in as a whole.
[68] This might not be true for every narrative, especially those that take place in a room/in a house or other

its strong mediation. Because the reader – contrary to the spectator – is unable to 'see' the written landscape, some instance has to 'see' it for him/her. And it is this 'seeing' which can again be layered on a number of levels. Depending on the narrational format, the final product may have gone through a number of interpretations and manipulations. The landscape is thus not only reproduced or represented, but is also aestheticized and even mythologised.

The Myth(s) of *Whiteness*

Mythopoesis is another important concept O'Sullivan introduces. As the title of his article slyly suggests, there is a level of "myth-science" involved. Not only will this be a significant tool in the construction of Afrikaner apartheid rhetoric and legitimisation, but it can also be used as a general mode of inquiry into *whiteness* (a central pillar within the apartheid system). In his acceptance speech at the BET Awards in 2016, actor Jessie Williams focussed on the inherent racism in the entertainment industry specifically, and in the Unites States in general. He referred to *whiteness* as an invention, something that a number of critics have tried to bring attention to. In this regard, Toni Morrison has argued that "the subject of the dream is the dreamer"[69], meaning that the authors under discussion write under the flag of *whiteness*. Joining Morrison in this discussion, bell hooks has targeted the 'invisibility' of *whiteness*[70] within discourses about race, while much work has been done by Critical Whiteness scholars such Robert Young (1990), Ruth Frankenberg (1993), Richard Dyer (1997), and George Yancy (2004) to expose the mechanics behind *white* privilege in different areas and fields of inquiry.

To garner a clearer picture concerning what *whiteness* is or can be, it is vital to dislocate it from its biologist conception and tie it to its social constructedness: "Like any other racial label, whiteness does not exist as a credible biological property. But it is a social construction with real effects that has become a powerful organizing principle around the world" (Rasmussen et al. 2001:8). Following Arndt's essay "Weißsein – zur Genese eines Konzepts" (2008), the invention of *whiteness* has its roots as far back as antiquity and was expanded upon during the Enlightenment era, while finding its ruthless pinnacle in colonial expansion and fascist race theories[71]. But as hooks' notion of "the myth of same-

---

confined spaces. However, as soon as characters are placed outside of these structures, the landscape receives a significant role. This can be expanded to include neologisms, such as cityscape, urban landscape, dreamscape, and so forth.

[69] *Playing in the Dark* (1992:17).
[70] She uses the notion of the "myth of sameness" (in Arndt 2009:174) focussing on *whiteness*' ability to 'hide' behind other discourses about race, such as the academic area of Black Studies.
[71] Complicit theorists in the construction and maintenance of *whiteness* are ubiquitous names such as Plato, Socrates, Kant, and Hegel.

ness" already implies, *whiteness* can be seen as a myth, an historic attempt to explain the world-as-it-is, bringing the argument back to O'Sullivan's idea of "mythopoesis" as "the imaginative transformation of the world through fiction" (7).

It appears as if *whiteness* is hidden in plain sight when looking at colonial and apartheid literature. *White* characters, designed and animated by *white* authors, are seldom marked as such and are set as the default. This absence of markers – yet the recognition of characters as *white* – is contrasted by marking 'Other' characters as Black[72], either through biological markers (assumptions concerning skin and hair colour, physiognomy), cultural markers (language, religion, traditions/rituals), or social status (enslaved person, servant). Fictions, and consequentially, myths concerning the 'Other' (whether the 'Other' is constructed or silenced) enter the world-as-it-is and influence it. This reveals the intense work that goes into creating categories of belonging, forming artificial boundaries between *white* Europe and what was then considered the 'New World'. And as Arndt has shown, looking, or more precisely looking *for*, has been a forceful instrument in creating these boundaries:

> Bodily differences were believed to embody mental, cultural, and religious differences, and formed the basis upon which cultures and religions were placed in a hierarchy. The construct of 'skin colour' was appropriated and declared a naturally given entity, which over the centuries created a 'regime of looking that has led people to believe in the factuality of difference [of 'skin colours'] in order to see it'. (2009:170)

Comparative to a number of scientific inquiries, the observable became a symbol of truth, as a number of fictional characters will attest to[73]. The ordering eye thus forms the basis in which people become comprehensible. Seeing comes before being, imprinting the observed subject with assumptions and theories before it is able to define itself. The scientific, organising gaze is therefore responsible for the construction of the subject before it has been given the chance to reveal itself. And it is literature that has helped in cementing the scientific eye's position within the construction of difference and the creation of a 'racial' hierarchy. Arndt (2009) shows how *whiteness* as an ever-present and yet absent category can be employed to trace the power of the *white* gaze while exposing how it functions within *white* literary productions. The myth of *whiteness*, its instruments of power (the scientific gaze and its reproduction), and its ability to be both absent and present, appears

---

[72] The capitalised Black references Gilroy's application of the term, "as a marker for all non-*white* positions which are faced with 'Othering', exclusion, and discrimination conducted by *whites*" (Arndt 2009:168, footnote 6).

[73] Crusoe understands that he is on an island after he *sees* its shape from atop a mountain, Peter Moor comprehends the Herero as the "enemy" only after he *sees* them in combat, and Jacobus Coetzee is only able to understand his position in the world and history after becoming a spherical eye, *seeing* everything.

as the focal points of colonial and apartheid literature. However, the literature by the powerful about the powerful and the (per design) powerless are not products appearing in and from a vacuum. The debate concerning whether Aphra Behn's *Oroonoko* (1688) or Defoe's *Robinson Crusoe* should be considered the first Western novel already shows that the *white* male has a historically privileged position vis-à-vis others[74], while the emergence of a literature of conquest privileges the West over the Rest.

Looking Forward

Because this book is reliant on the twin form of analysis of space and literature, the **Theory Chapter** will place both theoretical frameworks at the beginning. A first indicator of this will be a brief discussion of space and time as related and necessary categories of analysis. Both of these terms are central when investigating any form of cultural and historical products, since the tracing of any development is always linked to these elemental factors. Once these links have been established, I will isolate space as a philosophical term and sketch a brief and superficial genealogy. The aim of this is to situate the individual, social subject within thinking around space, locating its emergence within the different theories as they were designed and reworked from Classic philosophy to modern and postmodern European theories. The first thinker to be introduced is Gottfried Wilhelm Leibniz, who proposed *relational* space. As the name suggests, he points to a quality of space that is vital in contemporary responses to spatial theories, yet his conceptualisation does not include the introduction of a subject. Rather, his relational space has fixed points as a frame of reference, making a subject superfluous. What one can, however, take from this is the interplay between these fixed points, which is easily translatable into the interplay between various actors, be they objects or subjects. Leibniz is followed by Immanuel Kant's *a priori* space. Contrary to Leibniz' relational space, Kant argues that space is always already-there, and needs neither object nor subject to 'be'. Access to space is only on the basis of rationality, i.e. thinking about space. Because thinking (as well as orientation and navigation in the world) is always necessarily spatial, the subject can only think about space. Space can exist without the subject, but not vice versa.

It is Martin Heidegger's[75] *Dasein* space that transforms this *a priori* space, a space without a subject, into a space that becomes the space of *experience*. Thinking about space thus necessitates a conscious subject in order to be perceived as space. Here, space is an

---

[74] Generally, *Robinson Crusoe* is considered the first European novel ever produced. See for example *The Rise of the Novel: Studies in Defoe, Richardson and Fielding* (1957).

[75] The texts dealing Leibniz, Kant, and Heidegger are taken from the edited volume *Raumtheorie. Grundlagentexte aus Philosophie und Kulturwissenschaften* (Dünne & Günzel, 2006).

internal experience and receives a subjective dimension. Heidegger does argue that it is not an individual experience, but he does offer the subject as the focal point in considerations of spatial theorisation. Finally, with the continued emergence of the subject, Michel Foucault[76] argues for ideas concerning space to be applied in a social context, thus arguing for *social* space. This argument places society and its dealing with space at the centre of discussions concerning space with the focus on flows of control, discipline, power, and transgressions. He further reflects on time's influence on experiences on space, thus returning to my initial argument that these two concepts are inextricably linked. Foucault, however, argues for an egalitarian interrogation of these two concepts in respect to history's – and thus time's – prominent position.

The final theorist who will be introduced in respect to spatial considerations is Henri Lefebvre. The difference between Lefebvre and the other thinkers is his focus on space as a product, something that has the same value as anything that a society is able to produce. This difference is important when considering developments in societies, especially through the founding of abstract, and yet concrete, institutions such as capitalism, the nation, the state, and the expansion of these institutions. At the centre are society and its 'lived' spaces, and it is these spaces that are 'designed' by representational spaces that include maps, plans, and statistics. This combination is contested by a third space Lefebvre identifies, namely spaces of representation – the space in which art (and potentially literature) influences how the other two forms of space are interpreted, utilised, or rejected. Although Lefebvre is dismissive of literature as an agent of change, it is the spaces of representation which he identifies as the most potent instrument of possible innovation and as a revolutionary tool.

Once a working synthesis of Lefebvrian space and literary analysis has been established, I will venture into the sphere of the colonial novels. The three novels I have chosen, *Peter Moor*, *Heim Neuland*, and *Du heiliges Land!*, will be discussed together under the chapter heading **The Colonial Era: War, Toil, and Diamonds**. The themes I will discuss begin with a review of the landscape as experienced by the various characters. The focus is the idea of the 'empty' landscape (in this case the emptied landscape), and the various levels of spatial production identified through the narration as well as the characters' experience of these landscapes. From the landscape, the focus becomes the idea of the *whiteness* of the characters, mainly concentrating on the link between this *whiteness* and femininity because of the various arguments linking the industry of the female to her purity and her reproductive capabilities[77]. These qualifiers culminate in a European space, which these

---

[76] Foucault's ideas are taken from his 1967 interview "Of Other Spaces: Utopias and Heterotopias".
[77] Female reproduction has a number of levels, beginning with the biological (producing offspring), to the

female characters try to reproduce in the colony, namely the garden. The characters have different access to this space due to either their gender (Peter Moor), their industry (Etta Wibrandt, Gerda Ehlers, and Zoë von Gensdorff), or their status (Ingeborg and Carola Oberländer). However, the garden is a motif appearing in all three novels and is strongly linked to the *white*, colonising female.

Continuing chronologically, the Colonial Block will be succeeded by **The Apartheid Era: The Trust in Maps and Guns**. This section consists of two novels – although the Namibian novel *Born of the Sun* can be said to be part of this section, at least within its period. *Whiteness* will be revisited, but this time in another configuration. A first topic of analysis is the (de)construction of the *white*, male explorer as outlined in *A Twist of Sand* and "The Narrative of Jacobus Coetzee". An introductory foray into this stock character of colonial, and later apartheid, literature is interrogated via the idea of the 'empty' landscape discussed in the previous chapter. This time the question centres around how this idea is remodelled, seeing as the 'empty' landscape of the colonial imagination cannot fully be realised in these narratives. The *new* 'empty' landscapes must be produced under different circumstances and must be navigated and dominated in different ways. The sea as well as pre-colonial Namibia become the new spaces in which the *white* explorer can be situated and allowed to reproduce metropolitan fantasies while reflecting the dream worlds of the contemporary system. The fact that SWA as a territory was utilised very nominally as a setting for (English) apartheid literature makes these narratives important as products with which to understand the occupied territory as a laboratory for emerging concepts such as Afrikaner nationalism, SWA as space of adventure (as opposed to a space of settlement), and the covert desires and fears of the apartheid administration as propagated by the National Party. The themes discussed have a strong colonialist dimension, as numerous themes discussed in the Colonial Block are reflected in both apartheid novels. This begins with the primacy of *whiteness* in the construction and focalisation of the narratives, to the marginalisation and peripheral status of Africanist characters, to the forcing of European concepts upon the colony/administered territory. However, although there are a number of overlaps, the engines and legitimisation of power are starkly different as were the exercises of power.

The final chapter concerning the literary analysis consists of an antithesis, of a counter discourse to the previous novels, namely **The Namibian Era: Learning to Sing**. With the discussed novels all flowing from *white* European hands and written for *white* European eyes and minds, *Born of the Sun* creates a SWA which is in the throes of independence from South African administration. With its status as the first Black Namibian novel,

---

cultural (producing social beings), to the state (producing the nation).

and written from a Namibian perspective, the novel creates the conditions in which to interpret the history and the space of Namibia from a contrasting point of view. The fact that certain spaces are infused with resistant potential (such as the village, but also the jail cell) means that colonialist and apartheid spatial productions are ruptured or reconfigured. What this means is that the powerful metropole is disturbed, its authoritative tentacles are weakened. Namibia is imagined from 'the inside', meaning that local signs and symbols are either revitalised or redefined in order to create conditions for resistance and agency. *Born of the Sun* opens a space in which to challenge the arguments I have made in the previous chapters, especially since the novel does not comply with the *white* European gaze on Namibia. Furthermore, it allows a comparative look at how similar spaces are fictionalised by different authors and how different periods affect these imaginings. Lastly, the novel must be read as an answer to the productions of colonial GSWA and apartheid SWA, culminating in an independent Namibia – a process of development which must consequently end with the reclaiming of history and space in the service of those who have suffered injustices. In a way, Diescho's novel forecasts the establishment of the Heroes' Acre, or as President Nujoma put it in the inauguration speech: "At this Heroes' Acre we, the Namibian people, are writing the history of Namibia, the history of victory, the history of unity, the history of dedication, indeed, the history of nationhood".

2 Social and Literary Space

Where there is space there is being[1].
(Friedrich Nietzsche)

Nietzsche's assertion concerning space is a golden thread that moves through most contemporary spatial theories, especially since the social subject has become central. However, he neglects to add a second component that is necessary for his assertion: time. Time and space are the two aspects that are fundamental when thinking about being in the world. Without these two components, any existence is impossible. On the one hand, time is essential for the process of being as it maps trajectories from their start to the next point, culminating in an end (this can be natural as in death or artificial like a finishing line). There are arguments that positively postulate infinity[2] but these exclude realities such as life or any of its fixed temporal dimensions (ageing, death[3]). Because of concepts such as transience and durability, time is often accepted as a form of evidence for existence. Areas such as geology and physics place time centrally in their theories in order to prove processes or developments. Time therefore has an effectual dimension.

Space on the other hand is essential because it allows time – and therefore events – to unfold, to take place in a particular environment, not just as a backdrop, but as an essential participant. If time is the 'evidence' of existence, space must then be the setting wherein this takes place. A number of literary theories, for example, argue that narrated spaces can in fact be considered as characters in their own right[4], while new theories such as urbanism posit that space is a relevant factor in the formation of subjectivity and an understanding of the world at large[5]. Time and space – as a combination – can be seen as the foundation of being, and conversely, being is always a time- and space-related phenom-

---

[1] Quoted in *The Production of Space* (1974/1991:22).
[2] The accessible *Introducing Infinity: A Graphic Guide* (2012) traces the idea of 'infinity' from its proposition as an abstract term during the Classic period to its various guises within the contemporary period. The book illustrates infinity's simplistic dimension (the Möbius loop), to its paradoxical nature (Zeno's paradoxes).
[3] Notions such as the life cycle, age, decomposition, etc. can only function when coupled with accepted notions of time and sequentiality, e.g. the end of a life, phase, or stage (such as metamorphosis).
[4] Barbara Piatti (2008), for example, mentions Thomas Mann's *Tod in Venedig*, in which the setting has developed "Protagonistenqualitäten" (footnote 20, pg. 20). Here the space of action becomes as important as the characters themselves.
[5] For an Introduction, see "The People, Place and Space Reader" (Low and Seagert, 2014), especially chapters 4 & 7; as well as Liam Kennedy's *Race and Urban Space in Contemporary American Culture* (2000) for a look at how space also informs race and racism.

enon. It is this combination that produces the effects of sequentiality (time) and simultaneity (space) and allows for fields of knowledge such as history and geography. Time and space are inseparable and cannot be divorced from the idea of being in the world.

Time, however, does not only have sequential qualities. It possesses a circular logic that is expressed in the four seasons, the week, lunar timetables, and so forth. Space itself can be material, as in the interior of a room, and simultaneously abstract, as in the architect's design for this room. Because time and space are the foundations of human experience and existence, it naturally follows that numerous disciplines have contributed and tried to explain these two phenomena. And as these fields of knowledge have changed over time (some have only appeared more recently) so have approaches, definitions, qualities, and perceptions. Time alone has been broken up and fragmented into numerous different categories such as felt time, subjective time, lived time, social time, experienced time – all somehow connected to the individual feeling, experiencing subject. Categories have been further extended by theoretical physics, proposing things such as alternate universes (resulting in different time figurations), black holes (where time is slowed down), quantum mechanics (where time can flow forward as well as backward), and many more *theoretical* applications. Religious Studies have added to the debates as have various cultural developments concerning the recording, dealing with, and experiencing of time[6].

If all of these developments and hypotheses concerning time and its changeability have been set up and spread, then space itself should be just as diverse. Any discussion on space will reveal how different disciplines work with this concept, whether it is psychology (experienced space), social studies (lived space), religious studies (sacred/profane spaces), or physics (multi-dimensional space) or mathematics (plane space). As with time, various disciplines will deal with space (and its definitions) in a different manner, depending on what the aims are. Architects will deal with space on different levels (material space, abstract space, mathematical space) in order to successfully create buildings or structures. This will determine how engineers deal with space when deciding where to build roads or bridges. Artists who make use of public space through installations or graffiti may then use the same space. All these processes involve many different levels of spatiality and tend to be made up of a combination or cross between competing spatialities and spatial theories. These may allow for linkages between disparate fields, such as philosophy (for example social space) and literature (fictioned space).

---

[6] See for example *Religion and Time* (Balsev and Mohanty, 1993); *Time, Religion and History* (Gallois, 2007); *History, Time, Meaning, and Memory* (Denison, 2011).

If Lefebvre's arguments concerning the production of space hold then it should also hold for literary space, a social space that is produced on different and interconnected levels. On a formal level, the author constructs the narrative with his/her understanding of space as it appears or should appear in order to push the plot forward. This is further expanded through the narrator's conception of his/her environment and his/her position in the narrative. On a final level, the characters themselves are anchored in the space of the narrative and concern themselves with navigating that world. Subjective and personal experiences of space (via the narrating instance and the characters) come to the fore and can become central to the narrative. Katrin Dennerlein (2009) identifies exactly these methods of representing space in the novel. She however goes further in her assessment of these representations, arguing that "Raum kann in narrativen Texten auf viele verschiedene Arten dargestellt werden. Er kann unter anderem durch Figuren oder durch den Erzähler vermittelt, *anthromorphisiert* oder *allegorisiert*, *wahrgenommen* oder *beschrieben* werden und *Schauplatz* oder *Gegenstand von Reflexionen* sein" (my emphasis, 115). In other words, (literary) space has the capacity to be employed within an allegoric framework, referencing a place or space without specifically naming it. An example from my primary texts would be "The Narrative of Jacobus Coetzee", which uses pre-colonial Namibia to reflect upon apartheid South Africa via a number of overlapping themes.

In another example, Thomas Waszak[7] divides the spaces of fictional texts into two main categories and four further subcategories. The first main category is "Raum als materiales Konstrukt", divided into "kognitiv" and "territorial". The second category is "Raum als soziales Konstrukt", with the subdivisions of "symbolisch" and "metaphorisch". The various layers or literary space complement the various layers of material space. This creates the possibility of applying theories of the material to the literary[8]. He includes spaces that are psychological or that involve *thinking* about space, linking aspects such as *a priori* and *Dasein* space to the sphere of the imaginative. In a final comment, Waszak includes space as a construct, nearly echoing Lefebvre (who looks at it from a production perspective). Because subjectivities are at the centre of any literary analysis, so should ideas of power, power relations, and relevant relationships.

Space in literature achieves what 'real' space cannot, namely being produced outside the constraints that rigidly govern the real world (gravity, volume, laws, 'history'). But before we make use of the concepts of production and reproduction, it is imperative that a broad understanding of space and its elemental parts is achieved. The first part of

---

[7] "Umkämpfte Räume und (anti)kolonialer Diskurs in Eva Zellers afrikanischen Erzählungen *Die magische Rechnung*" in Arich-Gertz, Schmidt and Ziehen (2014:33–52).

[8] Literary theory provides an immense pool of terminology when dealing with fictional or representational space. For more, see the Introduction and Chapter 1 in Barbara Piatti's *Geographie der Literatur* (2008).

this chapter will therefore consist of an attempt to design a working understanding of space, relying on Leibniz, Kant, Heidegger, and Foucault. They represent a certain cohesion of thinking in the sense that they continue to build upon or reassess each other's work. Leibniz refers to Newton and Euclid, two prominent mathematicians and philosophers, in his conception of space, while Kant refers to Leibniz in his work. Heidegger in turn refers to Kant. This does not of course mean that there is an overarching theory or consensus. I merely posit that they are aware of a predecessor's work and try to improve on or disprove the theory. One can, nevertheless, identify a certain thread going through the theorisation of space in general (whether it focuses on mathematics, *being* in space, or space as an aesthetic product). These differing theories are evidence of the many faces that space has and has been given. It should prove fruitful to contrast the 'classic' ideas and concepts concerning space with those that put the subject in social space in focus (Foucault)[9]. What also seems to be quite useful is to follow the changing position of the subject within space, from being absent/non-referential (Leibniz), to it becoming central (Foucault).

With a shift in the subject's social and space producing theorisation, one should also consider that a shift from history (time) to geography (space) took place. Space, as a vital social technology, becomes central in an/the organisation of an/the urbanised world, especially since the number of urban centres is constantly evolving, as is the number of people who are moving to urban centres. Spatiality (at least according to Soja[10]) allows for the interrogation of societal processes which temporality might overlook or is unable to identify. In order to 'visualise' these theories or to visualise how they might work on a literary level, I will always link them to one of my primary texts. This link will remain fleeting and superficial, its only function being to show how these theories can be made visible within a literary setting while also showing how they can be used to interrogate literature. It is at this juncture that I would like to point towards the Eurocentric nature of these philosophies and theories. Because of my aim to place them within my project dealing with Africa and Africans, it should be said that these spatial conceptions merely serve to situate Lefebvre's social space within the wider network of European thinking about space. These theories emerged from a certain tradition in which European space and subjects are central, especially in their difference to 'Others'. A critique of such theories

---

[9] I would argue that Foucault's ideas of space can be categorized as both absolute-real (heterotopia) as well as mythical-aesthetic (utopia). Social space, however, seems to be the most prominent aspect of his thinking about space.

[10] Soja (1989) defines spatiality as "the created space of social organization and production" (79). Because space is social and society is spatial, spatiality allows for a further tool of analysis when looking at social developments.

will therefore be included when discussing this etymology. The final step in this chapter will be the proposed synthesis between Lefebvre's social space and what I have defined as literary space.

Lefebvre does not focus on literature as a 'space' in his theory, his arguments are only applied to the 'real world'. It is thus essential that the arguments inherent in the text are changed in such a way as to be consistent with literary spaces. Social space needs to be bound to the tools and concepts from the disciplines of narratology and narrative theory. Only once social space enters the literary world through the filters of narrativity and narration can literary space be interrogated. Fictionalised space can be treated as 'real' through this filter. History thus becomes predominantly spatial – as opposed to temporal[11]. One can then use this statement and apply it to the production of literature (produced in a certain space at a certain time, and necessarily anchored within a certain discourse). This would allow an examination of how dominant theories of space are reflected aesthetically and poetically and how these theories feed back into the construction of spatial understanding in a 'real world' setting. Following theorists and literary critics such as Bakhtin, space in literature has the potential to reflect current spatial debates and developments. His concept of the chronotope allows literature to be interrogated along the relationship between space and time, framing space as an aesthetic practice instead of merely treating it as a general fictional element. Although Bakhtin and his chronotope will only appear occasionally as an analytical tool in my literary analyses, it will be utilised to mark important spaces in the novels.

Through the chronotope certain narrative spaces will be foregrounded in order to connect the various fictionalised temporal and spatial levels while inquiring how these two interact. This may in turn help to garner an understanding of certain events and political processes. An example for this may be certain realities that are omitted when writing about a certain space. Geoffrey Jenkins' novel *Twist of Sand* (1959) is set *and* appears during the rise of apartheid in both SA and SWA. This is mentioned only once in the entire novel, although it is the force that defines and configures nearly every spatial aspect of these two states. Although the reflection of the time might be accurate (certain technologies, names of places, smaller historical events), Jenkins' dealings with space and mobility hide the racist-oppressive system of apartheid[12]. The high focus on the sea, along with its

---

[11] Ulrike Jureit's *Das Ordnen von Räumen* (2012) is an excellent investigation of this relationship, focussing on Nazi Germany's expansion eastward and the consequent destruction of the large sections of the Jewish population.
[12] "We must be insistently aware of how space can be made to hide consequences from us, how relations of power and discipline are inscribed into the apparently innocent spatiality of social life, how human geographies become filled with politics and ideology" (Soja, 1989: 1).

constant 'sudden' developments, may point to a territory which is as yet not as organised and stable as the body of maps, laws, and official statements would like to project.

The unpredictable[13] relation between the narrated spaces and the narrated time may therefore reveal certain real-time and real-space developments. Add to this the reliance of the protagonist on his vessel(s), a mobile space constantly threatened by natural occurrences, and the application of the chronotope becomes fruitful. What must be remembered throughout the literary analyses is what Arich-Gertz et al. have postulated: "Raum konstituiert sich zuerst in der Symbolpraxis des Schreibens" (11). In other words, it is the act of 'writing the landscape' or the narrative spaces that creates them – a process completed through the reader who animates these landscapes and narrated spaces. This is fulfilled by what can be considered the performativity of literature, or "the influence of fictional space on real space" (Arich-Gertz et al. 2014:20). The production of literary space can be equated with that of real space, the one affecting the other in one way or another.

One shortcoming identified by Bakhtin, however, makes the analysis of literary space decidedly more complex than its one-to-one relationship to real space, namely his concept of polyphony[14]. As will become clear when dealing with some of the various fictional texts, the voice of authority, of narration, of mediation in many cases stems from a single source. Other and 'Other' voices are silenced. This monologic production of (hi)stories and places creates a one-dimensional literary landscape. Bakhtin's polyphony – a term with its origin in music theory – opens up a definitive look at how the narrative voice dominates the text and the characters while simultaneously making the hierarchies between speakers and non-speakers visible. "The Narrative of Jacobus Coetzee" appears to be the exception, especially when considering the various levels of narration as well as the ideas concerning the non-speaking subject. However, the dominance of the I-narrator as well as the close proximity between narrator and colonising characters makes polyphony a vital tool in establishing the relationships between the fictional characters. These relationships, in combination with *where* and *how* they are formed, will steadily inform my spatial analyses. Before I open up a sample literary analysis, I would like to begin with a short introduction to the spatial theories that have influenced European conceptions of itself and the 'Other'.

---

[13] Not unpredictable to Captain Macdonald/Commander Peace, to a certain extent. He is at least able to 'read' the various land- and seascapes he comes across in comparison to the rest of the characters.

[14] According to Bakhtin, polyphony can be defined as "multi-voicedness" (*Problems of Dostoevsky's Poetics* 1972:279), and is strongly linked to "dialogism" (*The Dialogic Imagination*, 198: xxiv). In essence it focusses on the interaction between various 'voices' in which no one voice is privileged over another.

From Relative to Social Space

Time as a fact, as a reality, and as a concept, is by far more (omni)present than the idea of space. Time is constantly 'already-there' via daily routines, appointments, deadlines, and so forth. Because it is 'already-there' it appears to be measurable and therefore evident. Tools and instruments of measurement such as watches and clocks are pervasive and habitually invasive. And when they are not, there are further indicators of time's presence: the introductory music of one's favourite series, the arrival of a certain bus, the bells of a nearby church. In a way time is less visible because it is in plain view[15]. Generally accepted as a fact, time has become naturalised, meaning that its objective reality tends to overshadow its discursive and disciplining character. Because of this overstimulation of time or the feeling of now/later, space becomes concealed – it is hidden behind its omnipresence. Space becomes secondary, trivial. Space only seems to become noticeable when it is there in excess (e.g. lost out on the sea/in a desert) or extremely scarce (e.g. trapped in a submarine/in a tiny apartment) or when mobility is limited/restricted. And according to Lem[16], it is something that is solid, something tangible.

Accordingly, space is imagined as the exact opposite of time, which is invisible, fluid, and infinite. It is essentially locked in a binary relationship. This is far from the truth however, as classic and contemporary theories about space have attempted to show. Space is in fact not "less mysterious", it is not "monolithic". It has remarkably many facets and definitions. It has confounded and mystified thinkers since antiquity (and probably even earlier). It has been attributed godly qualities (for example Newton), been the subject of a number of thought experiments (for example Aristotle, Zeno[17]) and was the basis for some of modern philosophy's thinking (for example Descartes[18]). Space must therefore be placed on the same pedestal as time if one is to understand the world and, maybe more importantly, being in the world[19]. The theories of space that I will discuss should serve to build a basic awareness of spatial thinking.

---

[15] As is the case with *whiteness*, invisibility and hypervisibility (an excessive focus on making visible) appear to be two successful strategies to hide behind.

[16] "Of the two powers, the two categories that take possession of us when we enter the world, space is by far the less mysterious...Space is, after all, solid, monolithic...Time, on the other hand, is a hostile element, truly treacherous, I would say even against human nature" (Stanislaw Lem, *Highcastle: A Remembrance* (1966/2003).

[17] Some of the thought experiments focus on (paradoxes of) movement through space, speed, and motion.

[18] Descartes is a proponent of 'empty space' (in this case a vacuum) and has contributed greatly to modern physics through his ideas of "laws of nature and a conservation principle of motion; he constructed what would become the most popular theory of planetary motion of the late seventeenth century" (http://plato.stanford.edu/entries/descartes-physics/#3).

[19] "We are in the epoch of simultaneity: we are in the epoch of juxtaposition, the epoch of the near and the far, of the side-by-side, of the dispersed. We are at a moment, I believe, when our experience of the

This rather limited overview should in no way be considered as complete as there are numerous other theories that deal with space. A superficial scan of any volume concerned with spatial thinking will attest to this, especially as the categories may differ, for example. *Raumtheorie* (2006) by Jörg Dünne and Stephan Günzel might serve as a good example. The edited volume consists of six different methods of classifying space, ranging from the metaphysical to the aesthetic. One could of course argue that the various concepts of space inform each other and that any distinctions are artificial. However, this should not deflect from the important point that time also informs how space is conceptualized, either as a historic marker or as a theoretical element. Furthermore, it underlines the idea that multiple spatial theories can develop in parallel in different regions. My choices point towards an evolving spatial theorization and allow a certain level of continuity as well as innovation. Because of their relative temporal proximity to each other, they further signify certain shifts in the understanding of space. My immediate concern in the interrogation of my selected theories is the evolution of the subject within accepted notions of space, i.e. how space deals with the individual who shapes space and who is shaped by it. Although I don't approach these questions in this section, they will permeate the discussion of my literary texts throughout. Furthermore, I will not make use of these theories specifically, as my main focus is on social space as furthered by Lefebvre. My selection still serves two functions: 1) to trace an evolving understanding of space, and 2) to create a platform from which to interrogate social space through the evolution of the social subject. As *relational* space will show, the subject may be included in spatial processes, but is not constitutive of these.

Gottfried Wilhelm Leibniz' *Relational* Space[20]

Leibniz's considerations concerning space take the shape of a letter exchange between himself and Samuel Clarke, a proponent of Newtonian space, which in essence proposes a space that is transcendental and divine, existing as an extension of God[21]. However: space is not God, rather is it a container of his design. The debate begins with Leibniz opening with a Newtonian definition of space, which he gives as "das Organ, das Gott benutzt, um die Dinge wahrzunehmen" (2006:58). It is this statement that lays the foundation of his rejection of Newtonian space. As the discussion evolves, it becomes clear that Leibniz is designing his own definition against that of this generally accepted notion, especially in

---

world is less that of a long life developing through time than that of a network that connects points and intersects with our own skein." (Foucault 1967/ 1984: 1).

[20] Taken from "Briefwechsel mit Samuel Clarke" (1715/ 1716) in *Raumtheorie* (2006).
[21] [Space is] "eine Eigenschaft bzw. eine Folge aus der Existenz eines unendlichen und ewigen Wesens. Der unendliche Raum ist die Unermeßlichkeit, aber dies Unermeßlichkeit ist nicht Gott" (2006:60).

reference to the fusion between mathematical and divine space. He first questions 'godly space' by questioning its fractured and divided nature. He comments "[d]a der Raum aus Teilen besteht, ist er etwas, was nicht zu Gott passen kann" (60). This would refer to Clarke's previous explanation that God is everywhere at the same time and is therefore able to perceive everything which exists. This allows Leibniz a further platform to remove the metaphysical qualities of space. He bases his argument on the ordering principle(s) of space. As time orders things consecutively, space should therefore order things next to each other[22]. In other words, just as time regulates sequences, space regulates that which is side by side. This simple idea opens up space as being dependent and defined by the relationship between the *things* that occupy it.

Leibniz moves away from space as a given and identifies certain characteristics such as the impossibility to be empty and the impossibility for identical points to be reproduced. Furthermore, he is able to make an intangible and slippery concept graspable by filling it with 'things' instead of a transcendent being. Put differently: Leibniz's focus is the relation of things to each other, which then 'creates' space:

> Der Raum ist etwas vollkommen Homogenes und wenn sich in dem Raum keine Dinge befinden, so unterscheidet sich ein Raumpunkt durchaus in nichts. […] Ihr Unterschied beruht darum nur auf unserer trügerischen Annahme von der Wirklichkeit eines Raumes an sich. In Wirklichkeit aber ist der einzige Zustand genau der gleiche wie der andere, da sie vollkommen ununterscheidbar sind." (61–62)

Although this new understanding of space has a mathematical dimension (he speaks of 'Raumpunkte') and has the quality of being reproducible on paper – and therefore abstract – it also negates the idea of *empty space*, a concept which is deeply rooted in the colonial project. If one is to take Leibniz's spatial theory and insist that things create space, the fantasy of empty space becomes null. The absence of things in space would equal the absence of space. Without the relation between things there is no space to contain these relations.

Space can, so far, be defined as an organizing principle in that it is the relation between things. In order to gain access to Leibniz's idea of the 'relational things', it might be helpful to look at how he defines *Ort* (place) in relation to *Raum* (space). *Ort*

> [i]st das, was zu den verschiedenen Zeitpunkten für verschiedene existierende Dinge dann dasselbe ist, wenn deren Beziehung des Nebeneinanderbestehens mit gewissen existierenden Dingen, die von dem einen Zeitpunkte bis zu dem anderen Zeitpunkt als fest vorausgesetzt werden, miteinander völlig übereinstimmen. Fest existierende Dinge sind solche

---

[22] "Was meine eigene Meinung anbetrifft, so habe ich mehr als einmal gesagt, daß ich den Raum ebenso wie etwas rein Relatives halte, nämlich für eine *Ordnung des Nebeneinanderbestehens*, so wie Zeit eine Ordnung der Aufeinanderfolge ist" (my emphasis, 2006:61).

> Dinge, für die es keine Ursache für irgendeine Veränderung der Ordnung ihres Neben-
> einanderbestehens mit anderen Dingen gegeben hat bzw. (was dasselbe ist) bei denen keine
> Bewegung stattgefunden hat. (69)

Place is defined as a collection of *some* permanent, immovable, or constant things whose relation does not change drastically. On maps this would ideally present mountains, forests, rivers, or cities, amongst others. In outer space this would refer to constellations or planetary systems. Space becomes a collection of other spaces between these permanents and can therefore either move freely (clouds, meteorites, people) and through emerging patterns create new space. *Raum* has the function of placing these permanents in a relation to each other, becoming "das, was sich aus den Orten ergibt, wenn man sie zusammennimmt" (69). From these two definitions, one can now subsume that the most basic element in the production of space is not one singular *Ding*, but its permanent *relation* to another *Ding*. Leibniz does not define his concept of *Ding* (where it originates from), his most vital piece[23]. Space is not given a moment of 'origin' – how it came into being – but is rather described as it is at a specific moment. Space, like time, becomes infinite as it neither has beginning nor end, only a perpetual current state. The relational subject takes up a very minimal, potentially insignificant, role in the production of space because it is subordinated to permanent things (as it is itself not of such nature). In essence, the subject is only part of this construction *if* one includes it in the category of things. Leibniz, in his theory, does not see it as constituent to the creation or maintenance of space.

While moving through the seemingly endlessness of the African landscape, Peter Moor is continuously and without fail surrounded by the "bush" and the "enemy". Throughout the novel, these two factors are the most permanent and pervasive elements appearing in the landscape as well as in Peter Moor's mental processes. Although they are both able to move metaphorically, these two 'permanents' create the space Peter Moor inhabits for a short period of time. Peter Moor's movement is maintained and reproduced narratively as he constantly encounters these two elements, signifying his disorientation in an alien environment. He is, however, able to orientate himself[24] according to these two permanent narrative elements. The space of GSWA is produced (at least for the protagonist) through the 'fixed' points of the "bush" and the "enemy". These permanents are supported through other permanents such as the barren gardens as well destroyed buildings, both referencing the two original permanents. The burnt down houses are the result of the "enemy" while

---

[23] Could there have been a time without *das Ding*? And how was it produced/ reproduced?
[24] One can argue that this takes a temporal dimension, as Peter Moor is able to orientate himself in the world and history through the elimination of both the threat of the "bush" and the "enemy".

the "bush" encroaches onto the gardens that have been abandoned. The complication offered by the "enemy" and the "bush" is the fact that the landscape and accompanying spaces suddenly become run-through and overly reliant on these place-producing elements, eliminating other place-producing elements intrinsic to the 'real' landscape. The abstract and the implied are used in an attempt to empty the landscape by replacing the space-producing strategies in use by the original inhabitants, in this case the Herero.

A further development one must consider in respect to the permanents, especially if they are imagined as such, is that if these permanents are changed, so is the space. In other words: by annihilating the Herero (literally and figuratively), Peter Moor and company of course change the landscape of the colony. What was disorganised and barren becomes more organised and less barren (the end of the war is symptomatic of this linear thought process). After the threatening Herero are finally removed from a threatening landscape, the bush becomes lush with colours and scents while flowers begin blossoming. The groundwork for a new space, with new permanents (German farms, towns, railway tracks) has been laid for a European space. The imagined permanent link to the metropole guarantees this space since the metropole is fixed and, through the acquisition of the new territory, envisioned to remain in a dialectic relationship to the colony. The Herero find no mention after they are forced into the desert to their death, thus dispelling them from the narrative. What remains is the bush, but not as a threat anymore – only potential.

Although the "bush" is a colonial construct and a European imposition onto the landscape, its ever-presence is indicative of Peter Moor's understanding of his environment. Although Leibniz's theory speaks against the idea of 'empty space', it is unable to influence how this space is filled, especially in respect to the linguistic or imaginative. The over-reliance on fixed points of reference as space-forming elements creates the conditions to employ exactly these elements in order to negate the space that was previously conceptualised. The result is a colonial landscape in which the permanents are produced in such a way that their relationship is manipulated in order to serve a certain telos. The discursive space is contained within a certain network of places, which are produced and defined by the colonial explorer/military man. The disavowal of non-European *Dinger* allows for the effective projection of the symbolic onto colonial spaces and thus justifies their usurpation and reconfiguration. Setting up places such as borders, enclosures, military camps, etc. creates new permanent *Dinger*, which in turn produce new spaces, resulting in the alternate 'filling in' of the space. So, while Leibniz's theory has the potential to counter the fantasy of 'empty' space, it simultaneously creates the conditions in which the selective location of permanent *Dinger* produces spaces that can be filled with imperialist desires and fantasies. The dehistoricisation of the Herero, by refusing to name them or link them to their environment, justifies European control over their definition (solely as an "enemy") and access to their spatial resources, most notably land.

Immanuel Kant's *A Priori* Space[25]

Kant's thoughts on space take the form of an initial thought experiment, which is based on Leibniz's theory. The experiment consists of him proposing the 'reflection' of his hand on a surface. The outline of his hand would consist of points, which can be identically reproduced on some surface. Because of this mirroring effect, the points to be reproduced would be identical to their 'originals'. Kant employs this tool in order to disprove Leibniz's assumption that points in identical positions would in fact negate space. After his experiment he is able to assert that:

> [e]s ist hieraus [the thought experiment] klar, daß nicht die Bestimmung des Raumes Folge von den Lagen der Teile der Materie gegeneinander, sondern diese Folgen von jenen sind, und daß also in der Beschaffenheit der Körper Unterschiede angetroffen werden können und zwar wahre Unterschiede, die sich lediglich auf den *absoluten* und *ursprünglichen* Raum beziehen, weil nur durch ihn das Verhältnis körperlicher Dinge möglich ist, und daß, weil der absolute Raum kein Gegenstand einer äußeren Empfindung, sondern der Grundbegriff ist, der alle dieselbe erst möglich macht, wir dasjenige, was in der Gestalt eines Körpers lediglich die Beziehung auf den reinen Raum angeht, nur durch die Gegenhaltung mit anderen Körpern wahrnehmen könnte. (emphasis in original, 75)

He argues that things do not create space, but vice versa. Things can only exist because absolute and primordial space allows this. This inverts Leibniz 'creation' of space, returning space to the realm of abstract and transcendental (Newtonian) space. Kant argues that space, in its most basic sense, is something that orders all experienced phenomena and therefore bestows the individual with the ability to comprehend the external world through this process. To put it differently: space is already there, before we can prove it, before we can create it. But through its presence, it creates a matrix that gives the individual the tools to experience space. We can therefore only understand, think about, and 'create' space because it is already there.

This is necessary even when thinking about mathematical space, as Günzel explains, "[d]enn Raum (als äußere Form der Anschauung) ist die Grundlage jeder Beschreibung räumlicher Konfigurationen" (319). This is in response to Kant postulating that space can only have three dimensions (length, breadth, depth). This is highly relevant in respect to the idea of time (considered the fourth dimension), meaning that space remains timeless. Kant's space becomes something that can only be understood. The impossibility to

---

[25] Based on "a) Vom ersten Grunde des Unterschiedes der Gegenden im Raum" (1768), "b) Von dem Raume (1770), and "c) Was heißt: sich im Denken orientieren?" (1786) in *Raumtheorie* (2006).

remove space from understanding or contemplation is finally asserted with Kant's statement that "Der Raum ist eine notwendige Vorstellung *a priori*, die allen äußeren Anschauungen zum Grunde liegt. Man kann sich niemals eine Vorstellung davon machen, dass kein Raum sei, ob man sich gleich ganz wohl denken kann, daß keine Gegenstände darin angetroffen werden" (110). Space without reflection is possible, but not the other way around. Thinking, even of nothing, is inevitably spatial. For Kant it is the individual's calling to understand and think about the space that it inhabits therefore infusing knowledge into that space. This in turn can bring the individual closer to the concept that it inhabits and identifies as its world.

In essence, Kant's theory can be broken down into two main strands. Firstly, we need the *mind* so we can manoeuvre through space in thought, as well as physically[26]. It is something that is always there, pre-existence, and outside the individual. Secondly, space does not need to be filled – as Leibniz has argued – for it to be there. For Kant, merely the act of thinking about space, empty or filled, is already spatial. Rationality is not necessarily a prerequisite of space as any thinking, whether highly rational or irrational, must have a spatial dimension. The mind is the tool needed to grasp space, but not sanity. This becomes evident when considering exercises in logic. Even a person who believes s/he is made of glass will think spatially in order not to fall and break. One might psychologically exist in another space than that of the material world (i.e. in another place, in another time). For Kant then, the three dimensions are the basic denominator for spatial thinking, something which we as thinking beings are unable to escape. This essentially confirms Leibniz's position that space does not need the individual to exist, but that the opposite is most definitely true. Ulf Heuner (2006) summarizes Kant's attitude: "*Auf jeden Fall kommt erst der Raum und dann das, was wir mit ihm machen*" (emphasis in original, 7).

Like *relational* space, it seems appropriate to link this theory to a narrative. The narrative most fitting for this is "The Narrative of Jacobus Coetzee". Coetzee and Kant work on a number of levels, but it is the rational aspect of space which appears most powerfully in the narrative. This is first emphasised through Jacobus Coetzee's strong *rational* relationship to various spaces (the Cape Colony, topographies), while using space to rationalise a number of assumptions (the killing of the ~~Bushmen~~, as well as his 'superior' position vis-à-vis the Namaqua). Certain technologies play a significant part in these assumptions, ranging from his horse to his blue eyes. This rationalisation of his position in the world is taken a step further during his delirium. Although Jacobus Coetzee can be deemed to think and conceive of irrational arguments, he continues to think spatially. This culmi-

---

[26] The focal point for "c) Was heißt: sich im Denken orientieren?" (1786/2006).

nates in him 'becoming' the landscape, or in other words, him 'producing' the landscape through his rationalisation in it. His spatial thinking is more explicit during these moments, but it goes back to Kant's assertion that the subject is unable to think without employing space as a category, even if space does not need the contemplating subject to exist. Jacobus Coetzee complicates this somewhat, but this is only to replicate his earlier established god-like status. In order to rationalise this status, he is forced to remain in this construction, producing the landscape in which he is able to orientate himself even if only on an abstract and metaphorical level.

While Kant's ideas concerning space, especially its quality of being there before it can be experienced seemed revolutionary at the time, one must be aware of a number of links. The first is that the theory is a product of the Pan-European Enlightenment project. The fetishisation of rationality at the cost of a number of other mental processes (dreaming, intuition, irrationality) influenced European conception of non-Europeans, most detrimentally African subjects. By denying Africans any form of rationality, the *a priori* space in consequence denies Africans access to (Europeanised) space. By breaking this innate connection, Kant's theory reduces Africans' ability to negotiate time, locking them in a perpetual state of 'being' while they are understood as being unaware of this fact. Although Africans are seen to be able to at least think spatially, they are not understood to think *about* space. This allows Enlightenment philosophy to relegate African subjects to the non-human, paving the way for a plethora of further destructive and violent theories and processes such as colonisation, genocide, forced sterilisation, and cultural decimation. The theory itself has a comprehensible base (albeit one which has been dismantled), however, its application and the results of this application justified and accelerated imperial expansion.

Furthermore, Kant's philosophies in general placed Europe at the centre of the world, further placing *white* subjects at its centre. The effects of this are still felt today in a number of racist discourses, discourses in which African cultural practices and cosmologies are interpreted within an Enlightenment framework. By placing space outside of human influence, and by creating it as an exclusive sphere of reflection, Kant produces a space that is a purely *white* space. This form of European will to difference – and thus knowledge – can be summed up in Albert Memmi's words: "What is actually a sociological point becomes labelled as being biological or, preferably metaphysical" (1965/2003:115). He bases this observation on what he identifies as "three ideological components" used to support colonial racism. These are "one, the gulf between the culture of the colonist and the colonized; two, the exploitation of these differences for the benefit of the colonist; three, the use of these supposed differences as standards as absolute fact" (115). The neutral, rational quality of space is utilised to make space an exclusive subject while overwriting other/'Other' spatial configurations. The desire to locate difference and the production of 'truth' appear as the engines which fuel European racism in the colonies. Following Robert Zacharias' discussion of Enlightenment as being

> the logic through which entire continents get temporalized as 'New' and 'Old,' and through which the spatial binaries of colonialism – centre/ periphery, metropole/ colony, north/ south, First World/ Third World, and so on – are naturalized by their emplotment along a linear narrative of progress, geographies crushed into colonies by having 'the history of Empire laid upon them' (in Quayson, 2016:217)

it becomes clear how powerfully the concepts of space, time, Empire, geography, history, and logic are woven together in the process of colonisation, a web which is the consequence of Enlightenment rationality[27].

Martin Heidegger's *Dasein* Space[28]

"Wenn wir dem *Dasein* Räumlichkeit zusprechen, dann muß dieses >Sein im Raume< offenbar aus der Seinsart dieses Seienden begriffen werden." (141). This statement distinguishes Heidegger from the two predecessors by focussing on the individual who experiences space. Space can now be said to be experiential, originating in the individual's capacity to perceive. Although Kant argues that space allows for phenomena to be grasped, Heidegger argues that space itself is a phenomenon to be grasped. Herein lies the main difference between Kant and Heidegger: space 'containing' phenomena versus space itself 'being' a phenomenon. For Heidegger's *Dasein* to function, space needs to be external – so as to be experienced – and simultaneously needs to be internal – as a process of experience. This approach gives space a dual nature. It also gives space the quality to be the locus of all experiences, allowing it to form the blanket in which all experiences are covered. One could argue that space conceptualised like this has some echo of Newtonian space in the sense that it allows experience, albeit a god who experiences, to take place. In Heidegger's formulation, it is not God who is at the centre of experience, but the subject. However, the experience of space is not a subjective one. Because everybody is able to experience space, it is not a subjective experience, but a human one. This again has echoes of Kant, who posits that no one is outside space. Space is intrinsically linked to the mind,

---

[27] Quayson (2000) sums up this assertion as "the exclusionary forms of Western reason" is linked to "their complicity with imperial expansion and colonialist rule" (3). For a further discussion on the effects of Kant on Western conceptualisations of Africa/ns, see Piesche, Peggy "Der 'Fortschritt der Aufklärung – Kants 'Race' und die Zentrierung des *weißen* Subjekts" in: Maureen Maisha Eggers, Grada Kilomba, Peggy Piesche, and Susan Arndt: *Mythen, Masken und Subjekte*. (2009).

[28] From "Die Räumlichkeit des Daseins" in *Raumtheorie* (2006).

to the subject. It is in this vein that Heidegger posits that "[m]it dem In-der-Welt-sein ist der Raum zunächst in dieser Räumlichkeit entdeckt. Auf dem Boden der so entdeckten Räumlichkeit wird der Raum selbst für das Erkennen zugänglich" (2006:148). His main theory therefore argues that only once the subject enters space, is space there because it creates the conditions for experience. Once this is accepted he goes on to state that the

> Raum wird nicht allein erst durch die Entweltlichung der Umwelt zugänglich, Räumlichkeit ist überhaupt nur auf dem Grund der Welt entdeckbar, so zwar, daß der Raum die Welt doch *mit*konstruiert, entsprechend der wesenhaften Räumlichkeit des Daseins selbst hinsichtlich seiner Grundverfassung des In-der-Welt-seins. (emphasis in original, 2006:150)

In contrast to both Leibniz and Kant, Heidegger argues that space is a result of inner and outer experience of space. Kant's space is not internal because it is part of thought (a reflection on external stimuli) while for Heidegger space emerges from the interaction with the external world. For Kant, space demands reflection while space for Heidegger demands reaction. The subject and its experience becomes the focus of spatial understanding while moving away from the 'pure' spaces of mathematics and logic (Raumpunkte, the three dimensions). The subject is the locus of spatial theory, carried by the concepts of *Dasein* and *In-der-Welt-sein*. Space thus becomes reducible to questions of being and being in the world. This seems to locate thinking of space within the individual's ability to 'be' in space and experience it externally (as the world) and internally (as an immediate actuality). Space as it is, is always pre-subject. Even if I am never born, space will be there for at least someone else to experience. The space that I am born into, however, finds its definition in my experience of that space. Leibnizian and Kantian space have an eternal, unchangeable nature. Heidegger accepts this but argues that it is also experiential and therefore dependent on the subject itself. Space is not subjective; space is the subject. The thinking, feeling subject cannot create space, yet it can experience it. These two concepts are therefore inseparably linked through Heidegger's conception of space.

Du heiliges Land! provides an appropriate example to explicate Heidegger's *Dasein* space. The arrival of Ingeborg Oberländer in the colony has two different, but deeply connected, spatial components. Firstly, she enters a space connected quite superficially to her 'home' space, namely the German metropole. The encounter with this new space results in an emphasis of her internal space, which is projected onto this new space. An example of this is her homesickness manifesting itself as a sea of blooming flowers on the barren sands outside of her villa. Here, outside space responds to shifts taking place in her internal space. Inge's internal space is reflected onto an external, receptive surface. One must remember that the effects of external on internal space may vary and can be seen as being subjective. Yet, it is the process that is imagined as being universally human, namely the longing for one's home, and therefore not subjective – even if it is strongly linked to the individual.

Furthermore, Ingeborg's dreams, desires, and hopes are continually unlocked through processes of engagement with external space. Her internal space, more than any other character's, becomes locatable in the landscape. This is only recognisable to her though, as none of the other characters has access to her internal processes or to her projections onto the external space. Ingeborg's subjectivity is the result of the interplay between external and internal spaces and not only the result of relations (Leibniz) or thinking about space (Kant). Her production of the colony, although based on individual experience and sustained through her desires, must be read within the (supposed) universal act of leaving – and a longing for – home.

What makes Heidegger's spatial proposal so difficult to endorse is its universalist approach focussed on the individual[29]. The individual becomes the site of the universal, replicating Enlightenment arguments. His contemplation situates the individual within the 'experience' of a universal event ('being' in space), discarding that space can be a group or communal experience. When considering the horrors of the concentration camps (in GSWA and across Europe), as well as the conditions of the slave ships transporting kidnapped and enslaved Africans, 'being' in space according to Heidegger is basically nullified. Space under these extreme conditions is neither a subjective or individual experience, nor is it a universal experience; it is a communal and group experience, one that is essentially stretched into an experience of non-being[30]. *Dasein* is in effect reduced to only *Sein*. A further example of the problematic aspect of the *Dasein* space is that it is not relational, i.e. it does not provide a framework in which to discuss colonialism in respect to the hierarchies produced and the disparate experiences of space. Albert Memmi (1957/2003) reflects on being under French colonial rule in the preface to *The Colonizer and the Colonized*, stating "I was Tunisian, therefore colonized. I discovered that few aspects of my life and my personality were untouched by this fact. Not only my own thoughts, my passions and my conduct, but also the conduct of others towards me was affected" (4). The fact of colonialism defines and impacts one's relationship to the world and thus 'being' in the world. The chasm between individual, group, and universal practices of space becomes clear when they are stretched to the extreme. Tim Watson also links the focus on the individual as a source of the universal to imperial expansion[31]:

---

[29] A further problem is its so-called token 'human' concept, which tends to be linked to man/Man – making masculinity the exclusive 'human' gender (see for example Yekani (2011, especially Chapter 1)).
[30] For more on this, see for example Giorgio Agamben's *Homo Sacer: Sovereign Power and Bare Life* (1997).
[31] "The Colonial Novel" in Quayson (2016:15–34).

The historical shifts that enabled the novel to grow and attract readers were the same ones that allowed England, and subsequently Britain, to conquer and settle large portions of the world: an emphasis on the individual as a source of value and initiative" (2016:15).

Heidegger's inclusion of the individual subject within the frameworks of space and spatial thinking shows a progression from the previous theories by Leibniz and Kant. He is, however, unable to account for 'extreme' spaces[32] in which the universal is replaced by the communal and group experience of space.

Michel Foucault's *Utopian/Heterotopian* Space[33]

Foucault approaches the idea of space from a different perspective to those of the previous three theorists. He disconnects space from its mathematical-metaphysical and subject-experience figurations and focusses on its power-relational aspects. In other words, he is more interested in how space maintains/changes hierarchies or the locus of power than he is in imagining how it is reflected in the mind or on paper. This extends space's fluid qualities beyond those of designed and defined space, i.e. place. Questions of control, jurisdiction, use, supervision, and transgression outweigh the ideas of planes, containment, and experience. Foucault distinguishes here between the spaces of utopia and heterotopia. The main differences between these spatial terms are a) their scope and b) degree of 'realness'. Utopias tend to focus on and function from within a whole society or large parts thereof[34].

Any contemplation about an ideal world will undoubtedly lead to a new society, a new world, or the break down and rebuilding of the current world. Normally, this takes a theoretical, model-based form. When looking at the texts concerning themselves with utopia – especially by Morus, Campanella, Bacon[35] – they are all fictional spaces that are part of the existing world. They are part of the 'real world' space but have different spatial configurations compared to the societies which 'study' them or which are educated about these utopias. All three utopian texts are written as (travel) narratives that are set on an island, giving them a level of credibility. However, it is their insistence on being utopias

---

[32] 'Extreme' spaces are spaces in which the 'normal' functioning of a space is nullified, such as during a war or during captivity.

[33] Taken from his lecture "Of other Spaces" (March, 1967/ 1984) in *Architecture/ Mouvement/ Continuité* (1984).

[34] "Utopias are sites with no real place. They are sites that have a general relation of direct or inverted analogy with the real space of Society. They present society itself in a perfected form, or else society turned upside down, but in any case these utopias are fundamentally unreal spaces" (3).

[35] Utopia as a concept has been discussed by Morus (1516), Campanella (1602), Bacon (1627) (all three texts are published under *Der Utopische Staat*, Heinisch, 1983) and was later given new impetus by Ernst Bloch (1918).

that destroys this illusion. Because of this they achieve a level of non-space, which Foucault is intrigued by[36].

His focus is then turned to what he refers to as the "other-spaces" in society. He recounts six different classifications, qualities, or types of heterotopias[37], all of them relative to the space/place that they inhabit, represent, or contain. Examples of these qualities are deviation (crisis), multi-functionality, juxtaposition, a break from traditional time, opening/closing, and finally, their function vis-à-vis other spaces (1967/1984:5–7). In other words, a cinema (an example Foucault makes use of) is only heterotopic to the extent that in its own space it includes other spaces (the space(s) of the movie). Once however, the cinema building is destroyed or receives another function, it ceases to be that exact heterotopia. Furthermore, more established spaces (such as the home, the hospital) are not necessarily heterotopic, but can of course be. This happens only once their basic/essential spatial function is changed, extended, or transformed. At their root they are spaces that are defined by their social function.

The statement, which refers to social space most intently, is that

> we do not live in a kind of void inside which we could place individuals and things. We do not live inside a void that could be coloured with diverse shades of light, we live inside *a set of relations* that delineates sites which are irreducible to one and another and absolutely not superimposable on one another. (my emphasis, 1967/ 1984:3)

Again Leibniz is in some way conjured up. Spaces are always relational, in their position, in their function, in their conception. Going back to his definition of heterotopias, it should become clear that they function as absolutes. This may be because they are always seen in relation to what they are also not, or because they cannot be understood without the contemplation of the further heterotopias. This does have a Lefebvrian ring to it, as the control over social space will also concern the control over how heterotopias are used and understood. Conversely, it allows for digressions of norms and deviant behaviour. Heterotopias do not only allow for digression, they themselves are part of this digression.

Foucault discusses two types of spaces: the non-space (utopia) and the other-space (heterotopia). They do not necessarily exclude each other: a utopia may contain a heterotopia just as a heterotopia may have utopian elements. The main difference lies in their real-world existence, with the utopia having a much lesser degree of attainability, while

---

[36] Foucault further mentions the mirror as a sort of utopia as the mirror is a utopia that fixes much of Foucault thinking concerning this term. It inverts, is real and imaginative, it is reality and a sign, and so forth.

[37] "[T]hese places are absolutely different from all the sites that they reflect and speak about" (4).

heterotopias permeate most of society. This, however, raises questions concerning the relationship between utopia, society, heterotopia, and the individual. A hermit, living alone and cut off from society will most likely experience his life as an individual utopia (no wars, no violence, no oppressive laws and machinations) than a heterotopia (no laws to transgress, no 'traditional time', no juxtapositions). The individual in a society is therefore strongly linked to the heterotopia the society generates, changes, and/or maintains. Foucault's spaces are dependent on relations and relationships between the subject and its society.

One of the most heterotopic spaces (if there is such a superlative) in the various texts I will discuss is the colonial farm. This has many levels, beginning with its difference to the German *Bauernhof* (in size, in output, in labour intensity), to its ambiguous relationship to what is considered nature. Because of its separation from other spaces and places, the farm Ettenhof in *Heim Neuland* can be seen as a heterotopia. Also, its cultivation – and consequent separation from its surroundings – is subordinated to a system of organisation. This determines where what is cultivated and built, and who is allowed where. The farm can be said to have a number of attributes which one can use to define it. It is a fenced-in, autonomous space/place that has been imprinted with a certain telos through the introduction of symbols and labour. The farm is also the space of utmost enclosure and organisation, and therefore limitation. But just like the island, the farm is a space of infinite utopian potential. Because the farm is always at a distance from anything (the urban, the neighbouring farm, the home country), it allows for a very self-contained and self-determined lifestyle. This is one reason why the vastness of South West Africa – only so vast because of its initial enclosures: its borders – was so desirable. But because of its separateness from any other space, the farm needs to be self-sufficient. This is where the garden can be introduced. Orchards, vineyards, maize fields, etc. are all expanded replicas of gardens: a certain arrangement of plants. The farm appears to be an expanded model of the garden. The farm, being the subject of desire and survival in *Heim Neuland*, thus exhibits a number of heterotopic qualities.

One of the most prevalent critiques of Foucault's dealing with space has been his silence on one of the horrors of the 19th century, namely colonialism. Not only was this already discussed in relation to his examples for "Of Other Spaces" (his lecture, not the article), in which the war between colonial Algeria and imperial France was in full force. Rather than discussing this theme that has so many spatial components, he sidesteps African colonization in general and focuses on the Jesuits in Southern America. According to Robert Zacharias[38], Foucault also fails to show "how the conceptualisation of the

---

[38] "Space and the Postcolonial Novel" in Quayson (2016:208–229).

colonies as an 'other' space effectively positions the colonizer's space as normative" (209). This is taken further by Robert Young's critique that "Foucault had a lot to say about power, but he was curiously circumspect about the ways in which it has operated in the arenas of race and colonialism" (1995:1). These critiques point to his Eurocentric discussion of certain topics at the expense of Europe's brutal involvement on the African continent. Foucault at a later stage revisits the ideas and problems of racism, linking his concept of biopower to the state's definition and control of 'race'. This does not quite vindicate him from his earlier silence on colonialism. It does, however – like Lefebvre – offer a kind of toolkit with which to analyse certain developments that would fall under the categories of (European) 'colonialism' and 'imperialism'.

A Brief Retracing of Postulations

Let me summarize what I have opened up so far. By tracing the evolution of the theories discussed, certain assumptions can be made. This begins with the question "what are the qualities of space?". Because of the different spatial theories, this answer should contain differing conclusions. We can now state that space has both psychological as well as material qualities. These become evident when applying mathematics to space, whether in the form of volume, or a plan. Secondly, we can argue that space is an individual endeavour. It involves thinking, rationality, and being. It is constructed around the subject's ability to experience, perceive, and understand space. Real space finds its 'reflection' in the subject. And it is this experience and this 'reflection' that form societies. Societies are made up of individuals who perceive their role in space. These spaces are then in turn created, produced, and constructed. And these spaces again produce the individuals who inhabit them. This is how social space comes into being. The final answer should be obvious: from all the theories that exist about space, its fragmented state is its most defining characteristic. It can be carved up and observed from so many angles, that one cannot argue for one single space. Even the ever-present physical space cannot be defined as such if it is not filled with something. Leibniz, Kant, Heidegger, and Foucault cannot escape the fact that space is always there before the subject enters into it. It is only once the subject enters into space that its theorization is possible. Space is a given and will continue to be there before, during, and after the subject. Heuner's previous pronouncement concerning space connects all of these theorists more than their individual deliberations: space is there first and what follows is what we do with it.

Although these theories will not be discussed in detail when I reach my literary analysis, they are however evident in literature. The idea of absolute space (space as a container) cannot be divorced from any representation of the world. It is only how the limits of space-as-a-container are dealt with, i.e. is it a passive receptacle for action or a 'character' within the narrative? In Gustav Frenssen's *Peter Moor* the terrain plays a vital role. The novel's fusion of space and the future culminates in Peter Moor's ecstatic reaction to seeing a German woman and a baby on a veranda on a farm. The image is so overwhelming it elicits biblical symbolism and language from the observing/gazing protagonist. J.M. Coetzee's "Narrative of Jacobus Coetzee" focusses more on space-as-a-container. The main character is limited in his mobility due to a number of reasons. Also, the character's conceptions of his place (geographically as well as socially) are disrupted due to his immobility. Here space becomes a container, in which the character is imprisoned. Heidegger's spatial concept however is referred to when Jacobus Coetzee becomes one with his surrounding space while in a trance. He experiences the world mainly from an internal, a perceptual, and a reactionary fashion. Because of these many theories, space can assume many guises – sometimes more than one at a time – and thus affect narratives differently. It is difficult to look at space in literature and not locate any classical theories on space. They are always there because space as a concept cannot be tied down to one singular theory. Space is in fact not "less mysterious", it is not "monolithic". It is what literature wants and needs it to be.

The Social Space of Henri Lefebvre

Although Foucault's 1967 interview appeared seven years before Lefebvre's seminal work, Lefebvre's impact on spatial thinking is undeniable. The Marxist use of the term 'production' creates an arena in which concepts such as control over resources (modes of production) and the inherent power structures that accompany this control can be dissected. The neutral and objective façade of absolute space is dismantled in order to unveil spatial processes and how they (might) function in the service of (state) power. Lefebvre's theory that space is a product, i.e. the result of investment of resources, labour, and meaning, completes the previous theories in which space was treated as a neutral given that is used in the processes of production. However, it will take another fifteen years before the assertion of space officially enters into the theories of thinking about space. Döring and Thielmann (2008) trace the term 'spatial turn' back to Soja's *Postmodern Geographies* (1989), a term Soja combined with the Marxist concept of space. Günzel (2008)[39] understands the spatial turn in respect to Foucault's effort in creating a balance between history's overt importance and geography's relative secondary character in respect to world and historic processes. In this respect, the spatial turn is responsible for adding a spatial dimension to

---

[39] In Döring and Thielmann (2008).

time in order to fully understand how the world produced and reproduced itself at certain intersections.

For example, Lefebvre uses the example of the Greek temple (and its destruction) to illustrate how temporal and spatial concepts can be combined in order to understand certain developments. In his case, the temple is destroyed so that new relationships and hierarchies can be established. According to Lefebvre, the Greek temple was an exercise in the complete control and application of space. For Heidegger, the temple – and its consequent destruction – symbolized a historic juncture. Christopher Kul-Want states that "according to Heidegger, the temple served as a reminder, and even an imperative, to the Greek community to affect change by drawing to a close its own historical epoch" (2013:72). In other words, it was necessary to destroy the temple in order to create a new epoch that introduced new values, norms, and belief systems. Lefebvre also focuses on monuments, of which the Greek temple is undeniably one of the most prominent examples, in a different way. To him, *monumentality*

> took in all the aspects of *spatiality*...the previously conceived, and the lived; representations of space and representational spaces; the spaces proper to each faculty, from the sense of smell to speech; the gestural and the symbolic. Monumental space offered each member of a society an image of that membership an image of his or her social visage. It thus constituted a collective mirror more faithful than any personal one...Of this social space, which embraced all the above-mentioned aspects while still according each its proper place, everyone partook, and partook fully – albeit, naturally, under the conditions of a generally accepted Power and a generally accepted Wisdom. The monument thus effected a 'consensus', and thus in the strongest sense of the term, rendering it practical and concrete. (emphasis in original, 220)

As is evident, both Heidegger and Lefebvre see the temple as something linking a society to itself and to its understandings of power, of norms, and belonging. They therefore represent spaces serving the collective yet create and maintain centres of power. Although Heidegger's concept is not represented in his initial philosophy on space (here it is *Dasein* which is central), his ideas concerning social cohesion have a similar foundation compared to Lefebvre's. For Heidegger the temple is a tool that needs to be destroyed in order to create new social subjects. For Lefebvre, it is a space that was unified and reflective of its respective society. It is palpable and duly noted that the conceptions of space (as it is described, not necessarily produced[40]) have changed as time has moved forward. From relational space to *a priori* space to *Dasein* space, to concepts such as utopia and heterotopia, space has taken on many different forms.

---

[40] It is evident from the theories put forward by Leibniz, Kant, and Heidegger that space is always "already-there" that their theories do not deal with the production of space. Theirs is rather a description.

The thinking, perceiving subject's position within these conceptions has changed as well. Beginning as a potential *Ding* in space (Leibniz)[41], the subject itself has progressed into being central to how space functions and is experienced and produced. Although necessary as a receptor of space (along with its stimulus and *Empfindungen*) the subject is never part of the processes in which space is produced. The general consensus, as established via the philosophical theories I have put forward, is that space can exist without the existence of the subject. Not even Heidegger's *Dasein* can bring together the production of space and the subject that inhabits it. He does connect the subject to both internal and external space, yet space becomes the location where space-as-a-container for experience is tied to the space of *Empfindung*. It becomes paramount to focus on a space that allows the subject (in whatever form) to produce the space it experiences as well as give meaning to it. The shift from the abstract-mathematical space (the basis of both Leibniz and Kant) to the idea of symbolic or semiotic space (the basis of Foucault) means that space becomes endowed with potential instead of being a descriptive – even prescriptive – container or vessel. Space receives functionality, it becomes contested, is broken up and reconnected. Space is taken out of the bracket of being a fact, a given, and is remodelled into something that is fluid, tangible, and unstable. It mirrors the subject itself – they finally enter into a reciprocal relationship. The subject produces space while that space produces the subject. It is not *Raumpunkte* that matter or logic or being, but ultimately it is the subject within the space it is producing. With this in mind, we can now safely say that the thinking, feeling, being subject is at the centre of the next proposal concerning space, namely *social* space.

Although thinkers such as Georg Simmel (1908) and Foucault have advocated the idea of social space, it was Lefebvre's *The Production of Space* that took a different approach to the matter. Instead of looking at spaces in society that might be understood as being 'spaces of society' (e.g. Foucault's heterotopia), Lefebvre looks at the production of these social spaces. He does not by definition look at how individuals subvert or appropriate certain spaces in society, but looks at which forces in fact produce and maintain social spaces. It is this nuance that gave new impetus to spatial thinking[42], where the mathematical and metaphysical (and thus the space devoid of the subject-individual) is replaced by the social. Lefebvre attacks the institutions and systems of capitalism and their monopoly in producing space in the modern, contemporary world. He points the

---

[41] As argued previously, the subject only appears as a thing if posited as such. Space can exist without the subject being part of the constellation of 'places' and permanents that make up a space, depending on the theory.

[42] In the introduction to the chapter "Soziale Räume", Dünne describes Lefebvre as an "Impulsegeber" and "Resonanzverstärker" in respect of his contribution to the theory of "social practice" (2006:297).

spotlight on Europe, where heavy industry and their financial interests have their origin (feeding into imperial and colonial projects). It is here where space, previously seen as an abstraction, becomes part of the capitalist site of production and reproduction, but even more so, it has become reducible to a commodity[43]. This is, however, not the full extent to which Lefebvre pushes his theory. It also affects how a capitalist society reproduces itself, a system that has its own reproduction as its driving force, a term Denis Wood (1992) refers to as "conservative" (2). Here he takes the position that the reproduction of a certain class or group is directly linked to how (social) space is reproduced, and finally, how the control over spatial (re)production equals the control over social space.

It is important to acknowledge some of the elements found throughout Lefebvre's arguments are part of the production of social space. This begins with the idea of 'production', an idea central to everything spatial. And it is in this process that he is able to expand the building blocks needed to produce space and reproduce control over it. One of his focal points is the physical and the 'ideological' body. As Foucault has argued, power is always intrinsically linked to the body[44]. Lefebvre uses this and connects the body of the subject to the process of spatial production. This takes the form of the body *in* space (its relation to space/things in space), labour (the work a body does/can do/leisure), and the body *as* space (connecting the physical body to the state: symbolically, linguistically, and ideologically). His interest lies in the relation of one spatial body to others, and this unfolds most visibly in the urban centre. Because of the processes of production, urban centres are central to how commodity-based spaces work. The commodity is connected to the body through labour, a central aspect of production. This connection becomes functionalised – along with its spaces – in urban centres. Lefebvre is therefore concerned with how urban centres relate to their own spaces and the subjects inhabiting and creating these urban spaces. It is this analysis which then ultimately sums up or exposes what Lefebvre has identified as the elements needed to produce space.

Rooting his analysis of space in the social, Lefebvre looks at how space can be seen as a product, i.e. as something that society produces, and how the individual features in this production. One must, however, first understand Lefebvre's position vis-à-vis what he identifies as a shift from the 'philosophy' of space to the 'science' of space. He reduces this difference by asking the following question:

---

[43] Dünne summarises Lefebvre's position as "Lefebvre begreift Raum nicht nur als Teil der Produktionsmittel, z.B. als Rohstofflieferant, und somit der ökonomischen Infrastruktur zugehörig, sondern gleichzeitig auch als Produkt einer sozialen Praxis" (2006:298–299).

[44] Much of his work has focussed on the body, its discipline, and the containment of deviant bodies. Examples include *Madness and Civilization* (1964), *Discipline and Punish* (1975), and *The History of Sexuality* (1978). His concept of power is central to his ideas concerning the body. His work on the panopticon is also highly relevant as it describes the abstract but daily flows of power.

> With the proliferation of mathematical theories (topologies) thus aggravated the old 'problem of knowledge': how were transitions to be made from mathematical spaces (i.e. from the mental capacities of the human species, from logic) to nature in the first place, to practice in the second, and thence to the theory of social life – which also presumably must unfold in space? (3)

It is already deducible that he is not a supporter of 'pure'[45] space as advocated by mathematics. Lefebvre wants space to be released from its mathematical, logic-orientated shackles so he includes the concepts of nature – so far peripheral – and the social. These new ingredients already push the terms further. Thinkers such as Leibniz and Kant discussed the idea of space outside what we consider the world, as well as 'empty space'[46], theories in which nature was seen as part of space, not as space itself. Lefebvre asserts that this mathematical/mental space, supposedly "extra-ideological" (6), becomes "the locus of a theoretical practice which is separated from social practice and which sets itself up as the axis, pivot or central reference point of Knowledge" (ibid). Space is not material, but becomes a theoretical or an abstract container devoid of anything social, anything that is bound to the subject. This abstraction allows space to hide its ideological aspects with the aid of its scientific character. This might actually be of no consequence, but only if it stays in the realm of the abstract and is not presented as 'the truth'. It becomes problematic when the abstract is equated with the material, ignoring or overlooking the social.

The idea of 'empty space' propagated throughout the colonial project speaks volumes on this. Landscapes, understood through the gaze of the colonial eye, appeared empty because of the lack of recognisable or familiar space-filling and space-creating elements. This allowed European nation states, which had developed certain spatial configurations for centuries, to read or imply a lack of these elements as an invitation to impose their spatial configurations onto these 'un(der)developed' spaces. Of course these spaces were never empty, they were merely conceptualised and understood differently by the original inhabitants who had different spatial configurations. Social space, as has been successfully shown by oral historians and theorists of orature, does not always necessarily manifest itself physically or in a concrete form. Annette Hoffmann's doctoral thesis *"It rains less since the Germans came"*, for example, focusses on the Herero's oral production of landscapes. Lefebvre's social space is utilised in order to explain this phenomenon, focussing on the

---

[45] The word 'pure' here refers to spaces that are 'empty', 'neutral', 'objective' and 'extra-ideological'.
[46] Leibniz discusses infinite space with Clarke (Newton's divine space) while Kant rebuts Leibniz for his assertion that space needs things in order to exist.

network of kinship and locations, both which are necessary in order to (re)produce the spaces that constitute the oral practice.

This difference between the abstract and the social becomes very important when we start to discuss Lefebvre. His claim that philosophy has been replaced by science when considering space has its own implications. Although both fields of knowledge rely heavily on rationality and a certain self-imposed detachment from their area of interest, science tends to have a use- or end-function that goes beyond mere explanation. This means that science employs knowledge as a tool that does not only describe the world (likewise a function of philosophy), but further attempts to create or recreate the world[47]. And because the world can be defined by the idea of nature (if we are to believe Lefebvre), science's function becomes the subjugation of nature in the service of reason. This process means that the space of nature is replaced by the space of science and its capitalist overtones. Lefebvre conveys this idea in his three propositions:

> 1. [The science of space] represents the political (in the case of the West, the 'neo-capitalist') use of knowledge. Remember that knowledge under this system is integrated in a more or less 'immediate' way into the forces of production, and in a 'mediate' way into the social relations of production.
>
> 2. [The science of space] implies an ideology designed to conceal that use, along with the conflicts intrinsic to the highly interested employment of a supposedly disinterested knowledge. This ideology carries no flag, and for those who accept the practice of which it is a part it is indistinguishable from knowledge.
>
> 3. [The science of space] embodies at best a *technological utopia*, a sort of simulation of the future, or of the possible, within the framework of the real – the framework of the existing mode of production. The starting-point here is a knowledge that is at once integrated and integrative with respect to the mode of production. The technological utopia in question is a common feature not just of many science fiction novels, but also of all kinds of projects concerned with space, be they those of architecture, urbanism or social planning. (my emphasis, 8–9)

From these propositions one is able to identify Lefebvre's fascination with knowledge and how it is used as a product to produce certain social practices. In his second proposition he gives knowledge an ideological dimension, meaning that it is a tool of a certain group of privileged people (those in power or the dominant class). This has the result that social practices are steered by a certain group of people who are invested in reproducing these practices and thus maintaining their power and elitism. These three points become relevant in the analysis of my selected literary works. The idea of the purity of science (especially of those of 'race' and *white* supremacy) and its spatial manifestations are a

---

[47] A look at fields such as cartography, genetics, botany, physics, etc. should suffice.

focal point of my work. Colonial (and to a certain extent apartheid) literature tends to reproduce the accepted notions of European superiority through various literary methods. These usually have a fantastical dimension[48] and mirror and support ideologies 'back home'. Science and technology are manipulated in order to discredit spheres that do not fit these constructs (i.e. the non-scientific/the 'irrational') while conversely positioning them as liberating, civilizing tools.

In order to move forward from these propositions, let us have a look at how Lefebvre works with the idea of social space. He first asserts that "(Social) space is a (social) product" (22) and that the space

> [t]hus produced also serves as a tool of thought and action; that in addition to being a means of production it is also a means of control, and hence of domination, of power; yet that as such, it escapes in part from those who would make use of it. The social and political (state) forces which engendered this space now seek, but fail, to master it completely; the very agency that has forced spatial reality towards a sort of uncontrollable autonomy now strives to run it into the ground, then shackle and enslave it. Is this space an abstract one? Yes, but it is also 'real' in the sense in which concrete abstractions such as commodities and money are real. Is it then concrete? Yes, though not in the sense that an object or product is concrete. Is it then instrumental? Undoubtedly, but, like knowledge, it extends beyond instrumentality. Can it be reduced to a projection – to an 'objectification' of knowledge? Yes and no: knowledge objectified in a product is no longer coextensive with knowledge in its theoretical state. (26–27)

Beginning with the concept of social space (as a feature of every society), Lefebvre begins to unpack and unravel certain relationships of power, especially those rooted in the spatial. He identifies a certain combination of concepts guiding the production of social space. These form a triad and are described as social practice[49], the representation of space[50], and representational space(s)[51]. These three concepts are then applied to urban space, where the forces of production (labour, the body, raw materials) and the methods of production (industry, markets) are concentrated. Furthermore, it is here where metropole and periphery (whether local, national, or global) are shaped and created, and where

---

[48] These can stretch from the protagonist's control of his environment (*A Twist of Sand*), the characters' interaction with non-Europeans (*Peter Moors Fahrt nach Südwest*), the space for speech allowed to Africanist characters (*Heim Neuland*) or the non-reference to the oppressive system (*A Twist of Sand*).

[49] "[E]mbraces production and reproduction, and the particular locations of spatial sets characteristics of each social formation. Spatial practice ensures continuity and some degree of cohesion. In terms of social space, and of each member of a given society's relationship to that space, this cohesion implies a guaranteed level of *competence* and specific level of *performance*" (1974/1991:33).

[50] "[A]re tied to the relations of production and to the 'order' which those relations impose, and hence to knowledge, to signs, to codes, and to 'frontal' relations" (ibid.).

[51] "[Embody] complex symbolisms, sometimes coded, sometimes not, linked to the clandestine or underground side of social life, as also to art (which may come eventually to be defined less as a code of space than as a code of representational spaces)" (ibid.).

the production/reproduction of space is at its zenith. This again has repercussions for social space as the urban space's perpetual production and reproduction of social relations, social practice, the representation of space, and representational space(s) are responsible for the maintenance of certain power structures. These of course try to reproduce themselves via the spaces that allow for these processes.

Lefebvre anticipates certain questions pertaining to social space, especially to those relying on certain terms (abstract, concrete). He attempts to answer these questions, but comes to the conclusion that social space cannot perfectly fit any one definition – it has numerous facets that do not tie it down to one explanation or interpretation, visible in his triad which has a strong mix of abstract and concrete. Not only is this counter to what the previous theorists have tried to posit (forcing space into a single definition) but allows space the potential to remain real *and* theoretical, abstract *and* concrete. Because (social) space is a (social) product, the product must therefore change according to the society. The spaces proposed by Kant, Leibniz, Hegel, Heidegger, and the likes can therefore not be universal, they can only be a theory emerging from a certain society at a certain juncture. In essence, Lefebvre argues that these thinkers helped create a quasi-neutral (even 'empty') space that presented itself as objective and detached from ideology. But with the emergence of social space, this assumption was proven to be the opposite – a space that was used and manipulated in order to maintain a/the status quo.

For social space to be 'produced' and concretized, it needs a combination of the Lefebvrian triad. And in order to control the production of social space, one needs to control these three elements. It begins with how the cohesion and continuity of social practice is regulated and maintained. Although Lefebvre argues that *competence* and *performance* (33) are essential to this process, I would include *discipline* as well. While competence and performance are individual abilities, discipline is a social technology of control. And as Foucault has shown, it is also an internalised social process, which becomes social when subjects start to discipline others/'Others'. Of the three abilities, discipline is the most socially regulated, focussing on what is allowed or prohibited, proper or obscene. It would seem plausible that these are processes of socialization and therefore dependent on the society. And depending on the society, certain spaces may be used differently (roads, churches, parks, land, housing). There is however consensus concerning certain spaces that are outside the individual's direct control[52]. This would include, for example, not driving on the pavement, jumping red lights, or parking in non-designated areas. These illustrations prove that discipline, whether by the state, the self, or others affirm and

---

[52] Denis Wood (1992) identifies many a social contract when he locates his house lot on a map and discusses the obligations and responsibilities he has vis-à-vis his neighbours and the municipality (9–10).

maintain certain spatial practices. Furthermore, social practices are underpinned and managed on the level of representations of space.

To stay with the example of road use: the sign system differentiating pavement and street, whether on a map or in the material world, also indicates how it is used. The slight elevation of the pavement, the absence of vehicles, the absence of lines/directional arrows, and so forth indicate *where* one is located. These differences are then cemented even further by creating laws designed to monitor road and pavement use. This would include traffic lights (colour codes), signs, traffic police, and traffic laws. Here the space that is in essence real (it is quite difficult to argue against a road being a real space) receives an abstract dimension through the knowledge and the codes that govern the road and its use. The final step in this triad might be where ideology is at its most overt and simultaneously covert. A road can only be used by people who own/ have access to certain means of transport. This was challenged, for example, in Philadelphia during the birth of graffiti. Suddenly, those who were excluded from the public transport system for one reason or another were able to symbolically board the subway trains and trams. This happened by writing (tagging) one's name on the wagons, making the name (usually a pseudonym in order to avoid prosecution) visible to those who made use of the network.

Social practice (i.e. taking public transport) became infused with representational spaces. A name was able to travel from a disenfranchised area to a privileged suburb, making those from the former space visible to the latter. This led to a number of restrictive laws concerning tagging and spraying by removing the painted wagons from the network – thus negating the visual impact of the pieces and criminalising the artist. Guerrilla gardening, politicised comics, and reworked maps, can all be placed within the sphere of representational spaces[53]. The purpose is an artistic remodelling of given spaces in order to make them more accessible or to change their monologic character. However, management and regulation over space, especially public space, is always necessarily hierarchical. This is where discipline creates individuals who then acquire competence (learning the bus schedule, knowing the routes, bus etiquette) and internalize the performance (buying the tickets, waiting for the bus to arrive, passive behaviour during the trips, acknowledging the bus driver as a temporary authority).

Lefebvre's triad does exhibit a certain exclusiveness. To begin with, the subject is only really present in the sphere of social practice. The subject is excluded from the sphere of the spaces of representation. This is because this part of the triad is stylised as a top-down yet 'neutral' form of spatial control. City planning and architectural blueprints, amongst

---

[53] For an example of how one can work with representational spaces, see Eugene J. McCann "Race, Protest, and Public Space" (1999).

others, appear isolated from the subject and its possible influence. Furthermore, representational spaces become exclusive through their strong reliance on art as a resistant mode. Not only does this move power from a subject to the artist, but the individual subject is not necessarily constitutive of the artwork's resistant potential. Another aspect is the fact that the three concepts have a significant level of materiality. Social practice to high degree represents the exception, but the other two concepts rely on certain physical components. Maps, plans, statistics, cartoons, and graffiti, are all based on physical reproduction. What thus seems to be central to the triad is the control over the resources for the production of space, not the subject situated within the produced spaces.

One should, however, not forget that Lefebvre does not entirely reject or dismiss previous classic theories on space as a resource to his thinking. It is the use, (especially through capital and neo-capitalism), misuse, and appropriation of these theories that hides the ideological dimension of spatial politics. This becomes evident when he introduces Hegel together with Marx and Engels when trying to define 'production', a term that is central and fundamental to his whole argument. Hegelian production, as Lefebvre sees it, can be defined according to the following steps: "first, the (absolute) Idea produces the world; next nature produces the human being; and the human being in turn, by dint of struggle and labour, produces at once history, knowledge and self-consciousness – and hence that Mind which produces the initial and ultimate idea" (quoted in Lefebvre 1974/1991:68). This is interesting because man (i.e. the subject) emerges out of nature, is produced by it. Man then uses nature (according to Lefebvre: the world) as a resource and as a sight of labour to produce further abstractions. Production here is circular, as the Idea is at the beginning and the end of the process. However, struggle (over nature) and labour (against nature) form the backbone of Man's development. Marx and Engel take a similar approach, theorizing about consciousness and the world in their definition of production. According to them it

> has two senses, one very broad, the other restrictive and precise. In its broad sense, humans as social beings are said to produce their own life, their own consciousness, their own world. There is nothing, in history or society, which does not have to be achieved or produced. 'Nature' itself, as apprehended in social life by the sense organs, has been modified and therefore in a sense is produced. Human beings have produced juridical, political, religious, artistic and philosophical forms. Thus production in the broad sense of the term embraces a multiplicity of works and a great diversity of forms, even forms that do not bear the stamp of the producer or of the production process (as is the case with the logical form: an abstract form which can easily be perceived as atemporal and therefore non-produced – that is, metaphysical). (1974/1991:68)

In both cases we have abstractions concerning what is produced (the world, self-consciousness, history). Nature plays an important, yet rather supportive role, producing Man in order for him to produce (Hegel). Or, conversely, nature is the result of production (Marx and Engels). In both cases however, Man is the producer of his world and of his understanding of this world and him-/herself. And this is largely due to the labour invested in this production. Production is thus tightly linked to nature, and to labour.

Having established the role of production, labour, and nature[54], we can now focus on the body of the subject. The body is what connects the forces of production with the destruction/appropriation of nature. It is the body that needs to be spatialised (i.e. exist in space), but inversely, it also needs to create space for itself to be. This sounds similar to Hegel's understanding of 'production', yet in this instance, the body produces itself. Although this appears tautological, Lefebvre explains it as follows:

> [T]here is an immediate relationship between the body and its space between the body's deployment in space and its occupation of space. Before *producing* effects in the material realm (tools, objects), before *producing itself* by drawing nourishment from that realm and before *producing itself* by generating other bodies, each living body *is* space and *has* space: it produces itself in space and it also produces that space. (emphasis in original, 1974/1991:170)

The body is intrinsically linked to production and reproduction, whether of itself, of other bodies, or space. It is unable not to produce. Now one could ask how 'more' space is produced when space is *a priori* and already-there. And how is it produced through the reproduction of bodies? The answer is anchored in the idea of the social body. If the body is the site of power, and if the body is the agent that links production and nature, then it should hold that the body cannot but produce the space it will at some point inhabit. This is of course not transferable to the physical-biological body (which also needs to take up space), but the social body, the body that is part of a general society. Even the mere arrival of a body in space (a newborn child) necessitates the production of space for the new body (hospital, home). This has a material as well as social dimension (kindergarden, school, the family). The newborn, for example, is produced in a certain space (for example the traditional nuclear family) and creates its own space (as the newborn in the family). It receives an identity (consisting of data such as date/place of birth, name, nationality), but also a social identity (gender, 'race', class). This insertion into social space

---

[54] It should be said at this juncture that nature is a construct, as Katie Soper points out. She argues that "the one thing that is not 'natural' is nature itself" (quoted in Carrigan, in Quayson 2016:82). Carrigan further adds that nature is "both a discursive construct and material fact that is bound up with issues of power, difference, and domination" (in Quayson 2016:82).

in turn requires the newborn to be socialized in order to a) reproduce itself and b) by extension reproduce social practices, which again influence representations of space and representational spaces. Institutions like schools and the job market are vital in achieving and maintaining this level of socialization.

It is through such institutions that the state is then able to transpose the individual's body onto its own identity. Terms such as 'Head of State', 'nerve centre', the 'heart' of a region or a country, roads as arteries, and transport networks as a nation's 'lifeblood' are inscribed into the functioning of the state. And because the state creates itself as a body (producing its own space *in relation* to the bodies it contains and other body-states) it allows the control of space and its inhabitants. The soil as a space that reflects its inhabitants is animated with the idea that it is part of the inhabitants, and vice versa. The space of the soil receives organic qualities, which allow it to become a part of the respective society. Lefebvre argues that this *urspace*, "implies a myth[55] of origins, and its adduction eliminates any account of genesis, any study of transformations, in favour of an image of continuity and a cautious evolutionism" (274–275)[56]. It is therefore difficult to divorce the 'original' inhabitants from 'their' *cultivated* soil. This allowed fascism and its obsessive connection of biology and geography (myths linking the soil to a certain group or race[57]) to influence thinking about "race, nation and the absolute nation state" (275). Ulrike Jureit (2012) discusses the eastward advances by the Nazi regime and its endeavours to link its 'blood' to the spaces it was occupying. These ranged from phantasies of 'emptied space' (as opposed to 'empty space') to their long history of 'cultivating' their soil and therefore 'cultivating' themselves. Legitimization did not stem from a historical right to the desired regions (although this was also integral to their argumentation) but by linking an exclusionary understanding of the soil of the desired region with that of the 'German' body. The body therefore becomes the site *and* tool of state power. A similar line of argumentation has been used previously when European settlers expressed the necessity for them to cultivate colonised soil. In this case the labouring body of the colonisers (accompanied by its cultivation of the soil) and the body of labour needed (in the form of the original population) fits this schematic perfectly.

---

[55] A strong example serving this myth is the Afrikaner nation, or more precisely the Boer nation. A combination of Christian rhetoric, a powerful focus on *whiteness,* and Othering processes assisted in the expansion into, and acquisition of foreign territories by Afrikaans-speaking South Africans. The culmination of these myths was the birth of the apartheid state.

[56] One can link this to the myth of *whiteness*, a myth that is atemporal and eternally perpetuated in various guises.

[57] German *Blut-und-Boden-Literatur*, the national form of literature of the Nazi state is a prime example of this, as is the Afrikaans *plaasroman*.

The control by the *white* colonisers over the soil (which now is infused with European culture[58]) and control over the workforce (with the support of national laws, police, punishment, regulations) is a vivid example of this type of thinking. In her study of South African apartheid literature, Rita Barnard (2007:70–73) refers to the circular logic imposed by the apartheid government in attaining land. First, it took away land belonging to the local population, which was then handed to European large-scale farmers who were given the privilege of working large arable tracts of land. This strongly reproduced the original mythic relationship between the Boers (the Afrikaans-speaking farmers) with the soil while guaranteeing control over the land and its resources. The displaced people were relocated onto patches of barren land, struggling to become self-sufficient. This struggle was then construed as proof that the original inhabitants were incapable of using the soil productively. This was then designed as a 'truth', reproducing and locking-in the myth of the Afrikaans-speaking farmers' inherent connection to the soil and thus to the state. Again, *white* European culture (with labour at its core) is linked to the cultivation of the soil, resulting in an imaginary relation between biology and claims to foreign land. *Heim Neuland* firstly, and *Du heiliges Land!* secondly, are excellent examples in which biology is directly linked to soil. Concepts such as labour and industry, on the one hand, and sacrifice and 'love' on the other, are evoked to justify ownership of foreign space(s). The long line of land ownership historicised by Etta Wibrandt and Dirich Dierksen is connected to the 'holy land' of Ingeborg Oberländer. Both cases exhibit attempts to legitimise to oneself the act of taking away other people's land; and thus social and identity foundations.

After having looked at production, nature, labour, and the body, we need to look at the space in which these elements occur in the highest concentration. This is of course the urban centre. This is where production and reproduction are at their most intensive. It is also where there is the richest collection of bodies and their social interaction. The urban centre can accordingly be identified as producing numerous spaces while simultaneously reproducing these spaces as well. Housing, the family, labour activities, as well as segregation, all help to produce urban spaces. Lefebvre's theory is most visible here, as all the elements he identified appear here in high quantities. But having accepted that new spaces can be produced in these urban centres, one must be aware that reproduction of spaces is the most common practice. In order, however, for a space to produce itself as urban, it has to achieve a number of self-imposed feats, which then allow it to continue to

---

[58] Jureit (2012) also argues that the difference between the populations in the east and Germany was the extent they cultivated the soil and therefore to what extent they themselves were cultured. This finds its expression in Jureit's term "Biologisierung des Raumes" (Chpt. IV), referring to the link between the soil and its occupants.

reproduce itself. One of these feats is the domination of the countryside. The countryside must become a supplier of raw materials (i.e. nature), of bodies, and of difference.

Here Lefebvre covertly makes use of the mirror analogy[59] – the urban centre is able to identify itself because of its reflection in the countryside. The mirror signifies the town to itself and thus reflects an actual space (that of the urban landscape) as well as an imaginary one (the urban-rural dialectic). The urban centre, *the* point of accumulation, produces the countryside as its own reflection and reproduces it in an urban space (in the form of parks, 'natural areas' and signs/symbols). This may pose a problem for the analysis of my selected texts, as they do not take place in the city or any urban centres. *Peter Moor* takes place in the interior of then-GSWA, *Heim Neuland* is mostly a farm novel, *Du Heiliges Land!* is set on a diamond mine, while *Twist of Sand* has a ship as its most prominent locale, "The Narrative of Jacobus Coetzee" takes place on the border between the Cape Colony and the territory of the Great Namaqua. The most complex relation between urban centre and its countryside reflection is to be found in *Born of the Sun*. Because Muronga's centre is not the metropole but his village, his relationship to that centre of power is one of resistance and opposition. This is clearest in his reluctance to be fully incorporated into metropolitan systems of discipline and authority, while maintaining his strong links to his home.

However, this may also be an opportunity to link Lefebvre to these settings and replace his idea of the city with that of the metropole. The metropoles in this case are of course imperial Germany and apartheid SA, with their need for natural resources, labour, and space. The city as such does not feature in the novels but the concepts of capital, trade, spatial production and control, as well its hidden ideologies all appear in the texts. The metropole mirrors the periphery, just like the urban mirrors the rural. This is also why Lefebvre states that

> a revolution that does not produce a new space has not realized its full potential; indeed it has failed in that it has not changed life itself, but has merely changed ideological superstructures, institutions or political apparatuses. A social transformation, to be truly revolutionary in character, must manifest a creative capacity in its effects on daily life, on language and on space – though its impact need not occur at the same rate, or with equal force, in each of these areas. (54)

This is the potential *Born of the Sun* therefore is allowed to carry. First, it reconfigures and remodels the spaces opened up by Frenssen, Kraze, Westerlind, Jenkins, and (to a cer-

---

[59] In "Of Other Spaces", Foucault identifies the mirror as *the* object which is able to connect utopias to heterotopias, stating that "[t]he mirror is, after all, a utopia, since it is a placeless place…But it is also a heterotopia in so far as the mirror does exist in reality, where it exerts a kind of counteraction on the position that I occupy" (1967/ 1984:4).

tain extent) J.M. Coetzee. The novel is revolutionary because it gives stagnant and fixed spaces new energies and new potential. Muronga and the other characters reinterpret the social spaces imposed on them (the mine compound, the jail, the forced relocations), and imbue them with his/their own revolutionary essence. Even the format of the novel is utilised and manipulated in order to reconfigure (G)SWA from a *white*-dominated dreamworld into a space that stands for liberty and self-determination.

One can compare how much of Muronga's SWA is in the current Namibia (i.e. how revolutionary the new spatial configurations have become), but the focus should first and foremost be on how Diescho's SWA is different to that of his so-called predecessors. This in essence sums up the power relations that define social space. Changes in society, in order to be termed revolutionary, have to concentrate on how daily life is lived and experienced. These must then be changed accordingly. The individual, his/her routines, gestures, and his/her relation to other individuals need to reflect the changes in space and the changes in the state institutions. Processes of production and reproduction, which are chained to the individual and his relations/ relationships, thus have to begin bottom up. The individual's space is the building block of social practices. The production of space from the top down, therefore, has to first be informed by the individual and not by those desiring to dominate and control space.

What must be remembered is that Lefebvre's theory on the production of space is a product of the leftist 1968 movement within European countries. These carried strong Marxist convictions and influences and focused on an interrogation of class relations at the expense of questions of 'race' and racism[60]. What this seems to suggest is that questions of 'race' and intersectionality (of gender[61], of sexuality) were marginal or neglected. European expansions on the foundations of 'race' and racism, as well as the accompanying technologies, are ignored while privileging economic factors. These economic factors are, however, not traced back to their most significant roots, namely the colonial and imperial involvement during the Industrial Revolution. The unimaginable increase in cheap labour and new resources opened up a new level of capital expansion, locking the colonies (and their (re)production) in a disenfranchising relationship to their metropoles.

Lefebvre's debt to Marxism and its critique of capital do not at any point refer to the basis of modern-day capital, namely colonialism. With the text being printed in France in 1974, and a small number of colonised nations having achieved relative autonomy, an excursion (however brief) into the influence of this type of spatial production would

---

[60] This can be viewed as a general critique of classic Marxism.
[61] Most obvious in the continuous use of the term 'Man' to denote humans.

have been extremely helpful – not only for my work but for the application of the theory. While numerous thinkers such as Memmi (1965[62]), Samir Amin (1976), and Gilroy (1993[63];1995) attribute economic expansion as one of the main directives of colonialism, Lefebvre does not include this fact in his etymology of European capitalist developmental processes. He does mention imperialism, fleetingly linking it to the *nation* (112) and the expansion of global capitalist markets[64] (277) (and their space-producing mechanisms), yet he shies away from linking these processes to the 19th and 20th centuries. These two eras formed the basis and framework for current global economic systems, with African resources at the heart of moments such as the Industrial Revolution.

A further problem is his reliance on Hegel, a philosopher known as much for his metaphysical discussion of History[65] and progress as he is for denying African subjects any form of history, abstract thinking[66], and humanity. Two paragraphs exemplifying his thinking deeply influenced later attitudes towards African subjects before and during the processes of colonization and the accompanying destruction of cultures and people. In a first contemplation, Hegel designs a classic 'we-and-them' binary in which the (*white*) 'we' is positioned as superior to the (Black) 'them':

> The peculiarly African character is difficult to comprehend, for the very reason that in reference to it, we must quite give up the principle which naturally accompanies all *our* ideas – the category of Universality. In Negro life the characteristic point is the fact that consciousness has not yet attained to the realization of any substantial objective existence – as for example, God, or Law – in which the interest of man's volition is involved and in which he realizes his own being. This distinction between himself as an individual and the universality of his essential being, the African in the uniform, undeveloped oneness of his existence has not yet attained; so that the Knowledge of an absolute Being, an Other and a Higher than his individual self, is entirely wanting. The Negro, as already observed, exhibits the natural man in his completely wild and untamed state. We must lay aside all thought of reverence and morality – all that we call feeling – if we would rightly comprehend him; there is nothing harmonious with humanity to be found in this type of character. The copi-

---

[62] Sartre's introduction to the 1974 version of Memmi's *The Colonizer and the Colonized* also comments on the economic exploitation of Africans by Europeans.
[63] Gilroy and Morisson locate Slavery as the beginning of the global capitalist system of exploiting Africans and links this to European colonial ambitions and Modernist discourses. This is echoed in Gordimer's introduction to Memmi's *The Colonizer and the Colonized* in which she posits that "Slavery was not abolished, it evolved into colonization" (2003:27).
[64] Lefebvre does mention violence, wars, and the army as "productive forces", yet he does not tie these to colonial expansion – although he posits that these elements produced "Western Europe – the space of history, of accumulation, of investment, and the basis of the imperialism by means of which the economic sphere would eventually come into its own" (277).
[65] History (as opposed to history) is here written with a capital 'H' in order to emphasise its construction as a philosophical concept used by both Marx and Hegel in their discussions of the processes of production
[66] His most famous example is arguing that Africans needed to be enslaved in order to grasp the abstract concept of 'freedom' as without captivity they were unable to appreciate and understand the concept.

ous and circumstantial accounts of Missionaries completely confirm this, and Mahommedanism appears to be the only thing which in any way brings the Negroes within the range of culture. (1956:93)

A number of tropes and arguments used in colonial rhetoric have already been predated by Hegel, tropes and rhetoric that have been multiplied and disseminated throughout the colonial project(s). Concepts such as 'Nature', 'Knowledge', 'Religion', 'Morality', and 'Law' are all employed in order to produce distance between Europe and Africa. This distance, realized through an ever-expanding search for difference[67], is maintained through the technology of temporal progression, a product of *white* culture. A second technology of maintaining this distance is through, first, defining Africa and the African and then, secondly, denying these Eurocentric constructions a place in the European 'timeline' of History.

Hegel's other utterance that

> [a]t this point we leave Africa, not to mention it again. For it is no historical part of the World; it has no movement or development to exhibit. Historical movements in it – that is in its northern part – belong to the Asiatic or European World. Carthage displayed there an important transitionary phase of civilization; but, as it is Phoenician colony, it belongs to Asia. Egypt will be considered in reference to the passage of the human mind from its Eastern to its Western phase, but it does not belong to the African Spirit. What we properly understand by Africa, is the Unhistorical, Undeveloped Spirit, still involved in the conditions of mere nature, and which had to be presented here only as on the threshold of the World's History" (1956:99)

now seems near comical. Africa was of course neither left, nor was it not *not* 'mentioned again'. In fact, it provided *the* space to reflect upon *white* Europe. Africa's place in the development of European history and History is undeniable. Not only that, but the fact of African histories and History is just as undeniable. Hegel's inability to completely silence African history (he is forced to at least include Egypt) also forces him to rewrite geography as he has to incorporate parts of Africa into Europe and Asia. What these passages show are a) the resilience of racist discourses and ideas (Hegel's ideas are from 1837) up to our contemporary era, and b) the incongruous nature of these discourses and ideas, having been disproved on uncountable occasions. All of these problematic and dubious constructions of Europe, Africa, and the accompanying constructions of difference are not in any way discussed by Lefebvre.

Lefebvre, for all of his efforts to disentangle space from its rational-'neutral' guises, falls into the same trap. His silence on the production of the colony as a European space of violence, oppression, and profit significantly weakens his focus on the idea of

---

[67] A search that runs on the production of knowledge.

production. The histories of European capital and industrial expansion are inextricably linked with the destructive accumulation of foreign resources and the control over foreign subjects. The racist and dehumanizing strategies employed by the colonialists and their supporting institutions are not touched upon, while the processes of capital and its production of space is couched in a European (read: *white*) context. Although Africa played/plays an intrinsic part in the development of a world History and the global capitalist system, not least through its 'nature'[68], it has not found a place in Lefebvre's theory. And while general trends within the globalised commodity system point to a seemingly Westernisation of Africa (especially following the city-countryside dialectic as proposed by Lefebvre), these are resisted on a number of levels (starting from state interventions to subjects on the ground). As the character of Muronga will show, the influence of the metropole is not all-powerful and all-pervasive, but a constant negotiation.

Social Space and Literary Space

Since the ancient Greeks produced and performed their tragedies and comedies, the elements of artistic time and space have generated much discourse, at least within Western academia. Moving from the very rigid unity that Aristotle proposed, to the collapse of temporal and spatial boundaries in postmodernism, these two units and their relationship have changed over time. Bakhtin (1937–1938) gives these two units an extensive arsenal of power. This power is concentrated in the concept he refers to as 'chronotope'. By tracing something he calls 'historical poetics' from the Greek romantic novel until the Rabelaisian novel[69], he argues that the "relative typological stability of the novelistic chronotope that were worked out in these periods permits us to glance ahead as well, at various novel types in succeeding periods" (85). In other words: an analysis of the chronotope in literary products can show shifts in historical poetics and by extension, society. For Bakhtin the main concern is not time and space in isolation from each other, but rather how they interact, how they are connected and function together[70]. Foucault makes use of this but ascribes literature a more subsidiary role, feeding into the general discourse of a society. It can however still be viewed as 'archaeological evidence'.

But instead of focussing on the effects of time in combination with space, I will try and connect the space of literature with theories of the material world, i.e. with that of social space as posited by Lefebvre (and extended upon by Soja, David Harvey, Christian

---

[68] 'Nature' first in connection to its resources, and second as a spatial resource that can be manipulated (as nature reserves, dumping grounds, testing grounds, etc.).
[69] His objects of interrogation in his essay "Forms of Time and of the Chronotope in the Novel" (1981).
[70] Although he asserts that time is more central in his analysis (86).

Schmid, and others). The reason I feel that this is necessary, is that this theory – not all of it – has its strong focus on a) the subject and its relation to space, as well as b) the network of relations between various spaces. This allows me to always make a link back to the metropole, even if it is a link that is not established within the narrative itself. But because it needs the colony, because it needs the foreign space (i.e. the "countryside"), it is always already-there, often hidden behind its over-presence. The colony and the administrated territory are only one part of a whole, even if it is an uneven whole, and include the other half without directly pointing to it. That which is silenced is made visible.

The first step in succeeding in this endeavour would be to establish the link between the spaces produced in literature with those produced in a capitalist society reliant on the mechanisms of racism and its most extreme form, colonialism. As I have tried to argue, Lefebvre's theory of social space – if we assume it to be 'true' – cannot be excluded from literary space. Literary space is another form that social space must eventually take as it reproduces spaces that already exist. Utopian literature, according to Foucault's understanding, would either reproduce ideal aspects of a society (equality, freedom of identity, statelessness) or turn it upside down (marginalized groups in power, a return to a prehistorical, pre-capitalist state). So even ideal spaces and places are informed and updated by current politics, ideologies, and paradigms. The same can be said for invented spaces, as their configurations must either reproduce or dismantle current paradigms. Because of my reliance on the theory of social space and how it conditions everyday life, my aim is to understand it as the bulk of my synthesis. However, I will still make use of certain ideas pertaining to literary space in order to strengthen the bonds that attempt to unify both theories. In order for that to work, there needs to be a basic understanding of the spaces of and in literature, as they are the locus of my investigation.

Sappok (1970) identifies three levels of space in literature. On the initial level there is the linguistic production of a space (*Raumdarstellung*). This is followed by the function of the *Raumdarstellung* for the various levels of the text, and finally the meaning of space for the whole of the narrative[71]. Just like we have with Lefebvre (and later Soja), the idea of space is built on a triad, each element connected to the other. Again the understanding of space is reliant on further propositions on space. And again this relation is relative, where one element is unable to exist without the other two elements. Sappok's idea is one that also moves from the formal (i.e. linguistic) level – the level of production, to a textual (i.e. meaning) level, to a narrative level (i.e. the end-product). Based on this, there is a strong connection between the process of production and the space in literature as a functioning product.

---

[71] Quoted in Katrin Dennerlein, *Narratologie des Raumes* (2009:24).

Space in literature has two further functions – one is the *position* of objects and persons in space, while the other is the *movement* of people and objects in space (Dennerlein 2009:74). These have both a geographical or mathematical, as well as a social and relative relationship. Position and movement are always dependent on power, competence, and performance, vital aspects concerning Lefebvre's social practice. Position and movement are also dependent on the narrated space (prison, woods, the moon's surface) and in relation to another location (home, road, utopia). Space in literature, therefore, bears some of the imprints of social space, especially since it cannot but produce/reproduce some aspects of this space, whether "dreamt up" or "speculated about", to rephrase Lefebvre.

First, one should consider the accepted notions of spatial understanding in fictitious worlds and universes. This may include invented worlds, manipulation of existing spaces, or realistic representations. Questions of orientation, influence of space on character and vice versa, as well as fragmentation are considered. This will be extended upon to look at how mental and abstract spaces are reproduced (e.g. maps[72], travelogues) and how these create and form the literary spaces. Although the spaces in the novels I look at (GSWA/SWA/Namibia) are in fact 'real' spaces in a geographical-historical sense, they are still able to contain invented spaces (the farm in *Heim Neuland*, the small island in *Twist of Sand*). It is this contradiction that makes literature so complex and its settings so revealing[73].

It must be noted when discussing Lefebvre and literature that he did not work with or on the aspect of literary space. He mentions the subject without elaborating. This may have numerous reasons, from him not being a literary critic to the 'un-realness' of the space of the novel. It may also be because literary space can be produced and manipulated more easily than the space Lefebvre is invested in. For him, literary space is "enclosed, described, projected, dreamt of, speculated about" (15). If taken in connection with his focal points concerning space, literary space is the exact opposite of what he discusses. The individual cannot penetrate literary space, as it is merely a mental-abstract space, a space that has no concrete existence. It can only be created and traversed in the mind, not physically. Even the places which are real and which do exist cannot be recreated in literature; only certain aspects can be represented. Literary space, in his analysis, should rather be seen as a discursive tool maintaining hegemonic power than a space that can actively

---

[72] See Robert Stockhammer's *Kartierung der Erde* (2007) in which he looks at fictional novels that include or make use of maps. *A Twist of Sand* is an excellent exercise in abstract spaces. Maps are created, manipulated, and reinterpreted by the main character, who is a master of his environment.
[73] Barbara Piatti has done extensive work in looking at the combination of the real and the speculative within the real in her book *Geographie der Literatur* (2008). Here, it is Swiss Vierwaldstättersee and Gotthardmassiv as it is reproduced in a number of literary texts, ranging from plays to novels.

change already-produced spaces. This seems evident when focussing on his assertion that aesthetics helps in maintaining abstract space's neutrality and objectivity:

> The dominant discourse on space – describing what is seen by eyes affected by far more serious congenital defects that myopia and astigmatism – robs reality of meaning by dressing it in an ideological garb that does not appear as such, but instead gives the impression of being non-ideological (or else 'beyond ideology'). These vestments, to be more specific, are those of *aesthetics* and *aestheticism*, of *rationality* and *rationalism*. (my emphasis, 1974/1991:317)

Aesthetics (a pillar of any artistic discipline) and rationality are identified as cornerstones of ideology. Ideology receives an artistic as well as a scientific reality. This does, however, not necessarily disqualify an investigation into their relationship within the sphere of the speculative; if anything, it strengthens the need for this investigation. The space in literature is made up of a number of elements, from signs and symbols, to subjective interpretations and individual orientation. It also contains and elaborates on features such as social practice, representation of space, and representational spaces. These three terms can be imbued with a new energy, a new perspective, and most importantly, their internal logic can be questioned. Literature further allows for the concrete examination of the links of temporality-time, spatiality-space and social being-matter[74]. These terms become malleable and fluid, allowing one to test their application in both 'real' and imaginative spaces.

Connecting Lefebvre to Literary Space
The main feature of Lefebvre's social space is the relation and relationship of all its parts, ranging from the singular individual to the whole globe. Production, labour, nature, the body, capitalism all play an important role. So the focus is not on the measurability or provability of space, but how it produces and contains power, how it dominates discourse and how it establishes control. On a very basic level one could argue that the space of literature (literary space) is a product. It is produced through various processes and is made with and from a number of resources. It is also where things are exposed and, more often than not, hidden. Just like abstract space, used in cartography, town planning, architecture, literary space can represent 'real space', but creating its own space with language. And because language is a social product, literature must be rooted in society – even when this does not seem to be the case[75]. This allows it to create spaces that do not exist (i.e.

---
[74] These are categories opened up by Edward Soja (1989) and are built on Lefebvre's own triad of representational spaces, spaces of representation, and social practice.
[75] There are numerous literary genres which are set 'outside' one's immediate society or time, such as science fiction, fantasy, fairy tales, myths, and the like.

worlds on foreign planets, below the Earth's surface), but also imbue certain spaces with excessive energy[76] and exoticism (i.e. colonial fantasies, travel literature).

Lefebvre does not focus on literary space, but because space is a product of social interaction (which close to any narrative can be reduced to), his theory should also be applicable to space produced in imagined worlds. Even the archetype of the colonising novel, *Robinson Crusoe*, a novel painfully detailing the protagonist's slow appropriation of 'his' island, and a novel ignoring other/'Other' characters for the majority of the narrative, still needs these marginalised characters to place the *white* protagonist at the centre of a slowly expanding world. Although Crusoe is alone for most of the novel, Friday's introduction gives him the power to define an 'Other' character whom he then enlists in destroying the threat of the ~~cannibals~~. Friday's death, just before Crusoe is saved, points to his limited involvement in Crusoe's life outside the island, i.e. his prevention from entering into European spaces. The island-space of the narrative thus opens up the asymmetrical relationship between coloniser and colonised, a spatial power relation.

Based on this, the first relationship that needs to be looked at are the subjects who produce space in the fictitious world. As Dennerlein summed it up previously, "Raum kann im narrativen Texten auf viele verschiedene Arten dargestellt werden. Er kann unter anderem durch Figuren oder durch den Erzähler vermittelt, anthropomorphisiert oder allegorisiert, wahrgenommen oder beschrieben werden und Schauplatz oder Gegenstand der Reflexion sein" (2009:115). In essence, space has many facets and can appear as a backdrop for the plot to unfold or it can itself become a character. However, the subject that produces the literary space is always of or in that space. Space cannot create itself; it needs the energy of the narrating instance or the characters to be produced. It only comes to the fore once a character or narrator is aware of its existence, of its presence. This would then imply that a literary space has diverse mechanisms of being produced. These can be divided into three main categories, 1) the space created by the author (is it 'real' or imaginary, current or historical, etc.), 2) the space created by the narrator (what details are the reader introduced to, what qualities are prominent), and 3) the space of the character (how does s/he orientate him-/herself, what is his/her relationship to the things, objects). Again a relative relationship among the different levels is important to the construction of space, as all three levels might be contradictory to one another. What is important for the production of the space in question is not necessarily the believability or realism of the space produced, but rather its internal logic. This refers to the characters' (and the narrators') ability to navigate their world even if it is alienating or disorganised. For example,

---

[76] An example would be Romanticism's concept of nature as a place/space of regeneration, contemplation, reflection, but also of divine creation.

the space of science fiction may seem to be absurd and impossible from a purely scientific perspective, yet it makes sense within the context of the literary produced space(s) of the narrative if the absurdity or impossibility remain consistent.

It is through Lefebvre's concept of social space that I will look at how the selected novels may and can function. This will take the form of interrogations concerning certain relationships: of narrative authority, character constellations, and the ability (and authority) to speak. Not only will this reveal the power constellation's structure in the production of the narrative, but it also reveals how the levels of author, narrating instance, and characters may interact. Because certain power is always inscribed to any of these literary personae, spatiality and its producer must always be examined. Soja (1989) argues in connection with spatiality,

> [a]s socially produced space, spatiality can be distinguished from the physical space of material nature and the mental space of cognition and representation, each of which is used and incorporated into the social construction of spatiality but cannot be conceptualized as its equivalent. (120)

If space can hide things from us, the interrogation of spatial relations in literature can help us find what is hidden. This can again help us open up questions, such as why is this or that hidden, who hid it, and why was it necessary to find it? Because literature can produce spaces and spatial relations which the 'real' objective world is unable to, it becomes a lab to test and query ideas on space. History and geography merge with the imagined, science meets fantasy, ideology meets its critics, and the real world is infused with the un-real.

So far literary studies have as yet failed to produce a comprehensive theory concerning space[77]. It therefore becomes necessary to patch together and combine certain approaches. The best way of doing this is by adopting terminology used when discussing literary space. Ideas put forward such as the chronotope and polyphony prove helpful – even if these terms are borrowed from competing fields of knowledge (namely science and musicology, respectively). Polyphony especially has strong anti- and postcolonial potential as it allows competing voices to be located within the narrative, disrupting the monologic colonial recording of events. Different voices inhabit the same space, complicating any form of authority of these spaces. It also inserts different perspectives and paradigms into the narrative, neutralising any form of complete narrative authority. What makes polyphony a difficult strategy is the need to 'look for it' in the narrative structure, which is further complicated by the colonial/apartheid narratives insistence on

---

[77] This should not be read as a shortcoming, but rather it should be seen as testament to space's refusal to being defined.

remaining monologic. Even the example of "The Narrative of Jacobus Coetzee", which is reconstructed through a number of narrators, ends up reproducing the voice of the *white*, male explorer. It is only the tone and the format that change, while the speaking authority remains the same. However, polyphony allows networks of kinship and spaces to be located even within monologic narratives, revealing the connecting potential of social space. *Born of the Sun* benefits from this concept, as a host of individual voices are given a space in which to speak and perform, acting as a competing format in respect to the colonial/apartheid novel. The plethora of voices creates a network of spaces, generating the conditions for a new form of community.

Furthermore, literary terms such as actant, narrator, and focaliser may work well when linked to the chronotope and polyphony. The introduction of the idea of fictioning, a potent theory connecting the material and the fictional, could complete my approach by offering another level of conceptualisation. These various concepts work well by themselves, but it is their combination and the resultant connection to Lefebvre's social space that ultimately allows me to add to existing literary space theories. In order to make my approach comprehensible (and give a possible outlook to how it may be applied), I will analyse a passage from "The Vietnam Project", the first section of *Dusklands*. Thematically linked to "The Narrative of Jacobus Coetzee", "The Vietnam Project" offers a different stylistic approach to these themes. The important thing is, however, to see whether both texts – set in a different time and space – can reveal the mechanics and strategies of *white* authority, especially in respect to 'Othering' and *white* achievement. This preview will consist of three, non-sequential steps.

First, there will be a short discussion of the space of the narrated passage. This creates the context from which to look at the power of the narrating instance (e.g. his/her position vis-à-vis the construction of the plot). Once it is established who/what is speaking, the relationship of the narrative instance to the (other) characters will be looked at. Like social space, literary space is highly relational, with these relations influencing plot development. A look at group relations is also relevant, as in many cases characters are designed as representatives of their specific group (along the lines of nationality, 'race', age, political conviction). This would open up questions concerning monologic vs. polyphonous narration, for example. Finally, the interrogation of literary space should reveal its relational ties to: a) other literary spaces (within the text as well as intertextually), and b) material spaces (either as a reproduction of such or its deconstruction). Ideas such as allegory, metaphor, or analogy expose the level of this relationship and further influence the preceding analyses. The narrated production of literary space becomes contingent with the production of material space, bringing them into a mutually inclusive relationship.

In the chapter "The Status of Style", Goodman (1978) begins with the proposition: "subject is what is said, style is how" (23). A bit further he argues that "[a]lthough most literary works say something, they usually do other things too; and some of the ways they do some of these things are aspects of style" (ibid.). The two artistic dimensions of any work, subject and style, are at first placed in a mutual relationship, covering two aspects of the same matter. The necessity and centrality of style and subject in the production of literature become tools in which to locate the concepts I touched upon in the previous paragraph. These two elements constitute the literary product, each with its own style and/or subject. *Dusklands*, consisting of two complementary and yet disparate texts, is thus an ideal starting point. The two narratives are linked through similar subjects such as *white* authority, the construction of the 'Other', and the failure of *whiteness* to maintain its own idealised reproduction. Be that as it may, it is the style that makes the two texts so different. Let us look at a sample passage:

> The photographs I carry with me in my briefcase belong to the Vietnam report. Some will be incorporated into the final text. On mornings when my spirits have been low and nothing has come, I have always had the stabilizing knowledge that, unfolded from their wrapping and exposed, these pictures could be relied on to give my imagination the slight electric impulse that is all it needs to set it free again. I respond to pictures as I do not to print. Strange that I am not in the picture-faking side of propaganda. (13)

On the level of narration, it becomes clear that the story is produced from the I-narrator perspective. Although not always the case, this would mean that the authority to produce the narrative and to push the plot forward is centralised in one person. This would reflect, for example, the metropolitan ability to produce its own myth as well as the spaces it will consume. What is important for this section, however, is the monologic production of every aspect of the narrative. This is further emphasised by the fact that the 'I' is in a position to (re)produce knowledge (via his report) and has a further interest in inventing knowledge. In many respects the 'I' can be considered either a personification of the producing metropole, or a metropolitan agent. Significant is his privileged narrative position as well as his position within an official knowledge-producing structure. His environment is representative of representational space – the space denoting knowledge. He is involved in a social practice on the level of his engagement with cultural products, namely written documents and photographs. He is also involved in incorporating these aspects into his work of writing. Finally, he is linked to spaces of representation through his photographs, principally due to their impact on his imagination, i.e. the sphere outside of the representational spaces.

The 'I'-narrator intimates that there is a strong link between the photographs he carries in his briefcase, his imagination, and the Vietnam project. He creates a space in which the production and dissemination of knowledge is his central occupation. His utterance that he should rather be in the "picture-faking side of propaganda" also gives away that he is in the business of manufacturing written propaganda. This is important for the passage as he connects the ideas of imagination and knowledge – however, in the service of an institution. He produces knowledge concerning the world-as-it-is (he fictions it), and produces knowledge concerning himself (mythologizing himself). This supports the idea that his voice will be the only one present in the construction of the narrative, making it a monologic textual production. The space in which he exercises his authority is left unnamed and unspecific. One can gather that it must be a powerful space due to its knowledge-producing abilities and aims, while also being a space which is able to reproduce other spaces (photographs) and archiving these other spaces (in the form of documents and photographs).

A certain power structure is also visible through the mention of a political space, namely Vietnam. Not only is the imagination strongly linked to the report, but the report itself indicates a level of definition of this political space. One can infer that the 'I'-narrator is situated in the heterotopia of the archive, a space in which time and space are forced into a number of competing relationships[78]. The character becomes part of these competing relationships as s/he contributes to or takes away from these relationships in the form of substitution. The replacement of one document with another, the addition of new information, the deletion of artefacts can all be said to change the makeup of the archive. Although the space still remains vague, it is possible to make certain assumptions. How, for example, does this space function in relation to other spaces? This is a difficult question, not only because the initial space is left open. Another reason for this is the lack of other spaces to connect it to – except for Vietnam. What function does Vietnam have in relation to the archive? Considering the need for a report on this political space, one can make further inroads. Firstly, Vietnam seems to be defined with a specific goal in mind. This may be political, military, or economic. The fact remains that certain technologies are utilised in order to gain access to this political space. The mention of propaganda in relation to the report points to an aggressive, crisis-orientated approach. The 'I'-narrator must be part of a group in power, its power coming from its authority to define. The focalisation of Vietnam into a report gives it an official dimension, meaning

---

[78] Foucault mentions the archive as one of his identified heterotopias due to its function of perpetuating history.

that hierarchies must be involved. Therefore, it can be argued that the 'I'-narrator is writing the report in the service of a higher instance, locking him in a hierarchy of labour.

On a final note, the narrator (although forceful in the production of the narrative) is subordinated within the larger group. Questions concerning his position of *whiteness* cannot be answered from this short passage alone due to the lack of visible markers. Yet, considering the exercise of defining and producing a particular Vietnam, one is reminded of America's political and military involvement in the Asian state during the sixties. The text does not reveal this at any point, but an extradiegetic interpretation of such an involvement can open up a further development in the passage. Considering this, one can now infer that the knowledge-producing character is part of an American institution, one that is implicated in activities surrounding the war in Vietnam. From here, it becomes much simpler in defining the 'I'-narrator's participation in the (re)production of *whiteness* and its privileged position.

From this short passage one is able to make a number of assumptions based on the form of narration (monologic) and the space in which it takes place (a space of knowledge production). The merger between material social space and literary space proves to be beneficial, especially when many of the details remain vague. Further assumptions can be made concerning "The Narrative of Jacobus Coetzee" due to the analysis of "The Vietnam Project", most forcefully through the association between the historic space of pre-colonial Namibia and its literary (re)production. The establishment of *whiteness* as a technology in defining and controlling the 'Other' connects the disparate texts, indicating the resolute and perpetuating position of *white* characters and narrators in the production of *white* literature. This is where one must deconstruct the efficacy of the *white* voice to control or erase the spaces in which the 'Other' is allowed to speak. One should, however, not confuse the narrator with the focaliser, the former being akin to a voice, while the latter can be described as the Seeing Eye. Although the 'I'-narrator is usually the focaliser as well (there may be exceptions), the focaliser is the figure through which the visible fragments of the world become palpable. Narrator and focaliser are the two most important interfaces of any narrative, especially since they are the mediating instances without which the narrative cannot function.

Seeing and Speaking

While *Peter Moor*, *A Twist of Sand*, and "The Narrative of Jacobus Coetzee" are equipped with a narrator-focaliser, *Heim Neuland, Du heiliges Land!* and *Born of the Sun* have separate entities for the two functions. *Heim Neuland* actually divides the job of focalisation amongst a number of characters, creating a denser network of character relations as compared to the other two colonial novels. The separation of the narrator from the focaliser creates separate entities that are able to produce space. This becomes clear, for instance when Etta and Dirich first think of going to GSWA, revealed in Etta's emphatic reaction to the colony's supposed endlessness (401). Her reaction is supported by the narrative voice during her and Dirich's travels, yet the voice includes its own opinion concerning the People of Colour who live in this endlessness (484). The doubling of this opinion through the narrative instance points to a voice sympathetic to the main characters it narrates into being. The movement to other focalisers (Detlef Welzin, Gerda Ehlers) shows a certain flexibility in the reproduction of the character's opinions and inner workings. Yet it is the over-arching narrative voice that connects these characters and forms them into a whole. The hierarchical ordering of the characters – most significantly in respect to their relation to *whiteness* – breaks up this homogeneous whole. This is already initiated when Etta and Dirich first encounter Black bodies. The reaction does not happen in her own words (although the passage ends with a colloquial "Oha!"), it is mediated by the narrative instance. The reaction to the People of Colour they encounter in the "*Eingeborenenniederlassung*" is again not Etta or Dirich's reaction, but a mediated one. The narrative voice has the authority to reveal information about the characters without them having to reveal it themselves. These two reactions will form a general tone amongst the *white* characters, marginalising the voice(s) of the 'Other'.

Du heiliges Land! operates along the same lines with Ingeborg Oberländer becoming the main focaliser. Further characters take turns of exposing the various narrative spaces and complications, but Ingeborg remains the main source of spatial mediation. It is also important to mention that she is the only character to originate from outside the colony, giving her different access to the literary spaces. Her alternating attitude towards GSWA underlines this, while the settled characters have already more or less formed their opinions. On a number of occasions, direct speech is used in order to verbalise these attitudes and opinions, contrasting this to *Heim Neuland*. Instead of forming an over-arching link between the characters, *Du heiliges Land!* actually links them spatially, however, leaving the characters the capacity to reveal their own reactions to their surroundings. This difference is significant in respect of the encounter between character and the landscape, as mediation distances the character from his/her own experience.

Du heiliges Land! can produce a more intimate relationship to the spaces of the narrative, a relationship denied by the interjecting narrative voice of *Heim Neuland*. This intimate relationship to the narrative spaces as explicated through the characters' own words and on their terms intrudes on the space afforded to dissenting voices. Black characters are only part of the experience of space, as objects within the space. Their reactions to the intrusion of Europeans into their spaces are buried underneath the experiences of the *white* characters. *Heim Neuland* and *Du heiliges Land!* employ different intensities of focalisation (and to a degree narration) in order to organise their spaces. The exclusion of Africanist characters from these organising mechanisms creates an intimate relationship between these produced spaces and the experiencing *white* characters, while forcing the space-occupying Africanist characters to the absolute margins.

Born of the Sun, in contrast, has a Namibian character as its sole focaliser. Access to other spaces is constructed around Muronga's symbolic relationship to these places, i.e. through mediating characters. He is informed about the spaces/places outside of his village by other Black characters. This strategy firstly links Muronga to these spaces through his social relations. Secondly, he learns about these spaces from the experiences of others, thus linking them to not-as-yet experienced spaces. These informants help Muronga make his world form the resources they give him, reinserting them in these spaces. The previously marginalised voice (marginalised in the other texts) permeates every space in the novel either through physical habitation, or through verbal reproduction. The narrative voice places the Black characters in a continuous social reproduction of the narrative spaces, contesting the perceived absence of Black bodies from the colonial and apartheid spaces. The literary spaces do not only result from the narrative voice, but are predominantly produced by the characters and their interaction. Although the narrative has only one focaliser, his access to the spaces of the narrative is guaranteed through his interaction with the other characters. This is markedly different in respect to the spatial production of the monologic production of space by the 'I'-narrators as well as the spaces produced in the multi-focalised novels. The social production of space reaches its climax in the figure of Muronga, who pieces together his world through personal experience and the experience of others. As the literary analysis will show, this is also its revolutionary potential as posited by Lefebvre.

3 The Colonial Era: War, Toil, and Diamonds

Writers of fiction have always had a very complex relationship with the spaces and places they dream up. Whether they themselves had visited these places, whether they designed these places as analogies, or whether they fictionalised certain places as a willing screen for (discursive) projections, writers have an impact on how real spaces can be experienced or observed[1]. This might be most pronounced or visible in colonial fiction. Because of its far-reaching social and political influence through the creation of 'new spaces'[2] of/ for *white* desires and fantasies, but also adding to discourses on various themes and topics, colonialist fiction is a literary genre in which the settings need to be looked at critically and through the lens of history. Although this has been done to a large extent and has had a significant impact in reading the social (and international) dynamics of the colonial period, Namibia as a doubly colonised space has received little attention. Dorian Haarhoff appears as an anomaly, having contributed to the study of Namibia through its periods of occupation by means of literary analyses, stretching from the pre-colonial era until the first years of independence. One can also mention Bruno Arich-Gertz, who is involved in two books dealing with Namibia under German and South African occupation[3]. However, his essays deal with a number of connected yet disparate topics (such as the relationship of the letter culture in colonised GSWA to the fiction of André Brink and Siegfried Groth).

Most noticeable concerning the work done to interrogate Namibia, or its occupied guises of GSWA and (to certain extent) SWA, is the prominent focus on the country as a space of German *literary* colonialism. This can be understood as the interest of fiction produced in and about the colony by German literary scholars. A number of reasons underlie this. The first and most obvious connection is the strong link between GSWA and its imperial nation, Germany. GSWA becomes a space visited and constructed by

---

[1] Tuan (1977:4) uses the conversation between two Nobel Prize winners, Werner Heisenberg and Niels Bohr as an illustration as to how literary space can 'fill' material space. Their conversation centers around the castle they are in and how their perception is influenced through their knowledge of Hamlet. However, extensive studies have been published concerning 'writer's' places (real and fictive), such as Thomas' Hardy's Wessex, Balzac's Paris, James Joyce's Dublin, or William Faulkner's Yoknapatawpha. See, for example Piatti (2008).
[2] These 'new spaces' can be divided into two categories, depending on their production. These two categories are the *terra nullius* (i.e. the fantasy of 'empty space'), or *Tabula rasa* (i.e. the desire to 'empty' space through methods of overwriting, disavowal, violence, and other processes).
[3] The first, his own, is *Namibias Postkolonialismus* (2008), while the second is a collection of essays he edited, *Afrika-Raum-Literatur* (2014).

Germans from the colony and from the homeland. This translates into a transnational dialogue through the focus on the colony by those who lived there and by those who were producing and reading literary products about this exotic place. As a resource and mirror of the time, literature emerging from and about GSWA can therefore give insight about the German colonial project – and continues to do so. Literature produced during the colonial era can be said to reflect German society at a specific time on a number of levels. Most notably, it is the reading habits of the colonising nation that allows insight into how the project of colonialism was received[4].

A second reason for the focus on GSWA by German scholars is the shift from the colonial to what is now known as the postcolonial[5] during the 1960s. Not only were a number of African nations achieving independence, but the uncovering of colonial crimes, coupled with the resurgence of African liberation and self-definition as well as anti-racist discourses, became a reason to revisit the literature produced since 1884 (and before). One of the reasons was the genocide of the Herero committed by the German colonial army, a genocide that would later also include the Nama. The later link to literature became significant as German historians[6] were the first to make this claim. It was this event that prompted a number of scholars to find links between the *Vernichtungskrieg* against the Herero and Nama and the literature produced during and after this time. Although historians initiated the uncovering of the genocide, a need for the analysis of the literature further fed into the examination of the general attitude of the German public towards those they had colonised. The focus did not exclusively interrogate the attitudes of the German government and the colonial administration towards Black subjects, but the attitude of the general public towards Germany's imperialist role[7].

A further, definition-based argument for the return to colonist literature is the question of its role in the broader field of German literature. German literary scholars[8] posed

---

[4] See for example Brehl (2004:80–81). Not only are authors, the texts, and the reading audience of interest, but so are publishers and distributers.

[5] This refers rather to the period of decolonisation, not the theory emerging as a response to this period. 'Postcolonialism' as a term is rather eclectic, as Quayson (2000; 2016) has shown and can denote a period, a way of thinking/theorising, as well as an intervention. Although it is right to claim that SWA was far from being post-colonial (i.e. not a colony anymore), I am using the term 'postcolonial' as a response to the dismantling of European occupation and the accompanying discourses of Pan-African autonomy and the movement towards independence. South West African opposition to apartheid is run through with these ideas, even if it can be said that Namibia only became post-colonial in 1989.

[6] Horst Drechsler (1966) and Helmut Bley (1968) were the first to discuss the possibility of a Herero genocide.

[7] Haarhoff (1991:74) mentions that *Peter Moor* was cited as evidence of German maltreatment of its colonial subjects.

[8] Nethersole uses the term "deutschpsrachige Literatur der Peripherie" to describe the literature to emerge around GSWA as a colony (in Keil 2003:12).

questions concerning its literariness and its acceptance into the canon of German literature as a result of postcolonial discourses. Because it was, and is, considered to be trivial, reactionary, racist, as well as of questionable quality, German colonist fiction has never featured in discussions concerning the question of what constitutes German literature. The analyses of classic colonist texts such as *Peter Moor* (1906) and *Volk ohne Raum* (1926) has to a high degree ceased to be exercised on a literary level. They are predominantly looked at in connection with their historical period, not as products that reproduced certain German fantasies and desires: their importance has shifted from a literary product to an historic artefact. Medardus Brehl (2004), for example, uses the discourses that were prevalent during the German destruction of the Herero in order to dissect and interrogate *Peter Moor*. The text is revealing of a certain ideology at the time, justifying its worth as an historical artefact, but it does not investigate the literariness of the text, i.e. how the levels of narration, character relations, and repetition of certain tropes and themes function. The result is that colonial rhetoric becomes comprehensible, yet the 'production' of the colony as an imaginary space/place is left more or less untouched. The example of *Volk ohne Raum* is also symptomatic for a 'longing' for the colonial era, a longing that is still present to this day. The plethora of safari adventures, African romances, and colonial novels is testament to this, as is the literary interest in colonial (auto) biographies and diaries.

Another reason for the retrieval of GSWA as a literary space is the current relationship that Germany has with the territory called Namibia. Although it has not been under German control since the Treaty of Versailles in 1919, Germany and Namibia continue to be strongly linked through their historic entanglements. This can be observed from the large sums of development and aid money given to Namibia, the medial interest in Namibia as a setting for various shows/films/novels/magazine programs, and the interest in the maintenance of customs and rituals through Namibian-German partnerships. This begins with the large number of German NGOs and NPOs operating in Namibia[9], as well as the various clubs and organisations that promote German culture and identity in Namibia. These are most present in schools and cultural centres such as galleries, cinemas, and on specific occasions (Karneval[10], Oktoberfest). Further examples include institutions such as the

---

[9] These organisations undeniably provide vital services and expertise (disease prevention, education, family planning, health assistance) but can also be seen to continue colonial influence (state policies, distribution of resources).

[10] The Karneval and Oktoberfest (celebrated in German communities across Namibia) carry strong racist/ *white* supremacist undertones. For a recent controversy concerning the Karneval in Swakopmund see: "Government condemns KKK 'glorification'" (*New Era*, 02/07/2015) "Die einfallsreichen Ku-Klux-Karnevalisten" (bildblog.de), and "Media Ombudsman says Kuska photos not offensive" (*The Namibian*, 11/07/2015).

Goethe-Zentrum and the Deutscher Akademischer Austauschdienst (DAAD). Problematic affiliations have also been maintained throughout the years, most notably between right wing and neo-conservative groups[11]. These oscillate between genocide revisionists/relativists, colonial war glorifiers and apologists, neo-Nazi partnerships, and colonial nostalgists. 2012 saw a number of German/Namibian authors attempt to deny or relativize the genocide of the Herero and the Nama with German books published in Namibia[12]. Descendants still strongly influence the memorialisation and discussions of the war, while colonial rhetoric and ideology is being reproduced and in some cases celebrated.

Furthermore, numerous German tourists travel to Namibia to visit places of relevance to the German colonial regime, such as the graves of German soldiers at Waterberg[13] or the *Reiterdenkmal* in Windhoek[14]. This type of tourism makes questions of decolonisation difficult as the tourists who travel to Namibia play a vital part within the larger national economy. Renaming of towns has been resisted on a number of occasions through this argument. Lüderitzbucht, the first official German colonial space and place, became the site of such a controversy when it was recommended it be renamed !Nami≠nüs[15]. Most of the *white* population of the town was opposed to the renaming, citing the town's German colonial heritage and its touristic worth as the main arguments to maintain the status quo. However, despite the opposition, the name did change in 2013. The powerful link between the maintenance and control over German colonial history in Namibia, and the enthusiastic (and problematic) tourists these cater for, has a strong colonial focus. This makes the complex and difficult processes of reconciliation and decolonisation extremely challenging. Although large amounts of aid money, experts, and tangible means are sent to and invested in Namibia by the German government, this is not to be understood as

---

[11] Two of these are the *Hilfskomitee Südliches Afrika* and the *Traditionsverband ehem. Schutz- und Überseetruppen*.

[12] Examples include Rainer Tröndle, *Gewisse Ungewissheiten* (2012) and Hinrich R. Schneider-Waterberg, *Der Wahrheit eine Gasse* (2012).

[13] The visitor's logbook contains a number of anti-Herero sentiments and glorification of the buried soldiers, usually written in either German or English.

[14] The *Reiterdenkmal* has been removed from its once-prominent position in Windhoek in 2013 according to Government decree. The negative reaction to this 'event' was shared by Germans in Namibia as well as in Germany, with both sections employing racist as well as discriminatory language to make sense of the relocation. The readers' letters published in the German *Allgemeine Zeitung* newspaper read the removal of the statue as a personal attack on the German community, positioning them as victims of a government plan to devalue German culture in Namibia. Ironically, the Herero also reacted to the removal with outrage as the statue was seen to be part of their history as well. Of course, no German letter pointed towards this at any point, placing the *Reiterdenkmal* firmly and exclusively in the sphere of German (historical) ownership.

[15] See for example: https://www.theguardian.com/world/2015/feb/26/luderitz-v-naminus-dispute-over-towns-name-divides-namibia as well as https://www.namibian.com.na/112868/archive-read/Nami%E2%89%A0N%C3%BCs-residents-against-new-name

reparation payments. These have been so far denied on the basis that the aid money and tangible means are "for all Namibians" and do not privilege a certain group.

Considering the Herero and Nama claims for reparations against the German government, instigated in 1999 and 2005 respectively, it becomes clear that the ties between past imperial power and its historically colonised territory are constantly being (re)negotiated. Based on these entanglements, past and present, one can detect a productive arena in which colonist fiction can be understood and considered. Namibia is still utilised as a setting for popular literature in which historic inequalities and violence are repressed and silenced. Furthermore, a desire to rewrite Namibian history by Namibian Germans and mainland Germans persists, making any form of closure or intellectual debate concerning issues such as the *Reiterdenkmal*, reparations, or the acknowledgement of the genocides a continually arduous task. Historical insensitivities emanating from colonial privilege and manifest in a form of a victim cult have so far prevented meaningful dialogue concerning the role of the *Schutztruppe*, the *Vernichtungsbefehl*, and the responsibility of the German state in the destruction of Namibian societies and their perpetual ridicule[16]. Namibia as a (German) setting must be seen as a product of the colonial era in which GSWA would allow for a number of fantasies and desires to take form, while continuing to deny that the territory had its own complex, extra-European history.

What emerges from the analysis of colonist fiction tends to be reflective of the home culture[17]. The acts of writing, publishing, buying, and reading these narratives points at a society willing to produce and consume such a commodity. This can be summed up through hard numbers by looking at sales figures, translations, reprints, awards, number of writers/works, and so forth. But these would only illuminate one side of the coin. What should be further considered are the linkages between the works/authors, the general public, state policy, contemporary ideas and concepts concerning aspects such as race, gender, class, sexuality, 'empty' space, the 'export' of people and ideas, the dominance of one people over another, and the production and spreading of knowledge. As will be noticeable in this chapter, I will open up a number of tropes that emerge through the writings of colonist authors. These may have been primarily theorised and discussed through the example of British writing of empire. However, seeing as theories and ideas concerning the hierarchies of 'race' and the domestic place of the woman were ubiquitous in Britain and mainland Europe (albeit with minor differences, impacts, and implementations), it does seem appropriate to apply some of these theories and ideas to the German

---

[16] The scandal at the Charité in 2011 (discussed at a later stage) is only one of many setbacks experienced by the committees arguing for the acknowledgement of the genocide of the Herero and Nama.
[17] Ulrike Hamann's *Prekäre Koloniale Ordnung* (2016) is a current example in which developments in the German colonies reflected various discourses concerning the 'home nation'.

context. Ideas and ideals concerning colonialism, *whiteness*, humanism, and patriarchal authority all emerged as a pan-European project with strong overlaps. Since male and female authors both wrote their fictions in and about GSWA, and because a number of tropes seem to recur throughout both bodies of literature, it becomes possible to link the theories emerging from the different geopolitical contexts.

Furthermore, the close proximity in Europe and the even closer proximity in Africa between these two nations[18] allows for a cross pollination of literary and real-world fantasies and anxieties[19] to some extent. These were located in both the Black as well as the female body, for example. The body should, however, not be the only focus when looking at colonist fiction. This becomes clearest when observing how characters express their first encounter with the newly entered space(s). Many times this is the very first direct contact with the 'new', preceding the encounter with the 'Other'. As all three novels will show, the majority of the main characters are those who have no prior knowledge or have had negligible contact with GSWA, except through secondary sources. This has been discussed by Memmi (1965/2003:51) and Said (1978;1993), for example, where literary and medial (re)productions of the colony influenced further productions of the colony and constituted a form of knowledge. Other technologies such as photography, postcards, calendars, documentaries, and landscape painting added to these colonial productions. The strong monologic nature of the colonial discourse, i.e. the similarity and sameness of the medial reproductions created a literary genre that ran on fantasies of an African 'empty space'[20] (and fantasies of producing this space). However, it is this initial confrontation with the perceived 'empty' space that opens up the chance to either locate or invest the views from 'back home' into the located society. This can either be in accordance with the society back home or in contradiction to it[21]. Both paths, however, tend to reproduce prominent aspects of the home society in order to orientate oneself in an unknown space.

The questions that the experience of 'empty' space opens up can be summarised along the lines of: what should be done with this space? How do I navigate this new space? How is it similar/different to home? These questions, especially the first, allow the characters

---

[18] German and British territories shared four common borders, while the British port of Walvis Bay was located within the borders of GSWA.
[19] These would include a crisis of masculinity, the limits of knowledge, disorientation in the world, and the constant undermining of *white* authority. These anxieties had their origins in European metropoles and were played out/reproduced in the colonies.
[20] I highlight African 'empty space' in order to contrast it to the encounter with foreign, Western spaces that were undoubtedly not considered empty. While Germans were traveling to their colonies in small numbers, many more were emigrating to the USA, a space that was already 'filled' and a space that they could not consider as either *terra nullius* or *tabula rasa*.
[21] A comparison between *Peter Moor* and *Heim Neuland* will testify to this difference.

to reproduce aspects of the home society, where 'empty' space seems to be an historic, bygone occurrence, an occurrence identified and located somewhere else. This again gives the colonialists a chance to rectify any 'mistakes' they had made back home (in the sense that they did not make use of the full potential of the space) and the chance to reconfigure the space before them as no one has any *legal* claim to it. Other non-legal colonialist claims to literary space may take the form of landscapes that are viewed and permeated by the colonial gaze. Another form is by creating a hierarchy of spaces (metropole vs. periphery, urban centre vs. rural enclave, garden vs. 'wilderness') or imbuing certain spaces with meaning/energy (such as the farm, a *trek* path, a war zone). One look at the numerous works focussing on colonist literary space is indicative of the distinct ways one can look at these spaces[22].

I will begin the discussion of the novels with a very brief summary of each work. This allows for access to the plot of the narrative. Furthermore, I will focus on the main narrative strands and the main characters only, except where the introduction of a secondary or menial character is necessary. The second part of this chapter will be the actual analysis of the narratives in respect to tropes they share. Certain deliberations as to how these tropes appear and function within each individual narrative are opened up, connecting the novels according to these tropes. As McClintock (1991), Haarhoff (1992), Noyes (1992), and others have successfully shown, colonist tropes (and the accompanying fantasies and reflexes) cannot be isolated or treated on their own. Because of various intersections, certain concepts feed into or strengthen other aspects. In the colonial context *whiteness*, for example, is also informed by gender, which in turn informs domesticity as well as the German construction of the 'Other'. These concepts again influence the way we can understand space (through inclusion/exclusion), the fetishism of purity (in a racialized, sexual, as well as in a personal sense), or the fantasy of the control over other/'Other' bodies (female and African)[23]. My aim is therefore to weave a web in which all three narratives are able to be in direct conversation with each other.

Lefebvre's city-countryside dialectic will form the setting in which this conversation may occur, thus allowing the relationship between the metropole and the periphery to form the background. The location of the metropole in the colony is indicative of metropolitan desires and production processes. Central to this dialectic is the process of pro-

---

[22] Stiebel (2001) focusses on the creation of landscapes in Haggard's novels, while Haarhoff (1991) is interested in the frontier as a concept and its relation to the metropole. Noyes (1992) deals with spatiality as a grid in order to interrogate colonial space(s).

[23] It should go without saying that this control is a literary fantasy and an imperial desire. This imperial desire was and is constantly resisted on a number of levels by those it desired to control. Homi Bhabha (1993) and Ashcroft (2001) discuss the various tactics involved in resisting colonial and imperial desires.

duction, the process that formed the basis and later justification for the various forms of violent occupation. And because dialectics implies a certain reciprocal relationship, it goes to say that the relationship between metropole and colony is mutually influential – although highly asymmetrical. The continuous metropolitan production of the colony is also reflective of the metropole's need to reproduce itself through this perpetual process. In other words: the colony is the engine behind the metropole's drive to reproduce itself, using the construction of the colony to reach this aim. In this way, the colonising nation and its colonised territories cannot be regarded as independent spaces, but spaces that produce and reproduce each other. As the metropole imagines and writes the colony into being, so the colony becomes entangled in the metropole's production (and definition) of itself.

The three motifs that will make up this web of intersections are elements central to the novels or spaces with a high repetition. It is the analysis of **the myth of an 'empty' landscape** that will begin my literary analysis. Because the characters enter the colony *before* encountering the people living there, the landscape is formative in their character development/description and their evolving relationship with the colony. It is also revealing of the fears/hopes with which the characters enter into the colony. Peter Moor is confronted by a landscape of war, while Etta Wibrandt, Dirich Dierksen, and Ingeborg Oberländer encounter a space that appears to be under German control. Through the insertion of *domesticity*, these spaces are transformed by the ***white* female settler**. In this case the colonial landscape is loaded with metropolitan markers such as purity, homemaking, and *whiteness*. These motifs are written onto the body of the female colonist, yet are implemented in order to serve/save the male body[24]. Domesticity in this case also has a racialised component, as the female colonist is responsible for preventing the mixing of *white* and Black bodies. The final space I will be looking at is the **colonial garden**. This has special value in the literature of GSWA, especially because of its harsh climate. The garden, as will become evident, fluctuates between its realisation (with special focus on labour investments) and as a space of desire (as a possible Paradise as well as a link to home).

Although these three tropes appear in the novels in one form or another, the emphasis differs between each novel. The colonialist garden allows entry into the powerful discourse located in the binaries such as wild/ordered, civilised/savage, nature/culture, and Black labour/*white* labour. The landscape is the central theme in *Peter Moor*, while the desire for land and private property is central in *Heim Neuland*. *Du heiliges Land!* picks up elements of the two previous narratives, yet its central theme is domesticity. The three novels

---

[24] "Domestic hygiene purifies and preserves the *white* male body from contamination in the threshold zone of the empire" (McClintock 1995:32).

announce their own central themes but also make it possible to compare how the other works deal with each of these themes. What is most interesting about the comparisons is tracking the changes in attitude concerning these themes as time and interests pass. The trajectory begins with the settlers in *Heim Neuland*, which was published after *Peter Moor*, but sets its plot before the war. The start of the war brings Peter Moor to GSWA and he and his fellow soldiers violently remodel the *Schutzgebiet* into a colony by eliminating the Herero. The trajectory ends with the discovery of diamonds, catapulting the colony into international renown. Temporalities overlap (*Peter Moor* and *Heim Neuland*), or are separated by years (*Peter Moor*/*Heim Neuland* vs. *Du heiliges Land!*), changing the spaces while conversely preserving certain aspects and technologies.

Introduction to the Texts

a) *Peter Moor*

Peter Moor is the story of a young German who enlists in the colonial forces in order to help suppress the Herero rebellion against the German intruders[25]. After the three-month journey by boat, he and the rest of the forces reach Swakopmund. The war situation does not go according to his expectations as confrontations with Herero soldiers are few and far between. Rather, his war accounts focus on the harshness of war environment and the exhausting conditions. In the few clashes with the Herero, he is able to prove himself and contributes to the successful subjugation of the "enemy". Because of his physical exertions and the subsequent decline in his health, a later return to the colony becomes impossible. On his return *Fahrt* back to Germany, he meets a family friend with whom he shares his story. In a narrative twist, it is revealed that his account of events is in fact the published version of his experiences of the war, made possible through the efforts of the family friend.

b) *Heim Neuland*

Heim Neuland follows the colonising aspirations of Etta Wibrandt and Dirich Dierksen from Germany to GSWA. Beginning in the small north German town of Hodrum, a great storm threatens to destroy the coastal town but Dirich's bravery saves everybody. His achievements bring the two cousins closer and they end up marrying. A banker misappropriates Dirich's fortune, setting the scene for his and Etta's move to the colony. They decide to become colonial farmers due to their long family history of being landed gentry

---

[25] He gives the deaths of German civilians in GSWA as the reason, yet it becomes clear that is not a war of retribution or protection, but rather of destruction.

and Etta's dislike of urban spaces[26]. Once in GSWA, they first buy a small plot in order to organise their entrance into the agricultural economy. This takes the form of cattle acquisition and soil cultivation, both utilised in order to finance a larger farm. Etta and Dirich manage to buy their own farm, "Farm elf", and rename it Ettenhof (sometimes referred to as "Neuland"). The two protagonists are also introduced to military personnel of the town of Okahandja as well as other farmers in their vicinity. The married couple completes the house on their property with the help of a former Hodrum local, Chrischan Möller, whom they save from his vagrant lifestyle. After Etta falls pregnant, she and Chrischan travel back to Germany so she can see her sick mother before she dies. While she is aboard the ship, Ettenhof is razed to the ground, indicating the start of the Herero uprising. Dirich is drafted into the German colonial army and is involved in the defence of Okahandja. Back in Germany, Etta has given birth to their son, Hans=Heim. Dirich joins Etta in Hodrum after the end of the war, with the couple resolving to return back to Ettenhof and continue their life in the colony.

c) *Du heiliges Land!*
Du heiliges Land! is a novel set around the coastal town of Lüderitz in GSWA, and is what Gudrun Thiel (1988) has coined a "diamond novel"[27]. The main protagonist is Ingeborg Oberländer, a young middle class woman who has been sent to the colony in order to be married off to a German man. Competing for her hand in marriage are the manager of a diamond mine, Hans Gothland, and the proxy holder of the same mine, Dr Herbert Klinger. Because the former is not in the social or financial position to ask for Ingeborg's hand in marriage, he decides to start stealing diamonds from the mine. This proves unsuccessful as Ingeborg has already chosen Klinger to be her future husband. After she informs Gothland of this, he is devastated and begins neglecting his work duties and starts drinking excessively. After a heavy night of alcohol consumption, Gothland commits suicide by drowning himself in the ocean. Ingeborg and Klinger's union is delayed indefinitely after Ingeborg becomes suspicious of Klinger's faithfulness due to his frequent visits to the Casino and the seedy Bar "Schloß Baux". Her suspicions arise because there is a rumour that Klinger was involved in a relationship with one of the women working there. The planned union is eventually cancelled after Adolf Oberländer's (Ingeborg's brother) heavy debt comes to light. In order to save her brother's social standing, Ingeborg decides to

---

[26] In this case, a life in Hamburg, the next larger city approximate to the fictionalised coastal town of Hodrum (based on the historic town of Husum), is rejected.
[27] This is a subgenre of colonialist literature that focuses on the discovery of diamonds outside the town of Lüderitzbucht. Thiel discusses three books concentrating on diamonds, namely Lene Haase's *Raggy's Fahrt nach Südwest* (1910), *Dina* (1913) by Hans Grimm, and the novel of this section, *Du heiliges Land!*

marry Oskar Vollmüller, the richest diamond trader in GSWA. This is to Carola Oberländer's (Adolf's wife) liking as she sees herself profiting from this marriage. This wedding, too, is cancelled after Klinger exposes Vollmüller's fraudulent activities, ruining him in the process. Adolf Oberländer dies shortly thereafter, leaving Carola, who consequently expels Ingeborg, in charge of the house. Without any securities, she attempts to find accommodation with friends in Cape Town. Because they are travelling, Ingeborg is forced to find employment in order to support herself. She works for an old lady, who fires her after the she suspects Ingeborg of reading her letters. Jobless and without any relations in Cape Town, Ingeborg becomes a singer in a reputable cinema. Klinger comes to one of her performances and convinces her that he has been faithful all along. He pays for her to be released from her contract with the cinema, freeing the way for their wedding and a return to Germany.

What immediately jumps out when looking at the novels is the metaphorical employment of space, noticeable in each of the titles. From Peter Moor's *Fahrt*, to Etta and Dirich's *Neuland*, and Ingeborg's *heiliges Land*, all three titles concentrate on the spatial component of their narratives. Apart from the blatant and overt racism concerning Africans and Africanist characters and the contempt shown to other nationalities (the British, the Portuguese, Afrikaners), the authors weave a net of ideas of what constitutes Germanness or a German ideal – constructions that are, of course, relational. The spaces these concepts come to the fore in the most are the war arena, expanded upon by the nostalgic quintessential farm life and complemented by the diamond novel. Various allegories are fused or dislocated, while the emphasis shifts from one topic or theme to the next. What unites these topics and themes, however, are two different practices.

The first practice takes as its starting point the question of what to do with the new space. In *Peter Moor's* case, the space is not German, it still needs to be acquired and, in a sense, earned[28]. The novel treats the space as foreign, as alien, as a space that needs to be conquered, including everything it contains. However, in order to overcome the space which is foreign and alien, the protagonist enlists the help of signs and symbols he has gathered from the metropole so as to order and organize the war zone. An Easter fire, a German oak tree, a German woman with a German baby, a garden – they all help Peter Moor to orientate himself in this 'foreign space'. These signs and symbols also help to displace the foreign and the alien. The initially overpowering and terrifying landscape is

---

[28] The rhetoric of "the right of the stronger" and the "chance of growth in a difficult space/place" are used as justifications for the terror brought upon the colony. This rhetoric is fuelled by ideas of progress, linearity, civilisation, history, Social Darwinism, and labour.

slowly but surely pacified. The "enemy", lurking at every turn and hidden in the "bush", becomes visible and manageable. Once these two objects of suffering are removed can the space become German, can the space become a colony. The "enemy" is finally banished from the space, from the "bush", from the narrative. The "bush" becomes the site/sight of victory, opening itself up to the vanquisher. The space now has the *potential* to become German.

Heim Neuland, however, deals with this question in a very different way. Although the "enemy" has been defeated (in a figurative and historical sense), it is not enough to make the space German. It is not enough to gain access to the space and to the land through military intervention. What is necessary to Germanise it is the prospect of instilling German-ness into the soil and into the local inhabitants and justify the *Deutsch* in *Deutsch Südwestafrika*. This is exactly the goal when the narrator mentions Etta Wibrandt's desire "ihre Leute nach und nach *zum Deutschen* zu erziehen, wie's in einer deutschen Kolonie nur recht und billig war" (emphasis mine, 445). This sentiment is echoed in Clara Brockmann's writings, arguing that the coming Germans have the mission to educate the African population (Wildenthal 1993:82). Contrary to Peter Moor, Etta Wibrandt and Dirich Dierksen's mission is not military, but cultural[29]. The best, most innocent space for this is the farm, replete with numerous signs and symbols from the metropole: the enclosure, the garden, the relationship between capital and labour, and the foundation of settling down, namely domesticity. The various colonial novels of course show a different extent of the aforementioned elements.

In *Peter Moor*, for example, domesticity is considered an exotic event due to the war conditions as well as the lack of German (female) colonists in GSWA. The gardens mentioned above are not connected to the *white* female colonist, only her reproductive ability is emphatically emphasised. Meanwhile, domesticity is a prominent and central trope in *Heim Neuland*. This is clearest when one considers the time spent by the narrator and the characters in order to position the *white* female colonist as a genuine homemaker and housewife. The different levels of domesticity, especially in respect to the farm gardens, also show how important the idea of the 'perfect *hausfrau*' is propagated in the novel. However, with the emergence of a product which is highly desirable in an international commodity and capital economy, *Du heiliges Land!* moves away from the war-torn and rural spaces which make up the initial German Southwest African landscape and ends up in the urban space of money, exchange value, vice, and wealth. The sand dunes, having

---

[29] I feel uneasy in trying to separate the various forms of colonial territorialisation. However, the novels clearly emphasise a specific strategy used in appropriating foreign space. Peter Moor's fleeting but brutal encounter with the colonial space is contrasted by Etta and Dirich's long-lasting and mythologised connection to the foreign soil.

protected the interior from invasion for millennia now produce myths of untold riches. Stiebel comments on the labour-free procurement of diamonds in Haggard's *King Solomon's Mines* (2001:78), pointing towards the colonial fantasy of infinite riches. In *Du heiliges Land!* this fantasy has, in fact, become a fictioned reality. Here the space of established German-ness receives numerous threats, from the outside (in form of *foreigners*) as well as from the inside (in form of *the foreign*). A 'true' and 'pure' German becomes the antidote and the necessary agent in order to maintain the work done by previous settlers and their administration. German-ness is not merely a bio-cultural given anymore[30], it has become a virtue, a quality that is at the same time fragile and durable, innate and learned, personal and communal[31]. As Brockmann goes to great lengths to explain (visible in her non-fiction as well as her colonial novel), it is the virtuous German (woman) who can survive in GSWA – exemplified by both Ingeborg Oberländer and Herbert Klinger.

Although the novels have strong themes connecting them (and which I will discuss in the coming section), I would also like to point to significant differences in the 'writing' of GSWA. On an initial level, this 'writing' of GSWA has a non-linear dimension to it. Although this does not appear to be the case when contrasting *Peter Moor* with *Du heiliges Land!*, it becomes observable when *Heim Neuland* is introduced. Peter Moor enters a space that is, according to the narrative, still 'wild' and unsettled. The fact that the "bush" and the "enemy" are the main referents and orientating principles shows the absolute lack of beacons for the protagonist. The territory is still empty and run through with potential, potential which Peter Moor is only able to secure, but not release. This potential is tapped into when Etta and Dirich enter the territory. Before Peter Moor even becomes a necessary character, the married couple has already created circumstances in which the colony's potential is realised. The establishment of orientating beacons (the farm, the garden, hierarchies) transforms the barren, unsettled spaces of GSWA into German and German-producing (i.e. by producing German offspring) spaces.

Both texts deal with the Herero-German war, but it is *Heim Neuland* which focuses on the pre-war GSWA, a space in which Germanness has started to permeate both time (via labour) and space (the soil). The colonial settlers arrive before the military and create a GSWA in which German-ness has started to take root, while offering a justification

---

[30] The character of Dr. Schleicher in *Du heiliges Land!* is reflective of the new forms of German-ness as they are understood both in Germany and in the colony. This will become clearer when I discuss *whiteness* in response to the German colonialist characters.

[31] According to Yekani, this phenomenon is also applicable to the idea of masculinity, arguing that "a certain paradoxical simultaneity seems to subsist that reads hegemonic masculinity as both the natural order of things as well as a cultural achievement" (43). This would explain how *white* masculinity in colonial fiction is always already implied but continuously reproduced through masculine achievements (hunting, war, dominance).

for the arrival for Peter Moor and company. However, Peter Moor does not identify the colonising work done by Etta and Dirich, only in certain instances (such as the colonial garden and the woman with child). And yet this is negligible as Etta and Dirich return to a GSWA which the army has now subdued and which has opened itself up to its conquerors. The landscape abounds with smells and colours, all of which Peter Moor will never enjoy – but Etta and Dirich as well as Ingeborg will. Ingeborg and the other characters of *Du heiliges Land!* will profit the most from Peter Moor's violence as the territory can now be considered a colony proper because initial colonial desires can now be realised: ownership and control over the territory, the exploitation of local resources and people, and finally, the establishment of a culture of German-ness in a distant far-off place. The colony has become settled[32] and its potential can now be extracted. The 'empty'/'emptied' landscape(s) serve a number of functions, depending on the time period as well as focus of the narrative (bravery vs. industry vs. love). The meaning of GSWA is constantly in flux, with the narrators and characters offering multiple approaches to the territory.

Emptied Landscapes

a) *Peter Moor*

Before Peter Moor encounters any human agents of danger in the colony, the landscape itself threatens him. His sighting of a mountain range generates fears of the menacing potential and violence of this gigantic, ancient structure:

> Right before us stood a monstrous, horribly wild mountain range. I had never seen mountains. Not only I myself and the other North Germans, but also the Bavarians were amazed at the sight. Quite close in front of us, and also receding into the distance, huge naked rocks rose to the sky. Some were lighted up by the evening sun, and shone bright and hard; others, gloomy and fearful, hung menacing, often directly over us. On all sides were evidences of the mighty powers that had ruled of old, that had knocked off pieces of rock and precipitated them into the depths, and had left other pieces, already split away, hanging at a frightful height, as though they might plunge down at any moment. Little powers could not exist here. We didn't see a shrub or even a spear of grass, and not an animal. We, the only living beings, were rolling along through this immense, dead wonder-work on our little creaking cars, ridiculous to look upon. (1908:43)

The adjectives he uses to describe the sight range from "dreadfully wild" to "monstrous" to "threateningly dark" and "terrible". Peter Moor reveals two very distinct impressions

---

[32] "Settled" in this sense has two equally important meanings, namely in respect to the influx of colonial settlers, and in respect to the destruction of various local societies (most notably the Herero and Nama, but not exclusively) and the resulting 'peace'.

of the landscape on him. Firstly, it becomes clear that the landscape is wrought with potential danger, symbolised by the "menacing" rocks which "might plunge down at any moment". He perceives the landscape as a threat, always carrying possible death or injury with it. This will become a motif throughout the narrative, with the "bush" being the most common antagonist. The mountains and the "bush", however, are not the only threats. The lack of water, the vast 'empty spaces' are all instilled with negative potential, resulting in lacerations, fever (due to rampant typhus), and unquenchable thirst. The huge mountain, a new experience for Peter Moor and others, takes the form of a monument that was formed across time by this 'new space'. Nature is instilled with some form of mystical power as it is able to create such a massive structure while being able to impress its power on it. The mountain dwarfs the small coach containing the focaliser, symbolising the difference between the timeless power of nature and the technologies of culture. The second motif that this passage opens up is the promise that if one is able to survive in this environment, one is no longer a "little power". One has defied the power exerted by the landscape and come out as a victor. One therefore 'deserves' to live in this dangerous setting. This fact is reiterated through the ending of the novel, in which the average, young, and inexperienced Peter Moor has survived not only the "enemy", but also the setting of the war.

The initial reaction that Peter Moor reveals highlights the binary between the ancient subliminal forces of the natural versus the newly introduced promise of the technological. The location of technology, or sign of technological advance, becomes one way of assessing one's position in this binary. A passage that discloses Peter Moor's disorientation and alienation from the natural territory can be found when he comments on this perceived emptiness of the landscape. He is unable to locate any markers or structures that are familiar to him, detecting only lack and absence in his surroundings:

> In these hard, hot days of marching, and cold, moonlight nights, when we were advancing painfully, but still not without courage, one week after another, through the wild, bushy land — there was not a house, not a ditch, not a tree, not a boundary in the burning sun by day or the pale moonlight of the clear nights; when I was plodding along, hungry and dirty and weary, by the sandy, uneven waggon-track, my gun on my shoulder; when I lay in the noon hour in the shadow of the of the great Cape wagons, and in the bitter cold nights, hungry and restless, in a thin blanket on the bare earth, and the strange stars shone in the beautiful blue heavens— then, I believe, even then, in those painful weeks, I learned to love that wonderful, endless country. (81)

He is trained to look at space and identify structures, any structures that confirm some form of spatial control. Yet, all he encounters is what he can only grasp as 'empty space', space that has not been filled by European/German architecture or meaning. He is confused by the lack of houses (the sign of property) and the lack of borders (the symbol for inclusion and exclusion). He can only understand the foreign spaces once they are filled with 'his' objects. Peter Moor's only response to this apparent 'emptiness' is a *belief* in *learning* to love the country. His inability to find any recognisable signs or symbols can only be countered by the irrational, unexplainable emotion of love. This love coming despite all the hardships and misery[33] he has endured. And even when he pronounces his supposed love, he is not sure of it – the only feeling that might connect him to the territory outside of what is considered rational, is something that must be learned, something that he must rationalise for himself. Peter Moor realises his relationship to the territory in one of his darkest, most depressing moments in the novel. Imagining a loving relationship to the apparent 'barrenness' that has so far been encountered compensates for the implied and imposed 'lack' of everything.

His longing for home comforts is further emphasised in another scene. At one point in the novel, the soldiers light a celebratory Easter fire. Peter Moor describes the scene as follows:

> The next morning, while it was still dark, we made a fine Easter fire of dried thorn-bush in the middle of the camp, and all stood about it and were glad that we were still alive, although our life was so dirty and friendless and painful; and we thought of home, picturing how the mother was giving out the Sunday clothes, and how clean the living-room was, and how festive the morning coffee, and how the church-bells were ringing out over the houses. (94)

Not only does the fire reproduce German (Christian) cultural rituals, but it grants Peter Moor the opportunity to contrast his time in GSWA with that at home. The tool for this is one of the most potent colonial discursive instruments – cleanliness. His African experience (having an imitation fire in the "bush") is contrasted to clean clothes and the clean home. Also, the experience is not his own, a singular experience, but a group or collective 'we'-experience. This indicates that the fire not only creates a common space for homesickness but that all parties involved long for the cleanliness that they can only experience at home. The metropole with its luxuries and hygiene is reproduced in the periphery. But it is reproduced through the idea of lack: the lack of good coffee, of church bells, of Sunday clothes, of a clean home. The fire is the only thing that is able to connect the soldiers with home as any 'homely' and familiar objects cannot be located. The periphery has not evolved into being yet. To Peter Moor, GSWA can only still become a

---

[33] This is of course at no point contrasted to the misery and hardship he is responsible for; neither does he contemplate his own responsibility for his own hardships and miseries. Peter Moor is completely oblivious of the horrors that are taking place while he tries to understand his 'love' for the country.

"periphery". This is why the war is so necessary: to gain control over the periphery as a complete and subjugated space.

Annette Gertrud Hoffmann did extensive research when locating Herero identity in the landscapes they produce(d). Her thesis focusses on the insertion of a network of history, kinship, and meaning into spaces which the Herero refer to as their own (*eri rOvaherero*). This process arises when "the land is cultivated into a landscape by means of orature, mostly in form of praise poems (*omutandu*, or *omitandu* in the plural) as well as through performative acts that constantly contest and negotiate history" (6). This process usually begins with the placing of a grave of a well-known Herero figure (in most cases male) and the connection of that person to the land as well as to his predecessors and ancestors. It is through this process that the actual community, those who were left behind by the death, and the 'imagined' community (those who have passed on) are united through the oral performance. Hoffmann contrasts this means of 'landscaping' with that of Westerners, arguing that "'landscaping' in Herero culture revolves more around hearing and narrating or reciting than it is concerned with seeing and pictures" (24).

Because the German forces that arrive in GSWA are receptive to the landscape, a consequence of centuries of scenic painting and, later, photography, they are unable to identify or locate anything that the colonial eye cannot observe. Here we have a clash of the objective camera, the recording machine of the German soldier; and the meaning producing, subjective mechanisms of the Herero. The narrative format privileges the former completely, giving the latter very little to no space. This has the effect that the Herero are divorced from their link to the land they originally inhabit and live on[34], and to the narrative, as the final chapters prove[35]. Emptiness in this case reminds the character of how far he is from home and how alien his new surroundings are. To put this in perspective: Peter Moor is still able to orientate himself in Madeira, a place that is different but not alien – "like a cousin one seldom sees" (34).

When looking at the language Peter Moor employs in his own narrative from a sheer quantitative perspective, certain words appear to dominate the linguistic landscape. The word "Graben" or its derivatives such as "begraben"[36] are mentioned roughly twenty times. In his study of the effect of the violent contact between Europeans and Africans, Esaïe Djomo identifies three forms of culture which the former implemented and repro-

---

[34] By producing the Herero as an abstract term, the narrative separates them from their cultural and social space. This separation then identifies the space as an arena of war in which the victor gains control of the territory. The abstract "enemy" becomes tangible as a defeated force and can now be identified and constructed.
[35] Once the Herero have been forced into the desert and Peter Moor witnesses their destruction, they are also eliminated from the narrative.
[36] Other examples of the word *graben* (to dig) reference the act of digging wells as well as trenches.

duced in the colonies, namely "Festkultur", "Körperkultur", and "Bau- und plastische Kunst sowie Totenehrungskult" (2011:233). The war allows very little of the first two expressions of culture, while forcefully creating the arena for the "Totenehrungskult". Peter Moor can thus only focus on that. As most of the characters die of typhus, burial of the dead seems to be the quickest solution. However, they are still sent off with traditional German practices, such as wooden crosses on the mounds and short sermons held by the military pastor. Although this is not the case for every burial action (the war arena does not always allow for this), this represented the ideal way of honouring the dead – considering the circumstances. These graves, however, become a powerful token of occupation as the question of the validity of the war arises amongst the members of Peter Moor's company. A freight-carrier dismisses Germany's ability to run a colony and urges them to sell GSWA to England (1908:80). He then receives a rebuttal from a young soldier, who argues that "[t]here'll have to be a thousand or two thousand graves in this country before that happens, and perhaps they'll be dug this year" (80). The answer, implying a consideration of the freight-carrier's proposal, is based on the number of casualties of the war. Not only that, but it also exposes the fear of numerous deaths arising from the war – the deaths as a result of the war against the Herero.

A further, more significant linguistic assessment of Peter Moor's vocabulary divulges his two main fears: the landscape (the "bush") and the Herero (the "enemy"). Although he is surrounded by the former and identifies it on numerous occasions, his confrontation with the latter takes an excruciating while to realise. In order to understand his surroundings as a war zone and as a space of danger, his reaction to both fears is to fuse them. Peter Moor's excessive and strong connection between these two words lays open a colonial anxiety: of being engulfed by the landscape *and* the people[37]. The landscape merges with the people who actually belong there and creates danger for all those foreign to the area. As an extension, this means that the "enemy" needs to be destroyed in order to control the space, to rid it of its inherent danger. War is needed in order to pacify both nature and its invisible inhabitants. That which cannot be seen and/or understood must be discarded or recombined in order for it to be comprehensible. The alienation in and by nature informs the response to those who reside in it.

One of the few times he identifies a plant or tree it is only as a reference to Germany. The identification of the oak tree – a highly layered German symbol – is able to improve the morale of the soldiers[38]. One can of course argue that this is a Romantic conception

---

[37] Walgenbach (2005:1713).
[38] "When we came, after some hours' marching, to a beautiful great forest, with trees which looked like German oaks, we were strongly reminded of our native land, and we became a little brighter and more lively as we passed through it." (1907/ 1908: 92–93).

of the regenerative qualities that nature, in this case Germanised nature, has. It also becomes relevant when looking at how Peter Moor is able to consistently and frequently connect the "bush" with the "enemy". The repetition of the two words creates a landscape in which GSWA becomes a "bushy" terrain hiding the Herero. Space becomes a danger, and must be subjugated and controlled militarily by removing its most dangerous element – the revolting soldiers[39]. In this comparison, the German oak tree represents a life-affirming space, while GSWA becomes the space of danger and potential death. The metropole must therefore reproduce itself in the landscape (through the imagined oak tree) and then produce a new space by clearing the way for this imagining and ridding it of potential disruptions.

Jean and J. Comaroff's article "Naturing the Nation: Aliens, Apocalypse and the Postcolonial State" (2001) could prove helpful when decoding how the tree (as a sign) is vital in understanding how discourses about plants are also discourses about the nation-state. Although the article focusses on South African local flora, its destruction in fires, and the consequent debates around (illegal) immigrants in South Africa, I want to use some of the arguments to discuss the future of the only *named* wild plant in *Peter Moor*. The article firstly identifies that there has always existed an "aesthetics of nature" (628), and that this has been used "in the service of nationhood" (Shula Marks quoted in Comaroff and Comaroff 628). This is exactly what the German oak tree has been mobilised to do – it reproduces the German state within the confines of a territorial war. Its image becomes an object which confirms and vindicates the soldiers' decision to protect Germans (while exercising retribution) in this hostile space. In essence, "geography is perforce being rewritten" (633) as the German oak tree has crossed seas and borders and entered the colonial frontier, momentarily displacing the local "bush". Germany has, so to speak, been exported into a perceived vacuum and germinates via the soldiers' new-found vitality. The military is pushed on to expand the frontier while increasing German/-ised space via the occupation of foreign space.

The German oak tree, however, only makes a fleeting appearance, serving as a symbol rather than an encroaching element. The treacherous bush remains the main environmental actant. The alien tree – having travelled thousands of miles over seas and borders – is not allowed to flourish or reproduce in a space which is dominated by foreign desires of control and acquisition. Here, the durable connection between a symbol of the nation-state (the German oak tree) and the new desired space cannot be sustained. Con-

---

[39] It is of course undeniable that a similar strategy was used in Conrad's *Heart of Darkness* (1899), when Marlow appears to locate Africans in the "bushes" and forests he travels along when on his boat on the Congo river.

sidering the assertion that GSWA was not as yet seen as a German colony[40], it becomes clear that the German oak tree could not remain as part of the landscape. Its role remains supportive in the war effort but it has no function thereafter. Its imaginative and symbolic nature ensures its brief appearance and its consequent immediate disappearance. Other signs (more concrete and lasting) such as state borders, a bureaucratic apparatus, enclosures, and roads will be implemented. The short life of the German oak tree is further compounded by a later and conscious return to indigenous knowledge concerning the environment, most notably plants. The alien sign-tree will be replaced just like it briefly replaced the local trees. Space is emptied by replacing/substituting markers.

This connection also infers that the terrain – already identified as empty on numerous occasions – needs to be *emptied* from the markers that Peter Moor and his company are unable to grasp. This would allow the Germans who will still be coming[41] to take control of the land and overwrite and/or re-inscribe meaning into the landscape[42]. But before the landscape can be emptied of its initial content, it needs to be filled by the imagination and fantasy. This method was already applied when the soldiers were imagining Africa, the war, and GSWA. In this case, the landscape needs to be emptied of the "enemy", meaning that it needs to be inserted into the (already threatening) landscape. Because of the type of war and because of the lack of classic warfare, Peter Moor starts to invent and imagine enemies at every turn. He explicitly reckons that there are enemies in every bush, always lurking (51). Yet, he waits for more than an hour, avoiding any shots, because he is unable to locate a single enemy (52). This imagining of the enemy in the immediate surrounding is also invested with unnecessary violence:

> Apparently the guardsman at last learned enough, for he said: 'The missionary said to me, "Beloved, don't forget that the blacks are our brothers." Now I will give my brother his reward.' He pushed the black man off and said: 'Run away!' The man sprang up and tried to get across the clearing in long zigzag jumps, but he had not taken five leaps before the ball hit him and pitched forward at full length and lay still. I grumbled a little: I thought the shot might attract to us the attention of hostile tribes who had perhaps stayed behind. But the lieutenant thought I meant it was not right for the guardsman to shoot the negro, and said in his thoughtful scholarly way: 'Safe is safe. He can't raise a gun against us any more, nor beget any more children to fight against us. The struggle for South Africa will be a hard one, whether it is to belong to the Germans or to the blacks.'" (234–235)

---

[40] See Jureit (96).
[41] The coming German settlers are of course an important reason as to why the war was necessary from a German perspective. A victorious war effort would bring stability and the land needed to entice German nationals to move to the colony. Etta and Dirich's, as well as Hans Gothland's consideration of coming indicate a willingness for Germans to come, even if it is in a fictional context.
[42] The renaming of towns, farms, and natural landmarks are the most obvious modes of overwriting and reinscription.

Peter Moor is not concerned with the death of an unarmed, hunted individual, but with the potential that his death may bring more enemies. Hiding, lurking, the enemy is everywhere, hidden by the land, hidden by the "bush", able to multiply instantly.

Peter Moor may of course, like so many settlers in the history of colonisation, lack the language to understand the landscapes he is moving through[43]. This may be an argument that one can charge the protagonist with, but not necessarily the other characters. If my argument that Peter Moor and the reader are simultaneously 'educated' holds, then we can assume that neither knows much about the plant life to be found in the colony. But this does not vindicate the other characters that have been in the country for a while and should at some level have knowledge concerning the plants. The "Afrikaner"[44] should receive a special mention. Also, Frenssen did have access to this information and might have tried to educate Peter Moor in this respect. Furthermore, Peter Moor makes no effort to learn whom he is fighting against (Brehl (2004: 90-91). The Herero, one of the bigger societies of GSWA at that time (the most populace after the Owambo), are at no stage identified as such. Peter Moor is only able to identify them according to what they are to him during the war: the enemy. He enlists in a colonial war, travels for months, suffers from hunger, thirst, and disease, without knowing (or acknowledging) his adversary.

This disables any identification with the enemy people in his narrative as they are consistently treated like an abstract concept. Even when they are not seen as enemies (for example when they find a small child or a group of non-combatants), they are still part of the enemy whole and therefore as collateral of the war. In essence this dehistorises the Herero people, denying them a history and a place in the history of GSWA[45]. They are discussed as nothing more than an obstacle that needs to be overcome in order to produce (German) history. Brehl (2004), analysing the discourses that were produced in colonist fiction in respect to legitimisation of the destruction of the Herero, argues that the arguments offered in the narrative support my claim. The anti-colonial war effort by the Herero is dislodged from its original context and inserted into the larger, philosophical 'universal history' or *Weltgeschichte*, as theorised by thinkers such as Kant, Herder, Schiller, and most famously, Hegel. This understanding of history as a linear, progressive, forward-moving development already excludes Africans from any positive contribution, but the example of Peter Moor explicates how this is done. The production of *white* his-

---

[43] This is what Coetzee might define as "[t]he literature of the empty landscape" (1988:7)
[44] Not to be confused with the Afrikaans-speaking Dutch descendants, also referred to as Afrikaner. In this case, it is a label for Germans who have spent some time in the colony.
[45] As the colonialist literature concerning the Herero war clearly expresses, the Herero are seen as a "proud people" but are relegated to a defeated force. This defeat ultimately leads to the claim to the territory. This is also an idea which is transmitted by *Heim Neuland*.

tory necessitates the exclusion of other 'histories' in order for it to claim supremacy and reproduce its truthfulness[46]. Retribution as a claim is thus rejected[47], even if it is the initial reason Peter Moor decides to travel to GSWA.

b) *Heim Neuland*

Etta Wibrandt and Dirich Dierksen's experiences when initially confronted with the landscape starkly contrast the fears and anxieties felt by Peter Moor and his desire to not be a "little power". One must remember that, on the one hand, the space that the two protagonists enter into is not yet German *soil*. On the other hand, Peter Moor and company have previously defeated the Herero[48]. This allows Etta and Dirich to enter a 'safe' space that has already been cleared of (most) dangers. This becomes most obvious through the lack of markers of menace (littered throughout *Peter Moor*) and the optimistic and confident attitude shared by the protagonists. Etta and Dirich enter the colony in order to remain. Their settler dream thus justifies the war Peter Moor will fight[49] but also inserts a German-ness into the pre-war colony. The colonising settler, who 'prepares' the initial grounds for the territorialisation, subsumes the role of the soldier in the founding of the state. Property and labour stand symbolically in the service of the nation-state before the military machine is invoked. The territory is German because of the farmer and his deep and industrious relationship with the soil – one of the basic elements necessary for the production and reproduction of a society.

Because *Heim Neuland* starts its excursion into GSWA before the war, the reader is introduced to the territory in a different way. Even prior to the first impressions of the land on the protagonists, Etta and Dirich earlier fantasise about what they might expect in the colony. When they first discuss possible emigration, Etta imagines the endless space as "[d]ie Freiheit! Die Größe! Demat auf Demat[50], alles Eigentum. Und alles unberührt. Neuland, in dem noch alle Möglichkeiten liegen!" (1908:401). The idea of the enclosure (*Eigentum*) is combined with the potential of German labour (*unberührt*). Thus

---

[46] German Namibian war commemorations reproduce this assumption. The Herero are constructed as 'proud' and 'organised', but are never understood as having been equal militarily or as having a justified reason for their rebellion. The reactionary trope of German victimisation (a trope prevalent in Germany's involvement in the Second World War and commemorated in the German cities that were bombed, such as Dresden) is also constantly perpetuated in respect to the need to 'protect oneself'. An example of this is the intense reaction to the relocation of the *Reiterdenkmal*.
[47] "'These blacks have deserved death before God and man, *not* because they murdered two hundred farmers and revolted against us, but because they have built no houses and dug no wells.'" (1908: 236).
[48] I use his argument in a literary sense as *Peter Moor* appeared before *Heim Neuland*, as did numerous reports and newspaper articles.
[49] It is the deaths in *Heim Neuland* which symbolically bring Peter Moor to GSWA.
[50] "[A]ltes, schleswig-holsteinisches Feldmaß (=5000 bis 6000 Quadratmeter)" (footnote, 401).

the corner stone for an expansionist but also idealised worldview is laid, one that ascribes ownership and property rights to 'untouched' spaces, spaces that belong to someone else. However, what gives the utterance a utopian capacity is the added fantasy of the new space, "das Land der Zukunft" (401). The potential space at hand is already projected into the future, where hopes and dreams may be realised. Although neither character mentions these views themselves, the narrator is able to deduce – or at least identify – this in their thoughts and reactions. By focussing on their genealogy as landed gentry and coupling this with their childhood 'games', the narrative voice presents Etta and Dirich as the ideal colonial settlers. This stems from their childhood fantasies: "Am häufigsten aber gefiel er sich in der Rolle des tüchtigen Bauernhofes. Etta und Dirich bewirteten den Berg als Mann und Frau. Er war der Grund und Boden, der sie nährte und ihre vielen Kinder obendrein" (381), which also nurtures the idea of the ideal family, one that is self-sufficient and large in number. And although this may seem like children playing and performing certain roles, it is again repeated when the two protagonists have grown up: "'Aber können Sie nicht nachfuehlen, daß wir uns danach sehnen, freie Bauern zu werden und den Laden aufgeben?'" (Etta Wibrandt to Detlef Welzin, 484). The wish to live a rural life – as opposed to one in an urban setting – is repeated until the end, emphasised in the desire to return to GSWA and to rebuild the destroyed farm. This may be because urban centres are already produced, i.e. the space for change and modifications is severely limited. The theories of *Lebensraum*, *Raumverengung* and *Raumschwund*[51] are the most common fears associated with space in the modern/modernist era. A flight into the rural landscapes, which the colony seemingly has in abundance, seems the most appropriate reaction.

Contrary to Peter Moor, Etta and Dirich are not frightened or oppressed by the vast 'emptiness' – they are elated by it. Not once does Kraze give the surrounding nature negative undertones, not once is nature responsible for any ills or afflictions. The exception is when 'their nature' is disturbed by foreign elements. Examples are the locusts, the razing of the farm, and the war effort[52]. Natural scenes are expressed in highly poetic language. This language can be experienced, as the narrator comments:

> Und dennoch — die wunderbare *Poesie* dieser Fahrten durch fremdes Land! Wenn sie beide nebeneinander auf der Vorkiste saßen und durch das *goldfarbene* Land fuhren, das so öde war, so *grenzenlos leer und verlassen*, daß das Gefühl ihrer Zusammengehörigkeit sie hieß, sich fest aneinander zu drücken. Gab es außer ihnen und ihren Begleitern noch Menschen auf der Welt? (my emphasis, 483)

---

[51] See for example Jureit (2012:22–23 & 71) as well as Haarhoff (1991:80).
[52] The farm is referred to as "ein Grab alles Glückes" (647), while the war descriptions take on similar language as *Peter Moor* (624).

Here, Kraze constructs a landscape and a space in which endlessness is seen as a positive quality, especially as it is cleared of any other subjects who can own or desire these spaces. Not only is the original population absent from these vast spaces but so are other nationalities and, even more surprisingly, other Germans. The endlessness can be enjoyed as no others and no 'Others' are present. This is reflective of *Großstadtflucht*[53] as well as the idea of ownership, even if this ownership is achieved through an aesthetic appropriation and not through property rights. The view is appropriated and becomes an exclusive event, reflective of the already-established desire of 'owning endlessness'. The aestheticisation of the foreign makes it comprehensible and clears the way for its acquisition. The emptiness of the landscape is celebrated, especially as it is connected to their solitude. This combination guarantees that the view (and the proprietary gaze) is an exclusive technology of the two protagonists, free from any interruptions and, more importantly, free from any contestation. *Heim Neuland's* protagonists need this emptiness in order to 'produce' their own landscape[54]. They do this by acquiring a piece of land and actively infusing it with their desired signs and symbols.

As I have also argued, it has the dimension or ownership, especially as there is the fantasy of being alone in the world[55]. It is the ownership of the view, of the aesthetics of the view. Photography and landscape painting are a form of this ownership. This ownership takes official form when they are able to buy their own farm, actually owning a space they are able to control. Now they have the house and the borders, so lacking in Peter Moor's landscape, and are able to expand on these spatial markers. Furthermore, they have bought an already-established farm (Farm elf) and renamed it Ettenhof (sometimes tellingly, referred to as *Neuland*[56]). This does two things to their 'own' space. Firstly, it rewrites the genealogy. Through (re)naming the space and, more specifically, renaming it according to oneself (see the example of *Lüderitzland*[57]) colonists inscribe themselves into the land. Their personal history and the way they want to be perceived are directly connected to the farm and vice versa. In this way, previous ownership is disavowed and overwritten, while insisting on the truthfulness of one's ownership[58]. Naming in this case

---

[53] *Großstadtflucht* is the flight from cities, as exercised by Etta and Dirich (they flee from Hamburg), but also experienced by Ingeborg and, to a certain extent, Peter Moor.
[54] This emptiness echoes an absence of visual markers such as settlements and visual man-made obstructions such as wind pumps and houses.
[55] Although Black characters, hired for their journeys, accompany them, they are not part of the visual experience that Etta and Dirich share.
[56] Ironically, Farm elf cannot represent *Neuland* as it is an already-established farm – even if it failed.
[57] The strip of land on the southwestern coast on GSWA that the merchant Adolf Lüderitz purchased from *kaptein* Cornelius Frederiks in 1883. Lüderitzland thus formed the foundation of what was later to become GSWA.
[58] Ownership/ propriety is further cemented through the law through the contract and other documenta-

links the legal act of ownership of land with the exclusivity offered by private property. As Henrichsen has argued, (European) farm names reflect dreams and anxieties of settlers and articulate a European claim to African territory (2011: xi). Sienaert & Stiebel (1996) give an overview as to how these temporal and spatial orderings take shape. The most powerful tool for this exercise is naming, the most fundamental form of assigning meaning.

The process of naming takes on a further dimension as the farm becomes a place that is different to its surroundings[59]. First, through the implementation of fences and gates. Second, through receiving an identity, it cannot be part of the spaces surrounding the fences and gates (it is not part of the neighbouring farm, or the constituency, or the town). This makes the farm – as previously mentioned – a relatively autonomous space. The use of the word *Hofstaat*[60] in *Heim Neuland* is exemplary of the desire for a self-reliant space that has loose ties to the metropole. By creating semi-autonomous spaces and configuring them to function like mini-states, Kraze unites ideas of the state, its sovereignty, and power. This is what Lefebvre points to when he argues that "[p]ower aspires to control space in its entirety, so it maintains it in a 'disjointed unity', as at once fragmentary and homogeneous: it divides and rules" (1974/1991:388). Power (through naming, the farmer, laws) carves up the farm. The farm shows signs of its unity (its name/inhabitants/produce) and simultaneously its separate nature (camps, house, garden, dam, roads) in order to manage it more easily. The farm becomes an exclusive space, devouring the signs and symbols which had previously been set up in this landscape, while disallowing these previous markers to be either accessed or maintained by its original.

After completion of the farm house after Dirich and Etta's arrival, reconstruction on the farm starts. The first object to undergo restoration is the well. The well becomes a vital technology in order to survive in the colony[61]. By fixing the well, the protagonists are able to begin herding and gardening. What follows is the *kraal*, the most important farm enclosure as it contains the most valuable commodity, cattle. Lastly, the farm has a *kraal* for smaller animals. Here, the land is first 'renovated' and then expanded upon through partitioning it and marking the partitions. The farm is finally made official settler territory when Etta, the *white* farmer's wife, arrives on the property:

---

tion, as well as visually through signposts at the entrance and the name on a map.

[59] Haarhoff (1991) starts his discussion of German colonist literature with the example of Adolf Kaempffer, who bought a farm from Hendrik Witbooi (*Harubeb*) and renamed it *Deutsche Erde*. Here the name dislodges the farm from its previous owner and gives it a German identity (61).

[60] The word is used to describe *Ehlersholm* (36), the farm Gerda and Franz Ehlers occupy.

[61] The importance of the well as a technology is discussed at great length in Dag Henrichsen's *Herrschaft und Alltag* (2011). Here the author creates a spatial concept, which he refers to as "topography of wells" (3).

> Chrischan war benachrichtigt worden, daß auch die Herrin den Viehtransport begleiten würde.
>
> Nun stand er mit den schwarzen Arbeitern zum Empfang aufgereiht, und ein riesiges gemaltes ‚Willkommen auf Ettenhof!' prangte zwischen zwei Pfählen, die zu einer Ehrenpforte errichtet und mit Schilf, Granatgrün und Oleanderblüten umwunden waren. (486)

It is however, not the farm as a physical territory that appears in the novel but the farm as an idea. Landscapes, the house, the Gran Canaries, Gerda Ehler's garden are all described in much more detail and more elaborately than Ettenhof. Rather, it is the idea/ideal of the farmland, the idea/ideal of ownership that are central. This manifests itself in the dream Etta and Dirich have, the actualisation of that dream, and the eventual collapse of that dream. The farm, as they have imagined it, offers all the desires they associate with property rights to them. This extends from the *"unvergleichlichen"* (my emphasis, (1908:487)) view that the finished house affords, to the endlessness inherent in this view (this endlessness is paradoxically contained on their property), and the ideal *Neuland* ('untouched' soil). Although the farm had a previous owner, its desolate state is the closest that Etta and Dirich can come to 'pure' nature[62].

As Esaïe Djomo has argued, "[d]er in die Kolonie einwandernde Europäer kommt nicht nur mit dem Gesangbuch und sämtlichen Sitten seiner Heimat dorthin, er bringt auch das Gesetzbuch" (2011:129). Djomo's assertion would make the farm a prime ideal heterotopia, as it now links the fantasy of expansive land and self-reliance with the law guaranteeing this fantasy. From arguing along the labour concept, the arguments evolve into a legal-judicial concept that historicizes the land only from the moment of its privatization. The general tenure concerning private ownership – as is visible in *Heim Neuland* – tends to concentrate only on the previous owner, while excluding the fact that it had always been there, just not in that format. Private property creates a new genesis and genealogy for the space. Instead of a progression of that space, it is separated from its initial surroundings (or its base: nature) and is reappropriated. The ideal heterotopia emerges as its design stipulates that the farm must be owned, separated and re-historicized, overwriting the traces of the original involvement in the landscape. The farm exists in multiple temporalities (the land/soil is always by far older than the farm), while it also exists in opposition to its (fenced out) environment.

The farm further becomes one of the most Germanised spaces in the novel. This not only becomes visible in the naming of the place but also through the architecture and the

---

[62] This house could be exactly what Stiebel terms "an oasis of 'civilisation' planted with flowers and fruit, both familiar and exotic, set on a vantage point overlooking 'illimitable lands' open to the gazer's eye" (2001:41).

imported plants and trees. In this way, Etta, who is mainly responsible for the cultivation of the flora (cornfield and garden), implants her German-ness into the soil. It is here where she is allowed the time and space to work the soil and inscribe it with German symbols. Not only are these symbols important, but also it is the labour she includes that transform the soil[63]. This cultivation turns the soil, through a combination of symbols and labour, into German soil allowing for a German to lay claim to it. Furthermore, it separates it from the surrounding non-German soil that is 'wild' and 'uncultivated'. This cultivation and consequent separation from its surroundings is subordinated to a system of organisation. This determines where what is cultivated and built, and who is allowed where. The farm thus has a number of attributes which one can use to define it. It is a fenced-in, autonomous space/place that has been imprinted with a certain ideology through the introduction of symbols and labour.

Labour in the colony, especially visible labour, becomes one of the markers of difference between settler and the 'Other'. As J.M. Coetzee has argued in the introduction of *White Writing* (1988), labour in the colony has to be divided into two opposing modes or styles of representation. The work executed by *white* colonists (both male and female; however, primarily *masculine* industry) needs to be visible. The eye/I should be able to identify the work that arrivals have done, whether it is building settlements, cultivating land, or implementing administrative and bureaucratic institutions. Etta's labour is concentrated in other spaces (their farm stall, the household, the garden), yet she is also always active in some way or another, contributing economically while maintaining the Dierksen's cultural centres. In order for *white* labour[64] to be seen, Black labour needs to be invisible. By denying that Africans were able of productive labour[65] and then linking it to their (lack) of culture, the first step to land acquisition was taken. As Ashcroft et al. argue in *Key Concepts in Post-Colonial Studies* (1998),

> the colonizing powers brought with them a particular view of land that had a philosophical, legal and economic justification. [...] For Locke[66], the very mark of property is the enclosure: the defining, or bounding, of a place that signals the perceived settling or culti-

---

[63] Albrecht Penck defines German soil as "Wo deutsches Volk siedelt, ist deutscher Volksboden, da hört man deutsche Sprache und sieht man deutsche Arbeit" (quoted in Jureit 2012:241).

[64] Memmi (1965/ 2003) discussed this already, linking colonialist activity and 'action' to ethics, stating that "[h]e who knows that he is in a bad ideological or ethical position generally boasts of being a man of action" (114). This is preceded by his discussion of "power politics, which does not stem only from an economic principle (show your strength if you want to avoid using it), but corresponds to a deep necessity of colonial life; to impress the colonized is just as important as to reassure oneself". In both cases visibility is of central importance.

[65] I use "productive" in its capitalist sense, meaning that the labour performed needs to somehow contribute to the trans-/national economy.

[66] Locke, John. *Second Treatise of Government* (1689).

vation of that place. Indeed it is the figure of enclosure that marks the **frontier** between **savage** and the civilized. Although nobody has an exclusive dominion over nature, says Locke, since the 'Fruits' of the earth and the 'Beasts' were given for the use of men, there must be a way to appropriate them before they can be of any use to a particular man, and this is the method of enclosure (Locke 1960:333). Because it is man's labour that removes the products from nature and makes them his[.] (Locke, quoted in Ashcroft et al. 1998:180, bold in original)

The argument here refers to private property, but it is rooted in the idea that this private property is the result of the cultivation of the soil/space that is enclosed. Thus there is a link formed which has a chicken-and-egg dimension: which is more important, the enclosure/private property which allows productive labour to take place; or the labour which necessitates private property? The enclosure was implemented in order to achieve a number of goals. Firstly, it was used to alienate the local populations from their own land, the engine of identity formation for many. Secondly, it paved the way for the mass acquisition of large tracks of land, leaving many local societies in spaces with barely workable soil. Thirdly, it created asymmetric relationships of power, as space became a minority commodity while the majority became more and more disenfranchised. Finally, the instruments of enclosure and property allowed colonialists to control the visibility of the labour that justified the enclosure.

It is at this juncture that literature becomes very important in substantiating the assumptions and processes of the colonial project. The *white*, mostly male, protagonists are always portrayed as being active[67]. Whether they are busy planting or cultivating crops, building or renovating their homes, trading, hunting, or travelling, the *white* colonists are always synonymous with action and industry. They are, in other words, always productive. And it is this productivity that is desired in the colony. Those, however, who do not fit into this category, the 'antisocial', are linked to markers given to local communities. Some of them can still be redeemed as the found-and-saved character, Chrischan Möller, proves. He has his vagabond life[68] changed after accepting the liberating force of honest, productive work. Language plays an important part in this marked difference. Phrases such as 'going native' and '*verkafferung*' show the powerful link between what is consid-

---

[67] Yekani (2011) points out that "[w]ithin narrative accounts, masculinity is not so much as something one can claim; rather, it is a position that needs to be achieved often in terms of a heroic struggle" (36), positioning masculinity as being continually and actively reproduced. This has a strong echo of the work that is needed to counter the regression in the Paradise of Africa, discussed in the section in this chapter dealing with colonial gardens.

[68] "Etta hatte eines Tages Kattundruck für eine schwarze Schöne abgemessen, als ein ziemlich *verlumpter und nach Spirituosen riechender* Mensch hereinkam" (emphasis mine, 1908:464).

ered *white* and what is considered non-*white*. And it is this link that also allows the question the idea of difference between *white* and Black labour.

Black bodies, whether they are portrayed/imagined to be busy planting or cultivating crops, building or renovating their homes, trading, hunting, or travelling, are seldom connected to these activities. While they may appear to be performing tasks, these tasks tend to be menial or superfluous. So, although the protagonist might reference the farm workers as planting crops or building a house, this work is generally not visible, only mentioned. The *white* narrative employs strategies such as evasion and silencing of Black involvement in order to create difference between colonising and colonised labour[69]. The ethical conflict, i.e. thinking about the effects of colonisation on the colonised societies, is overwritten with a focus on doing, i.e. legitimising the colonising settler's presence in the occupied territory. When the protagonists do make their way to the sites of Black industry, the workers are described as being on a break, or having deserted, or are busy with something else, less important (making food, drinking, singing/dancing). In this way, *whiteness* (without being mentioned) is constructed as the industrious binary to Black idleness[70].

Heim Neuland does have a high focus on the work which Dirich Dierksen and Etta Wibrandt perform. This allows them to be separate from the idle characters (the Ehlers, the von Gensdorffs), but especially the Black population. Dirich Dierksen, in his climactic speech during the war, focusses on the achievements that the German settlers have accomplished:

> Seht, wie wir es gewonnen haben: jeden Brunnen haben wir selber gegraben, jedes Gartenbeet selber bestellt, jeden Ziegel unsres Hauses selber formen helfen, und wie viele Frachtfahrten waren notwendig, ehe wir zu unsrem Viehstand gekommen sind! Alle Handwerker zugleich sind wir gewesen. Kaufmann, Landmann, Jäger und Soldat in einer Person. (619)

Not only does he emphasise the tasks they have completed, but he also reproduces the trope in which the colonial settler becomes the master of many trades. Their accomplishments are then contrasted to the 'barbarity' of the people they are helping, using the argument of a 'race war'[71] between the local communities and their European masters:

---

[69] "He who knows that he is in a bad ideological or ethical position generally boasts of being a man of action." (Memmi 1965/2003:114). Dirich Dierksen's speech reproduces this assumption. He admits that *white* colonists have taken the land of the different societies. He also lists all of the colonising settlers contributions to these societies, arguing that *white* involvement improved the livelihoods of these societies even though they have no land, and very little room to sustain their original way of life.
[70] For examples how to work with terms such as evasion (especially in a racialised context), see Toni Morrison (1992) and Arndt (2009).
[71] This was a military as well as national(ist) ideological tool, as Sarkin (2011) shows: "He [General von Trotha] insisted all along that Germany was fighting a 'race war'" and that "Germany depicted the Her-

> Wir haben unsre Pflicht an den Eingeborenen getan. Wir haben versucht, sie zu Menschen zu machen, daß heißt sie zur Arbeit und zu einer Art sittlichen Bewußtseins zu erziehen. Unsre Frauen und Töchter haben ihre Kranken gepflegt und ihre Kinder gelehrt. Wir haben uns bis jetzt nichts vorzuwerfen. Das, was uns in diesem Kampf einzig angeht, was hier sein tiefstes Wort spricht, ist der Rassenhaß. Die Eingeborenen hassen uns. Sie hassen den Deutschen, der gekommen ist und ihnen ihr Land genommen hat. Daß er sie von ihrer eignen Willkürherrschaft und Grausamkeit gegeneinander befreit hat, ist ihnen sehr gleichgültig. (ibid.)

Speaking as a high-ranking military official as well as a colonial settler with a high social standing, Dirich also represents the arguments that the military and the farmer classes believe and want to hear. He begins with the fact that some people had mistreated the Herero when they were collecting their debt. Yet, he fails to link it to the legislature that was introduced or the fact that it was a common practice, not something done by a select few. Dirich is also silent about the continual and accelerated processes of land loss amongst the Herero and the resulting increase in colonialist violence against them. This included 'legitimised' violence[72] as well as violence that the courts permitted[73]. Dirich also reproduces the trope of the civilising mission of the colonial nation, citing the introduction of European medicine and education as a legitimate response to colonial land acquisition. His final sentence, referencing the period of war between the Nama and the Herero, positions the *white* colonialists as saviours of the warring societies.

He of course neglects to mention that a number of colonial settlers, traders, and missionaries profited from these wars through intensified trading, social influence, and cattle acquisition, prolonging the wars because of their profitability. Like in *Peter Moor*, it is not the colonial project that is the reason for the war, but the simple difference in 'race'. And the argument behind this difference is productive labour, labour in the service of the nation. Instead of analysing the reasons for the war from a holistic perspective, meaning that he also considers the countless injustices perpetrated by the colonial government as well as the colonists, he reduces the war to the generally accepted argument of *Rassenhaß*. This argument (a paradoxical imposition, considering the overt racism of the colonists) overwrites and stifles any cultural, social, and political processes that led up to the war while vindicating the colonisers via this abstract reasoning. Dirich's 'analysis' of the processes leading up to this devastating war rests on the strongly held beliefs of *whiteness* and its potential to civilise and improve.

---

ero as the initiators of a 'race war'" (10).

[72] This included what is termed *väterliche Züchtigung*, a generally accepted form of punishment for Black farm and domestic workers involving whipping.

[73] *White* settlers were seldom punished for brutal crimes against Black people, crimes that included rape and murder. Conversely, a conviction of a Black person on these accounts usually ended with execution.

Linking Dirich's speech to "The White Man's Burden", certain tropes and arguments become visible. The strongest of this is the role of the *white* European populace in the development of a backward continent they have invented[74]. This 'help' is constantly written in the form of a liberation from something, but the damage done through this liberation (i.e. loss of lands, the destruction of cultures, the creation of strong master-servant hierarchies) are downplayed or relativised in order to emphasise certain achievements. Colonial horrors are designed as moments of self-defence and self-preservation without considering the effects of the general project of imperialism. The attitudes of certain military men and civilians are also completely ignored, such as Axel Gussow[75], as well as the soldiers who are conscripted at the outbreak of the war[76]. The war can thus not only be considered a result of the clash of two competing cultures, it is an event that is desired in order to establish *white* dominance. The paradox of a war being "frisch" and "fröhlich" speaks volumes about the attitude towards a development that undoubtedly has negative effects on those who are involved and the countless innocent people who have no choice in the matter. The argument of *Rassenhaß* is also dismantled by the desire for this war (conversely a desire for the imagined Black practice of *Rassenhaß*). The German aggressors can now position themselves as victims while celebrating their achievements, regardless of the effects on the Black population.

The achievements which Dirich recounts and spotlights are those in which *white* labour is employed in order to substantiate claims to Black land and territories. Identifying a 'lack' of Black labour, especially in the sphere of soil cultivation, further supports these claims. *White* colonial claims for land are expanded to include national claims for land, thus justifying expansion into Black-controlled territory. These claims take place on two competing and yet complementary levels, both highly reliant on notions of labour and *whiteness*/Blackness. Dirich's first effort in focussing on *white* achievement is centred on the civilising mission. He argues that their efforts "sie zu Menschen zu machen" has failed, although they have substantially invested in this undertaking, also involving 'their' women and daughters. The second level is the failure to make labourers out of the Black population, as the failed "sie zur Arbeit und zu einer Art sittlichen Bewußtseins zu erziehen". Dirich, Etta, and the other colonial characters failed on two levels, not due to a resistant attitude by the local populace or because of the undesirability of European

---

[74] V.Y. Mudimbe's *The Invention of Africa* (1988) speaks to this idea.
[75] "Axel Gussow fand, das Leben war wahrhaftig keinen Pappstil wert. Das beste wäre, es käme mal Krieg oder irgendwas und ein Haufen Menschen würde erschossen oder käme sonstwie um" (560).
[76] "Trotz aller Sorge um die Kolonie *lechzten sie alle nach einem frischen, fröhlichen Krieg*. So langes Stillsitzen machte stumpf. In fünf Friedensjahren lernt sich genug. Das mußte doch endlich mal an den Mann gebracht werden!" (my emphasis, 587).

temporal and spatial regimes, but merely because of an irrational, unsubstantiated claim of being hated for being *white*. This assertion and assumption is constantly undermined by the *white* characters' overt *Rassenhaß* in respect to Black characters.

The reason for a failure of the colony and the accompanying fantasies are a *white* failure to acknowledge its own violence, its own prejudices, and its own failures. This has the effect that the colony, as a project of prestige, is the only straw that the colonial Dirich is able to hold onto, a project he argues must continue at all costs. And the highest of these costs is, of course, the war. This war guarantees the continuation of the myth of *whiteness* while maintaining the strong discursive, race-orientated distance between *white* colonisers and the local population. On a superficial level, *whiteness* is reproduced through a victorious war effort, reproducing *white* superiority and supremacy via technological power. A military defeat would on a deeper level reproduce the racist tropes of Black barbarity and savagery – how else could these 'not-yet-human'[77] soldiers defeat an advanced enemy? Dirich's speech confirms – and deconstructs – a host of paradoxical tactics that *white* characters must rationalise in order to uphold the beliefs concerning the myth of *whiteness*[78]. The outcome of the 'sudden' and yet desired war will be twisted in order to be advantageous for the myth of *whiteness* – a myth that is unable to exist and function properly without the construction and then destruction of Blackness, both physically and symbolically. *Whiteness* both as a technology of the metropole needs Blackness in order to justify its intrusion into the world and the knowledge produced though and for this intrusion.

c) *Du heiliges Land!*
Du heiliges Land! makes use of the landscape in a very different way to the preceding novels. Although the landscape is conceptualised as being 'empty', the characters have a rather ambiguous relationship to the places they find themselves in. On the one hand, the ever-present sand dunes are likened to a prison (24) and to a lifeless scenery of coffins (68). The endlessness appears oppressive (34), while its apparent loneliness has deadly features (32). On the other hand, the oppressive endlessness is run through a type of enchantment no one can resist (11), it allows for beautiful views denied by the city (21), and

---

[77] This is a reference to the earlier passage, where Etta and Dirich doubt the humanity of a group of Black characters singing and dancing around a fire.
[78] This upholding of the myth is also a reproduction of "social positions determined by a powerful political and social grammar of difference" (Arndt, 2009:174). The fact that Dirich holds his speech during the occupation of Okahandja during the war, and the fact that he is a high-ranking military officer at this juncture, is revealing of *whiteness* military usefulness.

most importantly, it offers the chance of becoming healthy again (22). In one very telling passage, Hans Gothland's feelings become emblematic for this ambiguity:

> Unrecht Gut hatte er genommen, das Land bestohlen, das er liebte. Er fühlte plötzlich eine Liebe zu dem weiten, spröden, rauhen Südwest entbrennen, das ihm so vieles geraubt und eine irrlichternde Hoffnung gegeben. Er liebte dieses Land, weil er so unglücklich darin geworden... (148)

Peter Moor also experiences this contradictory logic when he thinks about the hardships he has endured in the war. Etta and Dirich echo this through the decision to return to GSWA. This novel, however, complicates the characters' relationship to the 'empty' landscape, especially as some have lived there for a long period, while others have just arrived. Depending on which desires are experienced, the desert and its incomprehension mean different things. For characters like Oskar Vollmüller it is the promise of endless wealth. For Ingeborg it means escape from Germany and its social rules. For Gothland it is the promise of a broken dream and the imprisonment in the diamond fields. Gothland's landscape becomes the prison of his dreams and fears, however a prison, which at another point he describes in contrasting terms.

In the opening chapter of the novel, Hans Gothland compares his time in Germany with his new life in the colony:

> Was hilft es mir, wenn ich inmitten ödester kleinstädtischer Biertischherrlichkeit den Reserveoffizier ausspielen darf? Sie sprachen von meinem Kollegen hier. Gewiß sind es Leute, unangetränkelt von dem, was wir Bildung nennen, aber ihr Gaunerblut oder ihre Freiheitsliebe – ganz gleich, das Einsetzen einer Persönlichkeit ist hier draußen doch Bedingung – stellt sie in meinen Augen zuweilen höher als jene stumpfsinnigen, kraftlosen, satten Philister daheim, deren Herdentrieb bei lebenslänglicher Gemeinschaft mit ihnen auch uns verkümmern läßt und alles und alles tötet, was einst in uns war am Stolz und Schöpferkraft. Was habe ich heute? Ein Leben in *Freiheit* in Gottes weiter Welt. Und *ich kann es formen und bilden, wie ich will*. Bunt wie ein Kaleidoskop, wechselnd, vielgestaltig, voller Tollheiten und Launen, liegt es vor mir. Und ein eiserner *Fleiß* wird mir dazu helfen, daß es sich in aufsteigender Linie bewegt. Sein Schicksal bezwingen, das ist etwas Wunderbares. (emphasis mine, 16)

The colony offers Hans Gothland a number of possibilities and opportunities, all of which can be achieved through industry and application. Although this is at another turn completely dismissed (when he talks about his dream of being a farmer), Gothland is convinced that the colony will offer him the chance to avoid the fate he would have suffered back home. The colony, as a 'new' world stands for opportunities denied back home. The foundation of this new world is freedom, an argument also made by Ingeborg. Hans Gothland begins to reveal an ambivalent relationship to his environment, a space which can be manipulated according to how the characters feel or the justifications for their migration to the colony. All of this is concentrated within the desert outside of Lüderitz.

And yet: this desert biotope must be considered as the most alien to any European emigrant seeing it for the first time. Because there is nothing like it in Europe, one can only experience it once one is physically in it, able to experience first-hand its vastness, its imagined lifelessness, and its immensity. And because there are no reference points that the metropole can offer, the metropolitan signs and symbols most closely resembling this space are employed. It is at this point that the narrator speaks of the desert in European terms, comparing the white sand to snow and the desert to a forest (25). A further example that has been introduced is the *Wüsteneinsamkeit* (23), referencing the Romantic term of *Waldeinsamkeit*[79]. Another example of this fusion is the term *Wüstenmeer*, where the complete absence of water (the desert) is linked to the largest body of water (the ocean/sea). These create a fusion between two antitheses, as the comparison links environmental concepts that could not be further removed from each other. And it is this unlikely juxtaposition that reveals the impossibility of speaking of the African landscape in European terms. This has the effect of emphasising its non-European-ness. Or to put it in Coetzee's words, this process is "a self-defeating process of naming Africa by defining it as non-European – self-defeating because in each particular instance in which Africa is identified to be non-European, it remains Europe, not Africa, that is named" (1988:164). This would also refer to what Henrichsen said about European/German farm names.

It reveals the lengths to which authors (amongst others) have to go in order to make new landscapes accessible to characters and readers alike. It seems that the only way to create a comprehensible landscape is to describe it in metropolitan terminology, exporting the excess of the metropole in order to first acknowledge the lack in the periphery and then to gloss it over. The 'empty space' of the colony becomes the site in which the limits of the signs and symbols of the metropole are countered, filling gaps in meaning created by the confrontation with the new and unfamiliar. In this novel, for example, a host of them are linked to the *white* female body and its reproductive capacity. The *white* female does a lot of work in bridging the massive physical distance between colony and 'home' nation, with the reproduction of rituals central to this. Aspects of traditions and rituals are imported along with the women graduating from the *Koloniale Frauenschule*. The skills acquired there are exported in order to adapt to life in the colony. Etta's troubles in baking bread are exacerbated by the dry climate until she learns how to do it in the

---

[79] *Waldeinsamkeit* can be used to describe the feeling of solitude (*Einsamkeit*) one experiences in the woods (*Wald*).

difficult conditions. This is replicated when Ingeborg's skills for social survival rest upon her domestic abilities. Although there is no mention of her doing any housework while living in Schakalswater, her skills as a homemaker working for someone else offers her the opportunity to begin a life in the so-called "Paradies" (Cape Town). Her access to the new space of the colony is not achieved on an individual level, but on a nationalist level. Her skills become national skills, both home and away. This link becomes personalised when she is lost in the desert and recalls soldiers dying of thirst here, connecting her, quite superficially, to a violent and bloody past.

Seeing as a place or location seems to enter into an *omutandu* once a chieftain or elite is buried there, graves receive a historic as well as artistic significance. This becomes even more evident when one considers the concept of memorial landscapes[80] that deal with the Herero genocide by the German *Schutztruppe*. In both communities, graves play a vital role in organising the events of the war and honouring the people who were involved. Because of the importance given to the Herero leadership and their place of burial, the war landscapes were strewn with a number of prominent places. The graves indicate that these burial places should fall under Herero jurisdiction (although not in a judicial-legal sense). This claim to the land housing the dead is at one point picked up in *Du heiliges Land!* when Ingeborg, in a very emotional speech, explains why the colony is 'holy land', also referencing the title:

> 'Und ich laß es mir nicht ausreden, daß wir auf heiligen Boden stehen', rief Ingeborg. 'Gerade weil hier die deutsche Jugend[81], die den Heldentod für dieses Land starb, in seinem Steppensand begraben liegt. Darum ist es so innig mit dem Mutterlande verknüpft und hängt mit tausend unzerreißbaren Fäden an der alten Heimat.' (141)

This passage is filled with what can only be described as metaphorical connections between the war and metropolitan Germany. The fact that the young imperial soldiers died a "hero's death" is significant in respect of their colonising role. Their interpretation as heroes further links them to the history of Germany as their sacrifice can now be included in the conflicts involving German forces and its connection to the securing of German soil – irrespective of the legitimisation of these wars. Ingeborg places these soldiers within the larger framework of German heroes, linking colonisation to the historic (and violent) formation of the German imperial state.

---

[80] See for example *Postkoloniale Erinnerungslandschaften* by Larissa Förster (2010) concerning the remembrance of the anti-colonial war, involving the remembrance communities of the Herero and the Germans.

[81] It appears that the German youth are the ones who symbolise the loss in the wars most intently. According to Ingeborg, it is their sacrifice that makes GSWA a holy place while Frenssen dedicates his *Peter Moor* to the German youths who had been killed.

Statistically, most of the soldiers were buried in the northern parts of the area, as north as to be just below the Police Line. The fewest soldiers would therefore be buried in the area around Lüderitzbucht[82]. What she is able to do, however, is link the conquered soil in GSWA with "der alten Heimat" because of the Germans buried there. This forges a compelling relationship between the newly-acquired territory and the home of the aggressor. Her appeal to the holy land echoes the Herero praise poem, but instead of fixing the graves to a specific space, she extends it to include the whole colony. This permits her to lay claim to everything within German borders, as opposed to pockets of space that contain the graves. The graves become the site and legitimisation for the simultaneous claim to foreign land and the mystification of the claimed land. The graves, as a site-specific symbol (i.e. the burial place), produce a German territory that consists of the spaces of war and death. The graves function as symbolic borders, littered all over the country and enclosing everything in German possession (read: occupation). Ingeborg employs the graves as an outpost that contains what is understood to be German space. They in essence enclose while not being enclosed themselves. What is important is that the graves, usually dug superficially or deemed unlocatable, become the outer bounds of the colony and are linked to both the soil and the *white* blood invested.

Enclosed and exclusive spaces in *Du heiliges Land!* receive an altogether different dimension as those in *Heim Neuland* and which were considered missing in *Peter Moor*. The first enclosed space encountered in the novel is the diamond field Gertrudenfeld. It is a space of wealth and a space of industry. There are a number of attempts to control the wealth of the space, such as division into the spaces to be excavated, security personnel, foremen and proxy holders, sorting houses, and on-site living quarters. Just as in *Heim Neuland*, the name echoes propriety and ownership. In this case, however, it is ownership by the German imperial state. Everyone on the field, from the lowliest employee to the top official, is subordinated to the German state. In this industry, there is no personal autonomy. The careful regulation by the treasury, which Gothland reveals to take the form of "strenge Kontrolle und Statistik" (28), makes the collection and accumulation of diamonds an alienating procedure because the employees will have no further interaction with the product. It appears to Ingeborg that a sorter, placing the diamonds in a collection box, "längst stumpf geworden sei gegen die Schönheit der kostbaren Steine und gefühllos" and that he "mechanisch seine Arbeit tat" (24). This 'mechanical' work ethic is again paralleled by the sorter's previous action of removing the stones from the sand.

---

[82] After the war against the Nama in the south, thousands of the Nama POWs were relocated to the notorious Shark Island concentration camp where large numbers died from malnutrition, violence, and the climactic conditions, amongst other reasons. The graves, as well as those who died in the south of Namibia during the war, therefore offer a counter-claim to Ingeborg's argument.

Here, the process is also "mechanisch, fast rhythmisch...in steter Wiederholung" (23). It becomes evident that the workers involved in the wealth-creating industry have become akin to machines, overlooking the beauty and value of the product they are working with. The fact that the stones are removed from the soil and sent to Germany, thereby dislocating them from their original place and context, means that the people working with the stones can only create a fleeting, fragile relationship to them. Here the enclosed space "commands bodies, prescribing or proscribing gestures, routes, and distances to be covered. It is produced with this in mind; this is the raison d'être" (1974/1991:143). The gestures are mechanical, perpetually reproducing themselves and therefore the space in which they appear.

The 'mechanical' workers become machines maintaining and preserving these spaces. This finds its epitome when there is talk of replacing the workers with on-site machines. Emptiness is countered by this reproduced space as the activity of removing stones from the sand, the mechanical work to follow, and the export to the metropole all inscribe value into the soil, while giving some form of compensation to those working this soil. The enclosure is accurately described when Gothland ends his thoughts of distrust concerning the sorter with "[e]r wußte nichts davon, daß er in den weiten, unermeßlichen Sandfeldern ein Gefangener war..." (24). 'Empty space' in this sense – the sand fields and the voyage the diamonds undertake – is run through with the idea of being in a prison without knowing it while continuously generating material wealth for the state.

The dunes of snow and the desert of forests are initial methods in which the characters can gain access to the relationship between imperial Germany and its barren colony. This relationship becomes stabilised through the influx of German money and goods. The metropole exports its most powerful signs, namely capital and the suddenly realisable dream of excessive wealth. It is the diamonds and their promise of wealth which both fascinate the characters (Ingeborg, Gothland), while they are also rejected (most vocally and paradoxically by Ingeborg), the reason being that the new-found wealth is corrupting those who desire it (167–168). This is analogous to the assertion that the corruption of the *Kulturträger* will spell the demise of the colony (usually women). Ingeborg becomes weary of the allure of the diamonds, especially as she is able to follow the fate of Hans Gothland, Oskar Vollmüller, and Adolf Oberländer. What is most striking about this is Ingeborg's initial joy in finding her own stone in the sand and her progressive distancing from the sites of wealth, the diamond fields. The only problem with this tactic is exactly that which she celebrates most about the desert: its endlessness. The endlessness of the desert also signifies, ironically, the potential for endless diamond supplies. Ingeborg, unmotivated by money[83], finds other uses for the supposed 'empty space'. Not only does she give it a higher placing than the bustling urban centres of Germany[84], she may insert her fantasies and wishes into it.

The Garden

The garden is a site of careful labour. Not only that, but gardens tend to exhibit a high level of order. This is mostly due to the fragility of the plants and to maximize aesthetic effect. Although there are numerous external factors, the garden is at its core inextricably linked to the soil. And as I have previously argued, the soil is always linked to the (modern) state. Whether it be linguistically, productively, or culturally, the labour undertaken by the individual in the garden always reproduces the state[85]. However, before gardening can take place, the ideal garden needs to be designed, to be imagined. More often than not, a recurring image enters once these preparations are considered: that of the Garden of Eden. This urgarden, equally functional *and* aesthetic, tends to be the model for most garden fantasies – it is the promise of abundance and safety. With the spread of European peoples into other territories, the potential to exceed these gardens increased. There was more space, more labourers, more abundance. Why then did Africa not fulfil these expectations? Coetzee (1988), referring to warnings made by visitors to the colony, explains why Africa could not become an Eden:

> [T]hey [the visitors] were apprehensive that Africa might turn out to be not a Garden but an anti-Garden, a garden ruled over by the serpent, where the wilderness takes root once again in men's hearts. The remedy they prescribed against Africa's insidious corruptions was *cheerful toil*. (my emphasis, 3)

What is striking here is the insistence on labour as a way to counter the regressive forces of the garden. In this case, one does not 'work' *in* the garden, but one works *against* it. This is the Garden of Eden of banishment, not Paradise with its salvation. In other words, Africa is the Eden in which forced exile – i.e. its loss – is a constant possibility and the only way to prevent this is through work. This work (both physical labour and a continuous belief in Paradise) involves constant work against the negative forces of vice and sin. These were

---

[83] This is one of the many inconsistencies of the novel as well as its main protagonist, Ingeborg: although she has no desire to attain wealth, she wants 80 diamonds for her dream necklace. It is this wish, which she intimates to Hans Gothland, that is ultimately the reason for his demise.

[84] "'Es ist kein Kunststück auf fettem Boden zu gedeihen', dachte sie [Ingeborg], 'wohl aber auf steinigem Pfad emporzublühen'" (32).

[85] These can range from geography, to the tools in use, language spoken, method of gardening. A brief look at American and German gardens, littered with national flags, is a powerful example of linking the garden to the state/nation.

located within the Black body; a body that was constructed around these ideas of vice and sin. This construction included laziness, sexual potency, violence, and excess. Biblical colour codes (light versus dark; white versus black) provided the basis for this form of thinking, while the production of cultural difference (through the gaze, language, customs, and rituals) maintained these binaries. One answer to the danger of the Black body was discipline – of oneself (through self-control and self-regulation) and of the 'Other' (through disavowal of land ownership and humanity). Work and discipline thus formed the backbone of (potentially) producing a Paradise outside of mainland Europe.

Louis XIV of France, also known as the Sun King, had a garden akin to the idea of Paradise. His garden, a playground based on consumption, excess and amusement, is contrasted by the garden of labour[86]. This marked difference becomes important when we add another dimension – that of time. The "African Eden" is imagined as being temporally behind that of the paradise garden of Louis XIV. In other words, Africa is the Garden of the original hu/man, one who has yet to experience the comforts of Paradise. In the Judeo-Christian time line, Africa is at the beginning of the great book, while Europe – to a certain extent – has already actualized some elements of the unreachable fantasy. This comparison, in my opinion, shows heterotopic potential. The initial idea of the ideal garden becomes the goal the colonists still need to achieve while avoiding the serpent and its seductions and temptations[87]. The colonial garden receives a different temporality to the European garden, while maintaining similar functions and elements.

a) *Peter Moor*

Peter Moor and company pass by an old outpost that has been destroyed. The reader is told that there is "a meagre little garden, where one could see traces of the care with which German hands had tended it" (47). Although the work the hands had done is visible, the labour is not. Peter Moor merely infers that the settlers there must have tended to the garden, rejecting black labour from the offset. This garden scene is somewhat reflected at a later stage when the company reach a small house with a woman on the veranda.

> As we rode by the first house that wasn't roofless or had burnt-out window-holes, we admired it very much, and when we noticed that proper furniture, a table and chairs, were standing on the open veranda, we stared in astonishment, and turned in our saddles to look

---

[86] Without a doubt, the garden owned by Louis XIV was indeed labour intensive. However, neither he nor his guests were involved in any stage of the manual labour needed. This labour was – as was Black labour in the colony – invisible.
[87] The colonists Coetzee refers to are those who have settled in the Cape Colony, whose function was to be a garden supplying fresh produce to travelling trade ships. However, this comparison works for most previous African colonies.

till we had passed. With wide-open eyes we gazed into the garden, which in former years the colonists[88] had laid out with great care. (128)

What becomes clear from these two examples is the visibility of *masculine* labour. The gardens in *Heim Neuland* are strongly connected to the female characters – and linked even more strongly to their fates. In these instances, the female is completely dislocated from this space. The second example is even more powerful, as the *white* woman only *is* in the space; she is not connected to it. Furthermore, the garden becomes a sight, the garden is reduced to a visual experience. What the *Schutztruppler* have achieved in the second scene, though, is to connect the soil to the timeless virtues of the garden, namely "simplicity, peace, immemorial usage" (Coetzee, 1988:4). Anonymous male labourers subsume the sphere of the domestic, symbolised by the *white* female and her investment in the home. The gardens in this instance become the site of male labour which is connected to productive labour. The first garden becomes an artefact of settledness and control over nature. It is infused with German-ness through the work done on the soil. This German-ness is then reproduced through the rhetoric of its destruction. This begins with the heap of "white stones" and takes material form through the graves of the settler and his wife on the property. The epitaph on the makeshift crosses on the graves reads "Fallen by the hand of the murderer" (1908:48), linking the death of the two victims to the loss of the garden. However, because the members of the *Schutztruppe* were responsible for the maintenance and harvest of the garden, the working of the soil takes on a military dimension. The fact is that when the soldiers also 'work' the soil it is always in reference to military exercises. They dig trenches, holes for fires in order to cook, holes for wells, or they dig graves. The garden allows for the only non-military connection to the soil – referencing its 'peace' function. The presence of the woman inhabiting a clean, intact house with a flourishing garden epitomises this ideal.

It is interesting to assess the spaces in which these gardens are laid out and tended to. In the first example, the garden is located next to a house that was completely destroyed. A group of sailors, who were stationed there, attempted to protect it but had to give it up. This house, occupied by the now dead colonial settler and his wife, was supposed to be a "stopping-place" for Peter Moor and his company. He mentions that they are "cheerful, despite our thirst" (47). One can infer that this stopping-place was chosen because it offered the chance to stock up on food as well as filling up on water. This garden becomes a strategically important place in the topography of war, as vital provisions can be replenished, while offering (potential) safety from both "bush" and "enemy". Just like the German woman with her child, this place becomes

---

[88] In the German version (1907) it is the *Schutztruppe* that had laid out the garden.

an "Oase des Deutschtums" (to quote Brehl, 2004), offering the contact with other Germans while enjoying the fruits of German labour. The second example of a garden in *Peter Moor* is again connected to a house. However, in this case, the house is not a stopping-place, neither is it destroyed. To the surprise of Peter Moor and his company it is in an impeccable condition. Placing a German woman with her baby on the veranda completes the picture of a sphere of safety.

The woman is linked to the garden spatially through her proximity, but she is also separate from it through the visible lack of labour. And just like the German oak tree and the initial stopping-place, this site/sight rewards Peter Moor and his company with new energies. What these gardens have in common (as space for provision, as space for respite, as beacons of orientation) can be seen as references to the initial African (literary) garden: the Cape colony. This garden, as political as it was aesthetic, had at its core the production of foodstuffs for the *Fahrt* from Europe via the Cape peninsular to the Middle East. Just like the soldiers who wander through the barren and waterless landscape of GSWA, sailors from Europe, especially the Dutch, arrived at a place that provided them with everything necessary. This included signs and symbols of the metropole such as European structures (van Riebeeck's fort, settlements) and European technologies of conquest (guns and ammunition, maps), so lacking during the long expeditions by ship. These were also complemented by the beauty and fertility of the Cape colonial garden. The garden becomes the site of three important, militarily significant functions.

First, it becomes an orientating beacon. It is a goal, a space linked to other spaces. The visitor is able to refer to the garden as a coordinate. Its difference to its surroundings via the enclosure as well as the vegetation separates it from other coordinates and makes it recognisable. Furthermore, it acts as evidence of human settlement, increasing its meaning and signifying power. The second military significance is the prospect of sustenance. This becomes important in an environment in which time or the surroundings do not allow for the procurement of food. This reflects the lack of access to nourishment afforded to the sailors from Europe (again reflected by the sailors at the first stopping-point). Control over space in the battlefield is supplemented by the organisation of space outside the battlefield. The final significance the garden has for a military endeavour is its regenerative quality. Not only are the products of the garden consumed, but also its aesthetic qualities. The garden's peaceful ambience and its safe-space qualities are the direct opposite of the thorns and dangers of the "bush". The "bush" is temporarily displaced/replaced, giving the soldiers the chance of a fleeting peaceful outlook. Even in its destroyed and ravaged state, the garden is still able to inspire, rejuvenate and orientate. This orientation becomes doubly linked in the garden scene with the German woman.

The scene gives them a short entry into a space that is not part of the war landscape due to its lack of war signifiers. It reproduces none of the war markers the characters have as yet encountered: there is no "bush", no sign of the "enemy", no evidence of violence or conflict. The clean woman and her baby symbolise a space dislocated from the general landscape shaped by war. The innocence and peacefulness of the scene is mirrored by its biblical vocabulary. Infant and mother are relocated into the narrative of Christ's birth, which is a space of promise but also serenity. The company is able to simultaneously locate themselves in the landscape (close to the fort), and within their culture (in the symbolic spaces of the Bible). The garden now offers the characters and the reader the possibility to locate cultural markers in a war-torn and barren territory through the introduction of the garden – the space of civilisation as well as the origins of Man.

b) *Heim Neuland*

What is special about the colonial garden, at least in *Heim Neuland*, is its position on/in the sheltering farm. Here, we have a space within a larger, organised space. The most important aspect of any garden is its soil. To be connected to the soil means being connected to the garden. This connection is based on a number of symbolic as well as physical relations, beginning with the labour invested. Turning the soil (unleashing its potential), planting flowers and shrubs (organising life), demarcating various beds (controlling space), and linking it to the house (creating a family-based genealogy) all form and in-form the garden space. These activities further link the activities in the garden to other (symbolic) metaspaces, such as the markets, the nation, and the family. Of these links, the symbolic focus on blood seems to be the most powerful claim to specific place. This link between blood and the soil can still be traced further back than merely its combination. Coetzee, in his analysis of Sarah Gertrude Miller's fiction, points out that the blood flowing in the veins is older than the body itself:

> [U]nlike the limbs and organs, the individual's blood is not property alone. Blood defines the inherited social status of the individual by flowing supratemporally through him and all his blood-ascendant and descendants: the blood of kings or slaves long dead can run in his veins. (1988:146)

The first instance of this philosophic-biological understanding of blood is Etta and Dirich's family history of working the land. From the start[89] this is introduced as being central to the characters, especially through their family property and as the descendants of people connected to the soil. Initially this takes the form of Hans (the wind), "ihr Schöpfer" (648), indicating that they are first and foremost descendants of their environ-

---

[89] The relations are established within the first five pages of the novel (359–363).

ment. Their origin, their place of belonging, is then specified by focussing on their lineage. Dirich's family has owned Annenhof[90] since 1780 (making the ownership roughly 120 years), thus fixing the family name to a specific space and linking the lineage to the soil. The families' connection to the soil is not as old as the house which was built upon it, dating back a further three hundred years (making its establishment to around 1600). One can assume that family Dierksen had bought the house and land after its conception and only later introduced agricultural activity. This process is repeated in Etta's case, who is the daughter of the local dyke official[91] (*Deichgraf*). Her connection to the space is one not just of protection, but of blood as well. And although Dirich loses his fortune, Etta maintains her link to her home through her mother, first, and through the birth of their (male) child on that property.

At the end of the novel, Etta, holding their son Hans=Heim, dreams of taking him with her and Dirich when they return to GSWA:

> "Und nachher, wenn der Schloßgarten sich mit dem zartlila Krokustuch deckte und die Bienen im Mittagsschein darüber standen und ihre Orgel spielten, dann wollte man Hans=Heim aus seiner grünverhängten Wiege heben und ihn bereit machen, die große Reise anzutreten nach der Heimat, die aufs neue gegründet werden sollte *mit Pflug und Schwert*, daß der Schwarze, vielleicht nach Jahrhunderten, den weißen Mann noch einmal segne." (my emphasis, 647)

Here the narrator opens up the scene to two relevant themes making up the colonial garden. Firstly, Etta dreams of rebuilding their farm, and most likely their garden. She will continue the familial link to the soil through her son, who will in all likelihood inherit the farm. Secondly, she asserts that they will rebuild their *Heimat* "mit Pflug und Schwert". The implementation of the plough can only mean labour, productive labour in the service of the colony; and by extension the imperial nation. The accompanying application of the sword protects the space – evoking the image of blood being spilt. Through sacrifice (on a literal as well as metaphorical level) and conflict (vs. intruders as well as the environment), the territory becomes permeated with German blood. This links the *right* to ownership of the soil, and by extension the land, to those who have their blood mingled with the soil[92]. The response to Dirich's speech further demonstrates this logic:

> "Ein jubelndes Hoch brach aus, als Dirich geendet. Eine starke, flammende Begeisterung hatte sich aller bemächtigt. Zwar manche Träne rann und schuf, daß die Hoffnung noch wie durch einen Flor verhüllt erschien, aber dennoch hatte Dierksen recht: Was so durch Blut besiegelt wird, hat Riesenkraft. Der Kolonie Treue trotz allem — immer!" (620)

---

[90] This is a *Bauernhof*, or a small farm
[91] The maintenance of the dykes falls under his responsibility and jurisdiction.
[92] See Ingeborg's argument concerning graves in this chapter.

The war creates an arena in which the ideology that propagates the loss of German life equalling the right to land. Labour *and* sacrifice (in the biblical sense) become central to the rhetoric of occupation and the claim to land. The control of the *white* foreign settler over the soil, which now is infused with 'his' culture, and control over the workforce, supported by national laws, police, punishments, and regulations is a vivid example of this type of thinking.

The first time Etta Wibrandt meets the soldiers Detlef Welzin and Axel von Gussow is at Gerda's garden on Ehlersholm[93]. This is the farm owned by Gerda and her husband, Franz Ehlers. Gerda meets Etta in the garden, which is described as follows:

> Die Orangenbäume in Kübeln auf der Terrasse, die ersten blühten, waren mit unzaehligen runden gelben Papierlaternen behaengt. Girlanden von Lampions wanden sich an den Staemmen der Akazien herauf und schlangen sich dann von Baum zu Baum in schillernd phantastischen Bogen. Auf hohen Postamenten schwelten Fackeln, und die Diener in ihren grün und goldenen Livreen leuchteten unter dem wechselnden Licht wie riesenhafte Gluehwuermer. Eine Geduefte der blühenden Orangen, Rosen, Fraesien und Lilien war über dem Garten, und die Toiletten der Damen blühten aus dem dunklen Grün wie seltene Wunderblumen (466)

This precise description can be read as a reflection of Gerda's character. Its most striking features are its beauty, while it abounds with smells and colours. It is highly sanitized, evident from toilets that are aestheticized in the same breath as the flowers and trees. This beauty, however, is merely superficial. Nothing in the garden is a product of Gerda Ehler's labour. She has no connection to the soil or to the enclosure she inhabits and has therefore failed to inscribe German-ness into her space. She herself is aware of this failure, commenting that "ich komme mir immer wie mein eigener Gast vor. So, als ob ich gar nicht zu Hause wäre" (467). Gerda is still linked to the property through her daughter Susi. This allows her to insert her own German-ness into these spaces through the reproduction of German lineage. Later on in the novel, it is this that saves her after the attack on her home and her consequent kidnapping. This is due to her child minder Klemen/Clemen[94] saving the child (as well as Gerda) and maintaining Gerda's German bond to her home. The fact that the assailants enter the house through the garden of Ehlersholm indicates how fragile the garden is as a space of peace and tranquillity. It seems to mirror a number of ideals imported from the metropole, such as the accumulation of the exotic as well as the maintenance and exhibition of hygiene.

---

[93] This is another example of a name being linked directly to an occupied space with the surname of the married Ehlers couple reflected in the farm name.

[94] Both versions of the name appear in the novel, possibly pointing to the exchangeable roles Africanist characters take up in the narrative(s), even if they save main characters.

An even more extreme example of a garden reflecting her character – and her fate – is Zoë, Baroness von Gensdorff. Her brother, Baron von Gensdorff, has already acquired the farm on which he and his disabled daughter, Elli, live. Zoë has no connection to the garden, yet she and it are strongly linked in a number of ways. A first link is established when Zoë and Detlef Welzin, her admirer, share their first kiss there. It is here that a 'forbidden' love starts to flourish. The love is forbidden because of the difference in social standing between the two characters. She tends to wait for him under a *Blutahorn*, a tree with fiery red leaves. The colour links her blood-red lips and her blond-red hair (507) to the tree and fixes her character to the garden. It is this garden setting which creates a space for Detlef Welzin to fully realise his desires for Zoë[95]. A later description of the baroness gives numerous indicators that she is as far removed from any physical constraints as possible, while her *whiteness* and beauty are seen as her most prominent features. This explains why she is overly reliant on beauty products:

> Mitsamt ihrer französischen Jungfer hatte sie halb Gensdorff in Bewegung gesetzt. Und erst nachdem sie drei Tage Bettruhe gepflogen hatte und die verschiedensten Mixturen, Cremes, Warm=, Lau= und Kaltwaschungen, Haarbehandlungen durch Sekt und Goldstaub, Puder, Massage angewendet worden waren, erschien sie wieder als die Nixe mit dem rostroten Haar und der blauweißen Haut, die es als Lebensaufgabe betrachtete, Männer zu betören, daß sie wie Lämmer an der Schnur hinter ihr dreinliefen, bis sie ihrer überdrüssig wurden. (507)

It is important to notice to which lengths she goes so she can maintain her looks. The luxury products (champagne and gold dust) reveal that there is no need for her to perform any productive labour as she is of aristocratic lineage, living off the labour of others. Compared to Etta and Gerda, she is the female character who is the furthest away from the garden labour. The final linkage – and punishment for her labour free connection to the garden – is her death at the foot of the *Blutahorn*. Zoë, like Gerda, enter into gardens already there – they are not part of the garden's history. The Baroness dies in a space that allowed her forbidden encounter, but also the space that had already announced her downfall. Her ambiguous relationship to Elli, her disabled niece, seals her fate. Here the garden works as a space of analogy. It concentrates Zoë von Gensdorff's *whiteness* in a mythical and aesthetic space, but punishes her for her inactivity. Her metropolitan labour free lifestyle cannot be sustained in the colony.

Etta has the most fertile relationship to her garden. Firstly, she is highly active in its organization – the plants to be planted, the labourers' work schedule, the protection and nurturing of the plants. This presents her with a large challenge that she manages success-

---

[95] "Es riß ihn näher zu ihr hin. In den Bannkreis dieser weißen Arme" (545).

fully, which is fixing the destitute state the garden is in initially. While Dirich works on their *Schloß*[96], her job is to take care of the garden. The labour investment appears to have been quite comprehensive, as everything needed to be covered and protected while the soil needed to be dug over (487). Furthermore, the vegetables and fruits have started to grow already – faster than they would have had grown *daheim*[97]. Her efforts on the colonised land are rewarded through the accelerated growth of her produce. Etta thus creates a strong relationship to the garden through the synthesis of labour and the soil.

Compared to her female counterparts, Etta has created her own site of work and productivity while creating a space for profit and sustenance[98]. Although there is the mention of Black labour, it is never witnessed. For example, it is through the Black labourers that her garden and her crops are saved. This is another example of a colonial garden reflecting the initial African garden of the Cape colony. It, however, echoes Coetzee's assertion that the "silence about the place of black labour…is common by and large…to the Afrikaans *plaasroman*, and represents a failure of imagination before the problem of how to integrate the dispossessed black man into the idyll…of African pastoralism" (1988:71–72). Dismissing the saving Black labour and locating the saving of the farm in Etta's contribution solve this paradox. It is revealed that she, not the labourers, chased away the locusts by speaking *Plattdeutsch* to them. Her cultural difference (in a linguistic level) augments her already-established difference (her industry) to the Black characters. The only evidence of Africanist involvement is Nikodemus, a farm worker, eating the intruders the next day. Etta's achievement in saving her land is complemented by Nikodemus benefiting from her heroics. Etta of course still profits from this labour by selling the grown and harvested vegetables and fruits to traders thereby generating an income.

It is her involvement that saves the crops *and* provides for the farm labourers. This is an opportunity to put distance between the *white* settlers and the Black population through their relationship to the locusts. For the *white* settler, they represent a nuisance, replete with strong biblical connotations. Here, one of the biblical plagues is staved off through the employment of German culture, in a sense confirming what Coetzee previ-

---

[96] The 'first' house Dirich has built is only a temporary abode. The two protagonists live there while construction of the *Heim* is finalised.
[97] "[A]uf einigen Beeten gediehen bereits Gurken, Melonen, Erbsen und Bohnen. Auch die Weinschößlinge, die Dirich aus Ehlersholm miterausgebracht hatte, hatten gut Wurzel geschlagen und taten ihre ersten Schüsse. Zwergobstkerne waren gelegt worden. Es würde langsam gehen, aber doch immer noch so viel schneller als daheim" (487).
[98] "Wenn auch die Gemüsepreise in den letzten Jahren heruntergegangen waren, so meinten Dierksens, in einem Lande, wo das Pfund Kartoffeln immerhin noch dreißig Pfennige kostete, müßten sich durch Gartenkultur doch nennenswerte Ueberschüsse ergeben" (563).

ously posited when dealing with the African Eden. For the original inhabitants, however, they are a frequent occurrence, apparently providing a form of sustenance and having no symbolic value or financial consequence. This is not as innocent or comical as it appears in this passage, seeing as food and eating habits were used as a means to distance Europeans from Africans (Haarhoff, 1991:38). The garden in this case creates an environment in which the desired partition between German, *white* culture and indigenous Black subjects is erected and maintained on a number of levels.

c) *Du heiliges Land!*

One reason for the absence of an actual garden in *Du heiliges Land!* might be due to the unsuitable, garden-hostile climate in the South of Namibia. Lack of water and fertile soil are large obstacles in creating favourable conditions for larger cultivation of plants in and around Lüderitzbucht, with the Namib desert surrounding this coastal town. The garden in this environment is therefore transformed into an object of luxury. The luxury of maintaining a garden in the desert is epitomised by Carola Oberländer, who requests a winter garden first from her husband (217) and later on from Oscar Vollmüller (283). As her husband lacks the means to afford her this luxury and seeing that Vollmüller is later unable to fulfil her wish, the *Wintergarten*[99] will remain an empty wish. This does not mean that the idea/ideal of the garden is therefore absent. The longing for a garden felt by Carola is echoed by another character, namely Ingeborg. This is visible in two scenes. The first is when she smells the final odour of the withered violets in her room on Schakalswater. This leads her to dream of a fairy tale castle during spring in Germany:

> Vor ihrem Blick tat sich ein weites grünes Land auf, erfüllt vom allewigen Triumph der Auferstehung. Sie stand vor einem weißen Märchenschloß hoch oben auf der Terrasse und sah trunkenen Auges hinab in einen blühenden Garten, goldener Sonnenglanz lag auf den Rosen und Narzissen und tropfte durch das Blätterdach breiter schirmender Eichen hinab auf grünen Rasen und Myrtenhecken, blühende Gummibäume und Agaven standen still und ernst neben der aufragenden Pinie und dem hungrigen Oelbaum, die Mandelsträucher waren übersät von rosigem Blütenschnee und ganz leise schwankten die Zweige im Sonnenwinde... War das das Paradies? Das heilige Land, der Unschuldsgarten ohne Irrtum und Schuld? (95)

The abundance and excess of the plant life on display is in stark contrast to the scenery that Ingeborg encounters on a daily basis. Having already been described in European equivalents, the landscape is now filled with European plants. The lack – or even absence – in

---

[99] In the novel, the *Wintergarten* is probably *the* German attempt to somehow bring the metropole and its superfluous signs into the colony. This climate and plant specific product appears extremely alien within the desert context, especially since it would also be a drain on the already scarce water resources.

the periphery is opposed by the surplus and wealth of the metropole[100]. Ingeborg has a similar vision once more when she walks through the desert to Lüderitzbucht in order to find Klinger. She is reminded of a scene she shared with him:

> Sie entsann sich, dass sie Klinger einmal entzückt eine Schlucht abseits der Pad gewiesen hatte: 'Sieh doch einmal her, hier ist es ganz grün…' Lächelnd hatte er dann auf ein paar armselige Moosgeflechte niedergesehen, die sich vereinzelt aus dem weißen Sand erhoben und leise Ingeborgs Stirn geküsst.…Und so wie damals erschien heute dieses öde Wüstenland ihrer kritiklosen Glücksstimmung wie ein blühender Garten. (362)

The empty landscape of the desert is again transformed into a space sprawling with plant life. This time the reason for this transformation is not nostalgia, but love. This aesthetic explosion is Ingeborg's desire to be with Klinger. Because of the unsuitability of a garden in the desert landscape, the only way to create it is through imagination and fantasy. It becomes clear that the garden as a spatial construction only appears as an object of desire, a desire which is always deferred. It is this deferred ideal – from the real *Wintergarten* to the garden landscapes that Ingeborg dreams up – which is the most prominent occurrence. Let me explain this through the application of an example.

The first mention of a garden in Ingeborg's surroundings is when Hans Gothland discloses to her his original dream (and failed attempt) of coming to GSWA to become a farmer. Through various bureaucratic struggles and a lack of funds, Gothland is forced ultimately to bury this dream. He had already imagined digging wells, keeping livestock, making clay bricks, building a home and *kraal*, as well as turning the soil (138)[101]. He is only able to work a small piece of land, barely surviving. His only occupation is the watering of cucumbers and tomatoes. The garden, with its limited array of plants, represents Gothland's failed dream (as opposed to Etta and Dirich's realised dream). Even his belief in his own strong work ethic ("und ich Tor hatte an den Erfolg ehrlicher Arbeit geglaubt!" (138)), is not enough to achieve the dream of owning a farm.

The garden here becomes the site of failed and futile labour. This can be read as a rejection of the naïve fantasies upon which colonial settler life, like the one romanticised by Etta and Dirich, is based. It can also be interpreted as a rejection of old values (i.e. honest labour) and the need to come up with a new strategy to insert German-ness into the colony. It may not necessarily mean a complete rejection of the farm lifestyle, just a rejection of that lifestyle as the only true one. It is this passage which identifies the garden of GSWA as a non-garden, possibly even as an anti-garden. A fantastical garden is imag-

---

[100] This projection of a European landscape onto an African landscape can also be interpreted as a form of fictioning.

[101] All these actions and activities reflect the work Dirich Dierksen undertook in order to get Ettenhof going.

ined onto the dune and desert landscape, as Ingeborg's example shows, while the physical garden is never achieved. It serves as a substitute for a desire that is untenable. A further example is the destroyed missionary garden that Klinger comes across during his travel through GSWA. It is only recognisable as such due to the residue of the cultivated plants (320). The dream of the garden was once realised but then becomes a relict, symbolising the failure of setting up a garden in the anti-garden of GSWA. The environment is a constant threat to this delicate biotope – whether due to the climate or intruders.

However, the garden still forms the basis of how Ingeborg is able to survive in a country that does not allow love, much to her own disappointment[102] as well as Klinger's[103]. This attitude is contrasted with the numerous occasions on which plant life (mostly domestic) is projected into and onto the barren landscape. This occurs, for example, when days of summer begin and "rotblühende Rosengärten" on the diamond fields "emporsprossen" (235). Rank soil becomes the fertile soil of Klinger's poetry, his "neue Gedichte" (ibid.). Furthermore, it is the combination of this imagined landscape plus his feelings for Ingeborg that transform this space that does not allow love into an idyll, a *Paradiesgarten* (238). However, this paradise garden can only be realised through Klinger's desire for Ingeborg. Klinger questions the idyll of GSWA as an illusion *because* it is founded on him being able to kiss Ingeborg. Again, the garden of GSWA is only possible through either a sexualised understanding of the landscape (i.e. by linking it to the *white* female body), or by inverting the encountered lack by imagining abundance in its place. The last strategy is most evident when Klinger reduces the lack of plant life and garden aesthetics with an abundance of incitement. When he and Ingeborg discuss GSWA at the end of the novel (after they have decided to get married in Germany), Klinger explains his relationship to the territory as follows:

> Die schweigende, urweltliche Größe der Namib, ihre stolze Herbheit — war sie nicht auch schön? Und war sie nicht von überwältigender Schönheit, wenn die silberweiße Mondnacht sie küßte? Blühte sie dann nicht auch ohne Blumen? ...Deshalb darf man die andersartige Schönheit unseres Südwest nicht schmähen — (464).

Again, it is a clichéd, heteronormative love declaration that transforms the impoverished landscape into a space of beauty and fertility. And again it is the fantasy of flowers projected onto the landscape that gives it its beauty – the sand dunes of the Namib are only able to offer the background of an imagined garden. The Garden of Eden and Paradise remain fantasies and desires that cannot be achieved. Therefore, the landscape needs to

---

[102] "Auch hier im Wüstensand um Lüderitzbucht fand die holde Wunderblume keinen Boden. Hier lagen zu viele Steine und Diamanten" (93).
[103] "Hier gibt's keine Liebe" (134).

be substituted with that of the imagination. GSWA is constructed as an anti-garden, as a space that cannot produce or maintain its own garden. The compromise becomes a fusion between endless emptiness and fantasy, which is finally resolved when the two protagonists return to the place where their fantasy gardens spring from – the metropole.

The unattainability of the garden and the focus of somehow realising it has other manifestations as well. Gothland exemplifies a first reference to the potential of the garden and its continual deference in a highly detonative and ephemeral scene. After Ingeborg finds a diamond, he praises her find and notices a certain enchantment in her eyes. He comments this – inaudible to her – with the words "'Eva, Eva'" (26). In this scene her innocent wonder in finding the stone transforms her into the cardinal female, threatening him at the same time. This is because the biblical Eve is the root of temptation while also being the reason for man's exile from the Garden of Eden. Ingeborg, in an initial act by Gothland, converts the sand fields into a type of garden, namely the *ur*garden of Eden. She then becomes a threat as her figurative Eve dimension has the potential to expel Gothland from their perceived Paradise. This threat is mentioned at a later stage when the figure of Pandora – responsible for the ills in the world – is invoked[104].

The newly-arrived woman, representing purity *and* temptation, disrupts the space previously rationalised. Her link to Eden, and the loss thereof, makes Ingeborg's character extremely ambiguous, especially as she is the most prominent personality connected to the gardens in GSWA, real and imaginary. This is in essence what Low has argued in connection to the *white* male colonial settler, who "domesticates the wild country into a safe pastoral one; here a man may live and work like an original Adam, creating and refashioning an Eden – trapped in a time warp – to his own image'" (in Stiebel 2001:69). A sort of Eden, an economic and laborious Eden, created by and for the *white* male colonial settler may be brought into disorder through the introduction of the Eve-Pandora female. The anti-garden of GSWA is thus conceptualised by introducing the female as intrinsically connected to the original garden, but also as a threat to the garden of the male settler. Gothland, Oberländer and Vollmüller's demises are linked to a female character in some way, exposing their innate weakness while underlining negative female involvement. The binary of organising male and disorganising female is touched upon by Yekani when she argues that "Victorian masculinity not only faced the growing demands for women's rights but also, more generally, the debate on a dangerous 'feminisation of culture' loomed large and male privilege as well as a 'healthy' masculinity were perceived and dangerous" (2011:19), while adding that "[t]he way masculinity is and can be imag-

---

[104] "[E]s ist eine alte Wahrheit dieses Lebens, durch ein Weib ist alles Unheil in die Welt gekommen. Nicht Ihre Persönlichkeit [Ingeborgs] klage ich an. Ihre holde Stammesmutter war schuldig..." (193).

ined is in close connection to the perception of women and femininity. Adventure heroes in their homosocial environment cherish only the company of other men" (59). Other men (vs 'Other' people) maintains some form of order and control, guaranteeing power is kept within the same social group. The introduction of femininity (also in the form of a perceived difference to Black masculinity or homosexual desire) may create an imbalance. Therefore, the ideal garden cannot be achieved in GSWA, but there are other spaces that allow for this.

It is this ideal that contrasts the Paradise garden of Cape Town with the non-garden/anti-garden of Lüderitzbucht. Cape Town is portrayed as *the* ultimate garden in the novel. Not only was it called *Paradies* (461) by Ingeborg, but her friends, Captain and Lene Schwarzkoppen, reiterate this. The Schwarzkoppen are visiting Lüderitzbucht and are having dinner with Ingeborg, at which point GSWA is introduced as Cape Town's foil. This is repeated at one point, when Lene compares Cape Town's beauty to the sand landscapes of GSWA (427). Ingeborg's only response is to reply that the sand dunes have their own beauty, remembering the moment she was kissed by Klinger (428). This opens up the chance to compare the two garden spaces – especially since GSWA remains a metaphorical/imagined garden, while Cape Town is described in real-world terms. One can evoke Stiebel's (2001) concepts of 'Africa-paradise' (58), Adam/Eve in Paradise (59), as well as the 'myth of Africa as a corrupt Eden' (a concept originating from Rice, quoted in Stiebel, 60). As should be evident, the gardens are either Paradise or Eden. Also, the gardens are not exclusive to one space or place, but run through the whole continent. In that respect, the trope of the garden extends across borders but is always linked to the main character(s). Ingeborg's first contact with Cape Town is described as follows:

> Je mehr sie sich der eigentlichen Stadt näherten, desto größer wurden Ingeborgs Augen. Durch *Gartenstraßen* und an weiten Anlagen fuhren sie vorüber, wo auf smaragdenem Rasenteppich die Veilchen blauten. Neben aufragenden Agaven und Gummibäumen breitete der Kirschlorbeer seine lederblanken Blätter aus. Noch mehr Grün nahm das Auge in sich auf, Oelbäume, Pinien, Zypressen.
>
> Ingeborg wurde ganz stumm vor lauter Bewunderung. Ihr war, als habe sie lange Jahre nur Sanddünen und Wüstenstürme gekannt. (426).

What then connects this image of Paradise to Peter Moor's orientation in the "bush"-landscape is the German oak tree. Ingeborg identifies the trees and is transported into a space and time of absolute purity and innocence: her German childhood. She proceeds to tear off a leaf and kiss it, remembering her "deutsches Vaterland, das Land, in dem ihre Mutter sie in den Schlummer gesungen hatte" (426). Cape Town receives similar qualities to GSWA by referencing the *Vaterland* through an abundance of green and fertility, but it is Cape Town that is able to facilitate this reference through a specific example.

Although Coetzee focussed on the idea of labour in order to counter the loss of Paradise, this is not a factor in Ingeborg's experience of Cape Town as such. She is forced to do domestic work and to her surprise, this entails physical labour[105]. After being fired from her job, she takes up singing under the name Renate von Hochheim in a cinema. Because she has lost the support of all male characters (Gothland and her brother have both died, while Vollmüller and Klinger are unavailable as patrons), she is forced to find a job for herself. This development is part of Brockmann's arguments concerning the female settler in the colony: that sexual purity is linked to economic independence[106]. The example of the promiscuous Monika[107], a prostitute in the *Kaiserhof* (as well as the other ladies in the establishment) is the clearest case for this argument. The added necessity for Klinger to symbolically buy Ingeborg's freedom from the cinema also substantiates this claim.

However, in spite of all of Ingeborg's misadventures and social sins, Cape Town remains a paradise. After working at the cinema and being saved by Klinger, she repeats the praise of Cape Town-as-a-Paradise. This may be due to Stiebel's argument that "the garden, bearing powerful connotations of paradise and order, is shown in sharp contrast to the turbulent beyond." (2001:68). The "turbulent beyond" is on one level the physical space of GSWA, the barren, dead, and inhospitable territory which allows very little growth and limited access to love. The second level is that of the disorganised spatiality of GSWA, where emptiness and endlessness are the main qualities of the landscape. Cape Town becomes the antithesis of GSWA through its organised appearance but also through its urban and metropolitan aspects. The only unifying trait both these garden spaces share is their ephemeral nature, their role as a character-forming, but short-lived, place. The garden which is Germany – signified through the yearning for a return – is designed as the ultimate garden, whether through projection (in GSWA) or as a copy (Cape Town).

The *White* Female Colonialist

So far, I have plotted the trajectory of how the colonists try to orientate themselves in their 'empty' surroundings while employing the abundance of signs and symbols of the metropole in order to replicate it in the colony. Labour and the enclosure play highly vis-

---

[105] "So wußte Ingeborg, daß man nicht ihre Persönlichkeit, sondern nur ihrer Hände Arbeit verlangte in diesem Hause" (436).
[106] "If a woman was not financially secure, she was sexually vulnerable" (in Wildenthal 1993:76).
[107] This is the woman Ingeborg accused Klinger of having an affair with.

ible and important roles. And so far, I have identified the places in which both of these processes can take place (the landscape, the garden). What I want to point towards now is how these places are affected by ideas of the self. By this I mean the qualities of the self that are marked as 'necessarily German'. My focus will be on *white* European women because they played a vital role within the mechanics and discourses of colonialism, whether as actors or as auxiliaries. I have already pointed to the rhetoric of the commodity market as linked to the *white* woman and her desirability within the colonial project. Back in Germany, the apparent lack of *white* women in the colony/colonies produced intense debates concerning their role in the home nation and the colony. *White* female contributions to the processes of colonisation, in the form of literature, discourses on 'purity' and reproduction, or as colonial settlers therefore should receive special attention. Of course, I am not proposing a break or separation between male and female colonialist involvement. What I am proposing is a look at how female perspectives reveal further colonial desires and fears, as well as generating further imaginations and fantasies. This is evident when one looks at the formation of women's organisations, such as the *Frauenbund* in Germany which used the colony as a springboard in order to discuss problems at home. Although the role of the colonist woman is rather ambiguous, it is revealing of a number of ideas concerning the control over other/'Other' bodies and is strongly linked to Enlightenment ideologies of (linear) progress, civilisation and the expansion/continuation of European values[108]. This took the form of two important forms of reproduction. The initial form of reproduction is on the biological level. Legally, biological reproduction was awarded according to patrimonial lineage as the child born to a German father received German citizenship. It was therefore the function of the German mother to guarantee her child had a German father.

The baby scene in *Heim Neuland* is reflective of the patrimonial lineage, as Guni (a domestic worker on Ettenhof) gives birth to a child, which, although deemed ugly, is marked as *white*. In this case, the baby is removed from the larger *white* community (due its lack of beauty), but is considered a *white* 'product' due to its German father and its *white* skin. Identifying it as ugly (the narrator gives no evidence to support this assertion) also comments on the undesirability of sexual relations between Black women and *white* men[109]. The colonialist woman's primary function here translates into producing German

---

[108] This started to take concrete form with McClintock's *Imperial Leather* (1995), in which colonialism was viewed from the perspective of women's roles in the British colonial project. *Wir hatten eine Dora in Südwest* (1991) by Tink Diaz is a documentary looking at the influence of the *Frauenbund* during Germany's colonial era. Hashemi (2016), leaning on Gikandi, discusses the ambiguous role colonial women inhabited, usually situated between the colonising male and the colonised societies.

[109] The basis for inter-'racial' sexual relationships was concentrated mostly within this framework, while sexual relations between *white* women and Black men were considered taboo on every level. The in-

offspring. Producing German children is deeply connected to the idea of maintaining the purity of German blood – and thus the German 'race', a concept rooted in bio-racist discourses and responsible for the genocide of a number of European societies in the 20th century.

The second form of reproduction is on the cultural level. As Brockmann has argued, it became the colonialist woman's duty to preserve imperial culture. McClintock identifies domesticity as a central mechanism of controlling undesired groups/people, while trying to fix male and female identities both at home and abroad. Again this is based on economic terms:

> Imperialism and the invention of race were fundamental aspects of Western, industrial modernity. The invention of race in the urban metropoles... became central not only to the self-definition of the middle class but also the policing of 'dangerous classes': the working class, the Irish, Jews, prostitutes, feminists, gays and lesbians, criminals, the militant crowd and so on. At the same time, the cult of domesticity was not simply a trivial and fleeting irrelevance, belonging properly in the private, 'natural' realm of the family. Rather...the cult of domesticity was a crucial, if concealed dimension of male as well as female identities – shifting and unstable as these were – and an indispensable element both of the industrial market and the imperial enterprise. (5)

This was achieved through dress and housework, but also through the export of domesticity. Domesticity includes the work done in/for the home, but can take other forms. Cleanliness (of oneself, one's family, the home, as well as one's morals) are further examples of domesticity. However, it also denotes the act of domesticating, i.e. to tame something. It is at this juncture that the garden comes in. The garden is a form of domestication as it makes that which is wild and untamed into something that is organised and controllable.

a) *Peter Moor*
When Peter Moor and his company finally reach that house "that wasn't roofless or had burnt-out window-holes", they do not merely encounter a safe space. It is also the place in which a *white*, German woman is sitting on the veranda and holding a German baby. This sight is described in biblical language:

> And there in the shade of the veranda stood a German woman, and she held a little child on her arm. How we looked! How we rejoiced over the light clean dress she wore, and her friendly face, and the little white child! We gazed as though at a miracle from heaven at a sight any one could see everyday in Germany— just like the holy three kings who came out of the desert and looked from their horses upon Mary and her child. She looked at us,

---

troduction of *white* women would apparently curb the sexual relation between *white* men and Black women.

> ragged, dirty, hungry fellows, and bowed in a friendly way, with big sympathetic eyes, when we all, as though at a command, raised our hands to our caps. (1908:128–129).

Brehl (2004) refers to this scene as an "Oase des Deutschtums" (87) in the desert, which allows the protagonist some semblance of revitalisation[110]. Brehl connects this recovery to the construction of the German identity, which he argues can only be attained once the subject moves from the individual to a group consciousness. The survival of the group is intrinsically linked to the survival of the individual (86). The *white*, clean German woman is placed in a familiar setting – that of the home. She becomes recognisable as Mary because she inhabits the space of domesticity, defining the desired concepts of settledness, cleanliness, hygiene, and homeliness. As McClintock (1995) and Haarhoff (1991:70) have both claimed, the *white* European woman is the site in which these concepts are most visible[111]. She is also a copy of the woman Peter Moor remembers during the Easter fire. He is able to create a feeling of 'we' and therefore identifies with the whole. The 'wild' and the 'uncivilised' become controllable through the labour of the woman in the home, reproducing home culture and home comforts. Not only was this argument central for the members of the *Frauenbund*, it reversed the dichotomy of woman = nature and man = culture (Walgenbach 2005:1713). According to Walgenbach, this is due to the cultivating effect women were expected/imagined to have in the colony. This took the form of the domestication of Black house servants (in some cases these were *white*, but had to be introduced to ideal homemaking). This involved 'teaching' the servant how to cook, how to clean, sow, and so forth. A further form of cultivation was that of the household. Reading, singing, and decorating, were activities that concentrated on recreating German homeliness in the 'wild' – of civilising the 'wild hut' of the male colonisers, so to speak. And lastly, the garden (and certain parts of the farm) were cultivated by the colonial woman. The male coloniser, who is linked to hunting and long periods in the bush, is now linked to nature[112]. These arguments placed the *white* colonising woman at the heart of the colonial project, with domestication and cultivation the main activities and technologies at the heart of the process.

Using Anne McClintock's (1995) interrogation of the intersections of race, gender and the economy, this passage is very revealing of these three dynamics. I will focus on the aspect of domesticity, which McClintock uses to expose the interplay between these three concepts. McClintock defines domesticity twofold: firstly, as "a *space* (a geographic and

---
[110] This was preceded by the revitalisation via the oak tree.
[111] Also in contrast to the dirty, ragged soldiers.
[112] "Die Virilität des Weißen Mannes wurde als nützlich angesehen, solange es um das Erobern und die Unterwerfung der Kolonien ging. Nun aber, so wird argumentiert, würde sich diese angebliche Nähe zur Natur zu einem Gefahrenpotenzial entwickeln" (Walgenbach, 2005:1713).

architectural alignment") and as "*a social relation to power*" (34, emphasis in original). The *white*, clean woman is the archetype for the idea of domesticity[113]: sitting on the veranda of the house and tending to her child. When analysing Peter Moor's encounter with the woman, certain features come to the fore. Firstly, the woman is connected to very little in the scene except for the child. There is no father or husband, for example. This means that the woman (who remains name- and voiceless) is designed as a subject who reproduces the German nation, yet is sexually unavailable to the coming soldiers. Although central to Peter Moor's comprehension of the significance of this site/sight, there will be no further mention of her as there is no need. Just like the oak tree, her role and function is fleeting – a brief symbol of the metropole serving a rejuvenating purpose.

Her role as ideal colonial woman is somewhat diminished when the narrator remarks that the adjacent garden has not been designed or tended by her but rather by previous *Schutztruppen*-soldiers. The woman is not included in the division of labour, referring back to what McClintock calls "the invention of the idea of the idle woman" (16). In essence, the encounter with the woman is primarily a visual experience that serves to replicate metropolitan domesticity where there is a lack of it. These two points underline McClintock's assertion that "[i]n the eyes of policymakers and administrators, the bounds of the empire could be secured and upheld only by proper domestic discipline and decorum, sexual probity and moral sanitation" (47). A further powerful argument McClintock is able to make concerning the connection between femininity and domesticity is the fact that it serves as a locating beacon for the male (24). It is no coincidence that there is a stronghold in the direct vicinity. Once the female and her home are located, masculine space is not far away. One must remember that the woman and the child Peter Moor comes across are both German and *white*. Furthermore, the woman is referred to as Mary, which desexualises her while giving her the ability to still reproduce. Not only does she reproduce, she holds in her arms The Saviour. Her body thus becomes a vessel in which German-ness is reproduced while imbuing the offspring with transcendental value.

It is at this point that I would like to return to the Easter fire Peter Moor and his fellow soldiers light in the bush of GSWA. This scene occurs just after Peter Moor and his company identify the oak tree in the bush, which gives the soldiers a much needed positive experience. They light the fire while it is still dark and reminisce about a possible moment back home. It is the Easter fire which lights the dark surroundings, mirroring the idea that Christianity and Enlightenment are able to bring illumination. The symbolic fire is employed as a way of separating the average, function-based fire (for cooking/warmth)

---

[113] As opposed to the laborious and industrious working class woman whose work does not allow entrance into this ideal because of the signs of their labour such as dirt, sweat and accompanying smells.

of the African subjects with the Christian, metaphorical fire. In this sense, the Easter fire enters the landscape not as a universal product, but as a European product immersed in cultural significance. And it is this significance that is substantiated through two equally relevant practices. The first practice is that of appropriation. The fire is started and maintained by burning "thorn-bush". This means that the fire becomes a make-shift Easter ritual because the original method of making it cannot be replicated. The "thorn-bush", the most constant tormentor of the soldiers and the container of the "enemy" figure, is given a similar potency to the 'authentic' Easter fire back home. The company is therefore able to exorcise the danger of the "thorn-bush" by including it its religious custom, pacifying and consuming it.

The second practice, which connects to the sighting of the German woman and her child, is the incantation of the mother-figure. Peter Moor does not identify *his* mother; he identifies *the* mother. The figure is placed on a representational level, especially as the whole company is able to imagine her via the fire. The mother figure, evoked through the communal Easter fire experience, connects all of the members of the company. This figure is responsible for a communal experience, in essence anticipating the appearance of a real female figure in the narrative. Another important point to consider is that the male figure, that of the father, is absent as well. The sole focus is the mother, the main character in the sphere of the domestic. She is connected to this domesticity through the "clean living-room", the "Sunday clothes", and "the festive coffee". This is contrasted by the "dirty", "friendless", and "painful" lives which the soldiers are experiencing in the war environment. Not only is the current situation juxtaposed with an ideal one (a cultural moment in the metropole), but this juxtaposition allows the characters to understand their current situation. Lack, absence, and scarcity are replaced by imagining a scene in the metropole. The sign of the metropole, in the case of the fire and the location of the German woman plus baby, is the (*white*) domestic female who is responsible for a bearable life in the colony. As Haarhoff put it, "[t]he frontier woman of fiction was cast in the role of keeper of culture, recreating the circumstances of home via hot midday meals and a German Christmas" (1991:71).

In both scenes of *white* female presence, it is these home circumstances that are mentioned and commented upon. Their manifestations both take place within prominent Christian contexts: the resurrection of Christ (the Easter fire scene), and the birth of Christ (the woman with baby scene). Through these manifestations, the German soldier is reinvigorated, especially on a symbolic, layered level. This occurs through the metaphor of resurrection and birth and linking the religious field to that of the German colonising soldier. The initial scene references the resurrection of the soldiers in the war landscape, created through the "home circumstances" offered by the metropole and the religious celebration. The sighting of the baby becomes indicative of the value of the German progeny, attaining the quality as a placeholder legitimisation for the continuation of the war. What connects the spheres of the religious with the male colonising project is the female (mother) figure which connects the German home with the colony, but who is also responsible for reproducing the home *in* the colony.

b) *Heim Neuland*

Heim Neuland replicates a number of observations that I have made concerning the *white* female colonialist in the domestic setting. Firstly, Etta Wibrandt has taken it upon herself to be involved in the productive life in the colony in equal measure to Dirich. She undertakes the long trips through the country with him and organises the running of the household and the laying out of the garden. She is present when the swarm of locusts nearly destroys their crops and sits behind the counter, selling commodities in their farm stall. All of these 'tasks' are supportive of Dirich's projects (building the house, buying and selling cattle, saving Okahandja, participation in the war), exemplifying the industry and activity that one could expect from the colonial settler wife. What differentiates the two protagonists, however, is the focus on the spaces in which they perform the tasks and the focus on their *whiteness*.

Because Dirich is not introduced as *white* and his *white* features are never mentioned, Etta's *whiteness* needs to be foregrounded[114]. Her *whiteness* is hypervisible[115], informing much of what she does. It also separates her from the other/'Other' characters. For example, her *white* hands are the object of desire for Detlef Welzin (486). Her *white* hands also link her body to her German home[116], having been formed through the harsh coastal conditions there. The hands, primary tools of domestic labour, become central when describing Etta. The combination of *whiteness* and female domestic labour create her German identity, explicated thoroughly in Nancy Reagin's "The Imagined *Hausfrau*: National Identity, Domesticity, and Colonialism in Imperial Germany" (2001). Here, domestic German labour is used as a marker to differentiate between various national and cultural forms of housewifery. Focussing on magazines produced for housewives, Reagin observed that these magazines

---

[114] This is argued according to the logic that the *white* female colonist would (and could) only be linked to a *white* male colonist.

[115] This term refers to the strategic and continued reference to her *whiteness*, especially with respect to the other characters.

[116] "Auf der Karre hatte sie sie [Hände] auch nicht grad pflegen können. Aber diese starke weiße Haut, den schmalen wohlgebildeten Nägeln konnte so leicht nichts angetan werden." (444).

introduced metropolitan readers to Germany's colonies and colonial subjects and presented the bourgeois housewife as a key part of the imperial project. But these depictions of colonial housewives also served as a mirror for metropolitan readers, reflecting back an 'essence' of German housewifery, thrown into relief by a foreign setting. (80–81).

Here we have the urban, found in the domestic setting. The metropole produces the conditions and definition of ideal German domesticity and supplants this in the colony. The reproduced conditions and definitions are picked up by the metropole, proving their desirability and durability. Guni, Etta's domestic worker, gives birth to a baby who was conceived with an unnamed soldier. The baby is deemed ugly, yet it is marked as *white*. This could be read as the *whiteness* of the German soldier overriding the Blackness of Guni, also hinting at biological superiority. The baby is not allowed a 'middle' space, while it is disconnected from its mother due to its 'skin colour'. This scene replicates the idea of the binaries perpetuated by *whiteness* in the colony: that it "functions as subject, norm, and engine of radicalizing processes" (Arndt, 2009:171), creating an exclusive space of *whiteness*.

A further aspect of the woman in the colony, and again linked to the *white* body, is the continuation of two equally important spheres: German cultural and biological spheres. Both are highly, but not exclusively, reliant on the *white* German female body. As Clara Brockmann argues[117], the introduction of the German woman was to prevent racial impurity through the sexual relations between German male settlers and African women. Although not explicitly pointed to in *Peter Moor*, it becomes an issue in *Heim Neuland* and a relatively central theme in *Du heiliges Land!*. However, it also hints at the sexual unions which were taking place in the colony but which were frowned upon, especially since

> [nach] der damaligen Rechtspraxis erhielten eheliche Kinder die Staatsangehörigkeit des Vaters, ehelich geborene, die deutsche Männer mit Frauen der Kolonialvölker hatten, waren somit automatische Deutsche geworden, hätten also auch alle staatsbürgerlichen und bürgerlichen Rechte besessen und so die Möglichkeit gehabt, General der 'Schutztruppe', Polizeipräfekt, Richter oder gar Gouverneur einer Kolonie zu werden – Szenarien, welche die deutsche Koloniallobby in Angst und Schrecken versetzt haben. (Momozai 2009: 16[118])

This not only led to the revoking of the official recognition of marriages between *white* Germans and People of Colour, but also led to discussions concerning the definition of what constituted German-ness. This is where Brockmann and the *Frauenbund* became vocal, citing these intermarriages as a reason for the degeneration of the German nation in

---

[117] This argument is threaded through most of her work, fictional or autobiographical. See Brockmann's writings (1910, 1912) as well as Walgenbach (2005).
[118] In *Frauen in den Deutschen Kolonien* (Marianne Bechhaust-Gerst (ed.).

the (settler) colony. The arguments suggest that this would dilute the purity of the German community, which in turn would end in the demise/degeneration of German cultural life and lineage. The *white* woman is imagined as a barrier against cultural and biological decline. This means that certain spaces need to be animated by the *white* German female in order to guarantee the prosperity of the colony. Spaces such as the home, the garden, the living room/bedroom, were areas in which the female is expected to operate and fulfil her role. Of course these spaces are part of a larger whole – the farm, the house, the territory, the nation – and to a certain extent are subsumed by these metaspaces[119]. One can argue that the feminine spaces are the building blocks on which masculine spaces rely. As long as these spaces are kept 'clean' and 'pure' it goes to say that the metaspaces are treated the same. The control of the *white* colonial woman over her prescribed spaces (Haarhoff refers to them as the three K's: Kinder, Küche, Kirche, 1991:71) creates the condition for control over the prescribed male spaces.

Etta is described as an excellent homemaker, controlling her home (through her Black staff) and organising cultural activities[120] for her guests. When she goes back to Germany, she is pregnant with Dirich's child. The child is born on German soil, guaranteeing its German roots. It also guarantees a safe, male lineage to the Dirksen bloodline. The name of the child, Hans=Heim, cements the connection between the town of Hodrum[121] and their new home (*Heim*). Through her various modes of reproduction, Etta Wibrandt is able to germanise her spaces and guarantees that they are maintained (her garden, her home, her child). Etta's role as the perfect female settler is briefly tarnished due to her trip home, though. This is because her child is conceived in GSWA, but it is born in Germany. Hans=Heim therefore cannot be directly linked to the soil (through his blood), only through his parents' relationship to the land. This relationship becomes interrupted as the signs and fruits of their labour have been destroyed and defaced. It is only the decision to return and fulfil their duty to the colony that allows Etta the opportunity to reclaim her position and status as a colonial woman. This can only happen via the home and the German woman within that home. In essence, the military man (Peter Moor) and the farmer (Dirich Dierksen) need the support of the housewife in order to complete the colonising mission. And once this mission has been fulfilled, the female settler forms the foundation on which the colony – and the colonist society – can grow and evolve:

---

[119] The 'female' spaces (e.g. the garden or bedroom) are only fragments of the larger spaces of 'male' spaces (e.g. the farm, the house). The *smaller* female spaces are necessary for the *larger* male spaces to function as such.

[120] "[M]an pflegte bei Dircksens am Abend zu musizieren oder vorzulesen." (486). In this instance they are reading Theodor Storm's *Schimmelreiter*.

[121] "Hans" is the name given to a stormy wind in Kraze's fictional town of Husum. It is also a very common male name that has a long literary and somewhat representative tradition.

"She... 'Germanized' the household within a colonial context, demarcating colonists from the colonized, linking housework to empire, building, and enlisting metropolitan women's support for German imperialism. Making 'German' homes in a colonial context, housewives thus contributed to the creation of communities of Germans in Africa that resembled the idealized, orderly small towns of the homeland, at least in literature for metropolitan audiences. (Reagin 2001:84)

The female colonial settler has her mission in a) providing a solid foundation for the colonising process, and then b) sustaining the process through her 'cultivation' of the male settler, the home, and the African subjects.

c) *Du heiliges Land!*

As I have pointed out, Clara Brockmann was a very vocal and active proponent of sending German women into the colony. Not only did her non-fictional writing focus on this aspect, but so did her fictional output. Many of the arguments made in *Die Deutsche Frau in Südwest* (1910) and *Briefe eines Deutschen Maedchens aus Südwest* (1912) can be identified in *Du heiliges Land!*. Although much of the focus of the novel is on the figure of Ingeborg Oberländer and her relationship to GSWA, Herbert Klinger, and Hans Gothland, certain claims are woven into the narrative. It must also be mentioned that the main female figures (Ingeborg, Carola, Rike Vollmüller) are at no point linked to physical home labour. Labour in this sense does not feature, but it is relocated in other cases and instances, as well as other spaces and bodies. The factors that play a vital role in Brockmann's construction of the domestic and domesticity are *whiteness* (representing purity as well as femininity) and the understanding or awareness of domesticity. Ingeborg and Carola, the only characters strongly connected to the home environment, show a domestic consciousness but are not linked to its active reproduction. Their domesticity centres around the assessment of the domesticity of others, for example Rike Vollmüller (Oskar's sister), their duties as bourgeois women, and the role of racial purity.

The most obvious and clear argument put forward by the narrator for the involvement of the German female in the colony is realised through the figure of Gothland. After he has finished work, he wanders through the houses on Gertrudenfeld, peeking into the small box-like homes of the *white* workers on the diamond fields. He is impressed with the state of some of the homes and the high level of homeliness they are able to offer. He puts this down to the arrival of a German woman in the home. Gothland observes that this was generally the case

> wenn ein Sortierer sich eine deutsche Frau mitgebracht hatte in diese Einöde, ihre geschickten *Hände* hatten mit bescheidenen Mitteln ein trautes Heim geschaffen. *Weiße Gardinen* umhüllten die Fenster, Wandbekleidungen boten Schutz vor Kälte und Zugluft, auf

sauberen Tischdecken stand weißes Porzellan, und Bilder und Blumenvasen zeugten von dem anspruchslosen Versuch, ein altgewohntes Bedürfnis nach ein wenig Schmuck und Schönheit zum Ausdruck zu bringen. Zuweilen war auch noch Platz für ein dichtverhangenes Himmelsbettchen da, drinnen schlummerte ein hilfloses kleines Menschenwesen — *der Triumph des Lebens in dieser toten Wüste.* (my emphasis, 34–35)

The contribution of the German woman is first and foremost in the service of her husband. Certain 'luxuries' are introduced to the home, such as cleanliness and protection from the cold. These are expanded upon through the beautification of the space itself, achieved through modest methods. The term "mitgebracht" (brought along) carries a very objectifying connotation, relegating the wife to the sphere of objects brought to the colony. Her role as a full person is denied, while it is her function which receives the attention. The vocabulary concerning the 'export' of German home makers carries a similar tone. Terms such as *Heiratsmarkt*, *Frauenüberschuss*, and *Frauenmangel* (Kleinau 2000:203) have strong economic undertones. The settler woman is thus placed in the sphere of the market and treated as a further commodity lacking in the periphery, but can be provided by the metropole. The last line in the quote (a reference to *Peter Moor* and *Heim Neuland*) is the new-born baby in the cot. Again, the responsibility of biological reproduction is mentioned in connection with the woman. In this case, it is also connected to the colour *white* through the drapes, the clean tablecloths, the porcelain and the canopy bed. And like the babies in the previous novels, the infant is symbolic for the survival of the German nation in an inhospitable environment (the previous two cases allude to the war environment), namely the "dead desert" (35).

Gothland's observations reference a further function the colonialist female is expected to perform. This function is not tied to physical labour, but to the moral integrity and pure character of the housewife. Her influence rubs off on the male settler preventing him from falling prey to the vices of the colony. These may have included idleness, drinking, and gambling as well as unsanctioned sexual unions. The positive influence of the 'pure' German woman on the weak colonialist male keeps the society stable and productive. That is why Gothland prefers to see his employees with a wife, because "die Macht der Versuchung, die hier in Trunk und Spiel und in Gestalt der widerlichen, schmutzigen Eingeborenenweiber war gebrochen" (35) and a "Mann mit Frau und Kind wurde nicht zum Verbrecher" (35). These assertions are to be found in the descriptions of the landscape, always locating in it some form of innocence and purity, in which the 'white' landscape is experienced as the quintessential innocent or pure space[122]. The empty landscape

---

[122] Examples include the white *Wüstenmeer* (52), the sand being compared to freshly fallen snow (52, 225), and the scene at the Paresis Mountains, where "in riesigen, weißumrandeten Halbringen, rann das Meer spielend und schmeichlerisch ans Ufer" (134).

and the ideal female settler are thus seen as connected elements, sharing a reciprocal relationship: the pure landscape is reflective of the female character while her involvement in the colony keeps the landscape pure. This purity is usually emphasised through the adjective 'white', which further carries the connotation of racial purity.

The first time Hans Gothland's feelings for Ingeborg are mentioned, they are described as follows: "Der Anblick *dieser weißen Frau* rief hier draußen weiche Reminiszen hervor; Gothland träumte wieder von girrenden Geigenklängen und marmornen Frauenschultern und goldhellem Wein. In *märchenhafter Ferne* lag das alles hinter ihm" (emphasis mine, 25–26). The adjectives connected to Ingeborg are focussed on her *whiteness*, which in turn open up a direct connection to the landscape and the surrounding endlessness. This endlessness is given a fairy tale dimension. This aesthetic strategy strongly links the *whiteness* of the woman to the aestheticisation of the landscape. It also introduces elements such as golden wine into the imagination, elements which come from another time and another space (indicated by his *Reminiszen*), but which Hans Gothland is able to link to Ingeborg. Another example in which the *whiteness* in the landscape offers a link to racial purity is the evening in which a number of guests of the ball on Schakalswater travel to Lüderitzbucht. Hans sits at the front of the carriage and gazes into the distance. His gaze is accompanied by a description of the relatively alien environment:

> Lautlos, in schweigendem Glanze lag das Wüstenmeer da, *weiß* und schimmernd, wie mit einer *Schneeschicht* übergossen. Der Atem der Poesie hauchte jetzt dem armen Land eine erhabene Schönheit ein. Blaß, in ruhiger Feierlichkeit sah der Mond vom mattblauen Himmel darauf nieder. Es war ein Bild von *fast biblischer* Größe und Heiligkeit. (my emphasis, 52)

Emotive terms such as "Poesie", "Schönheit", and "Heiligkeit" create an atmosphere of purely aesthetic proportions, yet certain foreign terms are also included, such as "Wüstenmeer" and "Schneeschicht". This can be linked to Gothland's intertextual references concerning Ingeborg in which she is first made *the* most prominent character in the Bible, namely Eve, and then remodelled into a modern-day Pandora[123]. In both instances, the *whiteness* of the landscape is connected to the female coloniser through the idea of her purity. This purity is broadened through the concept of domesticity, a construct focussing only on the *white* colonising woman.

Haarhoff identifies the function of domesticity and links it to the ideal of racial purity:

> Domesticity in the new domain emerged as an early theme in this [German colonial] literature and the writings of the women imported in the interests of racial purity were

---

[123] Both women are the first of their kind, Eve being the first woman 'created' by God, while Pandora is the first woman 'created' by the gods.

publicised by the pro-colonial societies. The first consignment of women arrived in 1898. By 1905 mixed marriages were made illegal and in 1907 the act was made retrospective to cover earlier unions. (1991:70)

At the ball that Carola hosts (as part of her domestic duties), the reader is introduced to Dr Schleicher, a physician with a fondness for African women. This is immediately made clear:

> Da war ferner ein Arzt, der sich einen ganzen Harem schwarzer Weiber aus dem Norden mitgebracht hatte und in dem Rufe stand, der weißen Frau Grazie und Schönheit abzusprechen im Vergleich zu den Negerfrauen. Neben ihren körperlichen Vorzügen rühmte er auch noch ihre scheue Leidenschaftlichkeit und die tiefen Offenbarungen ihres Geistes. (46)

Ingeborg comments upon this unappreciative attitude towards the *white* woman by questioning his attendance at the "Haus einer weißen Frau" (46). This introduction to the character of Dr Schleicher at first seems as a ploy in which to dismiss the unsanctioned sexual unions between German men and African women. Although the focus for this type of embargo concerning these unions was usually the single, middle or lower class male, the doctor offers an exception to this. And although his image of the African woman appears to be quite positive, his choice in partners is at a later further demonised. Klinger and Gothland try to reassert the virtues of *white* women during a heated discussion. This discussion is sparked as Dr Schleicher starts to rave about his current sexual partner, a thirteen-year-old Herero girl, called Gretchen[124]. Klinger and Gothland leave Dr Schleicher behind in the *Kaiserhof*, with Klinger's response to Schleicher's relationship being a downright outburst: "Skandal! Daß man das mit anhören muß! In einem *deutschen* Lande! Wo *deutsche* Frauen leben! Eine hohe Gemeinheit ist das!" (my emphasis, 80). This locks an imagined German-ness into *whiteness* and vice versa, closing it off to other definitions or rationales. Klinger continues to dismiss Schleicher's relationship, referring to African women as animals (81/82) and reminding Gothland of virtues such as self-discipline (82).

What this passage does, is open up a number of responses to the idea of mixed-race marriages and sexual unions. Firstly, the desire for an African woman is equalled with contempt for *white* women. The African woman's sexuality is only understood through the undesirability of the *white* female. This desire for the African female is then further constructed as unnatural by adding the dimension of paedophilia, an act which Klinger

---

[124] The name Gretchen has a long literary history in Germany, the most famous example being the Gretchen from Goethe's *Faust* (1772). The first part of the play is dedicated to her character (*Faust Teil I: Die Gretchentragödie*). Her character is also a victim of an unsanctioned sexual liaison.

understands as illegal in the colony[125], thus referencing the legal framework under which such relations can be rationalised. Schleicher cannot be alienated from the community because of his high social standing as a physician. However, he is discursively alienated through his exclusion from the ideal *white* community and through the wish for the state to intervene on a judicial level. And it is this judicial level which became a powerful tool in the struggle to maintain racial – and thus moral – purity. Schleicher becomes an enemy to the quest to sustain German-ness, thus becoming an enemy to the developing society and the state. His German-ness, through Klinger's continual focus on the "deutsche(s)", becomes disavowed. He is referred to only in respect to his relationship to African woman, not in respect to the development of the colony. The purity and morality of the *white* female settler is set up as an unbridgeable binary to female African sexuality.

An example where the moral superiority of the female settler is reinstated arises from Ingeborg's strong feeling for justice. After an Owambo worker from the mines is supposedly not paid his wages (it is never clarified whether he is victim or scammer), Ingeborg becomes enraged. The paymaster, unmoved by the worker's plea for his due wages, begins to argue with Ingeborg. His main concern though is contact with the Black bodies. He is afraid of the diseases he may pick up from them[126]. Again the ideas of contagion, but also purity (in this case linked to health) are invoked. Ingeborg, for her part, argues that she and the paymaster are able to treat this matter with more insight and intelligence. This is because as *whites*, they are able to control foreign people through "objektive Gerechtigkeit und Sorgfalt" (122). Her argument is that the Owambo are in *their* employ and should thus be treated according to European standards[127]. The main character however, continuously undermines this empathy for the workers[128], as she is unable to accept Black people as real people[129]. In this case they are only seen as an economic factor (as mass work force) which is diminishing at a steady rate ("Adolf erzählte kürzlich, daß sie fast

---

[125] "Das Kind ist dreizehn Jahre alt. Ich denke, wir leben doch in einem Staat mit *deutschen* Rechtsbegriffen!" (emphasis mine, 83).

[126] "Holen Sie sich nur kein Ungeziefer, Frau Gothland!. This fear is stated earlier by Carola: "wenn ich das Wort [Owambo] nur höre, ist's mir als müsse ich das Ungeziefer abschütteln" (112).

[127] Ingeborg, in a wish to help the workers, points out to Carola that "Sie arbeiten für uns". Here the "we" is understood to mean Germans, thus cementing the master-worker role of both groups.

[128] There are numerous examples in which Ingeborg reveals her racist and Eurocentric views, most notably when she discusses the workers in the house at *Schakalswater*.

[129] The "Hererojungen" are described as standing around with their "grenzlos dummen Gesichtern", while a group of girls there are likened to animals: "'Ob diese beiden ["Zwei Hereroweiber"] da unten auch wohl alle ursprüngliche Kraft und Eigenart den Informationen der Herzenskälte opfern? Sicher nicht. *Schade nur, daß sie meist Tiere sind*, die ohne das Bewußtsein ihres Rechttuns hinsterben. *Wir könnten viel natürliche Freiheit von diesen Negervoelkern lernen.*' So dachte Ingeborg, während sie hinabsah" (emphasis mine, 40).

täglich einen Owambo begraben" (113)). Here, McClintock's assertion that "race is not simply a question of skin colour but also a question of labour power" (5) is central.

The Black body is only recognisable in conjunction with the work it performs – in the service of the German colony. It is not given a space outside of that sphere, especially in reference to the spaces of the *white* body. *Whiteness* is employed in order to impose a racialised work relationship in which Black labour is exploited in the service of *white* capital and wealth. Racial purity is also subtly interwoven into the novel. Although Schleicher's relationships do not (evidently) produce offspring, these offspring must be imagined. In the discussion between Klinger and Gothland, the former mentions the degrading effect which relations with African women could potentially produce. There is the example of a Norwegian fisherman, who is married to an African woman. The response (again by Klinger) is one of disbelief: "Unglaublich. Und dieser Mann scheint keine Ahnung zu haben von seinem Verbrechen gegen die eigene Rasse!" (241). This is followed by an anecdote of an East African officer who marries a local woman and takes her on the trip back to Germany. She is ostracised and treated as a passenger of lower status. A final example I want to point to are the living conditions of the non-Germans (most notably the English and the Dutch) in the southern parts of GSWA. Here, through the influence of the local inhabitants, the Europeans have undergone the degenerative process of "'verburens'" and of "'verkafferns'". They have started to live in similar conditions as indigenous groups and are described as being dirty and uncivilised. The whole scene is described as follows:

> Auch in der Bevölkerung des Südens verstimmte ihn [Klinger] das vorwiegend englische und holländische Element; vielfach hatte er die Behauptung gehört, daß dem Süden des Schutzgebietes die Gefahr des 'Verburens' und 'Verkafferns' drohe, nun mußte er selbst die Wahrheit dieser Befürchtungen bestätigen. In niederen, wellblechbedeckten Lehmhäusern mit kleinen, vergitterten Fensterlöchern fand er ein schmutziges, verwildertes Volk, zwar weiß an Hautfarbe, aber doch bedenklich zu Sitten und Lebensweise der eingeborenen Bevölkerung herabgezogen. Nicht selten sah er eine Burenfamilie sogar in einer Art von Pontoks hausen, einer kegelförmigen Hütte, die die Wohnstätte der Farbigen darstellt, und die sie im Sommer mit Fellen, Kuhmist und Lumpen bekleideten, und im Winter mit Lehm vermauerten." (319)

Even though this passage fulfils a number of the requirements which qualify the European as appearing to 'regress', it is in stark contrast to the other characters in the novel. Gothland is introduced as living in a Pontok himself (7), while Etta Wibrandt praises the multiple functions of *Kuhmist* in the building of the house (1908:523). But because they are industrious and represent German-ness to a high degree[130], they are not treated as hav-

---

[130] I have discussed Etta's *whiteness* according her labour, femininity and domestic role. Gothland, at one point, is referred to as the "Urbild echten Germanentums" (12).

ing a degenerative dimension. Gothland does later exhibit a disjointed personality that consists of drinking, idleness, and diamond theft. In this case, however, it is the fault of the *Diamantenfieber* and his unreciprocated love for Ingeborg, not his own shortcomings.

The 'empty' space, into which the characters have entered, remains alien upon first contact. Various strategies are employed in order to escape its dangers, celebrate its beauty, or find some favour in this perceived emptiness. The strategies employed have greatly differed, especially concerning the question of how to insert German-ness into this 'empty space'. For the characters, the easiest way to accomplish this mission is by introducing metropolitan or urban markers into the territory which is slowly being conquered. Examples of this are the family, enclosures, and buildings. The military mission – the earliest of the narratives – provides a basis in which to observe which signs and symbols are introduced into the landscape and which of these will reappear or remain. The *white* woman emerges as a stable sign, one that is repeated in the other narratives. Another is the garden, also present in all of the works. This reflects which ideas of German-ness were overriding at the time, originating from political discussion to social-biological discussions some time later[131].

There are concepts and motifs that reoccur and prove the resistance of these motifs to change; yet they remain powerful vehicles in which the construction of German-ness (and its engine *whiteness*) can be interrogated. Because the repetition of the motifs of the *white* colonialist woman as well as of the garden are powerful reminders of colonial signification, it seems only consistent with the overall theme to interrogate them both. Although this interrogation has been done by critics such as Coetzee (in the introduction to *White Writing*) and Stiebel (in her chapter "Haggard's African Topography") and has been fruitful in understanding the literature set in colonial South Africa, my focus is the garden of GSWA. The dry, waterless climate, felt most painstakingly directly in *Peter Moor* but being most common in the desert environment of *Du heiliges Land!*, is in direct contrast to the lush and fertile spaces which parts of South Africa were able to offer. This is where Haarhoff's assertion that in "the [colonialist] fiction unutilised space is appropriated for the planting of gardens and the breeding of pigs. The land is vague, generalised and ideologised" (1991:71). Although very little pig breeding takes place in any of the novels (*Heim Neuland* does include cattle farming), it is the 'unutilised' space that is central, producing gardens, and with them, their tenders.

---

[131] For an in-depth discussion of the concepts of 'race' in Germany during the colonial period see for example Fatima el-Tayeb's *Schwarze Deutsche* (2001) and Ulrike Hamann's *Prekäre Koloniale Ordnung* (2016).

4 The Apartheid Era: The Trust in Maps and Guns

The colonial era in GSWA ended with the defeat of Imperial Germany during World War I, resulting in the loss of all her colonial territories in accordance with the 1919 Peace Treaty of Versailles. These territories were divided into three mandate categories, each category reflecting the mandated territory's presumed readiness for self-governance. GSWA was considered a "C"-class mandate, meaning that another nation, in this case South Africa, was given considerable power in order to "develop" the former colony and prepare it for independence. Guidelines as to how this was to be achieved were not specific, essentially paving the way for the incorporation of GSWA into the Union of South Africa. Consisting of four provinces, GSWA was envisioned to become the fifth province within the Union. This would mean a territorial acquisition that was slightly smaller than the Union itself. The Union would have practically doubled in size and gained significant economic and political influence in the southern African region. Especially since the neighbouring states were still colonies of European powers and because it now technically had its own colony to shape. On the surface, independence for SWA was envisioned, while political integration of the mandate territory was slowly being set up. Colonialism did continue — just within another framework and under a new name.

When comparing the now-ended German colonial experiment with the apartheid era that followed (including the preceding Mandate period), one thing is strikingly clear: the high degree of continuity between the two systems. These range from the construction and design of laws concerning groups and individuals, to the treatment of the various 'racial' and 'ethnic' groups[1] as they were defined and identified within the interpretation and execution of these laws. Furthermore, the (desired) complete control of space and its resources (the soil, landscapes, minerals, work force) also connects the two systems. Considering the legal frameworks set in place as well as the violence perpetrated by the state against the majority of its people and coupled with the relegation of the local population to a state of perpetual servitude, the links to and the mechanisms of colonialism within the apartheid framework are more than apparent.

Yet, these obvious continuities should not become the argument equating apartheid with colonialism[2] on a one-to-one basis. There are a number of reasons as to why this line

---

[1] Under apartheid's classificatory system, 'race' was used as an over-arching category which separated societies mainly according to their 'skin colour' (*white*, Black, Coloured, and Indian). These categories dictated nearly every aspect of life (habitation, mobility, social standing). The Black class was then further divided according to 'ethnic' belonging, for example Zulu, !Xhosa, or Pedi.

[2] A look at American segregationalism practised during the Jim Crow era could serve as an example of this.

of argumentation has a very fragile foundation. It is firstly the judicial and legitimised (albeit problematic) acquisition of the territory of (G)SWA and its integration into the larger whole of the Union (later the Republic of South Africa) that counters most claims of re-colonisation. It was a decision by the globally established League of Nations (admittedly by an international community dominated by the victorious Western powers as well as Russia) which guaranteed the transition of GSWA from a colonised territory to an occupied zone. The continual legal conflicts between the Republic of South Africa[3] and the United Nations (UN) concerning the form of rule over SWA as well as the directive for its independence is testament to this. This conflict reached its peak in 1966 when the UN declared South Africa's presence in SWA illegal and revoked South Africa's custodianship of the territory. South Africa ignored these developments and further strengthened its grip on SWA, resulting in international law suits over the future of the mandate territory.

In response, the apartheid structures SA attempted to enforce were vehemently opposed by most nation states, which was in stark contrast to the generally positive attitude with which colonialism was received both by imperialist European regimes as well as their respective general publics[4]. The sanctions imposed by South Africa's international trade partners (although not always respected by large scale companies and corporations) meant that there was an overall negative attitude towards this form of South African rule. The legal action which Ethiopia and Liberia took against South Africa also indicates that it was not only the West who opposed apartheid as a system, but that a number of African nations were also invested in securing self-determination for SWA and its people. In other words, while the colonising nations and their respective empires formed a sort of imperial community, the apartheid regime was near-completely isolated. Apart from some rogue nations, the only 'real' allies that apartheid South Africa had, were the various Bantustans. These were, however, in no way recognised by the international community, even after gaining 'independence' from South Africa.

Moreover, it was the immediate proximity of the mandated territory to its foreign administration that makes the classic form of colonialism difficult to sustain. The temporal and spatial vicinity in which laws, violence, and power oscillated asymmetrically between the two countries is indicative of South Africa's desire to expand her own state instead of forming a new one. It thus became an exercise in the erasure of a common border as op-

---

Independent from any form of formal colonialism, the positioning and privileging of *whites* over People Of Colour was a racial and racialist design, and not merely an imperialist simulation.

[3] From here on referred to as SA.

[4] It goes without saying that not every colonial achievement was celebrated in the 'home' countries, as the examples of Carl Peters and Lothar von Trotha show. The general tenure was positive, though, as new opportunities, prestige, and territorial expansion became the measure of colonial success.

posed to the erection of new borders[5]. The perception of new borders became a strategy for the maintenance of national power: borders were conceptualised internally rather than in response to SWA. The South African state was expanded, not transposed onto another space. The role of violence, the flag, and the Bible (technologies of conquest during the colonial era) became secondary tools of dominance – law took on the form of initial contact and power structuring in this context. The initial technologies of colonialism therefore became supplementary tools for the execution of laws. Where the gun and the Bible[6] had proven their authority during the colonial era, it was now laws, amendments and statutes that dictated fates. In other words: SA did not have to rely on wars in order to gain access to the space of SWA, but rather, it was through bureaucrats and law-makers that control was seized and maintained[7].

A further difference between these two authoritarian modes of governance was the way these systems presented themselves outwardly. While colonialism was deemed a natural and necessary progression at the centre of Enlightenment philosophy, the later implementation of apartheid seemed counter to the discourses of independent African states, although one can argue that these were forced into another dependent relationship with their former colonial masters[8]. Apartheid presented itself as a paternal method of governance, focussing on the 'well-being' of the original inhabitants of the land and using this rhetoric to justify the inhumane treatment of its subjects[9]. This approach was a global singularity and excessively reliant on public relations for its standing in the international community.

---

[5] The linguistic and ideological dimensions of this were manifest through the representation of South Africa's 'Border War', which did not reference the common border between SA and SWA, but between SWA and Angola. It is a strong indicator that SWA was thus seen as an extension of SA instead of an independent, sovereign state.

[6] In a strategic reversal, the gun and the Bible were utilised in order to oppose and resist the apartheid system and regime. For an analysis of the role of the church, see for example Philip Steenkamp's "The Churches" in: *Namibia's Liberation Struggle: The Two-Edged Sword* (Saul, John S. & Colin Leys (eds.) 1995) and *History of the Church in Namibia: An Introduction* (Buys, Gerhard, L. & Shekutaamba W. Nambala (eds.) (2003), especially "Section E: Growth of Prophetic Voice: The Namibian Churches and the Independence Struggle (1963–1990)".

[7] There were of course wars against the local populations during the mandate and apartheid periods, such as against the Bondelswarts and the Owambo. However, these should be considered as rebellions that were put down instead of wars in order to annex the land.

[8] Colonial structures were strategically replaced with neocolonial relations necessitating independence at some level for a number of African nations. African states still paying 'reparations' to France yearly serves as a good example.

[9] Hendrik F. Verwoerd, Prime Minister of South Africa and Minister of Native Affairs (1958–1966): "Our policy is one which is called by an Afrikaans word, 'apartheid'. And I am afraid that is being misunderstood too often. It could just as easily, and much better, be described as a policy of good neighbourliness". From: https://www.youtube.com/watch?v=vPCln9czoys.

The general (but superficial) boycott of South African products and her isolation from international politics (to a certain extent) further underline the difference between these two state ideologies. The fact that there were a number of colonised states at the same time South Africa was administering its apartheid mechanics, and the international outcry concerning these practices, serves as a final marker to distinguish the two systems. South Africa resigned from the UN as a member state (limiting the UN's ability to intervene on behalf of the Black population and also SWA) is indicative of the system's global disapproval. There is one more vital difference concerning the colonial and apartheid systems, one that I would like to open up at a later stage when discussing the novels. The argument focusses on the nationalisation of the soil, with the historic presence of Afrikaners in (G)SWA used as the core argument. The National Party was able to link its desire for the inclusion of SWA into the Cape Union via the large Afrikaner community in the territory[10].

Even though I have attempted to separate the two 'Namibias' according the mode of seizure of the territory, it is impossible to separate the two eras in one clean cut. This is because apartheid legislature and its enforcement had their roots in the colonial legal framework as well as that of the Mandate period. Examples of this would include the alienation of the Black community in urban areas[11], the forced resettlement of the African population in specific areas reserved for them[12], and controlling the labour and mobility of large number of African men[13]. Some laws were designed during the colonial period, such as mixed marriage laws (1905 & 1907), pass laws (*Passverordnung* of 1907), as well as land ownership (*Eingeborenenverordnung* of 1907). However, due to the political antagonism between the British and Afrikaner polity and the defeated German administration, some laws were relaxed or amended during the Mandate period. This was due to the Union elite seeing themselves as superior administrators of foreign territories and the strong focus on discrediting German colonial rule.

After the publication of the so-called *Blue Book*, known officially as *Report on the Natives of South-West Africa and their Treatment by Germany* (1918), the South African gov-

---

[10] A similar strategy was used by the National Socialist regime of Germany when invading dromer Czechoslovakia, Poland, and Alsace-Lorraine.
[11] Through the Natives (Urban Areas) Proclamation of 1924, as well as through the introduction of curfews for People of Colour in *white* neighbourhoods.
[12] This was achieved via the Native Administration Proclamation of 1922, making it a requirement for (Black) men to carry passports.
[13] This was controlled most tightly through a number of laws, beginning with Proclamation 3 of 1917 (focusing exclusively on mine work) and the Masters and Servants Proclamation (34/1920). These were propped up by the Vagrancy Proclamation (25/ 1910), which afforded greater power to employers concerning 'vagrants' in and around the reserves, and the Native Administration Proclamation of 1922.

ernment uncovered some of the atrocities that were committed during the 1884–1915 period. It was this book that both helped to discredit the German colonial administration and strengthened the claim to the ex-colony. The defeat of the German colonial masters, both militarily and politically, by the Union created the ground to assimilate the defeated territory within its own borders. A similar strategy had already been made use of after the Anglo-Boer War in which the 'independent' territories of the Transvaal and the Orange Free State were finally assimilated into a larger whole. General Jan Smuts' early and continued wish to have GSWA become part of the Union is indicative of the already-present aspiration to add to the Union's spatial and political territory.

The fact remains that, just like colonialism, the apartheid project was decidedly spatial[14]. The system had two focal points: the control of the movement of Black bodies within marked spaces and securing large pockets of arable and liveable land for the *white* population. Furthermore, the National Party, who introduced the concept of apartheid to South Africa, emphasised cultural difference in order to separate people of group affiliations. As stated previously, Black people were separated the most intensively according to this method[15]. The main reasons for this was the division of South Africa (and later SWA) into two territories, one for *white* South Africans and one for 'Other' South Africans[16]. The former group was provided with land previously held by the original inhabitants.

This practice had already been implemented after the Dutch settlers at Cape Town were making inroads into the 'hinterland'. The apartheid regime, however, made landgrabbing one of its main pillars of control. The disproportional distribution of land between *whites* and non-*whites* is evident of this policy as Rita Barnard (2007:92), amongst others, has pointed out. With *white* people owning or occupying 87 percent of land, it meant that the remaining thirteen percent was made available to the rest of the population. This statistic alone of course points to a system that in the long run was unsustainable, even through excessive force and coercion. What nurtured this irregular land ownership was the National Party's focus on the rural and its myth-creating and myth-sustaining potential. Soil, suffering and toil, and Christian iconography and rationale were manipulated in order to justify and legitimise the setting aside of land for the predominantly Afrikaner population. It is, however, important to remember how literature informed this type of thinking. The political and the trivial merged into a powerful tool

---

[14] I make this assertion with my thesis in mind. It is undeniable that control over temporal regimes was equally important for the implementation of the apartheid system.

[15] The category of the 'chameleon' (people who were put in different *racial* categories throughout their lives), however, exposed the arbitrary nature and porousness of these categories.

[16] As these were used as official categories and informed every aspect of apartheid developments, I will make use of these terms in order to point towards the powerful racial component in the system.

of self-definition and surface vindication, producing a discourse in which the minority narrated its rightful claim to lands into being, erasing and silencing the majority's dissenting voices.

As is visible from the evolution and final demise of the ideology of 'separate development', land-grabbing had two, relatively opposite, branches. The first was isolating the original societies from each other. This took many forms, such as the relocation of certain communities within urban centres, to the formation of the Bantustans or 'homelands'. The Bantu Homeland Citizenship Act of 1970 ensured that the non-*white* population was distributed within ten mini-states, each designed to be as homogeneous as possible. Because of the minority status of *whites* in South Africa, it became imperative to protect the *white* population from possible 'enemies' from within. These 'enemies', made concrete through the rather unspecific Suppression of Communism Act of 1950, were mostly those who opposed their forced removal or organised opposition against the laws introduced under the regime. The state guaranteed security by creating '*white* corridors' between the various locations that contained high concentrations of Black bodies[17]. A number of *white*-owned farms, for example, were placed between Black inhabited so-called reserves[18]. These corridors were then controlled (either by police or bureaucratic personnel), checking and limiting the movement of non-*whites*. The introduction of the highly unpopular passbooks made the surveillance and control of migrating workers easier (albeit not complete), while cities' controlling instances considered the control of Black bodies coming into urban centres high priority.

Strategies such as providing high-density housing (such as the hostels for industrial workers) or family homes (which were unavailable for persons without a family) became significant technologies in controlling the workforce. This was the second form of land grabbing. People of Colour in the reserves, who were unable to own or sell their land, were forced to move to the urban centres in order to gain employment to pay taxes and levies. Besides the urban centres, spaces experiencing a high influx of (internal) migration were the mining areas, most notably the Witwatersrand strip (Pretoria, Johannesburg) and Kimberley. The reserves thus became a labour pool, designed by *whites* to guarantee the safety of the *white* population, both at a rural and an urban level. As People of Colour were to a high degree unable to own land themselves (or if they owned land, they were

---

[17] These are the most visible and official mechanisms of control. However, as the system of apartheid became more and more difficult to enforce, newer and more brutal government extremities were introduced. This had the result of emerging militias, so-called third-force divisions, the militarisation of the police force, and an increased reliance on secret police.

[18] The term 'reserve' is indicative of its racial and objectifying nature. They were used as *reserves* for labourers but also as a resource in case certain things were needed (people, space, minerals, etc.)

unable to sell it), it became difficult for them to participate in any land and spatially related developments.

These mechanics were bolstered by the police and military, as well as an extensive bureaucratic machinery. As was the case during the colonial period, the apartheid state introduced laws in order to dislocate the original population from their ancestral lands (either physically or judicially). Ironically, in many cases a simulation of village life was introduced into the urban slots imagined for the African residents, designed to replicate the rural lifestyle people were supposedly used to[19]. This also allowed for greater control and surveillance through the lay-out, the location of natural boundaries (such as mountains or streams), and the inclusion of ~~Native~~ Commissioners within these simulation villages. It should be said at this point that the apartheid strategies employed in SA and SWA were at the core very similar, yet the scope and degree were not the same. A number of levels of segregation (urban apartheid and petty apartheid) were achieved to a relative extent but the overarching, large-scale state apartheid was never fully realised. My brief discussion of apartheid in SA here serves to contextualise and situate the novels in respect to the system being imposed.

While these developments were taking place, the *white* population used the new freed-up spaces to write their own history and myths[20], inserting their own pasts into the landscape and soil. The most powerful *white* literary product emerging from this amalgamation is the *plaasroman*, a genre Barnard (2007) likens to German *Blut und Boden* literature (73), the 'national' genre of the Nazi era. This type of literature was important in legitimising Afrikaner claims to ownership of land, but was equally important in forming a collective identity. As Cheryl Stobie (2009) points out, the *plaasroman* "sought to establish Afrikaner identity and dealt with such topics as landownership, tradition, white self and black other, and the lost son" (58), fictioning a belonging both in a spatial as well as in a social sense. Gideon Malherbe (2017) links the establishment of this literary genre as a response to processes such as urbanisation, arguing that "[t]his tradition in Afrikaans writing from 1920–40 focuses on a romanticised ideal of an agrarian lifestyle that was by then lost to the majority of Afrikaners" (11), adding that it "is the expression of a general longing for the perceived idyllic lifestyle that played out on the Cape Dutch *werf*" (ibid.), indicating that it is in essence a look backwards to an era that seems to be lost, but is also at the heart of apartheid discursive strategies.

---

[19] For more, see A.J. Christopher's *Atlas of Apartheid*.
[20] These two terms will be looked at in more detail when I discuss J.M. Coetzee's "The Narrative of Jacobus Coetzee" (1974) at a later stage.

A second, not quite as conservative, branch of literature started to develop, namely the Romance genre. Although not as vehement in its dislocation of the African population from its ancestral soil or linking the own past to this soil, the pastoral romance focusses on the subliminality of the landscape in order to put it under *white* control[21]. The focus on the aesthetics and subjective powers of nature disavow and erase the Black body from nature's most political manifestation, namely the landscape. This is also a point Coetzee made during his speech after he received the 1987 Jerusalem Prize for the Freedom of the Individual in Society. In his argument it is a *love* for the country, i.e. the non-human elements, which he connects to the erasure of the Black body as the landscape and its elements are pushed to the foreground:

> At the heart of the unfreedom of the hereditary masters of South Africa is a failure of love. To be blunt: their love is not enough today and has not been enough since they arrived on the continent; furthermore their talk, their excessive talk, about how they love South Africa has consistently been directed toward *the land*, that is, towards what is least likely to respond to love: mountains and deserts, birds and animals and flowers. (emphasis in original, in: *Doubling the Point*, 1992:97)

The landscape now creates the backdrop in which the love for a space is exclusionary of its 'Other', while employing the powerful emotion of love in order to feel as if to belong[22]. This love is employed as an abstract tool of appropriation, as is most evident in the Boer relationship to the soil. Suffering and toil inform this relationship most distinctly and is a strategy in which the landscape and soil are personalised and closed off.

Just as these myths and histories became a key thematic of colonialist literature, they became vital tools for the apartheid project (and of course the resistant movements and moments). This is most obvious when one looks at the rise of Afrikaner novels focussing on the deep relationship the Boer has with the soil, or the English romance employing apartheid South Africa as a setting for adventure, mystery, intrigue and love. Both cases make use of contemporary events (SA's isolation, the high degree of ruralism and increasing urbanism, rigid social and political borders, and finally, the strong focus on 'race' and miscegenation), while looking back at 'how things used to be' (traditions, customs, hierarchies, Black-*white* relations). The two novels I discuss make use of these popular tropes and themes by either affirming them (*A Twist of Sand*) or deconstructing and prob-

---

[21] See for example Johann Geertsema's essay "Imagining the Karoo Landscape: Free Indirect Discourse, the Sublime, and the Consecration of White Poverty" in *Literary Landscapes* (De Lange et al. 2008) where he argues that "the presence of the sublime in colonial contexts has aided…in the process of clearing the land of autochthonous inhabitants" (93).

[22] This emotion is also reflected in Peter Moor and Hans Gothland's relationship to GSWA. They love the land despite their ordeals.

lematizing them ("The Narrative of Jacobus Coetzee"). My analysis will take the form of briefly contrasting how the narratives deal with the *ideas of 'empty space'* (discussed in the section dealing with colonialism), the *technologies of conquest and domination* (such as the map and the gun), and finally, *the (de-)construction of the narrator-explorer perspective*. I will not focus on the empty landscape in detail as this trope was discussed at great length in the previous chapter. What is, however, strongly connected to both main protagonists is their ability and potency to uncover/fill 'unmapped' spaces through their engagement with their environments. Both spaces (sea and desert) are constructed as being empty in order to have the two explorers produce these spaces, reproduce their masculinity and with this, reproduce metropolitan engines of conquest, such as *whiteness* and spatial control.

The *plaasroman* has colonial roots in the way the Afrikaner 'nation' is described and produced. The most vital and central trope in this genre is the suffering and survival of the Boers, whether they were trekking through forsaken and barren land or while they were working this forsaken and barren land. The Christian motifs of suffering (hunger, thirst, war, persecution, violence) and survival (akin to Jesus in the desert, the Israelites surviving the Egyptians) are replete in these novels. In most cases, it is the resilience and the ingenuity of the Boers that overcomes these obstacles. It is also their suffering and survival which brings them their redemption, namely their own 'nation' and the promise of land/the Promised Land[23]. Various locations were envisioned for the latter, ranging from parts in South Africa to Namibia and Angola. This form of literature, the *plaasroman*, is revealing of National Party rhetoric and rationale, and is also revealing of the general Afrikaner attitude towards their position within South African history, its present, and the subsequent future. The strong claim to land, autonomy, and independence, all denied by the intrusion of the British but granted to a certain extent under apartheid, is a repeated mark of this type of literature[24].

The second literary genre, the Romance, has at its core the pastoral. This form of fiction focuses on the landscape being encountered for the first time – taking its cue from the travel writing of the Victorian era, while furnishing it with the modern day male explorer. Of course the landscape, along with its beautiful and majestic animals, its ferocious streams and impressive mountains, and array of curious and exotic people, serve

---

[23] This of course has a strong resemblance to Frye's assertion that the successful quest is the engine of any romance, an engine which is also present in the *plaasroman*. The difference between these two genres is the heavy focus on the soil as an actant – as the basis of Afrikaner identity and the resource for Boer access to the land.

[24] Unfortunately, the language barrier does not permit me to analyse Afrikaans literature. However, the discussions concerning this product and its reoccurring tropes within English apartheid literature seem very fruitful and can enrich the analysis of my primary works.

as a background on which to paint the masculine explorer-adventurer. As Yekani (2001) has pointed out, "masculinity – like all genders – is simultaneously and interdependently produced within a complex web of power relations" (26). Much of these relations are based on defining and othering, guaranteeing that *white* masculinities remain at the top of the hierarchy.

It is impossible to discuss "The Narrative of Jacobus Coetzee" without referencing, to a certain extent, the literature which allowed such a narrative to emerge. Coetzee's novella allows multiple points of entry, working and playing with both types of literary genre. *A Twist of Sand*, however, falls into the category of the English romance. The novel allows certain comparisons with classics such as Herman Melville's *Moby Dick* (1851) and Rider Haggard's African romances such as *King Solomon's Mines* (1885) and *She* (1886). The image of the independent traveller who sacrifices everything in order to fulfil his mission/arrive at a certain place is reflective of the examples of adventure narratives mentioned above. Further aspects, such as the absolute freedom of movement, the dominance over space and people, and the omnipresent threat of the natural environment (whether on land or sea), all make up or represent the romance. While Jenkins reaffirms and reproduces this protagonist and the elements that form him to a large extent, Coetzee offers a more nuanced and composite approach to this genre, however reproducing a number of *plaasroman* tropes. The fact remains, however, that both narratives emerge from a period in the world, and South Africa in particular, in which the methods of *white* rule in South Africa were increasingly questioned and contested.

Introduction to the Texts

a) *A Twist of Sand*

A Twist of Sand is a novel that lives off the imagined dangers of the Skeleton Coast and the captain who defies them to attain great riches. Told by a first-person narrator, it begins with a near-death experience for Captain Macdonald and his crew when they are illegally fishing in waters off the coast of South West Africa. After being questioned by the police concerning the death of one of his crew members, it becomes apparent that he is not who he appears to be. As his story moves between his past and current events, it is revealed that Captain Macdonald is a former war hero, Geoffrey Peace, who was first discharged from the Royal Navy and then fakes his own death to steal diamonds. His aim is to locate an island, which his grandfather left him. After his episode with the police, a scheming German scientist looking for beetles blackmails Captain Macdonald into helping him enter the Skeleton Coast. They are joined by Dr Anne Nielsen, the premier authority of the sought-after beetles, and Johann, a survivor from Captain Macdonald's past. During their excursion, Captain Macdonald manages to kill Dr Stein – who had killed Dr Anne Nielsen – as well as Johann, locating the beetles and, with them, a large deposit of oil.

b) "The Narrative of Jacobus Coetzee"

"The Narrative of Jacobus Coetzee" is a multi-layered account of the trip undertaken by Jacobus Coetsé, the Dutch colonial farmer who is considered the first *white* person to have crossed the Orange River. Centred on this historic figure, the novella incorporates a note by the editor, J.M. Coetzee, the narrative, an afterword by the historian S.J. Coetzee, and the official deposition of Jacobus Coetzee at the Castle of Good Hope. The narrative takes up the bulk of the novella, detailing life in the Cape Colony before beginning with the actual trek. Accompanied by five farm workers and a contract worker (who is left behind to die in a cave), Jacobus Coetzee leaves his farm in order to explore the colonial hinterland. His official aim is to hunt elephants in the areas north of the Cape Colony. The Orange River, the natural border between the Cape and the as-yet unexplored hinterland, proves to be a tough obstacle to overcome. However, at some point Jacobus Coetzee and his team manage to cross it. While travelling, they encounter the inhabitants of the Great Namaqualand – which is where Jacobus Coetzee has entered after crossing the river.

After an initially peaceful interaction, the Namaqua invite Jacobus Coetzee and his five journeymen to their settlement. Jacobus Coetzee is welcomed into the ill chief's hut once they arrive. The community has a feast in the evening in which Jacobus Coetzee is involved in a fistfight. Suddenly becoming ill, he orders his group to leave. They do not get far and the Namaqua catch up to them. The group returns after Jacobus Coetzee is promised that he will be taken care of. While he is nursing his fevers and a boil, he is involved in another scuffle. He bites off a boy's ear and is expelled from the settlement. One of his farm workers, Klawer, escorts him on his journey back to his farm. During their desert crossing, Klawer passes away, leaving Jacobus Coetzee to find his way back by himself. He endures feverish and delirious conditions until he finally reaches a farm and is able to return home. After a period of recuperation, he, Hendrik Hop, and their attendants return to the Namaqua settlement and murder the inhabitants.

Deserts and Oceans

I have previously touched upon the singular narrator and focaliser of *A Twist of Sand* and "The Narrative of Jacobus Coetzee", opening up a discussion concerning the deconstruction of the *white* explorer-narrator perspective. Focussing on the technologies that bring such a perspective into being, a host of assumptions concerning the production of literary space by this omnipotent figure can be brought to light. Yekani (2001), in her study on masculinity, argues that "Within narrative accounts, masculinity is not so much as something one can claim; rather, it is a position that needs to be achieved often in terms of a heroic struggle" (36). The self-definition of these explorers as well their achievements positions them as being able *because* of their *whiteness*, but simultaneously forcing them to perpetually reproduce their *whiteness* in order to be considered successful.

One of the reasons why *A Twist of Sand* takes up an entirely different position in regard to the other novels is its setting. With all the other texts of this study focussing on the interior of (G)SWA, *A Twist of Sand* travels outside of the land-based spaces and makes the sea its most prominent space. The 'empty' landscapes which Peter Moor, Etta and Dirich, Ingeborg, Jacobus Coetzee, and even Muronga dream up are protracted to include the "wilderness of waters" (1959:36). The colonial fear of natural forces, inherent in *Peter Moor*, prevents a safe space for the protagonist whether on land or sea. Captain Macdonald's strong focus on the omnipresence of sand shows his fear of the inland's most uncontrollable element. His only option therefore is to produce a controllable space. The *Trout*, the *Etosha* (replicating the safe, controlled environment offered by the game reserve), his personal maps – they are spaces he can completely inhabit and control. His historic links to these spaces are reproduced on a consistent level (half the novel takes place in Captain Macdonald's past). These links give him the ability to organise his produced spaces to situate himself in a superior position.

The first example of this is the map he has inherited from his grandfather, providing him with the advantage over NP I, the submarine he is hunting. The Captain's ability to situate himself as an adventurer is evident in his successes in procuring wealth for himself and his mastering of seemingly improbable situations. The main difference between Captain Macdonald and the characters from the colonialist novels concerns the question of land. His main interest is the control over a mobile space. His technology of spatial penetration, his seafaring vessels, has replaced the Land Rover. The emphasis thus moves from taming and cultivating the land to increasing the possible spaces of penetration[25]. One must remember that Captain Macdonald has sailed the whole world over throughout his career. During his days as Commander Peace, he has even gone underwater. His obsession with the danger of the Skeleton Coast may be because it is the last space left for

---

[25] The narrative is mainly set off the coast of the Skeleton Coast, yet Captain Macdonald has been present in Gibraltar, Malta, London, Wales, Germany, Cape Town, and Walvis Bay, amongst others.

him to uncover. Overcoming the "nightmare" of this final frontier of civilisation would elevate him above everyone; possible danger, granting him a god-like status.

Desiring a god-like status is a prevalent theme in "The Narrative of Jacobus Coetzee". The trip across the Orange River by the historic figure of Jacobus Coetsé is recreated on three different levels. While the deposition is concise, the work done by the historian and university lecturer S.J. Coetzee lifts the Dutch colonialist farmer to the level of a mythic hero. Cited as "[a]mong the heroes" (108) of South African history, Jacobus Coetzee's narrative is reproduced as a legacy of *whiteness*. The focus on *white* achievement in the trajectory of the plot culminates in its most potent weapon: history. The protagonist's disorientation in a seemingly signless wilderness, "where everything…was possible" is countered through his transcendence of this 'empty' landscape. His own stylisation as a divine being becomes his strategy to adjust: a god does not require signs, he invents them. With this in mind, Jacobus Coetzee takes it upon himself to invent the Namaqua. One reason why this invention is reproduced is because of Jacobus Coetzee's desire to produce history. His violent return to the camp and the subsequent murder of its inhabitants is interpreted by him as a history-producing moment, one in which his narration is the absolute truth. This history is, however, produced under the authority of the Cape Colony. With the Orange River[26] considered the official limit of the Cape Colony, intrusions into the hinterland could offer new resources to the metropole. The metropole provides Jacobus Coetzee with the official permission to enter into the 'space beyond', acquiring new knowledge in return. Jacobus Coetzee's conviction that he was making history is thus taken up by the metropole in its knowledge-producing mechanisms. The history constructed around Jacobus Coetzee (himself ultimately the only witness) is archived only to be mythologised. Mythology becomes necessary for the metropole to maintain and preserve its authority.

The control over history and the spaces of history are necessary elements in the organisation of society. S.J. Coetzee's reworking of the official deposition, his university lectures on the subject, the reproduction of a monologic account of events, are all shaped in order to justify current power structures. The story of Jacobus Coetzee is reworked into an adventure story, with the "hero's" success changed into national success. The tone of intimacy underlying Jacobus Coetzee's ethnographic study of the KhoiSan creates a fraternity of *whiteness*, with the focus on *white* history. A secret bond of complicity is devised. This bond is devised horizontally along a time line, which connects the historic narrator with the current reader of his narrative (and audience of the lectures). The bond is also con-

---

[26] Jacobus named it "Great River", but its renaming into "Orange River" points to the Cape Colony's power to override and appropriate the efforts of its surrogates.

structed on a horizontal line, according to lineage. Jacobus Coetzee, an "ancestor" (108) of S.J. Coetzee's, is also an ancestor of J.M. Coetzee, the translator of S.J. Coetzee's works.

The Texts

a) *A Twist of Sand*

A Twist of Sand (the 1959 version) has been described in the blurb as "A submarine exploit of smashing originality..." by Margharita Laski, and as a book which "[t]he reader reaches the last page panting" according to the *Sunday Times*. Ian Fleming praised it with the words: "Geoffrey Jenkins has the supreme gift of originality. *A Twist of Sand* is a literate, imaginative first novel in the tradition of high and original adventure" (in Britton, undated, n.p.). The central facets of the novel are thus its adventure quality and its popular appeal. As Northrop Frye has pointed out, action is at the heart of popular literature[27]. It is clear that Jenkins' novel may be placed within the confines of trivial or popular literature. When one considers the presence of novels such as this within the critique of pop literature[28], it becomes important to investigate apartheid's popular literature. As Stotesbury (1990) has argued, the interest for researchers of trivial literature is in its production and reproduction of social norms/values, especially through the idea of boundaries (74). In many cases, pop literature – such as the novel under investigation – affirms or argues for the implementation or dissolving of boundaries, whether social (as in *white*/non-*white* sexual relations/living conditions), or political (as in the border between RSA and SWA). Stotesbury (1989) also argues that "the totality of a popular novel, its narrative form as much as its reception, requires serious examination for its links with its historical and social context" (39). In other words, just as was the case with *Peter Moor*, it does not suffice to *only* dissect the text; one must place it within its period of production and discuss its reception to a certain extent.

What makes trivial literature an easy target to renounce as superfluous are a number of elements. These can be summarised as its formulaic composition, the simplistic resolution of complex situations and problems, and the rather surface-driven construction of the characters. Binaries receive a distinct power and authority, and these tend to support and aid in the perpetuation of these binaries. Even when narratives are complicated, they are usually resolved within the limits offered by binaries. These serve a number of func-

---

[27] Frye, in *The Harper Handbook of Literature* argues that romance is "in its broadest possible meaning, a continuous narrative in which the emphasis is on what happens in the plot, rather than on what is reflected from ordinary life or experience. Thus, a central element of romance is adventure" (quoted in: Dolzani, 2004: xxiii).

[28] For example in John A. Stotesbury (1990) Jenkins (linked to *A Twist of Sand*) is mentioned amongst a group of writers who are described as "a distinctive breed of adventure-thriller and romantic fiction writers" which have emerged since the 1950s within the South African literary landscape (71).

tions, but two seem very prominent. The first function is that of recognisability. Stock characters have a high chance of being recognised[29], while main characters can be fleshed out according to this background. It further works within the framework of stereotypes in order to push the narrative forward, usually through the figure of the hyper-masculine and at the detriment of the 'Other'. The second function is the characters' subordination to the plot. High-paced adventure has little time and space for the complex construction of rounded characters, especially when these characters need to serve some trivial, trite action or contribution. Not only would this offer the distraction from the main characters, but would also distract from the action of the plot.

Geoffrey Jenkins' novel takes place predominantly, but not exclusively, off the shores of the Skeleton Coast. This is interesting because the novel and the narrative leave the traditional (colonial) setting of the interior and places the hero-narrator out on the sea. This setting allows for a more intense understanding of 'empty' space, as there are essentially no human structures (which might invoke ideas of *civilization*) or living beings (which might invoke ideas of *discovery*). But just as the setting of the open seas, moving about on the surface will not give a clear picture of all the possible spaces one might encounter. And just like "The Narrative of Jacobus Coetzee", *A Twist of Sand* contains questions concerning history, the 'I'-narrator and how these two ideas are able to open further questions of power. Keeping this in mind, *A Twist of Sand* is a significant novel to include when discussing apartheid due to its popularity. Not only because one can decipher the rhetoric and the rationale of the state in this literature, but also because state ideology is not (always) central to the plot. While the colonial novel is exactly that, namely colonial in its construction, the romance and adventure novel during the apartheid era is not necessarily about apartheid. It hides its apartheid affiliation by silencing it, by not mentioning it. And this is where I would like to discuss and dissect *A Twist of Sand*, namely by locating apartheid – and its tropes – in a novel which takes place mainly on the sea, a space which *appears* infinitely far from the dehumanising system. I will make use of three different motifs, focussing them through the character of Captain Macdonald.

This approach is necessary as he is the only access to the text as the narrator. Furthermore, Captain Macdonald's attitudes concerning his crew, women, and outsiders, as well as his performance as South African, all have the potential to uncover general attitudes of the era. Also, the reference to classic European maritime texts (*Moby Dick*, "The Rhyme of the Ancient Mariner" (1866), *Twenty Thousand Leagues Under the Sea* (1876)) in the text

---

[29] The child-like 'Bushman' in Southern African literature is the best example of this, but not the only one. Although certain characters are repeated, it is mostly Black characters who are cast as types. Other examples, however, include the racist Afrikaner farmer, the German of noble descent in GSWA, or the dandy British explorer, to name but a few.

itself, coupled with the reproduction of the traditional British adventure formula propagated by authors such as Haggard, but also Ian Fleming and Wilbur Smith, amongst others, (challenge → success → foreign element → further challenge → great riches) appears near perfectly in this novel. Finally, the medial reproduction and reception of the novel, from its different versions, sales and reprints, to the production of a film, shows that an object such as a book is able to pervade numerous areas of society, and is able to reach multiple audiences while taking on a number of guises. Apartheid, nonetheless, does make a very brief appearance. The novel alludes to the system once, Captain Macdonald mentioning it while travelling from Walvis Bay to Swakopmund with public transport:

> There were half a dozen European passengers in the forward end of the bus, and in conformity with the creed of *apartheid* on public transport, a score or so of Coloureds and natives sat behind the wire-meshed dividing grill. Whether they were dustier or more uncomfortable than the European passengers forward, it is difficult to say. But the grill was certainly not enough to make one unaware of their presence, if such was its intention, for with the dust and oil fumes were wafted in heavy, ammonical odours of unwashed bodies, that repellent which may be one of the deep, unconscious roots of *apartheid*. It cuts both ways, however, and a non-European will tell you that he cannot bear the stink of a white (washed) European. Livingstone was the first to find that out. (42–43)

The only passage referencing apartheid shows just how arbitrary it is. Both political groups (*whites* and non-*whites*) are confined in the same space and yet officially segregated. This segregation in no way influences the general shared displeasure of travel. However, apartheid is not relegated to the realm of legislature. It relies on learned differences, focussing them within the system ("unconscious roots of *apartheid*"), historic encounters (Livingstone), and the supposed mirroring of attitudes ("It cuts both ways").

Throughout the whole novel, there is only one Black character, the Kroo boy Jim, who is responsible for steering the ship. He becomes the victim of a violent death when Dr. Stein shoots him. Although it does carry shades of what Barnard terms "repression"[30], (where that which is unneeded, undesirable is not mentioned although it is there), Jim remains dead and plays no further part. He is in a sense erased from the novel. A further reference to apartheid might be the actual access to the setting of the novel – the sea. The novel was published in 1959, shortly before the mandate of the Odendaal Plan was introduced, yet it foreshadowed certain developments. When studying the map proposed by the plan, it becomes evident that none of the 'homelands' that were proposed had access to the sea. This means that the inhabitants had no real way of connecting to the-world-

---

[30] Barnard (2007) uses this term when discussing Nadine Gordimer's *The Conservationist* in respect to a Black corpse which continues to reemerge throughout the novel (Chapter Three: Of Trespassers and Trash).

out-there. Just like in the novel, Namibians were part of the world but hidden away, either through partitions or language.

b) "The Narrative of Jacobus Coetzee"
Most of the texts dealing with "The Narrative of Jacobus Coetzee" take as their point of departure the 'construction' or constructed nature of the historic texts (the narrative, the introduction-afterword and Jacobus Coetzee's deposition). The insertion of the fictional into the real, blurring the boundaries of both, is of high interest for most critics and theorists negotiating the text. Although most critics and theorists place the novella in the larger context of the book *Dusklands,* or within the larger body of Coetzee's literary output[31] (including his interviews, essays, biographies and other fiction), my focus for this text is to link the territory north of the "Great River" to Namibia, not to South Africa/southern Africa, as most of the literature of "The Narrative of Jacobus Coetzee" describes it.

Furthermore, the focus of the critiques of this novella have a discursive or historic dimension, neglecting the fact that the violence occurs *outside* of Jacobus Coetzee's South Africa (and thus expanding on the analogous potency). So, instead of dissecting the discourses opened up by the interplay between the historic-fictional texts, I want to include the discussion of Coetzee's "penetration" (to use his term) into a space that was and has been incorporated into the history of SA. A first step in achieving this discussion is by attempting a synergy between the various Coetzees who are allowed to speak. This becomes necessary due to the gulf between the temporalities in which the various narratives and comments occur. As J.M. Coetzee, translator of the narrative, informs the reader the introduction by S.J. Coetzee has been moved backwards, becoming the afterword. On a formal level, this presents relatively unfiltered access to the narrative, a narrative which would have been influenced and tainted by the initial introduction. Naturally, the narrative itself is not completely unfiltered as the text has been tampered with via the restoration of "two or three brief passages omitted from my father's edition" and the reduction "of Nama words to the standard Krönlein orthography" (1974:55). A number of interesting and important points to ponder emerge from this. Firstly, placing the introduction after the main text allows the narrative to unfold without the influence or weighting of an interpreter. The narrative is allowed to exist on its own terms, free of the restrictive authority of any mediating instance – at first. Secondly, the layout of the texts places the historian S.J. Coetzee between the two accounts of Jacobus Coetzee.

---

[31] This ranges from Dorian Haarhoff's *The Wild South West* (1991), Rita Barnard's *Apartheid and Beyond* (2007), the 2008 edited volume of *Literary Landscapes* (Attie de Lange et al.), to essays such as "Speech and Silence in the fictions of J.M. Coetzee" (Parry, 1996), "Colonialism and the novels of J.M. Coetzee" (Watson, 1986).

The first lengthy and detailed account is Jacobus Coetzee's fully reproduced narrative, beginning with an ethnographic analysis of various original inhabitants (the so-called ~~Bushman~~ receiving the most attention), and then moving onto his journey. The reader is given an intimate and personal entry into Jacobus Coetzee's inner workings, most notably his fever- and thirst-induced philosophical musings. The second narrative, an official deposition, is much shorter than the first. This is due to S.J. Coetzee having constructed the *Relaas* by Jacobus Coetzee, supporting it with historic evidence and attempting to place it in the larger context of the South African explorers. This was the focus of his lectures from which the narrative results. The historian Coetzee thus produces a narrative from historical and archival evidence, and embeds it in a time of intense political change, namely the period in which the National Party has come into power. His text thus does two things, each equally powerful.

Firstly, he covertly wishes the party into power, which is evident in his civilisation rhetoric, his appreciation of the *trekboer's* resilience, and the need to separate the explorer-pioneer from the original population. Secondly, his text legitimises the party's rise to, and maintenance of, power by linking past accomplishments and successes to the present, for example positively commenting on the crossing of the Great River. The fact that S.J. Coetzee refers to Jacobus Coetsé as "[a]mong the heroes who first ventured into the interior of Southern Africa and brought back news of what *we* had inherited" (emphasis mine, 108) creates a powerful relation between the mythological frontier pioneer and the community of descendants in the present. By placing Coetsé amongst other heroes substantiates his position as an outstanding individual, while referencing further heroes – such as the Hendrik Hop mentioned in the narrative. This has the effect that the past is populated with heroes who can be manipulated in order to celebrate current 'achievements' (e.g. the apartheid state). His crossing the river – now a simple task – is celebrated as a communal achievement, one that tries to locate these achievements within the current situation: South Africa in the 1950s[32].

Another aspect of this text's constructedness is the competing levels of 'truth' or history. The initial narrative is placed next to the academic work done by an historian (and a descendant) and is supplemented by the 'official' deposition of the narrator. All three texts have strong claims to truthfulness and historicity, especially the deposition. This is because this document has been 'witnessed' and noted by official persons, while having been produced in *the* space of official power and authority, the Castle of Good Hope. The initial account thus competes with the *Relaas* while both are audited via the research

---

[32] For an in-depth look at the various levels of authorship, see "Looking backward to the 'new South Africa' – J.M. Coetzee's exploration of the protocols of travel writing" (Marais, 1994).

done by S.J. Coetzee. His position of authority as an academic (having given lectures concerning "early explorers of South Africa" (55)) gives him a privileged position vis-à-vis the two texts. Furthermore, his involvement in a) the uncovering of the "reality of this extraordinary man" (121) and b) his contribution to the narrative through his introduction extends the narrative's claim of authenticity.

The deposition takes on a supportive role while evincing an archaeological, evidential function. The novel's year of publication seems to reproduce and point to a number of South African actions since 1760, with the crossing of the Orange River being the most common. After Coetzee, a number of other explorers entered the as yet unnamed territory, culminating in the British founding of Walvis Bay as a harbour. Further crossings include settlers (English and Afrikaans) during the German colonial era, soldiers (during the First World War), the Mandate administration (including bureaucrats, settlers and soldiers), the 'Border War', in which South African soldiers even crossed the Cunene (another official border, this time between SWA and Angola), and finally, as tourists. Each of these crossings has culminated in some form of violence, always perpetrated against the indigenous population, with tourism being no exception to the rule[33]. The novel, it seems, is evidence for the cyclical nature of *white* South African violence against the Black population in Namibia, with the question of land and movement through it at the centre of the disputes and conflicts.

Emptied Landscapes (?)

Because of my central focus on 'empty' or 'emptied' spaces in the two previous chapters, I would like to briefly link these concepts to the novels discussed in this chapter. In contrast to the landscapes in the colonial novels, the apartheid novels cannot fully work with the idea of a so-called and desired empty landscape. This is because it would be impossible for the National Party and its administrative organs in SWA to 'overlook' the infrastructure put in place by the German colonialist regime[34], even if Black spatial regimes and land claims could be 'overlooked'. Train tracks, settlements, harbours, enclosures[35], (farm)

---

[33] This belies a number of reasons, from the treatment of locals, to the effects on the environment and its inhabitants, to the competition of resources (ranging from parking spaces, accommodation, access to certain places, to basics such as water and food).

[34] One could term this as a fraternal relationship of *whiteness* in which *whiteness* is visible but categorised. Peter Moor's placement of the Portuguese as 'cousins' indicates a fraternity of *whiteness* while soliciting difference as well, especially in comparison to what is considered Black.

[35] Dag Henrichsen (2011) does mention that "[d]ie Einzäumung von Landbesitz, welche Leute so markant ins Auge stechen, erfolgten in systematischer Weise erst nach dem 2. Weltkrieg. Dieser Prozess der Besitznahme durch eine koloniale Siedlergesellschaft unter der Ägide zweier Kolonialverwaltungen, der deutschen sowie südafrikanischen, implizierte Prozesse von Vertreibung und Enteignung der afrikani-

houses, dams, well systems, as well as mining activities, and transportation networks all point towards the influence of the European conquerors. Even spaces that had little to no German spatial imprints could technically not be 'owned' as products such as landscape paintings, photographs, laws, and proposed plans confirmed German involvement within the spaces in the colony. This does not, however, mean that the 'empty'/'emptied' landscape topos cannot be used as a trope within the chosen novels.

One way of sidestepping the apparent 'lack' of 'empty space' is by creating it. Both novels do this quite successfully but in very different ways. Again it is the landscape that serves to position the protagonists – exclusively male explorer types – in reference to their host society and their environment. Not only do the two protagonists both move through large, 'empty' areas during their respective travels (first the sea, and second the desert)[36], but they also assist in emptying these environments. Captain Macdonald does so by manipulating maps and his crew, erasing the things they see or imagine, in order to safeguard his personal history. Jacobus Coetzee goes even further by erasing the traces of people in the landscape, thus destroying their presence and overwriting it with his own personal history[37]. Both characters produce palimpsests through their narratives, however, palimpsests that are recognisable to the reader only. The oppressiveness of the *white* narrative, saturated with *white* history and *white* geography, covers the surface, preventing further narratives, histories, and geographies from interrupting these 'expeditions'.

Captain Macdonald/Commander Peace is most at home on the seemingly infinite ocean. He traverses it in his fishing trawler, the *Etosha*, having been the commander of a submarine in his (previous) life. He is an ex-military man with a high level of understanding of how the ocean works, using currents and depths to his advantage. Compared to his crew and the other characters, Macdonald is able to manipulate his ship in order to manipulate his surroundings as well. He is the only character who is able to 'read' the ocean landscape. Macdonald is thus the only one who can decipher the 'empty' landscape of the ocean, always to his advantage. Comparing the literary production of either 'landscape' within the narrative (sea vs. land), it becomes clear that the 'empty' ocean is the dominant environment. However, both landscapes fit into J.M. Coetzee's notion of the "literature of vastness". A paradox is contained in Coetzee's notion, as the "literature of vastness, examined closely, reflects feelings of entrapment in infinitudes" (1992:98).

---

schen Bevölkerung." (xi) The fences thus only appeared after South African control, however, there were significant 'boundaries' already set in place which demarcated territories and land possession.

[36] The size of the territory and the spaces that are crossed may of course encourage ideas of 'empty'/'emptied' space.

[37] See for example Paul Carter's *The Road to Botany Bay* (1987) and "Writing on the Earth" by Sienaert & Stiebel, (1991).

These 'empty spaces' (desert and ocean) are contrasted by the 'filled' space of the *Etosha*, the only space that is not empty from the beginning. The ship has a history, a secret, is involved in Captain Macdonald's quest, while supporting her Captain's efforts to maintain his own history and secrets. One could go as far as saying that the *Etosha* is an extension of her Captain and thus his instrument in spatial production[38]. She contrasts the infinitudes of the open sea, the endless sand, the constant dangers faced by Captain Macdonald and his crew.

Jacobus Coetzee, on the other hand, has to deal with a very different landscape. His crossing of the Orange River in 1760, from the Cape Colony to the unexplored hinterlands, a time in which neither GSWA or SWA exist, is informed exclusively by the 'emptiness' of the landscape. Firstly, the first *white* man constructs this through the movement across the natural border. This already indicates that the protagonist will at no point see or experience European markers such as towns, cities, or roads. Furthermore, following the analogy of the filling-in of a map, Jacobus Coetzee's/Jacobus Coetsé's movement through the map's 'blank spaces' uncovers them and thus produces them. This happens first and foremost through his narrative. As he is the first *white* man to cross the Great River[39], he is the first *white* man to return from this unexplored and uncharted place and offer information about a series of topics. Secondly, movement through the space and his examination of space, place, and people, further produces the spaces. By situating himself and his culture at the heart of the new space, Jacobus Coetzee tries to replicate the Cape Colony within the Great Namaqualand. These efforts take a number of forms, the most prominent manifestation being his unbreakable confidence in *white* culture. Apart from a discarded *kraal*, Coetzee does not encounter any man-made objects or structures until he reaches the Nama camp.

The narrative focusses mostly on the natural landmarks, in other words those which function within the logic of a map. Similar to the colonialist novel, this takes the form of an initial incomprehensible landscape which needs to be made comprehensible. This happens through the technologies of conquest, namely the gun and the ox wagon. These two technologies have been reproduced and reanimated across time. This is observable when Captain Macdonald and his friend Mark travel in a Land Rover while carrying guns (48–49). For Jacobus Coetzee, they signify his explorer persona, while maintaining his links to the metropole. It is after he is separated from them that he enters his feverish de-

---

[38] This is not completely true when Captain Macdonald is lost in the desert of the Skeleton Coast. However, the *Etosha* is lying in wait, awaiting her Captain's return in order to safeguard his new secret: his oil deposits.

[39] Offering him the unique opportunity to name the River, a town called Warmbad ("hot bath") as well as the giraffe (*kameelperd*).

lirium, praising the gun's ability to open spaces. These technologies allow the movement through space and imprinting marks on it (through the hunting of animals[40] or the tracks left by the wagon), while also offering the momentary inhabiting of this space. Jacobus Coetzee is thus allowed to enter into unmapped space and produce it first by carving various metropolitan signifiers into the landscape (language, commodities, hierarchies, tracks) and then through his imbued power of describing and reproducing the space on his return to the colony, resulting in the erasure of the village.

a) *A Twist of Sand*

The first chapter in *A Twist of Sand* is titled "Skeleton Coast". This rather ominous name was borne out of the numerous wrecks and accompanying skeletons of the dead seamen on the shores of the coast, a coast which is directly adjacent to the Namib Desert. Apart from these remains, as well as the surrounding mountains, the landscape appears empty. The lack of drinking water and the barren soil make any form of living difficult in these conditions, most notably for human life. This is the landscape, as suggested by the novel. This may serve the purpose of emphasising its danger to those who have become stranded on the shores, or to create a narrative space in which there are no people – and therefore no support for the protagonist. Whatever the reason, the complete absence of other humans in the Skeleton Coast (originally referred to as Kaokoveld/Kaokoland) are fabricated, as this area was traditionally inhabited by the ovaHimba, a subgroup of the larger ovaHerero people. The landscape can thus not be interpreted as empty. As Ingold (1993), Hoffmann (2005), and Henrichsen (2011) have shown, societies interacting with their environment always produce traces of this interaction. This means that the ovaHimba have in some way or other altered the Skeleton Coast landscape by including it in their society as a resource. Basic needs (food, shelter) as well as tertiary needs (social and cultural reproduction) have influenced the responses to their environment. The verbal maps (*omitandu*) of the Skeleton Coast, i.e. its network of relations, has already created a space filled with spatial and temporal regimes while linking places to other places.

The 'emptiness' experienced by Captain Macdonald is the emptiness of the colonial gaze[41]. Jenkins does attempt to include a human presence in this otherwise desolate territory by placing ancient, non-African cultures, which are long dead and extinct, within the Skeleton Coast. The first example of this is when Captain Macdonald describes his first excursion with Mark. They both travelled to the Brandberg, a mountain situated

---

[40] This is the original reason given for Jacobus Coetzee's movement into the land of the Great Namaqua.
[41] This, to some extent, echoes Etta and Dirich's first encounter with the foreign landscape, ignoring the African people who are travelling with them.

in the greater Skeleton Coast area. They locate rock paintings[42] there, which Captain Macdonald assumes to have been left there by "Europeans of Egyptian or Mediterranean origin" (44). This is of course mere fantasy, as the origins of the paintings have been accredited to the KhoiSan people. They painted these drawings roughly 2000 years ago. This 'lost cultures' trope is further extended when an artificial water dispenser, appearing out of place within a space that is near impenetrable, saves him. Its simplicity is impressive, which forces Captain Macdonald to ask "[F]or how many centuries had this ingenious source of life in a country of death been working?" (250). Not only does the Skeleton Coast act as a keeper of history, but it is also depicted as a space which has been forgotten by time (probably due to the difficulty of accessing it). Yet, this 'empty space' (filled mostly with death and danger) is furnished with highly unlikely Western signifiers. These signifiers provide conditions in which Europeans, at some time or another, entered into the interior of the Skeleton Coast and managed to leave behind a token of this entry. Running water and an antique stranded ship indicate an age-old European influence on the Skeleton Coast, however, the captain of the ship and the creator of the tap are both unable to share their history. It is thus up to Captain Macdonald to decipher and uncover these 'lost' histories.

One fact concerning Captain Macdonald's explorer attitude becomes clear when he remembers a trip he and Mark took to the Brandberg. A number of observations come to the fore, all linked to apartheid (and colonial) rhetoric and knowledge. In an exposé of the landscape (serving the function of detailing its dangerous and treacherous nature), Captain Macdonald describes the scenery in minute detail. What makes this interesting are the constant references to the territory being unmapped[43], yet Captain Macdonald is able to give an expansive description. And while he focusses on the people who have gone mad due to thirst after being stranded on the Skeleton Coast, Mark's reaction to the Geinas mountains is highly paradoxical: "'Moses viewing the promised land!'" (48). Although the Captain questions why anyone would want to go there, Mark responds with "'[f]or Malory's reason — "because it is there",'" (48). This exchange is revealing for a number of reasons.

Firstly, the danger of the Skeleton Coast is made central through it being unmapped as well as its unyielding terrain. This is supported, but also contrasted, by the fact that the territory has not been surveyed, allowing two things: it allows the territory to remain 'empty', unknowable, and therefore something that can be explored and infused with

---

[42] The rock painting mentioned here is called "The White Lady" which has been identified as a UNESCO World Heritage Site.
[43] "A 4,000 foot cliff beyond, we had decided were the Geinas mountains, but it was impossible to fix them for the Kaokoveld had never been surveyed" (48).

potential. This is clearest in Mark's exclamation that it is "promised land", a biblical reference but also a rhetorical device employed in the Afrikaner treks. Further, it opens up the territory to be filled with metropolitan signs, beginning with naming, mapping, and territorialising the space. This territorialisation takes the form of placing state authority into the space and thus exercising control over it. According to Captain Macdonald, this has already been achieved. The initial, powerful, authority is the state itself through the implementation of an "invisible border" (45) and secondly, by placing an official within this territory. He is responsible for the airstrip at a place called Ohopoho, the "administrative 'capital'" of the Skeleton Coast. This barren, unforgiving territory is thus included in, and extends, the state control of space – from as far as South Africa. Moreover, Mark's reference to Mallory's "because it is there" is a colonial fantasy in its purest form. Although Captain Macdonald questions the reference to the "promised land", the consumption of the landscape is justified through the argument "because it is there", i.e. it does not belong to anyone (yet) and can therefore be appropriated.

These attitudes point to an apartheid fantasy of *white*-dominated spaces. The whole of the Skeleton Coast is supposedly uninhabited, except by the administrator and two communities of local inhabitants, namely the "wild ~~Bushmen~~" and the "~~Strandlopers~~ (Walkers of the Beach)" (45). However, they are not further discussed, except in reference to their place within the racial hierarchy. The ~~Strandlopers~~ are briefly described as "believe[d] to be almost the lowest type of living man closest to the 'missing link'", while "[t]heir stink is worse than any wild animal" (45). It seems that the narrator could just as well be Jacobus Coetzee, who uses similar language to describe and discuss the ~~Hottentot~~ in his narrative. The colonial can thus be found to live on in the apartheid era. The two societies become part of the history of the landscape while their entrance into the 'now-and-here' is prohibited. Not only does the 'empty space' impose a certain timelessness onto the ~~Bushmen~~ and ~~Strandlopers~~, it puts temporal distance between the two 'explorers' and their objects of study. Jacobus Coetzee does something similar when he attributes timelessness *and* spacelessness to the ~~Hottentot~~[44]. Added to the fact that Mark and Captain Macdonald are armed with an array of modern technology (guns, a Jeep, binoculars, a compass), they are strongly contrasted with the ~~Bushmen~~ and ~~Strandlopers~~. This disavowal of the original inhabitants of this space, coupled with the desire to occupy and enter into the space, is indicative of apartheid mechanics. The Skeleton Coast is consumed, filled, and navigated via metropolitan technologies, embedding *white* desires onto the space. Possible dangers

---

[44] "The Hottentot is locked in the present. He does not care where he comes from or where he is going." (57–58).

and disruptions are overcome by operating with imperial language, references, and technologies, the map being the most powerful tool.

The maps (or lack thereof) of the territory further define the emptiness of the sea[45] and desert. Although it is mentioned that the Skeleton Coast has yet to be charted, and that most information concerning the space comes from crazed sailors who were lost in the terrain, Captain Macdonald is still quite knowledgeable about the territory. He is able to discuss multiple entry points into the Skeleton Coast, has knowledge concerning the people who live there, and is able to locate and identify a number of landmarks. He and Mark are able to enter the territory via their available technologies and are able collect information. This 'mental map', i.e. the map Captain Macdonald has drawn up in his head, is contrasted by a number of actual maps. The first to be mentioned is the map Macdonald manipulates in his favour. Here the idea of maps as a source of truth and objectivity is dismantled, especially as it is referred to as a 'masterpiece' by John Garland. Garland points to the artificial nature of maps and their contested role as a tool of knowledge production and control. This is also very much due to the specific language of maps, as they are mostly closed off to the characters that do not know how to decipher the map's code. Again, I am referring to the 'masterpiece' map the Captain has drawn. Although it is a falsification, its recognisable but distinct code is incomprehensible to Constable Venter. Not only is he apparently unable or unwilling to decode maps, he is reliant on the testimony of Captain Macdonald as well as Garland. This testimony is taken as the absolute truth compared to the potential testimonies of the crew members, who would contradict what the map and Captain Macdonald would present. The 'masterpiece' map itself is, however, the falsification of information of further, older maps. In this sense, previous data is reconfigured in order to produce a new 'truth'. The old maps are manipulated as a means to both hide, disorientate, and distract.

A final point I want to make concerning maps in the narrative is the role of ownership. The maps mentioned are always linked to a producer or to an owner. Captain Macdonald and his grandfather, Simon Peace, are both involved in the processes and power structures of map making. Their activity is one in which knowledge and space are continuously being produced. However, their spaces ultimately are exclusive and personal. Their maps function in tandem with their personal histories and can be seen to be artefacts linking the current generation (Macdonald) to a prior one (Simon Peace). The map as a link is further developed when one considers them to be a narrative tool: Captain Macdonald

---

[45] "I had ruled the South Atlantic off into tight little squares. I had plotted the position where the *Dunedin Star* had first been rent under water; I had patrolled day and night, night and day. For weeks I had not even seen a ship. There was, in fact nothing." (87)

can trace Simon Peace's movements along the coast and can imagine the story of his grandfather's adventures. This is a direct link to the explorer who rids the map of its blank spaces, filling it with details and facts. The emptiness of space is filled in the abstract through the expansion of knowledge, and infused with the subjectivity of desires[46]. The map in the 1959 version is a great example: without Captain Macdonald's efforts and mapmaking skills, Curva dos Dunas would still remain 'undiscovered', a fact which the reader helps in preventing through his/her engagement with the supplementary sketch at the beginning of the book.

b) "The Narrative of Jacobus Coetzee"

On the other hand, Jacobus Coetzee does not necessarily encounter an 'empty' landscape. However, he empties it, only referencing the landmarks and markers he decides are important for his movement from the south to the north, across the river. The importance of natural markers necessary for orientation is central to his mission, as no officially produced maps for his sanctioned journey exist. He is forced to recognise the markers that help him to orientate himself and his journeymen in an alien landscape. Furthermore, because he is the 'leader' of the group, he must also provide for everybody. Navigation is thus vital in achieving his initial goal of hunting elephants as well as making sure that his crew and the cattle are fed and looked after[47] so that he can pursue this goal. Jacobus Coetzee is only able (or willing) to include topographic features in his travelogue, mentioning the rivers and the mountains he passes, as well as the length of the passing. At one point, he does mention an abandoned Namaqua *kraal*, but this is left uncommented as well as undescribed. It is only once he is 'lost' in the landscape (lost physically and psychologically[48]), that it becomes central to him. Although I will discuss this scene in more detail when I discuss the *white* male explorer, it should suffice for now that this dislocation allows the landscape to enter the protagonist – and vice versa. The landscape becomes littered with markers that allow him to locate himself in this unexplored space. The Namaqua help him in achieving this but it is through their believed difference and their implied inferiority.

---

[46] The most obvious in this case being the location and possession of "Curva dos Dunas", a privately owned island.
[47] Derek Maus, in "Kneeling before the father's wand" (1999) discusses J.M. Coetzee's male characters exhibiting the tendency to see themselves as father figures, a trope which J.M. Coetzee himself discusses when linking the Afrikaner settler to the soil and to his farm workers.
[48] The landscape is initially produced on a topographic level with its effect/affect on the protagonist unmentioned. This changes when Jacobus Coetzee 'becomes' the landscape and everything in it. His orientation is not linked to certain landmarks anymore, but via his fusion with his environment.

Not only does Coetzee invoke Christian rhetoric[49] in order to position himself as an authority vis-à-vis the Namaqua[50], but also always in connection with the landscape. The fact that he decides to meet them on horseback, looking "like a god, a god of the kind they did not yet have" (71) highlights his privileged position on both a spatial and a symbolic level. This is due to his elevation (looking down from his horse) and the understanding of his unique status in the exchange (being the first *white* person). The horse also serves to underline his superior presence, as Jenny Calders argues (1976:103): "If the horse is an intrinsic part of the Western, and of the epic, he is also a highly important feature of historical fiction of all kinds…If the hero is on a horse he is half way towards convincing the reader of an irresistible manliness." (quoted in Haarhoff, 1991:177). While Coetzee is only partially able to reproduce himself in the empty landscape, it is the initial meeting with his 'Other' that he is finally able to establish himself and his metropole outside of the set colonial borders.

Furthermore, it is the 'Other' which confirms Coetzee's belief in his own supremacy while confirming the prejudices he has formed about this 'Other', first verbalised in the opening sequence of his narrative. His utterance "I cursed the Hottentots for their improvidence. They cultivated no grain" (84) reflects the selective colonial blindness to the cultural practices of what was deemed a primitive people: their absence of agricultural activity[51]. This absence, a locked-in feature of pastoral literature, usually forms the basis of appropriating land in order to 'make use of it properly'[52]. The fact that activities other than agricultural form the earth and the landscape seem to be secondary[53]. Activities concerning and involving the landscape take a number of guises, of which agriculture is only one. Although it is a material, productive, and visual engagement with the landscape, it only reflects one possible arrangement with the environment. What appears to be uncul-

---

[49] The *Encyclopedia of Nationalism* includes Judeo-Christian ideology as a central component in the establishment of Afrikaner/Boer nationalism (2001:5). This allows for a comparison between the Boers and the Jews (in form of expulsion and finding the promised land). This forms a strong link to the concepts of the *trek* but also incorporates the idea of suffering into the history of the Afrikaner people. Jacobus Coetzee uses Christian terms such as "destiny", "guilt", while making his way to "Golgotha", the place where Christ was crucified.

[50] He imagines this on two levels. Firstly, his position on his horse makes him look "like a god" (71). On a second level he styles himself as a fatherly authority after his "schoolmasterly threat" (70).

[51] This was already discussed in the Colonial Chapter in respect to similar assertions made by the First Lieutenant (*Peter Moor*) and Dirich Dierksen (*Heim Neuland*). Agriculture can thus be interpreted as a marker of *whiteness*, creating distance to the perceived agricultural 'inactivity' of the Africanist characters.

[52] This is a point Haarhoff (1991:136) makes.

[53] Ingold (1993) makes two points concerning the landscape and human interaction within it: "First, human life is a process that involves the passage of time. Second, this life-process is also the process of formation of the landscapes in which people have lived." (152).

tivated space is the foundation of a specific society which impresses its specific spatial (and thus cultural) expression onto the landscape. This emptied landscape, one in which the soil is not 'appreciated' by the original inhabitants, becomes the engine which empowers colonial, and then apartheid land-grabbing rhetoric.

Technologies of Conquest and Domination

a) *A Twist of Sand*

Namibia is often referred to as "the land between two deserts" due to the Kalahari and Namib Desert, both being part of Namibia. Gerson Uaripi Tjihenuna's Poem, "Cry The Land Between Two Deserts"[54] pays tribute to this fact. More recently, it has been incorporated in order to also refer to the long, dry coastline which borders on most of the Namib. Although this understanding of the extreme environments making up a large part of the Namibian landscape was only verbalized or constructed after Jenkins' novel was published, he uses exactly these two prominent features of the Namibian landscape as his setting. Throughout the history of this political space (from the harshness of the Skeleton Coast to the controlled access to the *Speergebiet*), the ocean and the desert have always had a complex symbiosis[55]. The uncountable stranded sailors and seamen who had the unwanted fate of being stranded at the Skeleton Coast faced two threats: drowning or dying of thirst. The ocean and the desert, environments that are seemingly designed to kill people, thus become arenas in which survival itself is the ultimate achievement. Survival in these environments become a testament to one's ability to weather and withstand the worst which nature is able to construe[56]. So, instead of fighting both environmental *and* human agents (like Peter Moor), the adventurer must now face only nature – and her most extreme elements. Because of this shift in 'enemy', there needs to be a shift in technologies of conquest and domination. Armed with basic supplies and an able guide, Dr. Stein is unimpressed with the supposed dangers of the Skeleton Coast. The reason for this is his confidence in his resources, especially his gun, a tool he expects to make his expedition significantly easier. At one point after traversing a small mountain range, this becomes clear when he downplays the dangers of the Skeleton Coast:

---

[54] In: Henning Melber *It Is No More A Cry: Namibian Poetry in Exile.* (1982).
[55] A look at the life cycles and food chains that are contained within this environment show how strongly they are connected.
[56] I would argue that according to this novel, after the subjugation of the original inhabitants, nature is restored as being the main threat to the explorer-adventurer.

> "The Skeleton Coast has a reputation and everyone who comes here builds it up, until the whole thing is a mumbo-jumbo of superstition. When someone fails through his own lack of foresight, he adds still another legend to the Skeleton Coast. We've broken it wide open. It's straight-forward going. Nothing of it". He looked at me quizzically. "Not much in the way of navigation required, is there, Captain Peace?" (223).

Testaments of survival are relegated to the supernatural, even the superstitious. He also argues that these testaments flow into a larger narrative of myth, one that he is suspicious about *because* he has been able to survive in it so easily. Considering that he does not survive the Skeleton Coast could be the punishment for his hubris. This overconfidence is repeated when the group encounters a pride of Cape Lions. Dr. Stein decides to shoot all of them – a plan he then abandons because of their sheer numbers. It becomes clear that the threats of the ancient, timeless environment are countered by the introduction of modern technologies, of which the gun and the compass appear to be the most important and potent.

Captain Macdonald also has quite an arsenal of these technologies at his disposal. First and foremost, one must focus on his experience as a maritime navigator. Although there is no information concerning Captain Macdonald's career as a commander of a military submarine, there are numerous indicators that he is of a maritime lineage. This is due to his grandfather, Simon Peace, having been a sailor as well as a fantastic mapmaker. Captain Macdonald becomes strongly linked to the sea, having a direct patrilineal connection to its exploration. Furthermore, Simon Peace does not only bequeath his grandson an unlocatable island in highly dangerous waters, but he includes in his gift detailed maps and charts of the surrounding area. One can thus deduce that much of what Captain Macdonald knows and has learned is as a direct consequence of his grandfather's involvement on the seas. Captain Macdonald is therefore able to improve on his grandfather's initial findings, while using his charts and maps as a foundation on which to produce his own maps and charts.

Captain Macdonald's relationship to the sea is constructed around two strong pillars. First, his family has a history of exploring and charting the sea and its coasts. He is destined (whether as a descendent or even genetically[57]) to live a life upon the open waters. The decision to sail ships and command submarines is taken as a tacit, innate decision, a decision that is based on the familial link to the sea. This would also explain Captain Macdonald's extensive and intimate knowledge of all things concerning the ocean. Ancestry and forefathers play a large part in the makeup of the explorer-adventurer. This is

---

[57] At one point this biological link to the sea is commented upon when Hendricks is talked about. Garland comments that Hendricks' life on the ocean is down to his Malay ancestry, a people who "love the sea" (1959:38).

in stark opposition to the 'ideal' Afrikaner, and therefore the ideal element of apartheid fantasies. Captain Macdonald is not linked to the soil, but to the sea. He is presented as an international subject, at home in the wide spaces of the world and not tied down to a specific place – but rather a space: the maritime. Captain Macdonald is, however, still a persuasive figure within apartheid rhetoric as he is able to unify a number of elements of Afrikaner nationalism. These would include the inscription of his family history into the various landscapes (in the form of Simon Peace's name as well as the use of his maps), the cordoning off of his history and space to 'foreigners' (women, People of Colour, Europeans, the authorities), the monumentalisation and documentation of his quest (the wreckages of the NP I and the *Phyleria*, the produced maps/logs/charts), and finally, the 'sanitation' of his space (the (violent) removal of those who are not part of the space).

Captain Macdonald is able to improve on Simon Peace's notations and 'discoveries' by making use of technological advances. The submarine, which he commands during the Second World War and during his chase of NP 1, allows him to enter into spaces closed off to Simon Peace's comparatively primitive sailing boat. Of course, this makes Simon Peace's achievements even more spectacular, especially since he dies due to old age and not on the high seas. This serves as a template for Captain Macdonald to achieve great things, especially since he is armed with his grandfather's knowledge. The dangerous space of the Skeleton Coast is blunted, having been charted and explored and because this knowledge has been passed on to the following generations. One must also consider that there is no mention of Captain Macdonald's father. The link to the sea and its explorers is quite old, while erasing or ignoring the direct connection between the old and the new.

And yet this missing link has no bearing on Captain Macdonald's belonging to the open seas[58]. His relationship to the seas is further cemented through his ability to command various seafaring vessels. Firstly, he is the commander of the submarine *Trout*, on which he and his crew celebrate numerous military triumphs. This leads to the High Command of the British naval war effort giving him a top-secret mission. The mission is constructed so that Commander Peace's death, along with his whole crew, is considered a very likely reality instead of a possible outcome. Conversely, it would change, possibly end, the war. However, even if he survives this task, his position and role as a commander of the submarine will be discredited. His death, actual or professional, is the guaranteed result. And yet this does not deter his continued endeavours on the sea, driven by his inheritance and Simon Peace's maps and charts. Even after being discharged from the navy and relieved of his duties, he still follows the singular aim of possessing 'his' island. This

---

[58] Dr. Stein is happy to put as much distance between the captain and the sea, citing the latter's ability for using the sea to kill his enemies (210).

leads him to become the captain of the *Phyleria*, a private vessel of a Greek businessman. And again it is his obsession with his inherited island, coupled with his deep connection to the ocean, that create the conditions for him attaining an immense treasure, even if it belongs to someone else.

Although the ship he manipulates in order to acquire the highly desirable diamonds is barely sea-worthy, he is still able to manoeuvre it through the dangerous waters of the Skeleton Coast. A tragic (or advantageous) change in the currents sinks the *Phyleria* along with its crew of twenty-seven (Macfadden is safe on the lifeboat with his captain), but it also hides the intentions of Captain Macdonald, and more importantly his deed. This allows him to reset his life, progressing from Commander Peace (who is presumed dead along with the crew) to Captain Macdonald. The stolen diamonds then provide the necessary capital Captain Macdonald needs in order to purchase his own ship with which to complete the charts his grandfather has left him. The purchase of the *Etosha* becomes the final stepping stone in a) locating his personal island, and b) the transformation from a relatively disgraced submarine commander to an inconspicuous captain of an inconspicuous fishing trawler. The ship also adds to Captain Macdonald's performance, which is of the highest concern for his personal mission as well as the regulation of his past. The first indication of this regulation – which is of course connected to his mission – is first revealed when he tries to hide his charts from his first mate, John Garland, but then involves him to a certain extent.

Initial suspicions of Captain Macdonald's character are further augmented in the scene involving Sergeant Venter. The interview takes place on the *Etosha*. Here the captain reveals that he is not who he is initially introduced as. The brief episode begins with the words "Now was the time for my act, carried out whenever I came to port" (29), complete with a fake birthplace ("Parys", 31), and the acquisition of both a South African English accent (29) and Afrikaans (31). He has thus not only started appropriating South African spaces (the Skeleton Coast, the seascape off the Skeleton Coast), he has produced *white* South Africanisms in order to conceal his true (British) identity. The interaction with Sergeant Venter also reproduces the idea of *white* fraternity within a space of *white* authority[59]. The social act of drinking is introduced into an accident report involving the death of a Black person. Conversationally, the death of the Black crewmember takes up as much time as Captain Macdonald's lies, while an atmosphere of camaraderie is created. The focus on what it means to be Afrikaans (birthplace, accent, language) also

---

[59] Constable Venter meets the highest ranking officers of the Etosha, Captain Macdonald, John Garland, and Macfadden.

points to the porous boundaries between what was officially considered Afrikaans[60] and membership of this group. The death of the crewmember is used to form bonds of *whiteness*. The *Etosha* is and remains the space of a number of *white* bonds, reproducing a mostly European and artificial South African safe space.

It should be now clear that the captain and his ship are a dangerous combination, and they both rely heavily on each other. Not only does Captain Macdonald need the *Etosha* to locate his island, he also needs it as cover in order to maintain his façade. *Etosha* needs her captain in order to complete both its superficial function as a fishing trawler, but also to navigate the dreaded waters off the Skeleton Coast. However, this relationship is not complete without the most powerful tool of conquest, namely the map and its auxiliaries[61]. As the narrative reveals, the map appears in and is supported by various forms and guises. Firstly, the narrative differentiates between what is deemed official and that which is unofficial. The first chapter points to this extremely relevant distinction, especially as the former is strongly linked to the law. Next to his pile of logs (recorded by various ships), is a map Captain Macdonald himself has drawn up. John Garland praises the unofficial map as a masterpiece (12), especially for "a coast which has never been mapped, or never surveyed" (ibid.). Captain Macdonald is shown to be able to produce (and manipulate) the space/s along the coast, using official records in order to confuse those who are unfamiliar with the reading of maps, charts and their language. This group includes Sergeant Venter[62] and his crew[63]. By giving Captain Macdonald this kind of power, the narrative forms a character who is equipped to successfully tame the Skeleton Coast.

He is a performer armed with a ship which is capable of more than just its fishing, with maps more exact than their official counterparts, and an audience which is not as qualified to read and interpret these maps. The most overt description of maps as a source of power is when Captain Macdonald employs Simon's maps during the sinking of the *Phyleria*. His words to Mac sum up a large portion of imperialism's fascination with maps and their use: "'See that chart? …That's a murder weapon, Mac.'" (156). The development and deployment of maps has had a large impact on the history of imperialism, summa-

---

[60] Afrikaner-ness was constructed around a number of ideas. These included the history linked to South Africa and its soil, its social status through the mechanics of apartheid, its detachment from Europe (as a metropolitan centre), and its exclusive relationship to other Europeans and People of Colour. The purely Afrikaner town of Orania, in the Northern Cape of South Africa, is an example of the concentration of all these points in one space.

[61] A map of the Namibian coast is included in the 1959 edition, with an inset revealing Curva dos Duna's location.

[62] "'I don't understand that sort of thing. I wouldn't know how even to write it down. Tell me something simple, just for the report'" (31).

[63] "'They could swear blind that they'd [members of the crew] seen dry land, but John and I could prove beyond any doubt that they were talking nonsense'" (Macdonald to Macfadden, 32).

rised by Barnard (2007), commenting on the discipline of geography: "maps, boundaries, the naming of places – indeed, the discipline of geography itself – is scarcely separable from the imperial project" (5)[64]. The plethora of available maps (constituting varying forms and degrees of knowledge productions) is caricatured in a later scene. In this way, the production of abstract space becomes a complex, even flawed undertaking, one that is easily manipulated and difficult to maintain.

This happens when Captain Macdonald, claiming that "maps have always fascinated me" (173), is confronted with a map of the Skeleton Coast in the possession of Dr. Stein, which he is not familiar with. In an ironic twist, Dr. Stein answers the Captain's "I've never seen this map before" with "I'm glad there are some maps of the Skeleton Coast which you haven't seen, Captain Peace. As a matter of interest, you can get this one for five shillings from the Trigonometrical Survey Office in Pretoria" (173). Captain Macdonald is surprised by an official, readily available map, one that is produced and kept at the central place of apartheid power, Pretoria. The reliance on 'personal' maps, always positioned as more trustworthy than their official counterparts, is briefly disrupted. However, once Captain Macdonald has taken a closer look, his distrust becomes apparent: "God help anyone who took this official map for his guide!" (174). The 'personal' map is again established as the proper instrument of navigation, relegating the official map to a supportive role. The maps produced by official state institutions, apparently inaccurate and incomplete, are continually undermined. The state's ability to produce any abstract space is mirrored by Captain Macdonald (and Simon Peace) through the act of mapping. He can produce more accurate maps, manipulate them, or uncover things undetected by the state. This allows him to constantly move outside of the law, an ability that lets him murder and steal without much consequence.

b) "The Narrative of Jacobus Coetzee"
While *A Twist of Sand* is filled – and based upon – with the successful manipulation of specific technologies linked to maritime navigation (ship, map, log, weapons), "The Narrative of J.M. Coetzee" has a rich focus on the technologies of the 'frontier', of which the gun and the ox-wagon are the clearest examples[65]. It should be mentioned, that it is Jacobus Coetzee who is always armed, and who discusses in great length the contribution of the gun's violence to the creation/production/maintenance of history. Furthermore, the gun is also part of the explorer's self-definition, linking its fantastic abilities to a specific identity:

---

[64] This is an echo of what Said (1993:7) had already proposed.
[65] Haarhoff (1991) discusses these technologies in the Chapter 1 of *The Wild South-West*, in which both gun and ox wagon play highly prominent roles.

> The gun stands for the hope that there exists that which is other than oneself. The gun is our last defence against isolation within the travelling sphere. The gun is our mediator with the world and therefore our saviour. The tidings of the gun: such-and-such is outside, have no fear. The gun saves us from the fear that all life is within us. It does so by laying at our feet all the evidence we need of a dying and therefore a living world. I move through the wilderness with my gun at the shoulder of my eye and slay elephants, hippopotami, rhinoceros, buffalo, lions, leopards, dogs, giraffes, antelope and buck of all descriptions, hares, and snakes; I leave behind me a mountain of skin, bones, inedible gristle, and excrement. All this is my dispersed pyramid to life. (79).

The gun takes on a sacred, Christianised form, as "saviour" as well as 'proof' of life through death. It also has a material function, turning the hunted animals back into their basic elements (skin, bones) and returning them to the earth (excrement). The violence of Jacobus Coetzee's syntax, concentrated in the near endless list of hunted animals and the endless repetition of the word "gun" is indicative of the protagonist's proclivity for violence and its realisation through the instrument of the gun. This technology not only affects the hunted animals (a process heavily linked to colonialism and, more currently, land appropriation for game and hunting farms), but the people he will kill (and possibly has killed). Hunting ~~Hottentot~~ was already discussed in detail in the first part of his narrative and will foreshadow his violent return to the encampment – with more 'hunters' and 'provers of life'.

The ox-wagon's role, the second important technology, is twofold: firstly, it is used as a mobile home, which allows the appropriation of outside spaces from the safety of a protected and moveable dwelling. In essence, the inhabitant of an ox-wagon is both 'unsettled' and settled, both independent and fixed. As was the case with Etta and Dirich, for example, the ox wagon granted them a number of luxuries such as trade, meal preparation, protection from the elements, and a secure location to consume and own the landscape. Secondly, the ox-wagon allows for the transport and consumption of metropolitan products, whether as a sign of 'civilization' (making coffee, sanitary products, sleeping comforts), or as commodities used in trade and wealth acquisition. The 'intrusion' into the ox wagon by the Namaqua also signals an intrusion into the commercial space of the metropole. This prompts Jacobus Coetzee to shoot, to exert his authority, and to attempt to control the situation. In this scene, wagon and gun are inextricably linked.

These two technologies thus represent – and make – the frontiersman/frontiersmen, whether as travelling individuals (as in the case of Jacobus Coetzee), or as a settler society (as in the case of the Thirstland Trekkers and the Great Boer Trek). Much of Afrikaner mythology involving the Great Trek as well as the Thirstland Trekkers is dependent on these two machines of exploration/expansion and survival. The concept of the *laager* became more and more important as the *trekboere* moved further away from the metropole and into territories inhabited by societies such as the !Xhosa and the Zulu. The battles for resources culminated in full-out wars, with the Boers largely outnumbered. This had the effect that the defensive strategy of forming a circle with the ox wagons came to form the backbone of any military strategy. This tactic was later used as a metaphor in which the Afrikaner nation – with the help of its apartheid laws and *white*-owned resources – isolated itself from the Black population as well as the international community. The *white* spots were organised like a *laager*, with laws and statutes employed as guns. This *laager* mentality is also manifest in the "we-versus-everybody" rhetoric used by the National Party in its disputes with the UN, as well as the neighbouring African states. The ox wagon remained a contemporary instrument of dominance, if only on a symbolic or metaphorical level.

But it is not only the physical instruments that offer Jacobus Coetzee his imagined superiority. The first 'instrument' that gives him safety, security, and the confidence in his mission, is the permit handed to him by the Cape Colony. This bureaucratic act gives him the authority to defend himself against those who might do him harm, while he has the backing of the Cape Colony in the case of an emergency. This would imply that a larger authority than himself would deal with the Namaqua in case of any accident, a scenario that is fulfilled considerably by the events at the end of his second return. It is this form of 'safety net' which Captain Macdonald is initially offered[66], but which is later denied in order to protect the higher-ups involved. Furthermore, this permission (which is granted from an outside authority, and not initially by the Namaqua), gives Coetzee access to the resources he encounters on his trip, such as grazing and water.

The protection allows him to inscribe himself and the colony into the new spaces through the imperial act of naming. Just like Captain Macdonald, this ability (acquired by the movement through unexplored and unmapped space) leaves behind the traces of *white* 'discovery', overwriting previous histories and discoveries. It also creates the conditions for inclusion/exclusion. As Clarkson (2008[67]) argues, "if the act of naming calls a world into being, it does so insofar as there is a taxonomic pact *amongst those who speak the language.*" (emphasis in original, 133). The Namaqua, who are not socialised in Afrikaans, but who have already been named and 'explained scientifically' (according to their appearance, the setup of the camp, their eating habits, social make up, etc.) cannot participate in the defining of their space. The Cape Colony gives itself the authority to

---

[66] After receiving his mission, Captain Macdonald is told by his superiors that "[t]he whole South Atlantic is yours" (75), and that "*Trout* will have a free rein anywhere in any port in the free world" (77).

[67] "Remains of the Name" in: De Lange et al. (2008:125–162).

send its own subject into the unknown under the auspice of hunting. This subject in turn begins to 'civilise' this unknown, planting the seeds of the metropole on the edges of its own borders. Finally, this subject returns with relevant information and knowledge, such as topography, geography, and ethnography and expands on the Cape Colony's ability to produce and disseminate this newly acquired knowledge.

Again connecting Jacobus Coetzee's ox wagon to Captain Macdonald's ship, one can observe the 'safe space' function of this technology. The ox wagon is constructed as a space which can be controlled and which allows a withdrawal from the threatening elements (sun, sand, night). This space is, however, intruded upon by the Namaqua when they begin taking tobacco. Jacobus Coetzee responds to this trespass with the threat of violence, employing his gun in order to recreate order.

> The Hottentots had fallen back in little clumps and were staring at us. I rode out to warn them. "The first person who lays a hand on my wagon or my oxen I will shoot dead with this gun! This gun will kill you! Go back to your houses!" They looked back at me stonily. The crowd was growing larger. Even women with babies were drifting over now from the village. (74)

A moment later, after his threats are revealed to be impotent, he opens fire on the gathered crowd:

> Lifting my gun in one easy motion I fired into the ground at her [an approaching Namaqua woman] feet. There was no echo and barely any dust, but the woman screamed with fright and fell flat. The crowd turned tail. I left her untouched where she lay and turned to supervise the inspanning. At once she scrambled off.

These passages reveal the strong connection between the ox wagon (his property) and the gun (the tamer of the wild). Used in conjunction, Jacobus Coetzee is able to maintain his god-like status amongst the Namaqua by threatening violence in order to maintain his safe space. Once he is removed from this safe space, though, he is unable to reproduce his god-like status. He is forced to reconstruct his godly persona, concentrating his thoughts on the power of the gun completely and linking it to the act of gazing. The gun, disconnected from the safe space the ox wagon offered, is now employed as a subjugating instrument, transforming a threatening outside world into a safe space. In Jacobus Coetzee's feverish thought patterns, the gun is elevated to the sphere of world-making machinery. However, the gun is only able to fully realise its world making potential in the act of killing, organising incomprehensible signs. His initial goal of hunting elephants is expanded to include conquering the spaces he moves through. The gun does not only offer safety (which is also the main function of the ox wagon), but it gives its wielder the capacity to remodel an incomprehensible landscape into a comprehensible sign. This function of the gun is summed up when Jacobus Coetzee argues that he is "a hunter, a domesticator of the wilderness, a hero of enumeration" (80).

The ox wagon and gun are also instruments of knowledge production, making the endlessness of the hinterland an intelligible entity. By organising his expedition (first according to the landmarks, then through his narrative), he produces a space with recognisable signs. The metropole and its abundance of signs are used in order to orientate and navigate. This changes during his sojourn in the village as his forceful reproduction of metropolitan concepts (*whiteness*, cultural hierarchizing, the potency of his self-definition, and the definition of the 'Other') cannot be realised. His resultant violent return reproduces the conditions in the Cape Colony (replicating what was described and discussed at the beginning of his narrative). The violence of the gun plays a central role in the defining of relationships and is developed in conjunction with the mobile safe space of the ox wagon. The colonial conditions created in the Great Namaqualand reproduces the colonial knowledge concerning the artificial divide between *white* colonists and the Black societies they try to separate themselves from. The faith in the dominant role of history (a powerful tool for the production of knowledge and, later on, myth) connects the metropole with the space it is trying to incorporate and legitimises the violence of the gun on the Namaqua and the violence of the ox wagon on the landscape.

(De)Constructing the *White* Male Explorer

a) *A Twist of Sand*

Considering that the main character, Commander Peace/Captain Macdonald, wholly narrates *A Twist of Sand*, understanding the mechanics of the novel is inextricably linked to its main protagonist. Captain Macdonald, as a knowledgeable man and as a rational and logical ideal, represents in most parts a reliable and trustworthy narrative instance. There are sequences where this is ruptured[68], but the general tone of his narrative style tends to be supported by the facts and information supplied by the events themselves. This does not mean that Captain Macdonald is omniscient – far from it. He is not distracted by subjective impressions or emotions. Even when these do occur, there is a rationale behind them, recognisable only to the captain himself and the reader[69]. However,

---

[68] Captain Macdonald does have passages in which his recollection is missing, especially when he emerges from extreme situations, such as his near-death at the Skeleton Coast (245).
[69] He tries to rationalize the emergence of two suns at Skeleton Coast. Although Dr Nielsen is immersed in this spectacular event, Captain Macdonald tries to explain this phenomenon using oceanography, history and marine biology (216–217).

the consequence remains: the only access one has to the narrative and the produced spaces is through the character of Captain Macdonald. And as a result, this has the effect that he remains the only source of information, interpretation, and mitigation. He becomes the sole agent of spatial production, of spatial interpretation. Like Peter Moor, he is the regulator and controller of the narrative, especially of the objects/matters included and excluded. Inclusion and exclusion in the narrative, relevant due to the period in which they occur as well as the space in which they are placed or removed, are vital in understanding the construction of, and construction by, the *white*, male explorer.

As the story progresses – achronologically[70] – it becomes clear that fisherman Captain Macdonald is not who he claims to be. He controls his own history (only one other person has access to this) and can therefore control his future[71]. Discharged due to a secret mission he received during World War Two, Captain Macdonald leaves his native England to look for "something to do with an old man I saw die" (14). Not only does he keep secret why his crew and he are in the location they are in, he keeps his past hidden from everybody. This allows him to mask his intentions and further allows him to deceive the authorities and those close to him. And while he is able to keep his own history secret, the sea helps him to obscure his crimes. Even when his past catches up with him, the sea makes sure that this does not happen permanently. However, the reader is slowly informed about Macdonald's character as the narrative and dangerous situations evolve. In an ironic twist, the name of the man who sinks a super U-boat and single-handedly saves the world is Geoffrey *Peace*. In light of his further actions and crimes, this name becomes more of a pun.

Furthermore, history is used as a tool to isolate Captain Macdonald from the other characters. His is the only character who is given an expansive history, evident in his two personas as well as his extensive travels across vast spaces. One could argue that it is his extensive connection to a number of spaces that actually allow this history to exist. His character is therefore deeply spatial in contrast to everybody else. His travels (i.e. moving in time through memory and via his vessels) are told from his perspective only, doubly guaranteeing his control over his own history. This places his narrative over any other narratives as these only feed into his. When Dr. Nielsen shares aspects of her own person (169–170) this only serves to explain herself to the Captain. Her history has a use-function for the protagonist only; it is not relevant for further events. Even Johann's biography is used in order to link Captain Macdonald to his own past. Killing Johann finally buries

---

[70] Certain chapters (Chapter 4, 5, 6, 7, 8, 9) are flashbacks and memories. They follow their own time and only appear in the actual narrative as story-within-a-story and as spectres of Captain Macdonald's past.

[71] 'Mac' Macfadden is a further character who knows certain parts of Macdonald/ Peace's history, but his knowledge is limited, and only due to his complicity in stealing the diamonds.

that past. His secrets, buried in his various pasts, remain intact while his knowledge of other characters constantly increases. Knowledge thus becomes *the* form of power for the Captain, a power that is spatially generated and controlled.

The novel's narrator is a first-person narrator who is introduced as the captain of a fishing vessel. From the outset it becomes clear that he is involved in illegal actions. What also becomes apparent is that the captain is a type of explorer. When asked where they are by his second-in-command, John Garland, during an oceanic eruption off the Skeleton Coast, he mentions "Gamatom", the "native name I gave a high pointed mountain ashore" (16). This small passage reflects a similar attitude taken up by Jacobus Coetzee (who named the Great River – now the Orange River –, a town which he called Warmbad, as well as giving the giraffe its Afrikaans name). It reveals that he is the first European person to chart and map an area that is historically inhabited by others. He names further landmarks, "Inyala Hill" (20) and "Diaz' Thumb" (ibid.). Inyala Hill "doesn't have a name on the chart", while Diaz' Thumb can't be found on the chart either (20). This allows for a navigation only known to Captain MacDonald while keeping those without this knowledge outside of the navigational process. The crew is constantly kept in a disorientated state, stated most clearly by a Kroo boy who exclaims, "Skipper, the compass cheats me!" (16). Naming the landmarks alienates everyone else from their orientating ability, while navigational instruments such as the compass lose their importance. The abstract spaces produced by Captain MacDonald in this instance are highly exclusionary while regulating access to physical space (the landscape, the coastline) as well the interpretation of space (naming). His navigational network overrides any official state-produced control over the coastline as well any other form of interaction with it.

The landscape and its markers are subjugated to the explorer's need for naming. The fact that he names one landmark "Diaz' Thumb" is also reflective of the fraternity of *whiteness* I have mentioned earlier. Diaz apparently did not see the "dark thing sticking out…despite having been here four hundred years before us" (20). Captain Macdonald retroactively places Diaz into the landscape by naming after him an object, unknown to him at the time. This receives a further dimension when one considers who Bartholomeu Diaz was: a Portuguese navigator who reached the shores of Namibia in 1488 – as the *first* European to do so. This European achievement is retroactively inscribed into the landscape by another European as a token of their maritime link. Another problematic naming takes place when Captain Macdonald navigates a rather tricky sandbank on the border between Namibia and Angola. Here he navigates the dangerous waters with the help of his grandfather's personal map. This leads him to name a rock formation after him, Simon's Rock. Here he inscribes not only his European descent into the landscape, he personalises it by referencing the original explorer of this area. He doubles his claim over the space, which he has inherited, by further inscribing his direct lineage into it. In this sense he is able to construct his own utopia by laying claim to the history of this area. First, through Diaz as the initial 'explorer' of this space, and then through Simon Peace by linking it to his family. Captain Macdonald, however, does not only name elements on land, but also those on the sea. Before the *Phyleria* sinks, he places it in a current, "'[t]he *Trout* current, I call it, just for old time's sake'" (155). This is just off his own private island. He has thus created a space he has produced, a place he is comfortable in, a place only he knows about and can control.

b) "The Narrative of Jacobus Coetzee"
Although *A Twist of Sand* offers numerous moments and opportunities to deconstruct the exploring male protagonist, "The Narrative of Jacobus Coetzee" is an exercise in exactly this deconstruction. The novella is set up in four parts, namely a translator's preface, the narrative itself, an afterword and a deposition. Jacobus Coetzee's original narrative takes place between 1760 and 1762. The publication date for *Dusklands*, which contains my primary text, is 1974, while the initial publication of the "narrative" (*Het relaas van Jacobus Coetzee, Janszoon*) is 1951. Also, the afterword, which is part of a lecture series, comes from the years 1934–1948. This construction already problematizes the narrative as a whole as it is translated from Dutch (by J.M. Coetzee) and then retroactively commented on by the historian and lecturer, Dr. S.J. Coetzee. These layers provide a kaleidoscope of different forms of interpretation of the protagonist as well as the periods in which the protagonist was placed. The strong ties accorded to the name (all contributors in the novella are called Coetzee) further complicate the narrative layers. Each generation has a strong subjective and personal connection to the original Coetzee as both S.J. Coetzee, and consequentially, J.M. Coetzee, are direct descendants of the name-giver of the Great River. Thus their contributions cannot simply be referred to as neutral offerings of historical nature.

Also, the three additional texts are all based on one original oral text and therefore there is a continual distancing of the initial document. 'Objective' distance is created through the reworking of the deposition, first by S.J. Coetzee, and then by J.M. Coetzee. Certain passages have been changed or omitted, words have been rewritten. Not only does this alter the first version of the narrative, but it adds a biased understanding of the account. This becomes evident when one starts comparing the various 'versions of the text', where the narrative itself contradicts both the afterword and the deposition[72].

---

[72] The initial exchange between Jacobus Coetzee and the Namaqua is peaceful, for example, while there is

One could therefore argue that the narrative is in fact the product of a fictionalised, manipulated history. It is from this position that one can begin to question how narratives function and how narrated events can be manipulated. By extension, historic narratives must consequently also be questioned, especially if they are produced via such complex processes and so subjectively. J.M. Coetzee, the translator, admits to making changes to the "original", albeit only to "restore two or three brief passages omitted by my father's edition and to reduce Nama words to the standard Krönlein orthography". The reader does not know what passages have been inserted or updated. The only thing that is known is the main premise of the travelogue.

What begins as a travel narrative ends up exposing a multitude of European fantasies focussing on understanding colonial space, 'Other' people, history, and power. The first ever meeting between Coetzee and the Namaqua – possibly the first contact between a *white* person and the Namaqua – starts peacefully. This changes however when the narrator positions himself, with the help of Christianity, as a god-like figure. He naïvely interprets his arrival as the arrival of some transcendental figure, a position he does his best to maintain, but one that is deconstructed and dismantled very quickly. But, it also gives an indication of further "gods" that might enter this space as well – once it has been cleared of resistance. What can be deduced from this is a mirroring of the initial assumptions that Europeans propagated when they started to move away from Europe and violently colonise foreign territories.

Christianity, with its plethora of coded symbols, became a great tool to inflate the understanding of his own, European identity while constructing that of the 'Other'. The identified lack in the endlessness of the African landscape is overcome through the employment of Christian ideology and iconography. Jacobus Coetzee's efforts in perpetuating his divine self-construction are at the core of his failed connection with the Namaqua. The focus on separating the world into Christian and non-Christian is indicative of its *white* organising potential. When this strategy fails, Christian organising potential is transferred to the gun, a "saviour" because it is "our mediator of the world" (79). In murdering the Namaqua, Jacobus Coetzee proves his theories to himself by creating history. History in this sense is his personal history placed into the larger context of *Weltgeschichte*, the gun being the instrument that makes this process possible. The divinity of the gun absolves him from his crimes as they are committed in order to extend *white* authority and cement the prevailing *white* Weltanschauung.

After the initial contact, and the cementing of difference, the narrator and his group spend the night at the campsite of the Namaqua. This is where he starts to become ex-

---

no mention of his second, violent return.

tremely sick and suffers from hallucinations. Although he positions himself as a rational and contemplative subject, his abstruse thinking patterns contradict this position:

> I was too weak to ride, perhaps too weak to shoot straight. My men bedded me down in the wagon with the gun at my side. I told them to have no fear, to keep to the open country, and continue northwards. They kicked oxen to their feet and harnessed them. We could make out our pursuers: thirty men, one mounted. The cattle shambled through the heat. If we stopped now they would not budge but would stand in their traces till they died. Held in position by Klawer I evacuated myself heroically over the tailgate, wondering whether the Hottentot wizards could divine my future form the splashes. A great peace descended upon me: the even rocking of the wagon, the calm sun on the tent. I carried my secret buried in me. I could not be touched. (74)

Even after he acknowledges that he is in a weak and vulnerable position ("too weak") and needs help in order to "evacuate" himself, he is still convinced of his privileged position ("I could not be touched"). He opposes his relegation to human status by positioning himself as a transcendental being that cannot become tangible and thus cannot be penetrated. During this, his second return, he is placed in a hut set aside for menstruating women. This mirrors the sick chief he visited previously as both figures are located in a space which is set aside for specific members of society. In Jacobus Coetzee's case, he is placed on the margins of the Namaqua community, plunging him into a deep crisis. The result of a fever as well, Coetzee contemplates his peripheral position in the social relations of the Namaqua and places this in the larger context of his role in an alternative history. He makes use of spatial metaphors so that he can gain access to a sign which remains outside of his comprehension.

> The African highland is flat, the approach of the savage across space continuous. From the fringes of the horizon he approaches, growing to manhood under my eyes until he reaches the verge of that precarious zone in which, invulnerable to his weapons, I command his life. Across this annulus I behold him approach bearing the wilderness in his heart. On the far side he is nothing to me *and I probably nothing to him*. On the near side mutual fear will drive us to our little comedies of man and man, prospector and guide, benefactor and beneficiary, victim and assassin, teacher and pupil, father and child. He crosses it, however, in none of the characters but as representative of that out there which my eye once enfolded and ingested and which now promises to enfold, ingest, and project me through itself as a speck on a field which we may call *annihilation* or alternatively *history*. He threatens to have a history *in which I shall be a term*. (emphasis mine, 80–81)

The inclusion in an alternate history, one in which he is not the narrator and therefore not able to control his reproduction as "a term" makes the production of history – annihilation – on his terms the only solution. By having been pushed to the bounds of a foreign society, Jacobus Coetzee reinstates himself in that society by subordinating it as part of his personal history. This allows the Namaqua entry into *Weltgeschichte* by being connected to a history maker, a supernatural one at that. He evacuates himself "heroically" (75) while being supported, he fouls his blankets with "pathetic bravado" (77), and is constantly fed and carried by those who are willing to help him. He has become a walking contradiction of his own definition. However, while he has lost control of his body and its functions, he starts to think and theorize about his place in the world and, more importantly, in history.

When we look at what Marais (1993[73]) refers to as the syntax of imperialism, the narrator seems extremely powerless. Marais argues that syntax of imperialism is "the subject of the narrative sentences is the explorer, the journey the verb, and African matter the direct object" (52). His only ability while in the hut is that of thinking, however incoherent it is. If the journey is the verb, Jacobus Coetzee has no action, and no object to force this upon. This is underlined through his 'sojourn' in the menstruating hut, where he is not only isolated from society, but is also at a point where he is not even part of that society. His resulting musings concerning history and his role in it become apparent when one contrasts these two attitudes. First, he invests the gun, his gun, with the ability to create history: "Every territory through which I march with my gun becomes a territory cast loose from the past and bound to the future" (80). This takes root in his arguments about the ability of the gun to make things countable and therefore understandable. His god-like powers therefore spring from his possession of a gun. Now that he is weak and vulnerable and without a gun, he fears that his historic relevance will die with him. "He [the savage] threatens to have a history in which I shall be a term". This fear is rooted in his fear that he is unable to control his history[74] (and by extension, the history of the journey). His position as the subject in the syntax of imperialism is threatened by his lack of the verb.

Once he is able to escape the camp once more with Klawer (his most loyal journeyman), he is again able reinvigorate his god-like powers. He becomes nature, he becomes the landscape. So it is through him that the nature and the landscape take shape.

> "I was alone. [...] Here I was, free to initiate myself into the nature. I yodelled, I growled, I hissed, I roared, I screamed, I clucked, I whistled; I danced, I stomped, I grovelled, I spun; I sat on the earth, I spat on the earth, I kicked it, I hugged it, I clawed it. Every possible copula was enacted that I could link the world to an elephant hunter armed with a bow and crazed with freedom after seventy days of watching eyes and listening ears." (95)

---

[73] "'Omnipotent Fantasies' of a Solitary Self: J.M. Coetzee's 'The Narrative of Jacobus Coetzee'" (1993).
[74] This is strongly contrasted to the figure of Captain Macdonald, who has a plethora of strategies of maintaining control over his own history.

Coetzee becomes the medium through which the world must be perceived (invoking Marais' title). Considering the first-person perspective this has obviously been the case anyhow, but it also turns the focus on how the narrator is positioned when first meeting the Namaqua people. Here it is firstly the narrator who is the medium, but secondly, it is his narrative as well that forces a one-dimensional perspective on the reader. The god-like powers that Jacobus Coetzee possesses – and by extension the colonial narrator in general – creates a world in which the Namaqua exist not because they exist, but because he exists. And because he narrates them and their world into being, it is he who can – or even must – destroy them in order for them to become history, and therefore become part of the world. As he puts it, "I am a tool of history" (106). He goes even further by asserting that "[t]hey [the people he left behind] died the day I cast them out of my head" (106). This is again reflective of his ability to narrate the world and its subjects into being and therefore giving him the capacity to define their impact on the narrative. The *white* explorer does not discover or uncover, he makes the world he sees and experiences. Once he has re-established his superior position by murdering the threats to this fragile identity, Jacobus Coetzee has retaken control of his world-making potential. The narrative elimination of the Namaqua is completed through their physical annihilation. This combination produces *white* history that is picked up by the metropole, transforming it into knowledge and its residue, myth.

5 The Namibian Moment: Learning to Sing

At the time of writing, Namibia has commemorated 29 years of independence, first from German colonial and then South African apartheid occupation. Although most African states were able to declare independence as early as the 1950s [1], Namibia had to wait roughly 30 further years to achieve full autonomy and self-rule. This was finally achieved through a complex network of national and international players. On a global level, this included the United Nations (mainly through resolutions and the involvement of member states) and the Western Contact Group (consisting of Canada, France, Germany, the United Kingdom, and the United States of America). They supported Namibian independence by putting diplomatic and economic pressure on South Africa and proposing solutions for a transition from illegal South African occupation to Namibian self-determination and self-governance. These efforts were reinforced through the work of socialist allies, most notably Cuba and, to a certain extent, Russia. The former was on-site during the Angolan civil war while the latter provided armaments, equipment, expertise, and training. Cuba also aided and trained the socialist MPLA (*Movimento Popular de Libertação de Angola*), allied with the PLAN (People's Liberation Army of Namibia) combat units. PLAN was led and organized by and around the South West African People's Organization (SWAPO) and was the military wing of the party. SWAPO was recognised by the UN as the official liberation movement of Namibia[2]. However, the influential Herero Chiefs Council (HCC) was not part of this dense network of actors, rather seeking diplomatic ends to the occupation. These efforts culminated in their participation at the Turnhalle Constitutional Conference (1976), under the leadership of Clemens Kapuuo, together with other traditional authorities of various local societies and denominations. The conference served as a minute compromise on behalf of the apartheid government, ensuring "that the South Africans retained some control over the territory" with Namibia remaining "a very broad defensive buffer between South Africa and the rest of Africa" (Wallace 2011:186). The two most prominent groups, SWAPO and the HCC, still focussed on the same goal: independence from South Africa. As should be clear from this dense conglomeration of external as well as internal forces and organs, and considering

---

[1] See for example "Ghana's Dubious Decolonization Distinction – The First Independent African Country" by Sitinga Kachipande (www.africaontheblog.com) in which the problematics of colonisation and foreign occupation are discussed in respect of dates of independence, especially concerning the first 'nations' to achieve this status.

[2] The UN declared SWAPO as the 'authentic representative of the Namibian people' (Wallace 2011:278), which was later revised as "sole and authentic representative" in 1976 (Wallace 2011: 382, note 19).

the different modes of activity, alliances, and contributions, emancipating Namibia from South African administration can broadly be deemed a global effort.

What this chapter will focus on is an 'in-house' view of the liberation struggle. By locating non-military moments of resistance, and establishing personal as well as collective imaginations of a freed country, I will not only point towards literature's liberating potential (especially if it is a product from 'within'), but also at its potential to dream a different dream, offering the opportunities of self-definition. Because the novels discussed in the previous chapters have a strong 'outward-looking-in'[3] dimension, the aim now is to change the trajectory of this look and produce an 'inward-looking-forward' analysis. Moving away from *white*, European writing, the source under examination is considered the first novel by a Black Namibian author[4]. Literature by Black Namibians about Namibia has of course existed before the publication of Joseph Diescho's novel *Born of the Sun* in 1988. However, this literature was usually either of lyrical nature (struggle or praise poetry; workers'/protest songs) or of non-literary nature (pamphlets/(auto-)biographies/diaries/political essays).

Fictional products had also been published, but these focussed mainly on oral myths and legends and were in many cases collected by Western anthropologists, ethnographers, or linguists and cannot be attributed to a single author or source. Chapman argues that the emergence of a Namibian literary tradition is rooted within the oral production of "the songs, stories and fables of the Bushman and Khoi" (22). In this sense, *Born of the Sun* takes up a unique position in the literary landscape and should be treated as such. The novel opens up a number of questions and investigations concerning Namibian history, individual understanding of concepts around independence, liberation, reconciliation, subjectivity, as well as the breaking up of binaries such as rural and urban, tradition and modernity, and most importantly, the individual and the collective. The timing of the novel (1988 can be considered a liminal period in Namibian history) allows the opportunity to look at how history can be employed in order to open up expectations of a common, inclusive future, even if that history is filled with oppression and violence.

Introduction to the Text

Because this chapter has a different build up compared to the colonial and apartheid chapters, the introduction to this novel will be more detailed. The reason for this is to open

---

[3] This would allow an entrance into questions of Namibian-ness, i.e. Black versus *white* Namibian dreams and future visions.
[4] Chapman (1995:25).

up a text that has so far been discussed to a limited extent – although it is attracting more interest as Namibian literature attracts more interest. Chapman was the first to place the text within an emerging Namibian national literary cannon. *Born of the Sun* makes a brief appearance in F. Abiola Irele's *The Cambridge Companion to the African Novel* (2009), being discussed within the 'subheading' of "Anti-colonialism: organized resistance movements: SWAPO and ANC" under the chapter heading "Protest and Resistance"[5]. The novel is placed within a larger time of "protest and resistance" in southern Africa. Harlow looks at the novel along the lines of its main themes, namely "the relation between labor protest and anti-colonial national liberation resistance" (56). A further examination of the novel is an article by Wolfram Hartmann, published in 1989[6]. However, due to material restraints I am unable to access this text. Diescho has also been discussed in reference to his post-independence work (*Troubled Waters*, 1992[7]), but he is now mostly known for his work within the socio-political sphere.

Born of the Sun follows the story of its main character, Muronga, during the nascent struggle years. With humble beginnings in a village in northern Namibia, the protagonist becomes politicized while working in a mine in the Transvaal, where he experiences the extensive power and reach of the South African apartheid regime. Muronga is the focaliser of the narrative, although the reader is given insights into certain elements that would be closed off to him, such as translations, feelings by other characters, and events that take place away from him. However, the bulk of the action is connected to Muronga, whether directly or indirectly, meaning that the events and occurrences take place within the vicinity of what Muronga can perceive or experience. This also means that he is the character who opens up the spaces of the narrative, either through his presence (such as his village, the mine compound, his jail cell), or through other means such as hearsay or memory (for example the village and Rundu). In essence, the narrative revolves around Muronga and his evolution from a background as a herder and family man to a participant in the liberation movement. It traces the sacrifices this requires of him in addition to the physical and mental tortures he has to endure at the hands of the apartheid regime and its operatives, both Africanist and *white*.

The novel is littered with historical allusions, hinting at the narrative period without fully pointing towards it. An example of this would be the mention of Botswana's ("Bechuanaland's") independence, as well as the mention of Malawi's ("Nyasaland's") president, Kamuzu Banda. These historical references are mixed with events open to interpre-

---

[5] This is the chapter by Barbara Harlow (51–68).
[6] The article appeared in *Logos* 9 (1) (1989).
[7] Most notably by Arich-Gerz (2008) in his chapter "Lucia aus Ovamboland", pp. 96–125.

tation. The most prominent illustration is the death of Archie Bokwe, who can easily be read as Steve Biko. I will return to this character and his funeral when discussing narrative spaces, focussing especially on spaces of resistance. What I can disclose is that a number of overlaps between the fictional character and historical persona are pronounced, most notably their deaths while incarcerated, their involvement in anti-apartheid politics, and their outspokenness. Another example is the organisation the Namibian mineworkers refer to, namely the United People's Organization. It does not take much to link it to SWAPO, especially since the acronym and their activities point strongly to this association. Further examples of specific historic references can be the introduction of certain laws as well as taxes (such which Muronga's village is informed about). The mention of SWANLA, the main labour resource institution also underlines the actuality of the narrative. The novel thus weaves together actual events and developments with fictionalised people and communities.

The novel begins in Muronga's village along the Kavango river, and the narrative moves along with him from there to Rundu, to Botswana, South Africa, and finally back to Botswana. Namibia (referred to as South West Africa by the protagonist) does not appear again once the main character crosses her borders. Certain spaces are repeated or reproduced nonetheless, with the mine compounds, jail, and transport vehicles the most frequent. Be that as it may, this does not mean that there is no return to his initial 'home'. This takes both forms, namely physical[8], but until then it is through memory, the imagination, and through fantasy that he may return. His letters to Makena, his wife, create a powerful bridge to his village, and their correspondence replicates certain homely comforts[9]. An immediate return is near impossible due to the distance between where he 'is' (South Africa and Botswana) and his imprisonment within these two states.

A number of themes dealt with in the novel (such as Christianity, the wish for education, and a reconciliatory future) formed the basis for a "Report on Consultation between SWAPO and the Representatives of the White Community of Namibia" from June 19–21, 1988 in Stockholm. One of the main themes is that of education (a central trope in the novel as well as further Namibian literature[10]). Muronga consequently singles

---

[8] The novel's end hints at Muronga's return back home, although it is constructed as open-ended.
[9] These take the form of greeting rituals, intimate exchanges, and personal news.
[10] This seems to be a constant theme in the collection of writings *Between Yesterday and Tomorrow* (2005). This collection of women's writing was edited and compiled by Elizabeth |Khaxas (Director of the Women's Leadership Centre). In her foreword the Deputy Minister of Education, Becky Njoze-Ojo argues "that writing, and in particular writing by women, can be used as a catalyst for change" (xii), with writing a significant result of education. Many of the short stories and poems in this collection identify education as a possible way out of poverty, domestic powerlessness, or cultural submission. This sentiment is shared by the SWAPO elite in exile, who, according to Wallace (2011: 283), were responsible

out education (or rather, learning to read and write) as a tool in developing oneself while also bridging the gaps within the Black-*white* hierarchies, usually founded on knowledge, knowledge production, and knowledge dissemination by the European authorities. He dreams of imparting these skills to his son, Mandaha, once he is able to return home. One of the first results of his education is a direct line of contact to his home village through a letter exchange with his wife, Makena.

Although the timing of the novel and the events which were taking place in the initial setting of Muronga's story (the north of Namibia on the border to Angola, would have offered the opportunity to focus on the so-called 'Border War', as well as the conflicts and skirmishes between the PLAN units and the notorious Koevoet[11] forces), *Born of the Sun* takes a step back and focusses on civilian travails and mobilisation outside of the war efforts. What is striking is that the novel begins by locating artefacts of colonial occupation and intrusion within the daily lives of the villagers. This takes the form of the Catholic mission in Muronga's village and all of the accompanying discourses around the mission's objective. From denouncing traditional marriages as 'real', forcing Christian names on the congregation, controlling sexual unions, to relegating traditional customs to the category of heathenism, Pater Dickmann exercises substantial control over the village. At certain junctions this control is challenged, but this will be discussed at a later stage. What is, however, apparent, is the easy transition from a colonial stage to an apartheid stage, without having to change too many fundamentals. Pater Dickmann's continuous distinction between Christian and heathen is later translated into a justification for apartheid by the mine's *dominee* (Afrikaner preacher) when he uses the Bible in order to legitimise and rationalise *white* positions of power (113). Christianity is mobilised in order to discipline and rationalise control over Black subjects while devaluing local traditions and customs.

A final characteristic of the novel is its reconciliatory tone. Muronga does not demonise or reject the *white* person as an individual. He accepts the oppressors and evildoers (just like their Black helpers) as part of a system. His critique is aimed at the system itself, of the institutions and discourses of this system, and not of the individual actors them-

---

for "education, health and defence", while the incoming SWAPO polity envisioned the universal right to education as a basic social service ("Report" 1988:6) and a reason to have begun and continue the liberation struggle. Hamutenya, in response to a question by Jack Albertyn, names the continued presence of segregated schools as one of three reasons why SWAPO might maintain its liberating ambitions ("Report" 1988:5).

[11] This was a special unit which "was founded as a counter-insurgency section of the South West African Police Force" (Wallace:295) and was military in its make-up and activities. Furthermore, it "consisted of up to 3,000 personnel – mainly Black Namibians, many were recruited in Owambo – under the command of *white* officers, and it was responsible for inflicting much of the worst damage on the civilian population of northern Namibia in the last decade before independence. Its activities included hunting down and fighting SWAPO guerrillas with patrols of *casspirs* (tanks)" (emphasis in original, ibid.).

selves. This is clearest when the narrative includes *white* characters as helpers to the cause of liberation. Practices of stereotyping and pigeonholing are avoided while incorporating *white* anti-apartheid moments and activities. *White* 'helper' characters are then included within the envisioned future nation by being included in many of the discussions and imaginations of the collective "we" when independence is discussed. This reconciliatory tone is strongly reflected during a "Speech by Sam Nujoma, President of SWAPO to the Namibian Consultation, 19–21 June, 1988, Stockholm". He first denies claims that *white* people are the enemy, and offers opportunities of collaboration in the future development of Namibia (3). He extends a hand of friendship to the *white* population by offering them Namibia as a "home" (ibid.), which is linked to a stipulation, namely that "they make their patriotic contribution to speeding up of the independence and future reconstruction of *our* country" (emphasis mine, ibid.). Although they have been responsible for many atrocities and injustices against Black characters and people, they still have a place in the new future.

Nujoma sees reconciliation as a foundation for a peaceful transition and national stability, arguing that "SWAPO believes that it will be an act of irresponsibility for us not to do our uttermost to seek and work for mutual understanding and reconciliation between this [sic] two sections of our population [Black and *white*]" (4). They are seen as equals, not as enemies who have to be destroyed. The rationale is that once the oppressive system of apartheid is dismantled, so are the hierarchies and differences that *white* people have invented and set in place. Equality thus becomes the foundation for the relationship between the two groups[12], with education – again – seen as the great equaliser. This would also usher in the abolition of historic inequalities, such as land ownership and the re-emergence of traditional customs and rituals. Furthermore, the wish for a pluralistic society involves the sharing of knowledge and resources, meaning that the Black population would receive access to spaces, metaphorical and physical, such as universities, government, urban centres, and public discussions, from which they were continuously and forcefully barred.

Main Spaces of the Narrative

This section will slightly digress from the methods employed in the previous chapters. This is because my aim is not so much to show how space is produced by 'foreign'[13] char-

---

[12] So-called coloured societies and people are absent in the novel, the focus basically being on Black and *white* people.
[13] I use the term *foreign* in order to emphasise the non-endemic dimension of the characters discussed previously. Of all the characters dealt with so far, none were a) born in GSWA or SWA, or b) of descendants

acters (and authors) as they encounter SWA, but to show how space is produced by those originally from the imposed *state*[14]. I am very aware of the problematic nature of this last part of my assertion, especially considering the validity of such concepts of 'state' to the disenfranchised local populace, as well as their own encounter with alien disciplinary spaces such as the mining compound and the jail cell. Both of these spaces are limiting by their initial definition, yet they play vital roles in the maintenance of the state apparatus. Through the accumulation and concentration of both desirable and undesirable subjects, the state can control the flow of labour and resistance. Governing the temporal regimes of these spaces become a powerful tool for maintaining power and exercising authority. The mining compound is produced in order to extract as much mineral wealth from the earth while controlling the bodies who do this. Barracks, communal washrooms, and communal eating halls point towards a system in which surveillance over a large number of workers is utilised as a tool of control. This control is further realised through what I will term 'liminal subjects', in other words Africans who extend surveillance work. The jail cell, on the other hand, has one purpose only: to keep away 'undesirables' from the general population under the harshest conditions. This is first achieved by accumulating undesirable elements in an environment that is designed for captivity and immobility. A second achievement of the jail is its collapse and compression of spatial and temporal experiences. However, the intention of this literary analysis is to establish how a character such as Muronga is able to navigate these extreme spaces while constructing his own subjectivity and position within these structures.

Furthermore, I will not discuss each narrative space. The reason for this is that the spaces I am most interested in, the spaces that should dominate this chapter, are the spaces in which resistance is the most palpable. In other words: the aim is to look at spaces in which the notions and understanding of spaces opened up in the colonial and apartheid sections are dismantled and reconfigured. Discourses propagated in the discussed novels (such as 'empty' landscapes, the submissive role of Black characters, the necessity of controlling Black bodies) are challenged in this section, beginning with general assumptions of the Black subject. By linking *Born of the Sun* to its predecessors and contrasting the different conceptualisations of space as experienced by the main protagonists, I hope to demonstrate the resistant actions of Muronga (whether conscious of them or not) as well as his fellow characters. Because of the high occurrence of rebellions and anti-apartheid movements, as well as the multitude of literature produced on these movements, it is my further aim to

---

born in GSWA or SWA. Each one arrived from Europe or South Africa at some stage, with the Africanist characters all receiving minor or menial roles.

[14] I use italics to show the foreignness of the system imposed by European colonialists.

focus on the 'smaller' instances in which the ubiquitous systems of both colonialism and apartheid were challenged in the everyday. Moments that will be interrogated range from the (forced) membership in the "village church" to the (forced) migration to the South African mine. I will look at performativity and positionality as technologies of integration *and* subversion, of self-definition *and* subjectivity, of appropriation *and* resistance. My analysis will be made up of the following points of discussion: Muronga's village (the exposé space), Rundu (his first contact with the urban), and Pretoria (the centre of apartheid power). Considering the place- and namelessness of the village, one could argue that it represents an ideal chronotope in respect to the other places. Local time regimes are explicated here, while the spatial and social structures are introduced and later contrasted with the named and fixed places of Rundu and Pretoria.

The village is not only the first space one is introduced to in the novel but it is also of course the space that has socialised the main character most intensely. It is here where he learns who and what he is, where he belongs, and where he is able to return. Everything of worth to him and everything he knows has its roots in this space, he is able to retrace his history here. It also instils in him a feeling of belonging, of safety, and of security. The village, together with its inhabitants and stories, accompanies him throughout his journey, so it is imperative that the village also serves as an anchoring foundation from which to discuss the other spaces[15]. Most importantly, the village serves as a centre to his world[16], the foundation from which he understands and experiences all other spaces. The space where he had spent his childhood and early adulthood then changes – briefly – to Rundu. Although this zone of activity and the numerous cars initially take him aback, Muronga feels alienated from the town. Not only are the factors that define the village absent (such as the familiarity of its inhabitants), but the urban space tires him and his friend out[17]. He cannot but help contrast it to his home, especially considering that the number of *white* people present is much larger. What links Rundu to his home is the mission just outside the town, which he observes "looks exactly like our mission, Andara. The buildings, the roads, everything is the same.'" (77). The colonial intrusion into the 'rural' is also repro-

---

[15] The idea is not to romanticise the village in any way, especially when considering the connotations associated with the concept of the village (innocence, tradition, purity) as opposed to the city. The village in this discussion serves mainly to locate the character and his values in 'the world', so to speak, with the village at its centre.

[16] At a meeting at the mine compound in Doornfontein, Muronga is introduced to a number of other South West Africans, all with different affiliations. He thinks to himself "I never thought I would be among so many people, all of whom are not known to the people of my village" (135). His home informs his links to the outside world – either through *hearing* about them (such as in the case of Rundu), or through someone connected to it.

[17] "Rundu is too big a place for them. There are too many people walking in all directions not talking to each other. It makes them tired to see all this." (1988:84).

duced within the 'urban', although not within the urban environment but slightly outside of it[18]. A final note to be observed is that the migrant workers, which Muronga is part of, stay on a compound outside of Rundu and do not reside in the town. They are not part of the urban centre, but contribute to it and its process of accumulation (through their consumption, the data they share, their labour potential). They are, however, introduced to the metropole's power when a prominent leader, Archie Bokwe, is killed.

After Archie Bokwe's funeral at Doornfontein[19], which was identified as an illegal strike action by the apartheid government and the mining officials, Muronga and other strikers are removed from the compound and taken to a jail in Pretoria. This time, he is in fact within the bounds of the metropole of power within his larger political-geographic context. He is unable to experience this metropole as his sojourn takes place exclusively in the confines of prison. And yet, it is in this environment – an extreme space due to its strong regulation of time and movement – that Muronga is able to think and dream most clearly. This comes after he has learned that previous inmates have gathered strength during their stays (verbalised through their etchings into the cell walls), while also having time to 'travel' back home or back in time because of their close confinement and repetitive routine. It is after a humorous-grotesque daydream (involving a character from Kavango mythology) that Muronga sees a purpose in his struggles and places these in a larger political and national context. Contrary to its constrictive nature, and its tiresome daily repetitiveness, Muronga is able to grow personally and position himself as an empowered individual in respect to the overpowering and oppressive system of apartheid. This section is where the main character connects his current desire to resist the past.

I will link the three main spaces (village, Rundu, Pretoria) to historic moments of resistance and subversion that may have served as examples for the character(s). The discussion of the village could therefore involve a focus on the community as it redefines itself due to external pressures (colonial violence, economic strains, challenges to traditional power systems), while maintaining its core identity. This will take the form of a look back at how the main societies involved during the colonial era (Nama, Owambo, Herero) coped with changes in the 'national' and intra-social dynamics as well as coping mechanisms after the catastrophic wars and their repercussions. Of course, this cannot be translated exactly onto the liberation movement due to the traumatic effects of near-annihilation of a number of these societies. However, technologies such as continuation, memory, mystification, reaffirmation, and reappropriation are vital in the recovery of

---

[18] Muronga's travel companion points to the fact that "Shambya, the Roman Catholic mission nearest Rundu to the east" (1988:77) is not within the official city bounds.
[19] This is the mine in Transvaal, to which Muronga has been sent, and which is located relatively close to Johannesburg and, more significantly for the novel, Pretoria.

identity. Muronga and his peers apply a number of these processes in order to cope with slow shifts within their communities while being carted off to far-off places in order essentially to work and take orders. This may take the form of the technology of dreaming (becoming his mythical hero, Tjakova) or the appropriation of markers of his oppression (his yellow overall, his Christian name).

What seems like a red thread connecting these three spaces[20] (the village, Rundu, Pretoria) is the role of the church within the systems of colonialism and apartheid. Muronga's attitude towards this Western tool of contact thus forms a prominent part of my discussion. What is also thread through the chapters and parts is the role of labour. Labour practices are contrasted within the dichotomy of the rural (where Muronga is responsible for herding cattle) and the two mining compounds. Although he does not work in Rundu, he is introduced to the mechanics of the apartheid system (surveillance, medico-biological interrogation, 'objectification' of the Black individual). Muronga and his friend Kaye are introduced to the town as follows:

> "*Originally* called Runtu, and meaning 'too many people squeezed together', Rundu is the source of all things foreign to the Kavango people; all things 'white'. In the beginning, the *white missionaries* came to civilize the heathens and save their souls. They came, that is, to pave the way for the white man's new system of *trade*, *finance*, and *justice* – all the ingredients needed to support a 'healthy' civil service. Rundu," he [an elderly companion] continues, "is the source of new ideas, new technologies, and the many new structures needed to house them – *hospitals*, *stores*, and *offices* where workers sift stacks of paper. But Rundu is also a breeding ground for much that is evil – it is a place where the survival of the fittest is the order of the day. So the white people made *laws* to control the evil, and jails for disciplining wrongdoers." Some of the things he says Muronga and Kaye do not understand, but they have often heard of the place Rundu. (emphasis mine, 78)

A couple of things immediately jump out. First of all, the reference to the missionaries can be directly linked to colonial practices. This initial contact then opens up further moments of contact, namely "trade, finance, and justice". While these were organised locally by the original societies (inter-cultural and transnational trade networks had existed long before the arrival of the missionaries), they became centralised and concentrated within the *white* urban centre. Certain institutions also force the concentration of people as well, as the "hospitals, stores, and offices" seem to do. The inhabitants of Rundu are thus collected within the spaces, either as patients, as consumers, or as workers. Their social identity becomes reduced to their identity within these spaces. The added dimension

---

[20] The three spaces/places are strongly contrasted in their urbane qualities, with a gradual progression from the rural (the village), to the urban (Rundu), and finally to the metropole (Pretoria). For Muronga this is a linear development, in which a return to village is impossible as long as the metropole remains as the centre of power and control.

of it being a place of evil, of "all things foreign to the Kavango" opens up a rural-urban dichotomy – with heavy negative connotations for the latter. This negative image is augmented through the threat aimed at "misbehaving children", who are "often warned that they must behave well, lest they see what Makombwe[21] saw in Rundu" (78). Furthermore, he and Kaye are socialised and disciplined in Rundu. This starts with the organisation of their daily routine ("you only sleep where you are shown to sleep" (79)), defined according to various practices (through the division into labour pools), entered into the bureaucratic machine ("[i]n the afternoon each man is fingerprinted and given appropriate papers" (86)), and then finally re-identified (not according to village or family ties, but according to their future place of work).

These divisions and demarcations are then intensified and strengthened in Doornfontein and will find their epitome in the jail cell in Pretoria. Muronga's labour function is reproduced in the various relationships he is able to form while also defining his position within apartheid policies. Just like his introduction to Rundu and its many alienating features, Muronga is introduced to Pretoria via the same procedure: through an accompanying prisoner. The severity of the prison is alluded to as the prisoners have arrived at the place "where Archie Bokwe died" (160). Although cooped up in the mining compound and experiencing the bare minimum of rights and privileges, the Pretoria prison will take these to further extremes. However, just like in Rundu and Shakawe (in Botswana), he is able to make use of resistant strategies and survival techniques. As I have argued before, the jail is an extreme space as time and space are subordinated in the service of containment and terror. The terror the inmates, who have been imprisoned together with Muronga, experience oscillates between explosions of physical violence and the drudgery of uneventfulness. Especially the second tactic takes its toll on the characters as their daily routine is severely reduced, while contact and exchanges between the inmates are initially non-existent[22]. The limited space for activity and expression is strongly linked to the mobility and freedom of the prisoners, while reproducing the main factors of discomfort and hardship:

> Sitting…thinking…wondering…dreaming. Every day it is the same. Every day…the same tasteless porridge and bitter coffee for breakfast, the same bland soup and beans for dinner.

---

[21] Makombwe is described as a villager who spent time in the jail in Rundu. The oral dissemination of narratives and legends such as this (it is never clarified what exactly happened to Makombwe) and the individualisation of these experiences strongly point to a communal and traditional response to the threat of the urban centres and its dangers.

[22] "During the first few days *no one speaks except through sign language*. Then, a few words at a time are uttered, but nothing is said about Archie Bokwe in case the cells are bugged. All of the men know that whites have ways of listening in on their conversations. So, the men have only their thoughts to keep them company." (emphasis mine, 161).

> A guard comes into the cell and tells the prisoners to squat on their mats while he counts them. Routinely, they are subjected to the taunting and insults of the policemen who guard the cells. Every day the stench from the hole in the corner gets worse and the daily discomforts and indignities go on. (163)

However, this strongly encouraged inactivity also offers the opportunity of flight outside the "grey drab walls of the prison" (161), most notably through the acts of "thinking", "wondering", and "dreaming". A nostalgic but powerful return to the village and its values can cater for certain needs within the apartheid prison environment that Muronga now experiences first-hand. It is this flight back to the village and its myths that instil within Muronga a new purpose and a new identity, changing him from a fearful and relatively subservient mineworker into a conscious liberation fighter.

The Far-Off Village as the Centre

The unnamed village is the opening space of novel. The village panorama is quickly interrupted by the presence of the village church, with its first mention being Makena's absence at the next church meeting due to illness (3). It is at this juncture that the difference between Christianity and local cosmologies is opened up when Muronga remarks that

> [i]f someone does not go to church for a reason that is good as far as we in the village are concerned, Pater Dickmann must be given some Christian reason, otherwise he believes that you are either still a heathen, or that you are showing some tendency to turn back to heathenism – a disease these missionaries say they came to eradicate. (3)

The church exercises control over its congregation by monitoring who attends sermons and who doesn't, while influencing behaviour through the introduction of the bell. This instrument seems ubiquitous throughout the novel, somehow following Muronga everywhere. The bell serves to inform the villagers that sermons will begin, thus locking time and space in a mutual disciplinary relationship. Even the so-called 'heathen' characters (like Uncle Ndara) are able to hear the bells and are aware of their significance. The bells also work as an interruption, as their ringing informs the Christians within the vicinity that they must stop what they are doing and start moving towards church. It impresses a time regime onto the village that competes with other time regimes – especially if the church events are outside of the 'normal' schedule, for example weddings or baptisms.

A further aspect of the church is its ability to define. It defines who is good and evil[23], and also influences how the villagers are able to view themselves. Pater Dickmann has the

---

[23] The colour scheme of the Bible leaves very little space for Africans to manoeuvre in. At one point Muronga questions this simplistic and convenient colour scheme: "He does not believe the stories about the black devil with long nails and long horns. How can a devil who is black be so bad, and not the sweet white angels? Muronga wonders. It is the white missionaries who are bad. Not the black people in our

authority to define who is considered a 'heathen' because that person has not received a Christian name – usually the name of a saint. These names are foreign to Muronga and Makena, who show some difficulties in remembering their 'new' names. They start constructing their 'own' Christian names in order to try and remember these enforced names, laughing at the absurdity in the process. A further striking feature concerning Muronga's (and Makena's) entry into the Christian community is its high levels of performativity. A first moment in which this is observable is when Muronga comes to church early. He reaches it but no one is around to greet him.

> Not baptized nor being accompanied by a Christian, he is unsure whether or not to enter the church. He climbs the few steps and hesitantly approaches the open doorway. Pausing, he glances behind him to be sure no one is watching. *Peering into the half-lit interior, he dips his finger into the bowl of holy water by the entrance, just in case someone is looking. Slowly he makes the sign of the cross on his forehead and chest. Cautiously, he takes a few steps forward.* (emphasis mine, 21)

This part begins with a performative sequence, namely mimicking the ritual of sprinkling holy water. This is accompanied by a feeling of being observed by someone, followed by the performance of the traditional Sunday sermon:

> Silently walking up the aisle, *his hands pressed together in a gesture of prayer, he kneels piously by the front pew and counts all his fingers and toes three times before getting up*. After standing there long enough, he decides to look at one of the pictures of the seven stops on the wall. Flanked by stained-glass windows, the picture shows a bleeding Christ carrying a heavy wooden cross over his shoulder. Its gilded frame has lost its lustre. *His hands still clasped together, he cannot help wondering how these white people came to be so cruel.* Look at this, he says to himself in dismay. And this man is white, too. I don't understand what this man did wrong. Is it any wonder that not many of us want to become Christians? (emphasis mine, 21)

But while he is 'seen' to be praying, he is caught in a deliberation about the contradictions within Christianity, focussing especially on Christ's crucifixion. The violence of *whiteness* seemingly knows no boundaries.

His performance during church service – when observation and surveillance are the most intense – becomes an extension of his earlier performance as he highlights his presence during the sermon.

> As the church fills up with parishioners, Muronga slides down to the end of the bench *so that Pater Dickmann can see him easily*. The service begins. Since Makena is not with him, Muronga says the important prayers *so loudly for Pater Dickmann to hear*. The priest likes such piety. (emphasis mine, 22)

---

village" (20).

His desire – or need – to perform is explained at earlier moment, after Muronga has talked to Pater Dickmann about Makena's absence from the previous church meetings, stating

> that Makena's head is still ill and that she will go to the clinic tomorrow. That is what he wants to hear. Well, he will get exactly what he wants – finish! Then the next thing you know he will baptize us, marry us, and baptize our child, too. Oh, and give us rings, of course. He thinks about the church service yesterday, and particularly about *how he told the priest a good lie. Yes, he thought, if you must tell a lie to make these white people happy, then tell it.*" (emphasis mine, 4)

What is at the heart of this argumentation is not the act of lying itself, but the environment created in which this lie becomes necessary. The argument is that he is not lying to the preacher in order to maliciously deceive him for personal gain[24], but rather because it his wish to make this *white* person happy. There are further moments of mimicry and simulation – most notably of prayers and the catechism – but it seems that the strategic acceptance of the church is the most constant form of resistant behaviour. At one point the narrator mentions that Muronga and Makena's Christian names "are only Sunday names, anyway. At home they will still be Muronga and Makena, or since their child's birth, simply *Wiha-Mandaha* and *Nyina-Mandaha*, Father and Mother of Mandaha." (27). The church has intruded into the village (socially and geographically), but not cosmologically or structurally. Using the narrator's words, the church is only a Sunday event, an institution linked only to a certain time and with a limited reach within the quotidian.

Although this 'performance' of Christianity is negatively charged in *Peter Moor* and *Heim Neuland*, as well as "The Narrative of Jacobus Coetzee", it achieves a liberating aspect in the context of this novel. The answer of the village – of which a great deal remains 'heathen' – to the hegemonic claims of the Catholic Church is a generally understood strategy of appeasement, while limiting the scope of direct influence of the alien institution. The village and the relationship between the inhabitants and the controlling desires of the Pater Dickmann arms and prepares Muronga for a possible life 'on the outside' (referred to as *Thivanda*). Not only do the returning migrant and contract workers share their knowledge and experiences with the uninitiated and inexperienced, they also recall stories that have a direct effect on their situation. This has the result that further colonial

---

[24] A look at colonial policies (especially those concerning land and concession contracts) shows a high frequency of this type of 'lying', in which personal gain and profit were central. This begins with Adolf Lüderitz buying land from Cornelius Frederiks. Instead of using land miles, the merchant used geographical miles, a term Frederiks was unfamiliar with. The size of property bought measured nearly five times the size of what was originally negotiated.

persons and groups are connected to the village, contrary to its relative remoteness (it is connected to the outside world almost exclusively through buses and trucks). It is through the tales of the elders of colonial horrors (as event *and* warning) that the name von Trotha, "who loved blood" (22) as well as possible atrocities against the Herero are shared and recounted. The retold story connects the General to the murder in a church of a group of Christian Hereros who were deceived into thinking they were receiving presents. According to Muronga, this is why "many people are suspicious about the church" (22), its intentions constantly being questioned. To Muronga, one can now argue, the village is more than the space he has grown up in and whose traditions and customs he is expected to reproduce and maintain. Rather, it is a place that protects him from the possible horrors of *Thivanda* while arming him with the necessary narratives and coping mechanisms for a world in which his traditions and customs are slowly being supplanted. The village's function is expanded to include coping mechanisms for a foreign and alien world while remaining the centre to Muronga's ever-expanding personal map.

Rundu and the Encounter with Apartheid

When we go back to Lefebvre's conceptualisation of the *urbane*, the focus is on the dialectic relationship between the city and the countryside (i.e. the urban and the rural) and notions of concentration and accumulation within the former. The fact that Muronga and Kaye are required to wait next to the main road outside the village in order to be picked up and taken to Rundu serves as a vivid example in explaining this asymmetrical relation. Firstly, through the transport, the workers become reduced to goods that are picked up from the countryside and transported to centre(s) of consumption and accumulation. The fact that the compound outside of Rundu is designed as a reservoir to host migrant workers also fulfils this conception. Furthermore, Muronga contrasts the high degree of organisation within the town itself (visualised through the uncountable offices, the implementation of laws) and of the networks at hand (transport and consumption, as well as structures such as the jail) to the village. Judging from the spatial arrangements of the novel, one can argue that Rundu becomes the first proper contact between the main character and the ruling and organising systems of European power[25].

Muronga's experiences of and in Rundu have a high degree of hearsay as he has no comparable examples to make use of or to connect to this space. His direct reference(s) to the village as well as the story of Makombwe – linking the village and the negative qualities of the urban centre – indicates his reliance on the village's customs, signs, and

---

[25] Although the church is in the village, it is part of it and does not dominate (but influences) the established traditional hierarchies or social structures.

symbols to navigate this alienating space. His experience is nevertheless not a negative one. He and Kaye are taken aback by the sheer number of people and cars just as they are impressed by the pace and activity of the place. These are greeted with wonder, which is exemplified through their attempt to count – and thus comprehend – the omnipresence of the cars. The things they are confronted with do not overawe them, rather they are invested in trying to understand the underlying logic. This process is initially introduced in Muronga's inner conflicts concerning church symbols and iconography. It should be said at this junction that the characters do not outright reject the Catholic church, but rather the many inconsistencies, for example its colour scheme, the crucifixion of Jesus Christ (as a *white* man killed by *white* men), and the devaluation of local culture. And lastly, Muronga combines his lessons from the Bible with the lessons from the village and is able to forgive his tormentors and to imagine a future together with them. The town of Rundu is Muronga's first proper introduction to apartheid in its full force, although segments of this have already been incorporated into village life. This episode is the reason Muronga and Kaye end up in Rundu, a continuation of the process of labour procurement from the rural areas.

At an earlier junction, the most powerful person in SWA, the Bantu Affairs Commissioner, comes to visit the highest authority in the village, Uncle Ndara. This becomes an exercise in self-presentation by the Commissioner, while the identity propagated by the village church is reproduced and reinforced through the collection of Christian names and the absolute obedience towards the attending officials. Secondly, the migrant workers are separated into heathen and Christian[26] while they are required to produce certain knowledge tied to their ascribed identity. The information collected starts with: Christian name, followed by the heathen name, name of the father, name of the mother, the name of the "kraalhead", the name of the "village headman", the name of the "chief", and whether taxes have been paid before. The compiled responses are designed as one-word answers that do not offer much information. Yet when one looks at the responses in a larger context – namely that a number of workers have given answers – the cataloguing of these answers gives a clear overview of the region in question. Who are the elites in a specific area? How many workers come from which village? Who is/might be related? Who is in contact with his church and who may become a nuisance? And where are the people situated? Kaye, for example, when asked why he is still a 'heathen' by one of the

---

[26] Of which the latter group has certain advantages, which were already hinted at early in novel when the leverage of a Christian conversion is discussed. Muronga argues that "things are no longer as they were in the days of our forefathers. To get married in the church, with a Christian name – or just to acquire the name – gives you more respect and better opportunities if you want to work in the white man's mines or on the farms" (4).

officials, answers "[w]e have two homes; one here and one in Angola" (60). The goals of these procedures were to collect data and transfer it into a general network of information relevant to the control of Black bodies and the maintenance of *white* hegemony. These strategies are interrupted and complicated through the porous borders between Angola and northern Namibia, the reluctance to completely accept Christianity, and conflicting information and data[27].

The highest South West African office bearer within the apartheid system is a harbinger and exponent of apartheid. And his visit does have the quality of a presentation of power. Apartheid implicitness is of course one of his functions (i.e. he is the personification of the laws and regulations), and he and his assistant are a guarantee that discriminatory labour and land practices will continue. Furthermore, the visit hints at certain events and situations to come, such as the treatment of the men by the *white* officials. At the same time strategies of resistance are being devised. Kaye's 'double nationality' is indicative of the porous borders between Namibia and its neighbour Angola and the flux and influx of movement between the two states, which in essence must exclude but influence South African authority and its envisioned labour practices. The confrontation with the *white* system of power, and by extension European language, reveals new desires and aspirations for both Kaye and Muronga. They are aware that gaining an understanding of this language is very beneficial to them and might be beneficial to their own society. They reference the initial conflicts between the incoming *whites* and their chiefs, conceding that

> [w]e are at a disadvantage, my friend, by not speaking the white man's language. Even today we could be sold and we would not understand what had happened until we were being taken away. It is still as it was in the old days when the Portuguese came to take our people away in exchange for tobacco and gifts. The chiefs simply nodded their heads without understanding what they were agreeing to and to the things they were offered. (58)

Of course, the process of enslavement – a further African trauma – is more complex than this extract tries to illustrate, but the power of language, of another language, is made abundantly clear. Using an immediate example of this power supports this argument. The example is Makaranga, who is the assistant and interpreter to the *white* official. According to Muronga, Makaranga "is important because he understands and speaks the 'white man's language'. He is the only one who knows both sides. He knows the truth. But who knows if he tells the truth to us or the white man?" (57). Muronga laughs at this utterance because the interpreter has taken liberties with his translations between Uncle Ndara and the Commissioner. This hints at the performative dimension of Makaranga, but is also due to the arbitrary and strategic manipulation of language as an intermediate. In this

---

[27] This will be discussed in more detail, especially as resistant strategies.

sense, Makaranga embodies at the same time the complicity with the dominant/dominating system while offering a way to undermine this system. Here the topic of education arises again. It appears to be the key to self-fulfilment and a way to navigate exchanges with *white* people. A skill like this becomes essential considering (urban) Black people's permanent contact with *white* superiors, whether as employees, as statistical material, or in situations involving the police and the army.

Rundu shows a more intensive relationship with the oppressive system. This manifests itself firstly through the transport of able men from their village to a collection compound. Relocation and the transport of people by the state was an intrinsic tool of power of the apartheid state. The 'legal' and 'necessary' to-and-fro of mainly workers was vital to the labour economy while also allowing a significant level of surveillance and management of local movement and mobility. In this way the rural resources (in this case labourers) are concentrated in one point and can then slowly be integrated into the labour system. Not only does Muronga leave behind his wife and newborn son, but he will also be separated from his close friends, as Kaye, for example, will be taken to a different mine. This is an initial separation along certain criteria (age, ability, 'ethnicity', socialisation) that is predominantly founded on biological markers, bureaucratically sanctioned and organised.

The town is designed as an intermediate between the village, the final labour destinations of the characters, and Pretoria. Here, the mechanisms of division, separation, and removal all have their bureaucratic and formalised beginnings. It is also designed as the first foil to the village, a space where everything foreign and unfamiliar is concentrated. For many, it is the first taste of *Thivanda*, of the world outside of the village and its routines and regimes. For those, it is also the first direct contact with the system's processes and methods of discipline – the ordering of individuals, of movement, of time. Although Rundu is neither a metropole nor a place of state power, it is a space in which state power is exercised and a space in which the control of resources – most notably capital and labour(ers) – plays a crucial role. The network of control, so far peripheral within the village bounds, is given a tangible dimension in this urban centre.

Pretoria and the Birth of a Rebel

Pretoria plays the most significant part in the development of Muronga's political and nationalist evolution. As mentioned previously, his first introduction to the seat of apartheid South Africa's power is in direct reference to the killed activist Archie Bokwe[28]. For

---

[28] This is an argument Mbembe (2003) makes when discussing the idea of state sovereignty. In essence he argues "sovereignty resides, to a large degree, in the power and the capacity to dictate who may live and who must die. Hence, to kill or to allow to live constitute the limits of sovereignty" (11). In this case,

Muronga this transforms the jail in Pretoria into a space in which he himself, as well as his peers, may be killed. The space presupposes harsher treatment and an escalation in the infringement of his basic rights. Not only because he is within the disciplinary construction of *the jail*, but further because he is in the jail *within* the centre of power. What also contributes to the understanding of the jail's significance (as opposed to Robben Island, for example) is the fact that the detainees are neither high-ranking political prisoners nor are they what could be considered terrorists. Their 'crime' was merely the participation in an unauthorised mass funeral[29] that took place at the mining compound in Doornfontein. In other words, Muronga and a number of funeral participants were arrested for basic insubordination – which was met with extreme violence[30]. However, the apprehended workers are not killed (not yet at least), but again loaded onto a truck at a jail in Doornfontein and taken to Pretoria.

Before they reach Pretoria, the group of prisoners is carted around in order to disorientate and confuse them. Not knowing where one is and where one is being taken creates an atmosphere in which time and space are used against those without control. This strategy takes away any certainties, meaning that the outcome of the trip becomes the focus of speculation. This speculation is of course rooted in the experiences of the violence and inhumanity of the system. Images of the violence at the funeral, in addition to the knowledge of what has previously happened to prisoners such as Archie Bokwe, creates concerns for one's own safety. Muronga echoes this when he analyses the need of the authorities to continuously move the prisoners. Not only does this (again) reduce the workers to goods which "are loaded into vans", this strategy has the effect that "they kept moving him [Muronga] around so that it was impossible to keep track of him. The idea is to keep the prisoners guessing until they are finally anticipating the worst" (159). Here, the constant disorientating movement of the 'prisoners' can be seen to contrast the ordered past time regimes at the mine and the coming condensed time regimes at the Pretoria prison. Again the characters are confronted with a foreign regulation of perceived time and space, a strategy that demoralises subjects in turmoil.

This ordeal paves the way for the creation of intimidated captives once they enter the prison complex. The fact that the first days pass without any significant communication between the group members, and a general feeling of paranoia, is evidence of the effec-

---

the state exercises its sovereignty by murdering, and thus eliminating, a possible threat to exactly this sovereignty.

[29] As A.J. Christopher (1996:166), amongst others, has shown public funerals became one way of political organisation and resistance.

[30] It is at this point that Muronga is convinced that he will be killed: "This is it, he [Muronga] thinks, the white man is going to kill me. I am going to die here, so far away from my home and family" (155).

tiveness of this strategy. The participation of other Black characters in the subordination of the captured workers is a confusing – yet ironically comprehensible – part of this process. However, the attitude towards these liminal subjects is one of pity, not one of accusation. There is a feeling of solidarity in which it is the system that is at fault, not the perpetrators[31]. Against the harsh conditions within the prison walls (which involve a minimum of repetitive routines, physical brutality, and humiliation), the inmates develop bonds of solidarity. The beginnings of this emerge from scribbling on the cell walls by previous inmates, etched testaments to resistance that create some semblance of hope. What is also striking about these scribblings is that they introduce Muronga to South African culture (in form of language) and their resistant potential, although some of the rallying cries are not as much an affirmation of an ideal[32] but reflect the harsh conditions of their captivity. Muronga is impressed by these short messages to him and those to come after him, stating that the authors of these lines are "brave men" (162). The fact that "strong men" (163) have been there and survived their fate gives Muronga the hope of doing the same. These inscriptions in the wall can also be read as an appropriation of the space through language and physical interaction. This is supported by the fact that these words come from other captives who have experienced the same violence and oppression as Muronga, captives who inspire and rejuvenate him through their words and their spirit.

However, it not merely his tangible environment giving Muronga hope, but also his 'return trips' back to his village. Not only does he revisit the days of his childhood, he revisits the time when the elders would share traditional tales. One tale he strongly remembers is the tale of two brothers, namely Tjakova[33] and Manongo. The first brother is seen as a positive propagator of village customs and values (industry, bravery, intelligence). The second brother is constructed as the antithesis, representing qualities of laziness and inactivity. Muronga recalls his dislike of being called "Manongo" by others, rather imagining himself to be more like Tjakova. Although a childhood wish, it enters his current situation and creates in him a renewed identification with his boyhood hero. Because the limited daily routine keeps activities, especially intellectual activities, marginal, 'escape' into dreams, memories, and fantasies remains a valid counter activity. A combination of memory and dream suddenly allow Muronga to become his hero, Tjakova. The episode takes a grotesque turn as Muronga and Tjakova merge to become

---

[31] "He [the guard] has been ordered to say these things and behave this way. He is pitiful, but no more so than Muronga and his fellow inmates, who are also just pawns in the white man's game." (159).

[32] Some of the writings on the wall are highly political ("Power is ours"; "Let us fight, men", and "We are not afraid"), while others are a straightforward allusion to the situation ("We shit here"; "Jail is a man's home"; and "Men sleep here") (162–163).

[33] For more on this, see Herbert Ndango Diaz's doctoral thesis, *A Definitive Edition and Analysis of the Tjakova Myth of the Vakavango* (1992).

a huge mouse ("Muronga-Tjakova, the Monster Mouse"), which in turn terrorises the prison guards. The positions become reversed, but through a mythical transformation and not through any form of violence.

This hybrid between the mythical figure of Tjakova and the imprisoned Muronga is quite revealing. Muronga does not become his hero – they together become one. He therefore does not sacrifice his identity for that of a fictional character, but rather maintains it. He does, however, supplement his own – momentary powerless – persona with that of a traditional, prominent character from his culture. The combination is realised in the shape of a mouse, normally the symbol of timidity and fearfulness. And yet this "Monster Mouse" is responsible for spreading fear, resulting in the liberation of the inmates and imprisonment of the prison officers. Memory and dreaming create a powerful combination which allows the 'dreamer' a chance at adjustment while imagining another possible future. Another outcome of this 'dreaming' is the creation of hope as a resource, leading to an empowering experience. It is no wonder that directly after his dream, "for the first time since being thrown into jail, he does not feel powerless against the authorities" (164). This liberating exercise has further repercussions as Muronga begins to meditate on questions of discrimination, knowledge, and the formation of a 'we' identity[34].

Taking a Look Around

Muronga first contemplates the laws that he and his peers are subjected to, questioning their validity and their application. He begins by questioning the links between *white* hegemony and Christian rhetoric, links he has previously encountered numerous times:

> I was also taught that laws were not made arbitrarily in favour of one person or group over another. It has been only over time that these lessons have been weakened as more of my people have come into contact with the white man. They have become the supreme authorities to whom we owe absolute obedience and they have assumed the right to take our land away from us. The white man has told us that he has this right because God made him white and he is therefore superior to us blacks. He has gone to school and can read and write and that, too, makes him better. Yes, we have been taught to feel inferior to the white man and to fear him. But are we inferior? I know many things the white man doesn't know, but does that make me a better man? Now that I have gone to mine school and can speak a new language and will go home to my people a rich man, does that make me better or superior to any other man? I wasn't taught that I am because of what I have. I was taught I am because of others. No…I am not superior or inferior to any man – not even the white man. (165)

---

[34] Muronga has at numerous stages questioned the meaning of his situation, discussing with others the problems of race, tax laws, and discriminatory practices. However, in this case he starts to contemplate these topics in a deeper and more meaningful fashion. He tries to form his own opinion on these topics, and is not reliant on outside influences.

What comes to the fore in this first meditation is the question of a God-given right to oppress. This stems from a Christian conviction that confers godly powers onto the proponents of the apartheid system. Not only has Pater Dickmann argued along these lines (using the division of Christian and heathen to support his argument), but so has the *dominee* during his first sermon at Doornfontein (114). According to the *dominee*'s sermon, the government has been selected and installed by God and demands absolute obedience. Furthermore, Muronga laments the fact that this logic and rhetoric have conversely replaced or weakened local laws and thus created the conditions for subservience.

Muronga does not, however, see himself in this mould. Now more than ever he is convinced that education will offer him the prospect of becoming equal to *whites* within a future society, one in which Muronga and the UPO have dismantled the limiting and unjust conditions. He argues that

> [t]hey [white people] are feared because they have gone to school – and that is what I will do. I will learn to read and write, and I will learn the white man's ways and then I will not need to be afraid of him or hate him. I will not become a slave to him. I will learn everything I can, and when I get out of this stinking hole, I will return to my village with all of my knowledge and tell everyone about the United People's Organization. We must not be afraid of or hate the white man, nor should we allow ourselves to become his slaves. We must fight to get our land back. We must fight for our right to be equals with the white man." (165)

His desire for education does not stop with himself. As is observable, he intends to share his knowledge. The village – seemingly isolated from educational potential – becomes the first place Muronga wants to bring education to and thus liberate. This does not mean, though, that his desire is to bring Bantu education or *white* knowledge to his village. What he proposes to do is learn (and by extension teach) English and/or Afrikaans in order to speak *to* power. The devaluation of local and indigenous languages by the system has taken away some of their potency, but the acquisition of Afrikaans or English will permit a space in which to transport the ideas of freedom and autonomy to those in power. When he refers to "noise"[35] he does not necessarily have to point towards violence as a means, but rather he is referring to the verbalisation of dissatisfaction pronounced in a language that is undeniably comprehensible to decision makers and office bearers. Noise in this case carries a positive connotation as it allows a channel of communication that

---

[35] "We need to resist and talk day and night in a new language – in a language that the white man understands. Our language alone is not enough. The white man does not fear wisdom, he fears noise. So, when I go back I will teach my people to make noise…to sing for our land." (166). It is possible to locate this term within colonialist discourse. "Hottentot" and "Barbarian" became discriminatory terms referring to the *white* European societies inability to decipher the languages. In Muronga's case, this discourse is reversed in order to return to a local language and use that to make demands.

was previously closed off. And this noise will contain all the contradictions of the apartheid system; all the discomforts and injustices will be listed and disclosed. Noise will also be created by verbalising claims to occupied land while reaffirming the value and worth of the lost lands. Muronga's conception of noise thus takes on two guises, one as official (through the confrontation with official institutions and powers), and one as cultural (through the affirmation of one's own language in the form of praise songs). One can thus argue that these two different forms of noise are symbolic of two different movements of consciousness: one as a resistant mode that positions itself against those in power and one as an internal, re-affirmative mode which revitalises one's own culture while placing it in a national context.

Resistance and Disobedience

Haarhoff's first chapter of *The Wild South West*, which deals with early contact between colonising individuals (missionaries, explorers, traders) and the original inhabitants of the land, indicates relatively egalitarian modes of contact in which domination and submission seem to be the exception rather than the rule[36]. Because of the disparity concerning numbers between Europeans and the local population, an outright hegemonic assertion by the former was a utopian dream at best. Contact as well as the maintenance of networks and relations between the various local societies was more of a concern than the emergence of the *white* presence. Although seen with suspicious eyes[37] and identified as possible tools for power and riches, African elites did not consider the slow increase of a *white* presence as a serious threat. Certain elites even profited from their connection to the colonial administration, with Samuel Maharero the most famous example. Of course evidence of *white* influence as being destructive was evident in the Cape colony mainly through the first violent encounters between Dutch settlers and the Nama[qua] communities that had fled the colony and settled north of the Orange river. However, the desire to partake of the global trade system – especially with the emergence and consolidation of the Nama communities in southern Namibia and their consequent wars with the Herero – became a central motif in tolerating Europeans within the different traditional territories. The missionaries, who provided access to the trade networks locally and internationally, were in many cases integrated into the local structures[38], offering contact

---

[36] This assertion goes along the lines of trade and hospitality, although many racist assumptions and Enlightenment tropes were still reproduced in these Afro-European relations.
[37] Most notably and prophetically by Hendrik Witbooi.
[38] A number of *ovahona* and *kapteine* had their 'own' missionaries who also migrated with the congregations. Witbooi had Reverend Olpp, for example. Usually, they had a trader who supplied arms and

with luxury goods as well as guns, ammunition, and horses. All these developments were slow in influencing long-standing systems of organisation, however influencing them to large degrees.

What became a reason for concern to the local inhabitants was the founding of foreign centres of power, disrupting previously established authorial and governing spaces. The location of Windhoek, for example, as the capital indicated a change in spatial relations between the Cape colony, the territories in GSWA, and further colonial states such as Angola and Botswana. With the erection and control of borders and the accompanying state apparatus, the new German administration intruded into previously instituted trade routes and inter- and intra-societal dynamics. Although historians clearly show that it took the colonial administration an extended time to fully implement and consolidate its claims to authority within its territory[39], local societies maintained a semblance of power during European expansion. Nonetheless, the constant flow of settlers and military personnel as well as the intensification of trade in order to facilitate the acquisition of cattle and land, created an environment in which power relations started to become unbalanced. The introduction of laws, prohibitions, punishments, and taxes created a territory in which local influence slowly regressed and was replaced with a dependence on European products and goods. A slow and creeping influx of Europeans (mainly Germans) from the pre-colonial to the height of its sovereignty (culminating in the destruction of a number of original societies) therefore necessitated responses to the continuing effects of disenfranchisement, impoverishment, and political marginalisation. The most radical and extreme responses to this were the anti-colonial war efforts by the Nama in southern Namibia first, and then the well-documented Herero war. Nevertheless, war cannot and should not be seen as the only form of resistance to systems of oppression. Numerous other responses, which attempted to break out of the cycle of control, were introduced (some more effective than others).

The various societies and communities in Namibia developed different counter discourses and reactions to the ever-expanding intrusion of Europe's racist and colonising ideology into local systems, especially after the disastrous anti-colonial war. These can be divided into two connected yet contrasting modes of resistance: immaterial and material resistance. Immaterial resistance can be understood as a non-material response to events within the territory. This strategy would rely on cultural products that don't have a cor-

---

luxury goods.
[39] The fact that "Ovamboland" was never under direct colonial rule as well as the need to manipulate the larger Nama and Herero societies in order to gain their compliance is evidence for a relatively weak and powerless colonial government. Most historians pinpoint the end of the wars against the Herero and Nama as the moment in which something akin to control over the colonial territory was finally achieved.

poreal, tangible base, such as oral reproduction of identity and kinship. This includes an array of approaches in which language (but not only) is employed in order to counter colonial discourses and violence. I have mentioned the Herero praise poems, which may be viewed as one of the more potent examples of this strategy. However, the mythification of heroes, the commemoration of events, appropriation of dominant/dominating language, and naming can all be included within the project of creating counter discourses. A further result of immaterial resistance might also be the appropriation of technologies of authority, such as writing.

What defines immaterial resistance is its reproduction in the sphere of the abstract and in the realm of ideas, and therefore its 'invisible' and intangible nature. One should, however, be aware that immaterial resistance is always strongly linked to its complementing strategy, namely material resistance. As the name suggests, this form of resistance is developed within the sphere of objects and things. Physical objects are relocated within the realm of the symbolic and are then employed within the general framework of cultural resistance. Objects, which may fall within this definition, are the *Schutztruppen*-uniforms Herero soldiers wore during the war, the claiming of destroyed artefacts (such as graves and bodies), the reintegration of lost symbols (such as the white band worn by the Witbooi *kommandos*), as well as reclaiming and protecting the images of fallen heroes. The assimilation and re-appropriation of colonial status symbols such as the gun and the horse, as well as the reproduction of colonial markers such as square houses and colonial clothing also point towards a reworking of these objects within the cultural contexts of each group.

Considering these strategies, one can argue that the focal point of these interventions is first and foremost to maintain the authority of identity construction. For example, even though the Herero had lost nearly all of its people, lands, and cattle, they reversed the master-slave relation to the German colonisers. They referred to them as *omutua*, which roughly translates to 'slave'[40]. In essence, although much of the *material* basis for identity formation was destroyed or dismantled, surrogate strategies were formed in order to preserve some form of self-definition, whether individually or communally. The intrinsic and innate link between immaterial and material resistance should not at this point be broken up, but in this instance these two forms of counter-action should be dealt with individually in order to locate them and their expressions within Muronga's strategies.

---

[40] "Der arrogante Hererocharakter bezeichnet jeden, der kein Herero ist, als ‚omutua' (der Sklave)…Wenn ein Deutscher einen Herero ruft, sagt der Herero: ‚Omutua ue ndjii' (Der Sklave hat mich gerufen). Sie sagten es ganz offen, so daß die Deutschen hören sollten, daß sie Sklaven seien." Kuaima Riruako, "Das Leiden des Hererovolkes unter den Deutschen" in: *1884–1984. Vom Schutzgebiet bis Namibia*. Klaus Becker, Jürgen Hecker (eds.) (1985).

This would allow a (brief) tracing of these strategies from the pre-colonial period to the more recent war of liberation – of which Muronga will ultimately become a part. If possible, old and past strategies can be compared to their newer exponents. Furthermore, one can trace which strategies have 'survived', which have been reorganised, and which strategies receive a national character (considering the progression from conflicts during the colonial era and the nationally supported liberation struggle[41]). With the transitions from the pre-colonial to the colonial to apartheid, strategies needed to change, while the reproduction of the traditional remained a powerful engine in forming alternative discourses and modes of being. Looking backward thus allows ways in which to navigate a troubling present and imagine possible futures.

Past Words for Current Problems
Muronga's reference to Von Trotha and the atrocities committed against the Herero while they were gathered in church locates the past within the present and is employed as a cautionary tool for future developments. What this allows is a retrospective look that may offer protection in the present *and* the future. What is also striking is the fact that the Herero in the story are defined as "a different group of people who had a different chief" (21) and who are located in a different space. The plight of one group, which is per definition "different", is applied within one's own context in order to contemplate potential dangers to one's own society. The story, with its strong connection to Christianity and violence, must be interpreted as a warning. The strong links between the church, colonial power, and colonial violence also have a relevant basis in Muronga's village. Pater Dikmann's vehement opposition to non-Christian culture is reflected in the *dominee's* legitimisation of the state mirror the cruelty of colonial (and later apartheid) violence. However, using past occurrences that happened to other "groups" is only one strategy to be made use of.

A second strategy, discussed by Patricia Hayes in "'When You Shake A Tree'"[42], is the return to 'traditional' solutions to 'modern' problems. The focal point in her text is the oral rendition of King Mandume ya Ndemufayo's proclamations during a period when "[c]olonial overtures were made, and aggression was felt to be imminent, especially after

---

[41] It is possible to argue for a 'national' anti-colonial war if we consider Witbooi's assertion that the Nama should be viewed as an independent *nation*. He allocates this term to all the communities within Africa and compares his Witbooi nation, and the other African nations, with those of Europe. His letters first to Maharero (30.05.1890) and then later to Gouverneur Leutwein (18.08.1894) advocates autonomy for each 'nation' in the world. In: *The Hendrik Witbooi Papers*. Heyward, Annemarie & Eben Maasdorp. (1996).

[42] In: *Recasting the Past. History Writing and Political Work in Modern Africa*. Peterson, Derek R., Giacomo Macola (eds.) (2009).

the Herero defeat by the Germans in the south (1904) and the conquest of Ombandja and Evale by the Portuguese to the north (1908–1911)" (75). In order to counter these destructive events and the influence they would have on his kingdom, King Mandume started by locating historic practices and values and implementing them during his own reign. The results were a (brief) revitalisation of the Kwanyama polity, with power centralised in the person of the King. As Hayes explains, this centralisation had as a result that "[t]he problem of control in the kingdom is reversed, heightening the flow of power back to the king for the benefit of the land and hence...back to the people" (78). Moreover, Hayes argues that the return to past methods of control and organisation were the results "where both illness and cure are sought from *within* a particular history of the body politic and not in external forces" (emphasis in original, 91). If one further interrogates the text, the methods employed by King Mandume had internal as well as external considerations. This is clearest when one looks at the problem of raiding which the *omalenga* [headmen] orchestrated. The victims of these raids were usually Portuguese settlements in Angola as well as smaller communities along the Kavango. They may not be considered entirely as 'external' to the search for a solution as they were considered to still be within the empire of the Kwanyama, yet they receive an external dimension due to the people involved (being Portuguese and thus European). At the core of the problem are the activities of their own society, especially those who wield power.

What Hayes' text is able to show is that developments within indigenous communities are not always directly linked to outside factors and influences, but that an examination of the internal circumstances and the application of previous solutions can have far-reaching effects. Hayes received her information not from an archive in the classical sense, but from an oral historian (who might be considered a human archive). The relevance of this is that the successes of King Mandume are deeply embedded in the verbal transportation of history and tradition, placing the narrative in the realm of the immaterial. This realm of course has a long history within the African context, but it has received much more urgency and potency due to the developments of imperial and apartheid expansion. There are numerous reasons for this, such as the destruction and theft of material artefacts[43] (houses, shrines, graves), the dissolution of traditional hierarchies[44] and cultural capital (devaluation of indigenous products, theft of valuable goods such as cattle, metal work, etc.) and the removal of groups of people from their communal lands. Through the destruction of numerous physical markers of identity and group cohesion, the founda-

---

[43] Not only did von François raze Hornkranz (Hendrik Witbooi's capital) to the ground after numerous attacks, but a large number of Herero settlements were burnt down and looted during the war.
[44] "With Mandume's death, the kingship was abolished and a council of headmen was installed" (Hayes, 81).

tions of societies were forcefully and violently reconfigured. As Djomo (2011) has shown, one way for colonial powers to gain influence over the subordinated societies was "ein Vorgang, an dessen Ende Ausschaltung, Sterilisierung der fremden, einheimischen Kultur steht. Dabei gilt Entfremdung durch gezielten Eingriff auf die Identitätsstrukturen des überfallenen Einheimischen als *Modus Operandi* dieses Vorgangs" (10–11). In other words, the destabilisation of local societies and hierarchies was the main process of enforcing one's own culture on a foreign space and people.

The destruction of material artefacts as well as mass trauma is countered through the revaluation of other necessary immaterial artefacts. These 'new' artefacts are revitalised by incorporating them within an oral history and the reconstruction of what has been destroyed. The most well-known example of this form of revitalisation is the continuation and expansion of the locales produced and reproduced in the Herero *omitandu*. The idea of *ehi rOvaherero* ("land of the Herero") was first officially referenced as a claim to space during the 1870s when the Cape colony was making inroads into pre-colonial GSWA[45]. This was repeated when the German administration was broadening its administrative network during the 1880s[46]. Oral histories (of chiefs, cattle, locales, and events) thus achieved the status of a 'map', *the* imperial tool, that had the function of bolstering the Herero claim to lands they saw as their territory. The praise poems had the further effect of placing Herero history and genealogy within the realm of the landscape and creating a dense system of relations between the different locales. Names of famous chiefs (but not exclusively) as well as their cattle thus began to populate 'empty' landscapes, creating powerful claims to the territory and its history. Although not as innocent as it would seem on the surface (other groups had of course been displaced from "land of the Herero" and opposing claims by other societies were ignored), the praise poems opened up an alternative conceptualisation of central Namibia and the rightful ownership of the space. Even though the Herero did not own the land *per se*, their claims to the space were focussed on the resources which were located within the borders of *ehi rOvaherero*, whether material (wells, graves, pasture) or immaterial (history, autobiography). The oral, immaterial reproduction of claims to a space, located within the signifying powers of the target group, was expanded upon to inform other collectives of these claims. The invocation of proverbs and oral transmissions of knowledge create an immaterial arena in which resistant acts and actions can be transported.

---

[45] Henrichsen (2011:19).
[46] Ibid.

In a letter to Samuel Maharero, Hendrik Witbooi makes use of the phrase "to carry the sun on our backs"[47] in order to describe the ever-increasing shadow of German imperialism over the space of GSWA. The strong reference to a Nama folk tale in order to assess and predict the potential dangers that this foreign power within the territory symbolises is indicative of the potency of myths and legends. Although Witbooi later relies on dense Christian iconography and rhetoric to illustrate his opposition to the colonial government, a return to days past seems a successful strategy to (initially) comprehend and counter colonial intrusions. This invocation was used at the moment in which Witbooi, in essence, turned his proverbial back on the German colonial authorities, thus linking this expression to a mode of action. Furthermore, the expression emphasised and underlined his dedication to his break with the German colonial state. His letter to Samuel Maharero is a strong example of how the verbal has a direct influence on actions, most powerfully when used within a communally understood function.

Sigrid Schmidt collected numerous Nama and Khoisan oral renditions[48]. These renditions create a communal history of origins, but also imbue certain areas, animals, and persons with symbolic significance. As Schmidt rightly notes, the high mobility of these two societies, in addition to their spaces of movement, make certain settings prominent within their narratives. Thus the veld, with its semi-arid climate and sparse vegetation, forms the most repeated setting for their tales and fables. The veld thus becomes the locus of the culture and history of these two societies, while informing how other spaces are/will be identified and navigated. The mobility of the Nama and Khoisan forms a 'map' in which the interaction with other communities (which may take concrete or metaphorical form) are constructed and evaluated. Certain reasons and justifications for rituals (such as eating, storytelling, and hunting) are informed by the reproduction of pre-modern narratives but which remain relevant in modern times. The creation of the earth, linked to the deity Haiseb, offers a genealogy of the Nama and Khoisan people, while setting up further narratives building upon this creation-myth. Even through changes in space (e.g. displacement[49]) and through the intrusion of Enlightenment rationality into these societies, these myths offer alternative world paradigms and reinforce social cohesion and belonging. Furthermore, these myths offer icons and heroes which and who may relieve the distresses of the colonial and apartheid eras.

---

[47] Letter to Samuel Maharero dated 30 May 1890 in *The Hendrik Witbooi Papers*. This reference comes from a Nama folk tale in which the Sun fools the Jackal to carry it on its back.

[48] Of the eight volumes of folk tales compiled by Schmidt, six deal directly with oral narratives as recited by these two societies. The one I am referring to is volume no 8, *Tricksters, Monsters and Clever Girls* (2001).

[49] One should not forget that a number of Nama captives were exiled to other German colonies. See for example Walter Nuhr's Article "Die Deportation Kriegsgefangener Nama nach Kamerun", accessible under *www.traditionsverband.de/download/pdf/deportation.pdf*.

One of the figures who appears to spawn resistant potential and capacities is the figure of the trickster, a literary figure which is widely spread throughout the oral literature of numerous African societies. The main feature of the trickster figure, as the name might already suggest, is his/her ability to overcome more powerful adversaries through his/her intellect or ability to adapt to the situation. Usually concentrated in the figure of Haiseb, who can be equated with the Christian concept of God, the trickster is central in the resolution of conflicts and problematic situations. Examples of tricksters include the rabbit Zomo, the spider Anansi[50], as well Raven and Coyote[51]. The trickster figure is not always necessarily a person or god but may come from the animal kingdom. The unifying facet of the trickster is his inferior physical stature in comparison to his 'enemies' and his creativity and ingenuity in overcoming these. A further important newer fictional figure is the 'clever girl', who is reliant on her intellect and intelligence. The difference from the trickster, however, lies in the latter's need to first educate herself in order to overcome her problematic situations. The clever girl is a more recent addition to the cannon of oral narratives, which may again indicate a need for newer and more appropriate characters to counter the challenges of the times.

The importance of the oral tradition is of course not limited to its reservoir of past strategies. Orature also involves social aspects: the sharing of common stories and experiences. The fact that Muronga can dream of Tjakova is because the figure has a long history within his community and is passed down from generation to generation and from person to person. The myth becomes more than just a story, it becomes the expression of a communal and culture-specific social product. This helps in grounding Muronga's social identity and helps in resisting the defining mechanisms of apartheid as experienced through his encounters with the various representatives of the system (*dominee*, labour recruiters, compound managers, jailers). Orature is able to maintain and strengthen the networks, which the system has attempted to break up or dissolve. The stories shared in the village (and *Thivanda*) help to organise and navigate the 'outside' world[52], sharing this experience with members of his community. It also helps him to counter certain strategies employed by the church. His reiteration of Christian phrases and gestures is contrasted with his continued belief and trust in his 'old' god – a god that strongly links him to his ancestors, his current elders (such as Uncle Ndara), and his fellow villagers.

The need for historic personalities, even if they are fictional, is replicated in the post-war context within the Nama communities. Because of the heterogeneous factions

---

[50] These are popular tricksters occurring mainly in West African tales.
[51] These are popular tricksters occurring mainly in North and South American tales.
[52] I use this term only because Muronga had not been outside the limits of his village, not to contrast it to the village itself.

involved and their multiple motivations for taking up arms against the colonial government[53], one cannot simply speak of a 'Nama' war effort. Although the leaders considered it a collective effort to rid GSWA of the German presence (not by extermination, but by expulsion), most of the military activities were not a cohesive battle plan but were up to the individual *kapteine*. Their friction with the German and the British colonial governments, as well as their inter-group influences also affected their activities. Their post-war fates go a long way to substantiate this, with Witbooi, considered the greatest threat, killed relatively early in the war, but Simon Kooper, who had a significantly smaller force, was put on a state pension and allowed to return to ancestral lands with his people. However, it is the commemoration and the post-war discourses within their own communities that elevated the *kapteine* from fallen heroes to strong communal identifiers.

The cults around the anti-colonial heroes were augmented by the inhumane treatment of captured Nama soldiers and civilians (transported into concentration camps on the now notorious Shark island, off Lüderitzbucht) and the transportation of a number of prisoners to other German colonies, which most did not survive. Added to these events were the bounties that Von Trotha placed on the heads of the Nama *kapteine*. The fact that Witbooi's bounty was twice that of any other *kaptein* is testament to the threat he posed to German colonial authority. The relocation of the heroes, especially those who were endowed with an air of invincibility by their colonial counterparts[54] and within the post-war societies through tales of their bravery and tactical acumen, laid the groundwork for a return to a resistant self-definition. Like its predecessor, the Herero Days, the Witbooi commemorations pay tribute to the leader of the anti-colonial struggle.

Naming, like the reclaiming of space, has constituted a reliance on immaterial methods of self-definition. Muronga's assertion that his Christian name is only a 'Sunday name' reflects one way of dealing with the gaining influence of the church in the diverse villages. However, naming oneself (as opposed to spaces and places) was a possibility of manoeuvring within the highly organised and restrictive labour networks. The fact that the defeated Herero were subsequently reintegrated into the economy of GSWA as a *lumpen-*

---

[53] This would also apply to the Herero war effort, although the group was largely gathered under the leadership of Maharero, with few exceptions. The groups under Zeraua and Ouandja attempted until the end to avoid participation in the war. For more see "*Ovita ovia Zürn* – 'Zürns Krieg'" (Jan-Bart Gewald) in *Namibia-Deutschland. Eine Geteilte Geschichte* (78–91).

[54] A glance at the correspondence between the Colonel Nylan (Upington) and the Commissioner Cape Mounted Police (Cape Town) during the war is revealing on a number of issues. The lack of reliable news concerning Witbooi, for example, creates a scenario in which the *kaptein* is considered dead, but then reappears alive and well shortly after. See, for example, a letter dated 28.12.1904. Morenga (mentioned as Moringa) at one point seems to be defeated, which is then defined as "pure fiction", Confidential report by Lieut. Colonel Neyland, dated 03.08.1905.

proletariat, working on farms, in mines, and in German households, further changed the power relations between the two groups. The need to record and log relevant information concerning these new disempowered workers played a significant part in organising the labour network. However, the bureaucratic machinery was unable to fully gain control of the movement of those it was seeking to distribute. Examples include a constant refusal to be employed in this manner as farm and mine workers suddenly disappeared and moved into areas that were outside of the reach of the German administration. What made this strategy successful were two interrelated conditions. Firstly, because of the size of the territory it was difficult for the police force to patrol all designated areas. Secondly, many Herero workers were registered under multiple *names*, thus allowing them to be at multiple 'allocated' places and not being fixed to only one permitted place[55]. In this way they maintained their mobility while creating an opportunity to improve on their cattle possessions while preserving familial and social affiliations. Language thus became one of the most potent instruments of immaterial resistance, with strategies of renaming and re-locating the material in the realm of the symbolic. Returns to traditional and pre-colonial symbolism and icons added another dimension to the vigour of resistance.

Another powerful instrument of immaterial resistance was the production of counter discourses, i.e. discourses that were in opposition to colonial and apartheid discourses. One of the strategies of 'defining' and then exercising dominance over Black subjects was the production of 'universal' truths concerning identity. Mbembe (2002) traces the obsession of the act of defining back to Enlightenment rationality, focussing on "defining human nature in terms of its possession of a generic identity" (no page), attributing certain characteristics to certain groups. This process opened up the possibility of forming a *universal* understanding of humanity, consisting of fixed racial-cultural hierarchies located on a time line of development. Strategies defining the African subject were demonization (i.e. treating Africans as demons or devils), animalisation (i.e. linking Africans to animals and nature), and infantilisation (i.e. affording Africans human status but relegating this humanity to a nascent, underdeveloped state). These three strategies were used in order to justify extreme violence as well as legitimising imperial and colonial aspirations. However, these strategies were then adopted and re-appropriated by Africans, showing the arbitrary designs of these categories of humanity. One example already mentioned is the inversion of the master-slave relationship in which the Herero, though in the service of Germans/*whites*, referred to the 'master' as a slave, disrupting and inverting the supposedly stable binary.

---

[55] For more on this see Selmeci, Andreas & Dag Henrichsen. *Das Schwarzkommando. Thomas Pynchon und die Geschichte der Herero* (1995).

A further example refers to the act of infantilisation in respect to a very serious topic: the army. When Herero saw German soldiers and officers doing military drills and exercises, they placed these activities within the definition of playing. A typical observation might have sounded similar to "'[s]ie drillen, wie Kinder spielen. Wir haben noch nie gesehen, daß große Menschen spielen wie Kinder'" (quoted in Selmeci & Henrichsen 1995: 48). In this way, an activity that is designed for a war scenario and in preparation of violence is downplayed and interpreted as being harmless. A further reaction to these exercises was the fact that they were superfluous[56] within the context of the landscape of GSWA in which guerrilla warfare was much more of an advantage than classic European formation-based tactics. Although the German military was to a certain extent underestimated due to these misinterpretations, the reversal of powerful European racist discourse was at least redirected at the aggressor while the obsolescence of European military exercises was connected to the current environment.

The response to the seemingly redundant parades was supplemented by the land claims. In many instances these were constructed and presented within a European framework but using personal artefacts. As substantiation to the land claims, the territory was defined along borders, with the official document signed and then sealed with the house seal of the House of Kambazembi, as one example shows. Technologies of European diplomacy and power were employed to present and reproduce a case of land ownership. These cases were handled differently in respect to what Europeans were accustomed to. This lay in the small, but significant, differentiation between the ideas of 'belonging' and 'ownership'. The land claims made by the Herero relied on the concept of the land *belonging* to the community, and not their ownership over it. This created tensions as ownership of land guaranteed the unrestricted access to the available resources. This access was officially sanctioned and therefore justified the expulsion and removal of bodies not allowed within the demarcated area. Paramount Chief Riruako gives a succinct summary of how these two concepts created tensions between the Herero and the German farmers. He gives his account as follows:

> Um auf die Deutschen jener Zeit zurückzukommen: Der Zeitraum kann erbarmungslos genannt werden. Die Deutschen nahmen den Menschen das Land, ohne irgend etwas dafür zu zahlen. Sie behaupteten, das Land, das die genommen haben, sei irgendwie von Maharero allen, ohne Wissen seiner Berater, gekauft worden, was wir bezweifeln. Im Fall von Walvis Bay waren 56 der Ältesten zusammengerufen worden, als das Übereinkommen geschlossen wurde[57] – warum war das beim Weideland der Deutschen nicht der Fall? Aber

---

[56] These were remarks made by Herero to commissioner von François in respect to the efficacy of the drills. In: *Das Schwarzkommando*, 1995: 48–49.
[57] This is a reference to a previous contract that 56 Herero chiefs had signed with Commissioner Palgrave

diese Ländereien werden jetzt als deutscher Besitz anerkannt, trotz des Betrugs, der stattfand und durch den die Hereros Weideland verloren. Dann kam es dazu, daß Hererovieh abgeschossen wurde, weil es angeblich auf deutschem Land geweidet hatte, während das Vieh von Deutschen, das auf Hereroland weidete, ungeschoren gelassen wurde. Das Schießen nahm kein Ende und entzürnte die Hereros schließlich *so*, daß der Krieg zwischen den Hereros und den Deutschen begann. (emphasis in original, 247)

A reflection of the war practices used by both sides is recognisable in this passage. While little concern was expended upon differentiating between Herero civilians and combatants (i.e. shooting trespassing 'cattle'), Herero units focussed mostly on German soldiers and farmers (referencing the "ungeschoren" German cattle). This difference is mirrored in the official war declarations made by Von Trotha and Samuel Maharero, revealing the opposing war discourses. While the German General Staff, embodied by Von Trotha and his backers, fantasised about an 'end solution' in respect to the confrontation with the Herero forces[58], Maharero's goal was in effect favourable negotiations after the war. His declaration therefore made assurances for the safety of non-Germans (Boers, European traders), as well as children and women.

Reading Riruako's passage together with Maharero's declaration offers strong counter discourses against colonial concerns in which ownership became the basis from which to organise and justify a number of violent practices and fantasies. After the German administration had brutally struck down the Herero war effort, the dominant discourse on ownership survived. However, with a change of era (colonial to mandate to apartheid) and a change in administration (colonial to mandate to apartheid), older strategies employed by the Herero (which were reproduced by numerous other communities) emerged again as new identities, affiliations, and confidence were created. Immaterial resistance, in the form of language, symbols[59], and conceptualisations formed the backbone of another form of resistance, namely material resistance.

---

of the Cape colony. The contract guaranteed that the British would protect "das Land" and in return would receive Walvis Bay. This is also taken from the text by Kuaima Riruako, which is quoted above.

[58] Historians such as Bley, Zimmerer, and Zeller have pointed out that the military strategies involving the *Vernichtungsbefehl*, the pursuit of fleeing Herero in the Omaheke, the implementation of the concentration camps, as well as the unrestricted violence against surviving Herero non-combatants (hangings, shootings by death squads, and habitual and ruthless bayoneting) all indicate a wish to inflict as much damage against this enemy.

[59] The example of the highly esteemed Ovambo King Mandume should be mentioned at this point, especially his stance against the integration of the Ovambo kingdom into the colonial set up. His role will be discussed in more detail in connection with Muronga and his repeated incarceration.

Past Symbols for Current Identities

In 2011, a small number of the bones stolen by German colonists that were misused for experiments, and archived in the Berliner Charité, were 'returned' to Namibia[60]. The results of negotiations between the Namibian and German governments resulted in a symbolic hand-over, which took place at the Charité. Cornelia Piepers, State Minister in the Department of Foreign Affairs, caused a scandal in her handling of the situation. Her brief speech contradicted itself when she first mentioned that Germany "knew their historic and moral responsibility[61]" and then argued that the special relationship between Namibia and Germany rested on the latter's large number of tourists visiting the former[62]. Having enraged the 60 Namibian delegates, she left without listening to any of the proceeding speeches by the Namibian officials. Add to this the on-going legal battles over reparations and the acknowledgement of the genocide, this moment in the 'special relationship' between the two nations discloses the continuation of a colonial position. Piepers' disregard for the attendant delegates, the superficial and senseless reference to tourism (which can only be seen as a consequence of colonialism), and Germany's reluctance to return what was claimed and acquired through extreme violence, all represent a refusal to deal with a violent past. The responsibility of remembering this atrocity seemingly falls on the shoulders of the Namibian people.

Dag Henrichsen (2004; 2011), Larissa Förster (2004; 2010), Annette Hoffmann (2005), and Memory Biwa (2012), amongst numerous others, have examined how memory and commemoration have contributed to the reconstruction of a decimated community. While Henrichsen, Förster, and Hoffmann predominantly focus on the Herero, Biwa discusses the Nama in southern Namibia and Northern Province of South Africa. Although strategies had already been employed against colonial Germany before the colonial war, they found their zenith during and after the fateful crossing of the Omaheke by the Herero and the subsequent period of the concentration camps. These events are arguably the most traumatic in Herero history, as close to all resources for Herero identity and self-definition were destroyed or destabilised. The huge loss of human life, the masses of dead cattle, the loss of home, the dispersion of the 'nation', the loss of the traditional hierarchy, and the post-war treatment of the survivors all point towards a long-lasting effect of this harrowing historical episode.

Consequently, with the establishment of new forms of expression, remembrance and commemoration, modes of resistance against an oppressive historical metanarrative were

---

[60] These practices were in no way new, as the story of Sarah Baartman (better known as the Hottentot Venus) tragically shows.
[61] Arndt 2012:124
[62] ibid.

incorporated into the everyday. With the passing stages of Namibian identity (from colony to independent state), changes concerning the national character of these tactics have been either incorporated into the project of nation building or have resisted the act of incorporation. Furthermore, the commemorations and memorial periods are strongly linked to the specific groups, meaning that the incorporated symbolism and material representations present during these celebrations have a firm *internal* logic and transport predominantly communal assertions of an historic identity and future vision. Nonetheless, these strategies are essential as coping mechanisms. A (shared) violent history as well as similar losses of culture, influence, and land connect the main societies of the Herero and Nama, although the methods of remembering and celebrating are quite different.

Biwa[63] makes reclaiming the images of the headmen one of the most potent post-war reconstitutive strategies. This begins with von Trotha placing bounties on the heads of Nama *kapteine*, prompting civilian and non-combatants to hunt Nama elites. Severing and collecting of heads for medical and biological experiments became *en vogue*[64], with a large number of these heads being sent to Germany for cataloguing and safekeeping. Biwa (92) gives examples how these heads then became a sign of resistance, as they began to be appropriated in diverse media such as t-shirts, on scarves, and posters. The repatriation of the heads – through intense campaigning and diplomatic activity – was seen as the culmination of resistance to ownership of the heads. A final, nationally significant, medial reproduction and therefore claim of ownership of the heads within a modern state is the incorporation of Hendrik Witbooi's head[65] on Namibia's bank notes. Not only does he become an omnipresent symbol of Namibian independence (although in commodity form), but his international fame is re-established[66] through his image's participation within the global economy.

---

[63] Her chapter "The Afterlives of Genocide" (61–94) describes the genocidal events, also making a case for the genocide of the Nama people. The last part of the chapter, however, deals with the strategies of resistance to the genocide, with the claim for reparations by both Herero and Nama as the successful culmination of this resistance. Biwa further deals with 'smaller' acts of resistance such as memorial days in which colonial space (e.g. Lüderitz' inner city) is symbolically occupied while strong associations to the past (in form of dress, colour codes, artefacts) are paraded and made visible.

[64] This practice has strong links to the science of phrenology and what general physicians were later doing in the concentration camps under the Nazi regime in Germany.

[65] Although the term 'portrait' seems more fitting to describe Witbooi's picture on the bank notes, I am staying with Biwa's wordplay focusing on the reclaiming of Nama leader's 'heads' by the general Namibian society.

[66] The *kapteine* (Witbooi, Morenga, Kooper, Fredericks) who fought against Germany in the south of GSWA received a lot of international attention due to their continuous border crossings between GSWA and the Cape Colony. Not only were they the topic of security concerns and diplomatic clinches between Germany and England, they became mythologised as their elusiveness and trickery caused significant distress for both imperial nations as well as putting strain on their relationships.

A further, powerful mode of resistance against the ever-diminishing cultural spaces of the two communities most significantly affected by the genocidal wars is the symbolic reclaiming of certain places. Okahandja, capital of the Herero, went through its reclaiming stage once Samuel Maharero was successfully buried at his traditional place of belonging in 1923. The numerous spectators and participants, combined with the flags, uniforms, saddled men, and ceremonial activities (singing, reciting *omitandu* and *omitango* (praising people)) replicated the pre-colonial days. This was repeated to a certain extent in 2005 and 2007 when Nama factions paraded through Lüderitzbucht and commemorated the internment on Shark Island[67]. Thus, the spaces which were responsible for the worst moments of the (post-)war were incorporated into the tradition of remembering those who perished under the most inhumane conditions.

Of course, as time progresses so too do the resistant practices. Förster traces the evolution of the Maharero Day commemorations from their inception to their current guise. Although certain implementations stay relatively fixed (the participation of the *oturupa*, the spaces of memory[68] and memorialisation), other aspects have changed along with changes in the administration of SWA[69]. The political climate allowed for the return of Paramount Chief Samuel Maharero's body from exile in Botswana back to SWA. Symbolically, this act had the result of reuniting the disparate and dispersed Herero communities. Although the pseudo-militarist appearance of the *oturupa* did cause slight distress to the mandate authorities and the settler community of Okahandja[70], the effect of this demonstration of unity and, more importantly, survival was tantamount in the re-establishment of Herero self-understanding. The appropriation of German army uniforms (the uniform of the enemy), endowed with personal signifiers and a colour coded group identity, created a space in which to assert *Herero-ness*. The first step in achieving this was acquiring cattle, once *the* marker of Herero identity[71].

Furthermore, the establishment of a community through the efforts and influence of the *oturupa* is a significant factor in the creation of a new Herero nation and self-definition. What I am trying to argue is that the destruction of material culture does not necessarily spell the end of a culture. Strategies of reorganisation and the creation

---

[67] For more see Biwa's "Chapter Two: The Afterlives of Genocide" (2012) in which she focusses on Nama post-war commemorations and memorialisation practices.
[68] For example, the battle of Hamakari features prominently within the Herero recollection of the war although the venue for the commemoration has changed occasionally. For more, see Förster (2005).
[69] One reason might have been the hopeful outlook the regime change could potentially bring with it (most notably the return of ancestral lands), as well as the elimination of the German threat.
[70] Culminating in a ban during the 1930s.
[71] Cattle plays a huge role in the daily routine of a number of Herero, while being central to all festivities, commemorations, and social events (weddings, funerals, births, etc.).

of new networks have rejuvenating potential. By locating past symbols (innate or foreign) and incorporating them within a contemporary context, it is possible to maintain a strong link to the past while creating a space for a new future. The acquisition of cattle posed a number of challenges (not least the economic factor of an impoverished group), most notably the proclamation barring the Herero from keeping larger herding animals. However, as with most draconian laws, this was circumvented by keeping to spaces outside of police surveillance, and also requesting payment for work in the form of cattle. The restocking of cattle herds necessitated the opposition to other laws as well (such as labour laws and the laws concerning habitation); loopholes within the legal frameworks were exploited. Furthermore, the limited reach of the colonial police, augmented by the laxer control during the mandate period, created an opening in which an old hegemony could – at least symbolically – be reinstated. Past rituals were reanimated in order to recreate a community *after* most of its symbols, practices, and resources were reduced to next to nought. The wish for a return to the days *before* the genocide and the destruction of the Herero way of life, to a time when Herero hegemony was a reality, thus became the driving force in the formation of old-new (to put it bluntly: recycled) identities.

One can trace this reinstated hegemony back to the very first Herero Days, the moment in which Samuel Maharero's body was returned to its original place. With this return came a return to previous traditional practices such as the lighting and maintenance of the ancestral fire, male circumcision, female puberty rituals as well as polygamy[72]. Old ties were revitalised and a traditional way of life was utilised in order to cope with the events of the past. Moreover, the past was reinstated in the present with the hope of securing a future based on previous accomplishments and achievements. This form of recasting the past is evident when one looks at the grave of the Tjamuaha-Maharero family in Okahandja. The headstone is cast in the shape of a bullet, thus offering a number of associations and interpretations. Not only is it a reminder of the turbulent times under the colonial administration, it can be seen as a "Reflex dieses Kampfes [of African independence] in Namibia zwischen 1966 und 1989" (Salmeci & Henrichsen, 141), also referencing the liberation struggle. The Herero war against German colonialism is – in the form of the grave and gravestone – included in the renewed struggle against foreign European occupation. The slab on the tomb contains a cut-out in the shape of Africa, with special emphasis on Namibia. One can again reference the position and rhetoric of the past (this time of Hendrik Witbooi) concerning the idea of self-governance and autono-

---

[72] "Erloschene Ahnenfeuer wurden wieder entfacht, die Beschneidung der Jünglinge, die Pubertätsrituale der Mädchen, die traditionelle Heirat und die Polygynie wurden wieder eingeführt" (Selmeci & Henrichsen, 1995:95).

my, especially through the concept of the *nation*. The tomb can therefore be categorised as a monument, a cultural product that simultaneously connects the past, present, and desired future, while linking various communities (i.e. nations) to these temporalities[73]. The linear progression of history is at the same time reproduced and contested through the cyclical reference of violence both in Namibia and Africa. Furthermore, the tomb can enter into the national conversation of liberation while preserving its definitive social identity and history (through the Tjamuaha-Maharero names). In essence this creates conditions in which historic identities and events are able to survive and flourish in a contemporary world.

As the examples of Herero and Nama post-genocide identity (re)construction show, and as Hayes has pointed to, relocating the past within the present is a powerful tool in creating new forms of community while forming a foundation for a liveable future. These strategies created the conditions for a general anti-apartheid movement through the conjuring up of anti-colonial struggles and placing them within a contemporary context. The retrieval of prominent and historic personalities alongside the numerous original societies provided fertile ground to create current personalities. The strong connection to the horrors of the colonial era through lineage (especially of the survivors), memorial practices, as well as oral and archival documentation all had the effect that access to the past influenced the projections of the future. Post-colonial interventions such as the Heroes Acre in Windhoek are strong arguments for the success of the past within the present. The (symbolic) graves of Nama (Hendrik Witbooi, Jacob Morenga) as well as Herero (Kahimemua Nguvauva, Samuel Maharero, Hosea Kutako) and Owambo heroes (Nehale Lya Mpingana, Mandume ya Ndemufayo, Lipumbu ya Tshilongo, Kurukaza Mungunda[74]) are located in one single space at Heroes' Acre. Although the anti-colonial struggle takes on the form of a national project, it is not merely the mention of these leaders in a war context, but as a part of a *unified* state. This unified state produces a space in which communal histories flow into the general history of the now established nation state. The anti-colonial struggle is mirrored in the anti-apartheid struggle (and vice versa).

---

[73] Exhibiting the Lefebvrian dimension concerning the monument's potential as a strong organisation of time and space.
[74] According to the inauguration speech given by Sam Nujoma at the opening of the Heroes Acre, Mungunda is the exception to the rule in respect to the people who were 'buried' at the symbolic space. Contrary to the other names mentioned, she is the only non-elite, i.e. civilian person who was honoured at the site.

The Resistance of One, the Resistance of Many

So far, this chapter has opened up brief discussions on resistant spaces, followed by historic moments/movements of resistance. The two can and should not be separated, especially as the one is intrinsically part of the other. Any form of resistant behaviour is always spatial, meaning that space and resistance are inextricably linked[75]. The use of space against the intended hegemonic purpose, especially by marginalised or disenfranchised groups, is always resistant. However, my aim was to first identify specific spaces in the novel and link these to Muronga's resistant strategies. These can then be identified in relation to past practices and habits. As a result of the uncovering of the dynamics of these spaces and Muronga's responses to them, finding templates of/for Muronga's strategies is a vital aspect if one is to understand how Muronga and his peers offer resistance to apartheid. Because of a host of previous pre- and colonial moments of resistance – besides military conflicts – from which Muronga is able to draw from, it seems appropriate to separate the fictional spaces, however real they may be constructed, from historic resistance – on an initial level. What this separation can achieve is a separation of the fictional and the real in order to shed light on each concept individually. Because of the separate fields of inquiry[76], a sufficient foundation is necessary to enter into an examination of the resistant elements in the novel.

The first resistant space, which I identified and examined, is the village where Muronga lives. Not only does it briefly introduce the reader to Muronga's routine and his connection to the other villagers (his wife Makena, his friend Kaye, the village headman Uncle Ndara), it also gives insights into the daily routine of the main character. The first instance of contact with what can be deemed foreign elements are the church and its preacher, Pater Dickmann. As it seems, he is the only *white* person in the village and appears to have a significant position in the village community. However, this position is covertly questioned, especially in the form of critical stances in respect to church logic and symbolism. At one point it is affirmed that the traditional spiritual authority is still in a position of power, that "what the nganga [traditional healer] says is more important to the young couple than all the sermons and admonitions of the priest" (4). From the onset the authority of the *nganga* is reinforced, even with the emergence of a stable Christian

---

[75] Schlögel argues that „All unser Wissen von Geschichte haftet an Orten [...] Es gibt keine Geschichte im Nirgendwo. Alles hat einen Anfang und ein Ende. Alle Geschichte hat einen Ort" (2003:70, quoted in Piatti, 2008:16). The dual meaning of Geschichte of both a story *and* history is even more relevant for this book.
[76] Postmodern writing, especially, blurs the lines between the fictional and the historic. "The Narrative of Jacobus Coetzee" is an example of this in my work, while Thomas Pynchon's *V* (1963) and *Gravity's Rainbow* (1973) would offer further material in the study of the Herero and their place in fiction.

congregation within the village community. And yet, the state apparatus slowly but surely penetrates the space of local power, as the relatively isolated village becomes the site of labour recruitment. The highest administrative personality, the Bantu Affairs Commissioner, has personally arrived at Muronga's homestead and, under the supervision of the headman Uncle Ndara, introduces new laws and explains the addition of new taxes. These developments force the young and able men (women are excluded from the recruitment process) to leave their homes temporarily in order to sell their labour so they can pay the new taxes. This economic exploitation forms the basis of the initial integration of Black bodies within the labour system, while later forming the basis of general disobedience and resistance.

Muronga's first response in respect to being forced into the migrant labour structures is one of opportunism. The possibility of attaining (relative) wealth and improving one's social standing seems more like an opportunity than it does a restrictive practice[77]. The fruits of work are strongly linked to providing for others, as the wish to buy hats and fabrics for his family and friends clearly indicates. And it is this wish to provide for others that is manipulated in order to gain the following of the potential migrant workers. An experienced worker explains the procedure to Muronga, but it is his appeal to the relationship to his wife that proves the most convincing:

> "We go to sleep tonight, wake up tomorrow morning…and on the road we go to the Tribal Community Bureau office. There we will get registered…ready to 'climb the lorry', and then, off we go to wherever. We come back…different, with plenty of money, clothes, Vaseline and everything. All right? Now, don't put your wife to shame please!" (51)

The idea of labour is constructed around the idea of masculinity, a trope that will be repeated multiple times. The link between work and masculinity becomes a central argument in maintaining one's position within these structures, while the dream to improve one's social standing and material wealth supplements this. This in essence predicts the homosocial and male dominated spaces that are all connected through the exploitation of male-based labour. It is in these structures that male-on-male relations and organisation becomes central to the overthrowing of South African occupation.

The spaces Muronga enters into, apart from the village, are all male domains, and therefore spaces in which the masculine has to be continuously reproduced. This may take the form of exercising power over others, such as by the mining officials and their lackeys, the police forces, and the prison guards. On the other hand, the ends of ex-

---

[77] "Usually contract labourers who come back with heavy trunks are highly respected, especially if they bring thick coats and hats for their fathers, and long, dark, colourful fabrics for their mothers. This whole idea energizes the young men. The sooner they go, the better" (51).

ploitative labour also confirm a form of masculinity. Most significantly, competing ideas of masculinity are reproduced within these realms in order to gain access and control of the future. The *dominee's* assertion that if the workers accept the authority of God and his substitute, the government, they will have nothing to worry about (113; 114). This stabilises the European, male-dominated hierarchies of the apartheid system while guaranteeing the continued compliance of those which have been integrated. On the other hand, by focussing on future advantages of the work in the mines, on farms, and *white* households, the workers are able to find meaning and purpose in their work and sacrifices[78]. At one point these practices are historicised when a cyclical link between ancestors and labour is constructed. After the meeting with the Commissioner, Kaye tells Muronga "that we will do the elders' work one day" (61). What he is pointing at is the now-established practice in which men go 'outside' to work, returning at a later stage in order to negotiate work terms with the responsible 'outside authority'. It also gives the experiences that they can share with the next generation, preparing them for the dangers and pitfalls if *Thivanda*.

The fact that the work force is exclusively male and that these males come from all corners of the country means that new relationships have to be forged. Not only is this evident when one looks at the political organisations that are found throughout the narrative (most prominently the UPO and Archie Bokwe's Black Promotion Movement), but also in corporeal relations between men. Shortly after arriving in Doornfontein, Muronga witnesses an example of this type of relationship, one that he is unable to fully comprehend. This passage can be interpreted as a highly resistant scene, not only in reference to the fixed meanings concerning masculinity and femininity. The powerful idea of solidarity is evident in Muronga's brief confrontation with a sexual union outside of the traditional male-female partnership.

> One of the doors of the barracks closest to him has been gently eased open by the pleasant Transvaal breeze that blows over the compound. There, inside the room, Muronga sees two men who are both naked from the waist down sitting on a bed and touching each other in a manner that is unusual for two men. Or, at least, that is what Muronga thinks he sees. Unsure whether the setting sun is playing tricks on his eyes, he quietly bends over and, with his hands on his knees, he squints he eyes to see more clearly. It appears that an older man is applying vaseline jelly to the inner thighs of a younger man, who sits passively on the bed. *The two men are apparently unaware that they are being watched.*
>
> "What is the matter, Muronga?" asks Nyangana, who has finally rejoined his comrades.

---

[78] "Earning money for his family and for the taxes allows Muronga to persevere, to endure the pain of separation and degradation. But that is true for all men working in the mine. They must find comfort in each other's company" (123).

"Nothing...ehm...just *looking*," Muronga replies, *looking* ashamed and disgusted.

"Nyangana, *looking* toward the barracks, can also *see* the two men. The younger man is, by this time, lying on his back with the older man on top of him. "Ah, I *see*, yes of course. You must be shocked if this is the first time you have *seen* this sort of thing," Nyangana says sympathetically. "I myself was certainly shocked, too, when I first *saw* that."

"But what is this? Men...together?" (127)

The fact that two men appear to be doing what Muronga and his wife usually do confuses him. However, his friends Nyangana and Ndango, who have previously witnessed these acts, help him come to understand this.

"You see, Muronga, many of these men have been here a very long time and they are sexually starved," explains Ndango. "That is what they call *matanyuna* here. There are no women here, so men turn to other men. They sleep with each other as if they were sleeping with their wives, you see."

Ah, *matanyuna*! I have heard about it. The priest at home said that it happened in Sodom and Gomorrah; in some white people's country. "But...but...what if one of them becomes pregnant?" Muronga asks.

"No, it doesn't happen that way. I don't know why not, but it has never happened. They do it between the legs, just like you saw," explains Ndango.

Muronga is dismayed. How can a man do such a thing with another man? He wonders.

"*But these are men, real men, like we are.* And they are friends who stand by each other while they are here in the mine. When they return home, they remain good friends...family friends, although they do not tell their wives about what has happened between them. This is what I have *heard* from different people."

"I have *heard* that too," interrupts Ndango. "I have *heard* that when they leave here, they do not sleep with each other any more. They go back to their wives and children. But while they are here in the mine they are more than just friends or brothers. They take care of each other. Perhaps it is like what we have with our wives." (127–128)

I want to first point to two different strategies utilised in this passage. What begins as a visual event for Muronga, with strong emphasis on the act of seeing, becomes an attempt to comprehend this scene with the help of oral references. Not only is the term *matanyuna* used to link the village to the act that is taking place between the two men, but the different stories heard by Muronga, Nyangana, and Ndango create a web of connections and affiliations. The solidarity exercised between the two men is expanded to include those who are not directly connected to this practice, creating an imagined community of solidarity and one which has its roots in the village and finds its reproduction in the confines of the mine compound.

Homosexuality, as a form of interpersonal contact, is not explained or evaluated. Rather, it is placed within the larger system of oppression in which alternative relationships may be formed[79]. Although these relationships do not fit the traditional, historic conception of male-female unions, they are accepted within the extreme circumstances which apartheid, through its dislocating labour system, has introduced. The statement connecting the working men with oxen also has strong associative currency when one looks at the significance attributed to cattle in the development of the various original societies in GWSA, most notably the Herero. However, this time the strongly denoted animals become substitutes for the inhumane conditions experienced by and forced upon Black workers. Both associations reflect the intense conditions under which males have to adapt, while emphasising their sub-human import within the strongly confined and segregated political system.

Merging the Past, Present, and Future

The emergence of the *oturupa*, the reclaiming of 'stolen' bones and skulls of Nama and Herero people, and the formation of national cross-communal organisations all reflect the need to form new relations, relationships, and kinships. The disruptive events of a full-on colonial war and its horrific results combined with the near decimation of traditional structures and practices effected a number of coping mechanisms. A return to traditional forms of identity construction have created platforms for coping with the events and losses of the past – and a number of them are reactivated in order to deal with developments in the present. If we return to *Born of the Sun*, it becomes clear that Muronga and his peers make use of the past on numerous occasions[80] in order to navigate the 'new' world they are forced to enter. They create new meaning and value by re-appropriating some of the objects that symbolise their confinement within the labour and apartheid systems.

One example of this is the meaning associated with their uniform, especially the gumboots[81]. Muronga is very impressed with his yellow overall that relegates him to the position of labourer of the lowest classes. It also symbolises his place within a very fixed,

---

[79] Texts dealing with traumatic and events (such as the Slave Trade and forced labour camps) also discuss same-sex relations as a way of coping with the destruction of previous relations. Examples would include "Black Atlantic, Queer Atlantic. Queer Imaginings of the Middle Passage" by Omise'eke Natasha Tinsley (2008) as well as the collection of essays *Defiant Desire. Gay and Lesbian Lives in South Africa*, edited by Mark Gevisser (1995).

[80] I have alluded to them briefly when discussing Muronga's confinement in the Pretoria jail, while also pointing to the village as a source of orientation.

[81] The well-known South African gumboot dances are a form of cultural expression that emerged from the mining communities, incorporating the rhythms of traditional dances and the unique soundscape generated by the boots.

racialised hierarchy. But through it, he becomes part of a group, of a community. The yellow overall creates a bond with the other workers, creating a space of belonging. This space is further strengthened when one considers that Muronga is part of a historic community of workers, a fact that links his position to those before him[82]. He becomes connected to a past that is not merely institutional (i.e. consisting of a state organisation moulded by laws and regulation), but also communal. These connections are later translated into a national consciousness, linking current (and future) suffering to that of the past. The role of trade unions and work groups in the struggle for liberation cannot be ignored, as they played a vital role in civil disobedience and organising official resistance through strikes. Furthermore, the largest camps within SWAPO structures (apart from combatants) were student and worker's associations. Thus one can argue that the initial spark was ignited by civil disobedience borne from the large trade union networks.

The appropriation of the yellow mining overall can symbolically be linked to the uniforms of the *oturupa* and their fondness for German *Schutztruppen* uniforms. The rationale behind the use of signs and symbols of the tormentors, and their assimilation into own forms of identity construction, lies in the potency of its connecting potential. In other words, the integration of the signatures of power of the enemy strengthens one's own position. The paradoxical 'celebration' of the genocide repeated year for year by the Herero may serve as a template in order to gain access to Muronga's relation to his new uniform. His only remark concerning the overall is connected to the village and the response of the people who might see him wearing it. Although he only mentions this item once, he "constantly wishes that they could see him now, in his new yellow uniform, talking a strange language, and crawling around underground like a termite" (119). He wants to be seen *with* it, especially as this acquisition includes the acquisition of further skills (lingual and physical). This places him in the community of those who share the same clothing. It also places him in the tradition of people who left the village and endured the same hardships. The overall thus becomes a symbol that links Muronga to his informal community (his work associates) as well as everybody who came before him. Being seen wearing the overall at home thus gives evidence of his belonging to an imagined community, while it further works as a strong statement of survival.

In the context of the 'resurrection' of the Herero army[83], the proclamation is that 'we are still here', that one has withstood attempts at destruction. The echo of Audre Lord's assertion that "we were not meant to survive"[84] is undeniably contained in this practice.

---

[82] There are a number of scenes in which Muronga learns about *Thivanda* from older workers and elders.
[83] Borrowed from Selmeci & Henrichsen (1995:84).
[84] Taken from the poem "A Litany for Survival" (1995).

Assimilating the uniforms of the *Schutztruppe* as well as further structures and symbols (organisational structures, titles, names, insignia) transfers the power of these structures and symbols onto the Herero *oturupa*. The remembrance targets the previous owners and wearers of the uniforms. These included the elites who were given the uniforms as tokens of their position, those who were in the services of the *Schutztruppe* (as auxiliary forces or servants), and those who amassed the uniforms on the battlefields. In essence, the uniforms form a multi-layered reference to the past and the present by remembering and commemorating the fallen soldiers and non-combatants while animating new identities and strengthening the links to past heroes. Signifiers meant to oppress are reconfigured to proclaim one's own historic past, diluting the original oppressive power of these signifiers. The strong connection of the appropriated signs and symbols also reflect spatial re-appropriations (evident in the parades as well as naming) and thus constitute historic claims to land.

One theme Muronga continuously links to his oppression – and that of his people – is the question of land. At a meeting of the South West Africans at the mine compound, Muronga speaks about *white* tactics in maintaining their dominance. The first tactic is identified as money (185). The second tactic is identified as land:

> "Every day the white man takes more of our land and claims it as his own. If we do not stop him, he will keep taking it until we haven't even a place to lay our heads. 'But how can we stop him?' you ask. I say to you the must unite behind the United People's Organization". There is strength in unity. We must be willing to make sacrifices and take risks, for there is no gain without risk. And we must begin at once. I call on you now, to stand with me as we demand our land and our freedom from the white man. Our children will have no land and no future unless we do our duty to them and to our ancestors. We have only one chance to demand our freedom – for we will walk this earth only once[85]. Each one of us has been born only once and will live only once – as a slave or as a free man. The time has come. It is now or never!" (185–186)

What Muronga does in his speech is connect the themes that have been utilised in nearly every war of resistance in Namibia (and elsewhere). Just like the Herero concerns of unsuitable and insufficient land were central to their decision to take up arms[86], so too was this the main reason for Witbooi to dissolve his contract with Germans[87]. This past

---

[85] This is a response to Christian priests' assertion that the people who accept Christianity and leave their heathen lifestyles behind are "born again" (27).
[86] Land, however, was not the only reason for the war, but it was a significant factor.
[87] This was most evident in Witbooi's early letters to Maharero and Leutwein, which I have alluded to already. His decision was a combination of a godly mission handed down and the wish for autonomy and the recognition of the Nama as its own 'nation'. Günther Reeh's *Hendrik Witbooi: Ein Leben für die Freiheit* (2000) extensively discusses this dual argumentation.

concern is located in the present ("we haven't even a place to lay our heads") and then relocated into the future ("Our children will have no land and no future unless we do our duty to them") while the historic community ("our ancestors") are invoked. He thus places the land question within the long history of occupation and invokes previous as well as future generations to augment his argument. It is his rhetoric (as well as his resistant activities in jail) that allows him to enter "his new role as a leader of the United People's Organization" (188). When one looks at a common factor linking the 'uprisings' against the colonial and apartheid regimes it becomes impossible to move beyond loss of, and control over, land. Muronga is sensitive to this issue, claiming that the church in his village desired "the most strategic spot for their mission, the missionaries tricked Chief Ndara of the Hambukushu tribe with gifts of guns, mirrors and clothes until he gave them the plot of land on which the mission now stands" (20). The loss of land through trickery and for ephemeral status symbols[88] of course has a long tradition in the colonial enterprises as do false promises and ignoring contractual obligations.

South Africa's obsession with bringing land under its control is unmistakable even in the mandate era as is evident from the focus on the connection between the local population and their lands. The progression from "The native question...is synonymous with *Labour* question"[89] (emphasis mine) to "The native question is the *land* question"[90] (emphasis mine) reveals a powerful triangle in which the control over one of the three elements will result in the control over the other two. The need to transport labourers from their traditional homes to far-off places of work can therefore create conditions in which land may be brought under the management of the administration. Conversely, however, this triangle is able to open up strategies in which the three elements can be used. In an immaterial fashion, the elements can be used to counter current discourses concerning race and labour. This would potentially weaken the bonds keeping the triangle in place. Secondly, the collapse of the forced labour recruitment would ultimately lead to the collapse of the other two elements. In essence, a direct head-to-head conflict with the massively superior military machine, combined with massive South African military presence in Namibia meant that disrupting the apartheid regime's economic strategies would remain the most effective local weapon against a much stronger opponent. While the laws

---

[88] The gun might be considered an ephemeral status symbol as its function is diminished without bullets. However, Henrichsen (2011) has shown that the Herero over time incorporated guns into their rituals (becoming a *Gewehrgesellschaft*) while Patricia Hayes' (2009) essay mentions the presence of guns at Kwanyama celebrations such as weddings.
[89] Annual Report for SWA for 1920, pg. 13, quoted in "Blacks to Wall" Robert L. Bradford. In: *Travesty of Trust* (Segal, Ronald & Ruth First, (eds.). (1967: 91).
[90] Annual Report for SWA for 1921, pg. 13, ibid.

regulating movement, habitation, and access to basic social services such as education and health were tightly overseen, the size of SWA as well as the unmonitored spaces (including the exile spaces of Angola, Zambia, Botswana, and Zimbabwe) allowed certain groups and individuals the opportunity to escape these laws. What does remain is that labour laws basically impacted every aspect of Black life in SWA and thus would create the space for the most intense forms of friction and resistance. One aspect, apart from the organised downing of tools or absence from work, became the deconstruction of the labour policies and identifying their destructive, yet connecting, nature. The awareness of *how* these laws functioned created an arena in which to reverse power and hierarchical structures.

During discussions concerning the labour of Black workers, Uncle Ndara reverses the common European rhetoric concerning African subjects as well as their role within the labour economy. His comments question the relationship between *white* preachers and their understudies, revealing the contrary and divisive strategies employed by the *white* government and its extensions. While talking to young Black Christian understudies from his village, he identifies *white* bosses as children, stating that

> 'White people are like children. They want everything to be easy. When I worked far away in the mines, we black men did the hard work while they lazed around and told us what to do. They are afraid to do hard work. It is as if they think they would melt. I just don't know what they would do without black people. It is good for our young men to and work for the white man. Then you see how they live. Then you understand why these two [mission boys] behave like this. (36)

This is the sentiment shared by the Herero who were amused after seeing German soldiers during their exercises and parades (they were deemed to be "playing like children"). Questions of laziness and of access to material wealth are problematized and placed in the context of race. Uncle Ndara's questions aimed at the mission boys confirm the segregated nature of space, labour, and resources:

> 'Tell me, mission boys,' Uncle Ndara asks the boys before they leave. 'What do you eat at the mission? Do these white people eat with you?' 'No, they eat inside their rooms,' one of the boys answers. 'We eat outside. And they do not eat the food we eat. It's only for us and the dogs. They have different food that the sisters cook. We're not allowed to eat it.'" (36)

The two young men, in the service of the church, are not part of its space. They receive their own space while their exclusion from meals echoes what Haarhoff has argued concerning the conscious colonial differentiation between European arrivals and Africans. Based on the reports by hunters, emphasising the romantic, yet ascetic, life in the bush, he asserts that "[d]istance is maintained through diet" (38), while preparation of said diet should also be included. Christianity's inherent contradictions are easily exposed, as are the dividing social instruments, most notably food. Food, however, is evoked as a strong survival tool at another point in the novel. And again it is strongly linked to religious expression. This time, though, it is the traditional god whose name is central as well as his services to 'his' subjects. After being confronted with the disdain shown towards him by a liminal subject, Muronga turns to Kaye, reminding him of the important religious structures of their village: "And I am not going to change. I am what I am, and shall always be. We have our land, our cattle, our *mahangu*, which gives us the porridge which keeps us alive. We are not hungry yet, thanks to the God of Our Forefathers!'" (57). The benevolence of the 'old' god far outweighs that of the 'new' god.

A further seed of the past germinating in Muronga's present are King Mandume's words before his death. After Muronga is again jailed (this time for his organised anti-apartheid activities – he is labelled a 'troublemaker') and is isolated and beaten, he thinks to himself that it is "[b]etter to be free and dead than imprisoned and alive" (194). Although not a direct citation of King Mandume[91], it accurately reflects the sentiment. And although the King's quote does have the theme of resistant violence at its core, Muronga takes up the argument that death is a more desirable alternative to being a captive. This idea invokes the concept of individual sovereignty by offering one's life as a weapon, as a sacrifice, complicating the existing power structures. By being able to decide for oneself whether to choose life or suicide[92], choice has become a theme that has entered into postcolonial discussions.

A good example concerning the Herero – to be found in Pynchon's *Gravity's Rainbow* – is applied on a number of levels. The first being their decision to be involved in the dangerous work of constructing the V2 missiles for the Nazi military (the fictional Herero division is responsible for the projectiles under the name *Schwarzkommando*). A second level is the physical regression of the Herero women in respect to childbearing. A final level is the self-imposed sterilisation, based on the argument: if the colonisers were unable to destroy us, we will do it for them[93]. What at first seems to be a death wish is a claim to authority over life and community. Furthermore, by removing oneself from the sphere of influence of those wishing to do harm, this has traits of self-preservation[94]. The

---

[91] His words are "it is better to die fighting than to become a slave of the colonial forces" (taken from Sam Nujoma's inauguration speech for the Heroes Acre).
[92] The ability to choose to end one's life is a vital aspect concerning autonomy. With state sovereignty forfeiting some of its authority, some power flows back to the subject. The subject's life can thus be considered its highest form of sacrifice and its most valuable resistant asset.
[93] The final chapter in *Das Schwarzkommando* deals intently with this reversal of a destruction discourse, as does Bruno Arich-Gertz' *Namibias Postkolonialismen* (2008), especially chapter three "Mimikry in der kolonialen Zwischenzeit".
[94] This is also evident when looking at examples from the Middle Passage, where pregnant mothers threw

control and authority over one's own life (and consequently death) is the highest form of sovereignty. The confirmation of this (in the case of Pynchon's fictioned Herero and King Mandume) affirms that a life in the service of liberation is in fact the highest form of sacrifice.

Earlier at a village meeting, Muronga inquires why a certain headman has been replaced contrary to custom, which dictated that a chief stays a chief until he dies. Uncle Ndara then answers that

> [t]here are some things we have to accept that we do not like. When an old elephant can no longer reach the highest branches, it lets the young stretchy ones do it. And that is why chief Dimbare was elected. The people wanted a chief who could hold a pen. He is good, this man of the pen. He is here for the people whose tongue he speaks. He is very clever and his head is full of ideas. He goes to this thing, this church to speak to the white man's God. He is very strong because he gets his power from our God, Nyambi, and from the church God. He knows the white man's tricks. (17)

It is nearly impossible not to think of Hendrik Witbooi (as well as the other elites who were able to write) and his impact on the culture of letters in Namibia. His high standing within the colonial administration (most notably during Leutwein's tenure) and the value afforded by his found diary substantiate this impact. Furthermore, the diary created a clear picture of the political situation in GSWA as his correspondence included elites from other factions (e.g. Hermanus van Wyk of the Rehoboth Basters, Samuel Maharero, the governors, as well early letters to the administrator of the Cape colony) in addition to traders and various missionaries. His writing gives a direct, unmediated (although subjective) perspective on the developments within the colony as a whole and not merely within the Nama communities. The writing of letters had further implications, such as those put forward by Arich-Gertz concerning the participation of literary elites within the colonial postal system[95]. Not only were the elites participating by sending and receiving letters, but the postmen were to a large extent recruited from the original societies. Through the concentrated participation of both elites and civilians this meant that the postal system was already imbued with a resistant potential. The tone of the letters, the addressee, the contents all created spaces in which to organise different strategies. Witbooi's request to Maharero to avoid signing a treaty with the Germans (30.05.1890) as well his letters to the other Nama leaders informing them of the termination of his protection treaty with Germans (01.10.1904) are only two examples in which the power of the written word was central in the politics of the colony.

---

themselves or their children overboard in order to prevent them of having to live a life of enslavement.
[95] *Namibias Postkolonialismen*, chapter one "Telekom Namibia".

Muronga has identified this potential when he decides to become an active member of the liberation movement. After Uncle Ndara's explanation as to why a chief had been deposed of, Muronga is continuously intrigued by the power of the pen. His first official encounter with this power is at the labour recruitment in Rundu. After giving his data to a clerk, he wonders whether "there is power in a pen" (61). The complementing instrument of power, the book, is also given an omniscient function, namely that it knows everything about him and Kaye ("'That man in the office wrote down everything about us. There is nothing about us that the book does not know.'" (62)). The role of education – as previously discussed – becomes ever more present in Muronga's life the more he is forced out of the comfort zone of his village. The act of writing, traceable to the historic Nama and Herero elites (amongst others) is revitalised and reintegrated within the structures of resistance. Not only are Kavango chiefs, in this case the village chief Dimbare, embracing the written word, but so are the members of the community, in this case Muronga and Makena. What this allows is a way of directly communicating with another person, as opposed to sending verbal messages along with someone else. It allows the bridging of huge distances, for example from the mine to his home village.

Yet, it still gives Muronga the strength to continue, especially as he receives words from someone who he is slowly forgetting[96]. The act of writing (and reading) strongly links him to notable figures of the past, to his community, and to the future[97]. The act of reading and writing helps Muronga to cope with his imprisonment in Pretoria. Although the engravings in the prison walls are in a language he is not able to speak or understand, his position within that specific space connects him to the authors. What his cellmate then does for Muronga is to translate the writings and thereby translating the space as well. Muronga can, like the Herero did with Okahandja and the Nama did with Shark Island, claim that specific space for himself. The past is recreated (via affiliations with past prisoners as well as the Muronga-Tjakova Monster Mouse) and transformed into a present of solidarity. The unstable jail environment, in which violence is a constant and real threat, is furnished with symbolic 'home comforts'.

---

[96] "He realises that his memory of her has grown dim" (195).
[97] "Tell them that I am fine here and that I am learning to name things. Tell them that I am going to learn to read and write. Tell them that one day I will also teach Mandaha to read and write." (Muronga sending home goods and words, 169)

6 Conclusion

From Peter Moor's first encounter with the "large forces" of GSWA to Jacobus Coetzee's final comment concerning his position in the world, it becomes clear that occupied (literary) space is reflective of a number of aspects. This begins with the fear of the alien landscape, replete with ever-present dangers, and culminates in the production and organisation of this landscape, augmented through knowledge production and regimes of looking and gazing. Connected to these two extremes are strategies that attempt to rationalise and appropriate African spaces, especially in the service of an ever-expanding global economy. Spaces controlling large-scale industry (farms, mines) become chronotopes, compressing the temporal and the spatial. Their link to graves and prisons serve to underline this compression. Gothland, for example, kills and buries someone in the desert and essentially creates the conditions for this burial to be considered a grave[1]. He has buried his dreams in the desert sands[2], making it an abstract burial ground. His hopes concerning the future (as a temporal inscription into the imagined landscape of GSWA) cannot be realised. He becomes caught up in the temporal regimes of the diamond industry, a regime that reproduces processes and expectations in an infinite loop[3]. These spaces are constantly reproduced through reiterated and repeated activities and gestures. Time is constructed as a prison, prohibiting forward movement due to its strong relationship to the spaces of reiteration and repetition. These spaces become heterotopias in respect to the other/'Other' spaces they mirror, creating powerful binaries that feed concepts such as nature/culture, civilisation/savagery, and progress/stagnation. Examples include the mines and the desert, the desert and the casino, or the casino and Schakalswater.

As discussed when analysing the novels, these dichotomies cannot be separated cleanly but reflect asymmetrical relations depending on their design. A strong example is Jacobus Coetzee, who "goes from dominator-explorer to humiliated victim to vengeful dominator again" (Salván, 2008:149). His understanding of the concept of 'savagery' is projected onto the Namaqua he encounters. He (and the *white* 'race'), on the other hand, are positioned as a metonymy of *white* fantasies of 'civilisation'. Yet, his actions against the Nama-

---
[1] A number of factors prevent this from being defined as such, most notably the absence of witnesses to the crime and the fact that the person killed was a Person of Colour.
[2] This is verbalised when Gothland confides in Ingeborg his previous hopes and dreams of coming to GSWA as a farmer.
[3] These previously mentioned process and expectations take the form of digging, sorting, selling, and the stock exchange, amongst others. The machine-like disinterest shown by the sorters and the consideration of introducing machines into the digging activities points to the cyclical and circular activities on the mines.

qua[4] and, at a later point, against some cattle and a lamb, reveal the porousness of this dichotomy. As David Atwell (1991) has rightly observed, the violence of the narrative, both linguistic and physical, are committed by a narrator-protagonist who constantly observes himself executing these actions. Although Jacobus Coetzee exhibits a high awareness of his own internal processes, he is unable to understand them in relation to the categories he has created, namely those of his authorial position vis-á-vis the Namaqua. This position is generated spatially (his initial heightened position on his horse) as well as discursively (his need to locate and reproduce forms of lack within the Namaqua community). His powerlessness and impotence are spatially reproduced through his detention in the menstrual hut, which connotes a triple ejection from the Namaqua society. Jacobus Coetzee, however, is unable to accept this ejection and tries to maintain his god-like self-image, even when crazed and lost in the desert. Another character who is unable to uphold *white* ideals such as progress (vs. stagnation) is Hans Gothland. His demise is the result of a failure to progress beyond the role society has created for him and whose social position is the result of a failed dream. This failed dream dictates his forced entrance into a system of global capital (as opposed to self-sufficiency). The former crux of the colonial space, namely agriculture, is replaced with a system of labour alienation. Reproduction of labour relations, as well as the strongly controlled activity of diamond procurement, creates a prison from which Gothland cannot escape. The wealth-creating sand dunes become a prison and a graveyard, the two central social spaces of stagnation. Economic spaces (the diamond mines) in contrast to possibly utopian spaces (the farm), are unable to reflect the idea of progress. It is only capital and its networks that may progress in the setting of this "diamond novel".

Furthermore, economic spaces in conjunction with non-economic spaces mirror a number of assumptions of the occupying nation. This takes the form of the insertion of *whiteness* into the landscapes via the technologies of language (through naming, through explaining, through categorising), labour (the appropriation of the soil), and reconfiguration of local spatial structures (enclosures, exclusive spaces, relocation). Dirich and Etta Wibrandt are the prime examples of these strategies. Both are active in reproducing a number of colonial tropes, employing *white* fantasies[5] as well as fears[6]. The fear of the "bush", as a colonial metaphor of space that cannot be controlled due to societal resist-

---

[4] Apart from (and before) the violence perpetrated against the Namaqua on his Second Return, Jacobus Coetzee is also responsible for biting off the ear of a child, shooting at an older woman, and beating another adult with a whip.

[5] These would include the fantasy of infinite lands to work with, and the projection of the future onto these infinite spaces.

[6] These range from the fear of the uncontrollable Black body to the preservation of *white* social and biological purity, and finally, the fear of being marked as 'inactive'.

ance by the local populace, has subsided; the fear of Black bodies remains. This fear is rooted in the failure of the *white* civilising mission[7] as well as in the failure of *white* control over desirable spaces. These spaces are the various farms, their gardens[8], the fortress-town of Okahandja, and most importantly, the trade networks. In order to gain control of these spaces it becomes necessary to 'purify' them through the myth and strategy of *whiteness*. On a basic level, this takes the form of defining Africanist characters with the help of legitimising approaches. The first, most basic approach, is defining Blackness. First encounters therefore create the circumstances with which to initially define the limits and essence of the non-*white* characters. Markers of Blackness become categorised and produced in respect to *whiteness*.

Producing the 'Other' (and oneself)

Peter Moor's first experience with Black characters leads him to negatively comment on their language as well as their eating habits. 'Skin colour' becomes strongly linked to cultural markers (indecipherable to the main characters) and projected onto the whole group. This elemental classification of the 'Other' is further constructed and defined according to an internal, introspective perspective. In this instance, the protagonists define Blackness in respect to what it means to be *white*. Etta and Dirich as well as Jacobus Coetzee, for example, rely on Christianity with its pro-*white* symbols as a strategy to differentiate themselves from the 'Other' characters. Etta and Dirich employ Christian rhetoric in order to create an impenetrable border between themselves and Africanist characters. Like Jacobus Coetzee, they believe that the Christianity practised by Africanists is a performance, a ploy. This distrust opens the door for the influential and destructive mechanism of *whiteness*: the privileged position to define 'Others' in respect of their 'humanness'. The narrator in *Heim Neuland* asks the question whether the Black people dancing around an evening fire are human (1908:484). The answer is: no, not *yet*, even though some have become Christian (ibid.). Their 'humanness' is constructed as being consigned to the future, but a future in which their genuine acceptance of Christianity will guarantee them human status. A Christian telos becomes the argument, propped up by abstract concepts such as "destiny" (1974:57). This border cannot be considered hori-

---

[7] This fear is most clearly visible in Dirich Dierksen's speech during the war.
[8] Together with the farm, the garden represents the epitome of the ideological landscape of colonial desires and fantasies. The strong emphasis on difference to the disorganized surroundings reproduces the powerful dichotomies of civilization/savagery, progress/stagnation, industry/idleness, amongst countless others.

zontal, i.e. a division between equal cultures. Rather, it is constructed as a vertical border, producing an authorial position in regard to the construction of difference.

These privileged positions are reproduced and further guaranteed through narrative power. Captain Macdonald solely narrates *A Twist of Sand*. Not only is he in a position to manipulate the plot, he controls what is seen and who speaks. This power – an imperialist fantasy – gives Captain Macdonald the authority to construct all the characters according to his needs, while frequently reinventing himself as the situation demands. In respect to this, he is the only character to be given an historic background. The other main characters either have no history (Dr. Stein, John Garland), or their history is designed in order to serve the plot (Johann, Dr. Anne Nielsen). Furthermore, Captain Macdonald is in control over the access to his history, having erased most of the evidence. The control over personal history contributes to one's own myth and reciprocally helps to aggrandise this personal history. Peter Moor is a similar example. He controls his own history to such an extent that he is even afforded the opportunity to become his own historian. The second edition (1907) of his narrative underlines this well. While the first edition (1906) reads more like a peek into someone's diary, the 1907 version confirms that one is in fact reading *his* novel[9]. With Peter Moor pointing out that what one is reading is a product from the narrated world, his personal history becomes public. This is, however, only mentioned in the absolute last sentence, indicating that the whole narrative might as yet have been a peek into his diary. In either case, Peter Moor is the author and authority of his own history. This gives him the power to create his own myth. The objective, rational narrative style as well as the high focus on externals (the "bush", the "enemy") distance him from the actual spaces. His interaction with the world can be contrasted by that of Jacobus Coetzee, for instance, where much of this interaction is internalised. The same can be said for Ingeborg, whose grappling with GSWA appears to be as much internalised as it is externalised. The myths produced remain the same: one's own personal history is linked to the territory and therefore creates legitimate claims to the territory.

Peter Moor's claim is his duty to the killed Germans in the colony. Although a return for him is out of the question due the war's effects on his body, Peter Moor can still make a claim to the territory. This occurs when he imagines visiting the colony again. Of course, this would imply that the territory has come under German control through his sacrifices. The war means that his time in GSWA was limited, but it also means that he can always return. Having survived the war and having served his country, he has left his trace on the territory, even if his claim is not for land. Captain Macdonald and Jacobus Coetzee

---

[9] "I related to him all that I had seen and experienced, and what I had thought of it all. And he has made *this* book out of it." (emphasis mine, 1908:247).

both stake their claims as explorers and namers. The claim is deeply inscribed into 'their' territories: through the violence of language and the language of violence. Their acts of naming overwrite previous associations with certain objects and places, exemplified by Captain Macdonald's naming of "Gamatom" and "Diaz' Thumb" and Jacobus Coetzee naming the giraffe (*kammelperd*) as well as "Warmbad". The characters produce a symbolic and linguistic bond with these named objects and places, expanding on the network of the already-named. Naming also legitimises the act of 'discovery', an act that can only be interpreted as a repeat of a previous discovery.

These discoveries, and the strong focus on *white* achievement[10], create a platform on which foreign space is run through metropolitan signs and symbols. The non-material links to the land become material through interaction on a number of levels. On a superficial level this takes the form of ownership. A bureaucratic certificate guarantees private property. The property, be it a farm (*Heim Neuland*) or a mine (*Du heiliges Land!*), becomes exclusive. It is separated from its surroundings and is highly organised. All of this is necessary in order to introduce labour regimes. This is where the *real* relationship to the land is created – through the soil. The soil, invested with intensive labour, is dragged into a co-dependent relationship between what it can produce (food and diamonds) and the coloniser (farmer and miner). A cycle of production is created: the soil is 'nationalised'[11] in order for the metropole to reproduce itself. Then, metropolitan signs and symbols are invested into the space (architecture, landscaping, naming). The food cultivated and the diamonds mined enter a national and transnational economy and network of relations. This in turn legitimises the activities of farming and mining. These in turn legitimise the usurping of foreign territories and exploiting the available resources.

In order to impose the desired labour regimes as well as legitimising the claims to land and territory, further concrete mechanisms of control were implemented. These can broadly be categorised as state legislature and state-sanctioned violence. Colonising immigrants supported and enforced laws regarding land ownership (discriminating against local inhabitants), equality before courts (disadvantaging local inhabitants), and mobility (a strong control of access to certain spaces to the detriment of the original societies). Disciplinary measures such as *väterliche Züchtigung* (fatherly caning) reveal the attitude prevalent in respect to the relationship between punisher and punished. The infantilisation of Black people and the reciprocal authority of violence (and by extension: law and

---

[10] *A Twist of Sand* references a number of feats *white* men have achieved/not achieved, while "The Narrative of Jacobus Coetzee" is centred around the crossing (and naming) of the "Great River" by a *white* man. Peter Moor is impressed by what the *Schutztruppler* were able to achieve in GSWA and Dirich Dierksen's speech summarises the successes of the colonisers.

[11] In reference to Germany fantasising a replica Germany in GSWA.

order) is concentrated in the father-figure of the coloniser, reaffirming patriarchal notions of (*white*) masculinity that distinguishes itself from concepts closer to nature such as femininity or Blackness. This position is compatible with the idea(s) of Christianity, where the highest power is the Heavenly Father. He combines benevolence and malevolence, two qualities the average coloniser also exhibits. The argument, however, is that the benevolence afforded (food, 'wages') authorises the malevolence (violence). Each of the novels has moments in which infantilisation, 'fatherly authority', and the accompanying violence reveal the highly hierarchical role of the disciplining coloniser.

In Peter Moor this begins with the utterance "[d]iese Schwarzen haben vor Gott und den Menschen den Tod verdient" (1907:200). The "Schwarzen" are the Herero who have dared to revolt against their father figures. The evocation of God as witness and judge indicates that the extreme violence committed by the *Schutztruppe* is authorised by the highest power. This is echoed in "The Narrative of Jacobus Coetzee", where the protagonist is not only styled as a father figure. At the end of the novel he justifies his crimes by stating that he is "a tool of history". Connecting this to his previous differentiation between himself (as a representative of *white* Christians) and the H̶o̶t̶t̶e̶n̶t̶o̶t̶s̶ (as a people without a destiny), Jacobus Coetzee evokes God as a witness and even as a guiding force to his actions. The link between his "destiny" (to destroy a whole camp) and his own definition of being "a tool" explains his strong, undeniable link to the idea of serving *the* father while also *being* a father-figure who is able (and authorised) to punish.

Discipline, however, does not only entail physical violence. In *A Twist of Sand*, language is used in order to define encroaching characters. In a first example, Jim, the steersman, is constantly referred to as "Kroo boy", thus referencing his nationality[12]. Captain Macdonald calls Dr. Anne Nielson, a renowned scientist and expert in her field of study, "a girl" on a number of occasions. These two examples show the paternal position Captain Macdonald has taken up. This enables him to place himself on a superior social standing. Although he does not include Christianity in the construction of own subject position, he cements his father-figure position linguistically (by making others children) and by eliminating potential father figures: his own father is never mentioned. His grandfather dies shortly after he is introduced. The admiralty removes him from their authority. Dr. Stein (who appears as an older competitor to Captain Macdonald) is also eliminated.

A further example in which 'fatherliness' is employed as a tool of discipline and (labour) regulation occurs in *Heim Neuland*. This occurs when Etta and Dirich are busy with the planning of their house. On the advice of Chrischan Möller, they decide to limit

---

[12] The Kru or Kroo are a society originating from Liberia.

the festivities and payment for the Black labourers concerning the building and completion of the house:

> In zwei Monaten, wenn die Regenzeit vorbei war, konnte der Hausbau beginnen, und man würde herausziehen. Das war überwältigend. Aber Chrischan erklärte, die Hauptsache wäre, die Schwarzen niemals feiern zu lassen, sonst wär's gar aus. Sobald während Dirichs Abwesenheit nichts Dringlicheres vorlegen, hatten sie Ziegel formen müssen. Nun, sie sollten aber auch ihren Lohn haben. Der Baas ließ sie noch einmal versammeln und versprach ihnen ein Fest am Einzugstag, wenn sie so weiterarbeiteten. Ein paar Kapather (Ziegenhammel) sollten geschlachtet werden und jeder so viel Reis und Kaffee bekommen, wie er wollte, und ein Präsent an Plattentabak obendrein. Sie grinsten vor Vergnügen und versprachen Welten. Wenn sie nur den vierten Teil davon hielten, war's genug. (487)

Although the Black labourers are responsible for the construction of the house in which they are not allowed or welcome, their efforts are strongly controlled on a material level. The section is run through with an attitude of discipline ("die Hauptsache wäre, die Schwarzen niemals feiern zu lassen, sonst wär's gar aus") as well as a feeling of extreme benevolence ("jeder so viel Reis und Kaffee bekommen, wie er wollte, und ein Präsent an Plattentabak obendrein"), which is then finally contrasted with the general assumption of laziness and performance ("Sie grinsten vor Vergnügen und versprachen Welten"). Etta and Dirich's benevolence is further emphasised during Dirich's speech, in which he admonishes those farmers who used violence in order to collect the debts owed to them. Not only does he position himself as a father-figure in respect to other Germans (invested with the power to chide fellow colonisers), he offers other disciplinary measures which might further the colonial project:

> Und wenn wir bisher vielleicht nur aus dem uns angeborenen und anerzogenen Rechtsgefühl eines Kulturmenschen heraus ihnen gegenüber gehandelt gaben, so wollen wir von jetzt ab unsre Verpflichtungen immer im Bewußtsein tragen, um uns selber niemals einen Vorwurf der Härte oder der Ungerechtigkeit machen müssen. Doppelt streng gegen uns selbst wollen wir sein, wenn wir es gegen die Eingeborenen sein müssen. Dann werden vielleicht einmal Zeiten kommen, in denen es ihnen wie ein Ahnen aufgeht, daß sie uns danken werden dafür, daß wir in ihr Land kamen. (620)

The rhetoric of discipline, of oneself and of the 'Other', is central to his argument. Etta repeats this idea when she says that they will return to the colony – with "Schwert und Pflug", two powerful technologies of control and discipline.

The character who is the most father-like (and also sees himself in that vein) is Dr. Herbert Klinger. This is exemplified through his relationship with Ingeborg and in his concern for Hans Gothland. His treatment of Ingeborg as an unintelligible individual is mirrored in his pet name for her, "Dummes". "Dummes" can either mean 'dumb' as in unable to speak, or 'dumb' as in lacking intelligence. Both meanings link her to colonial constructions of African subjects. Klinger also discusses Gothland from an elevated position, especially as he considers his suicide a disqualifier from society (260). Klinger categorises Gothland after his death, stating that he was one of many "Halbmenschen" and a "Wundersucher" (464), arguing that it was his own personal weaknesses that brought him to his fateful demise. His father-like position in respect of characters considered weaker than him (Ingeborg and Gothland) is further expanded to include nearly everybody. He destroys Vollmüller and his accomplices, while judging Black characters, and those he deems to be 'suffering' from "~~verburens~~".

It would be naïve to claim that the process of discipline and punishment originate and stem from the *white* father figure. This would substantially marginalise the influence of the *white* female coloniser, most notably the influence exercised on the most ideologised spaces and places. Take for example the incantation of *the* mother figure in Peter Moor, the *white* mother figure as a placeholder for a group experience. Peter Moor does not see *his* mother, but a mother figure. She represents generally held assumptions concerning the dichotomy of 'home' and 'wilderness' and is able to reproduce the former in the latter. The focus on aspects such as cleanliness, homeliness and familiarity is starkly contrasted by the alien space of the "bush". Yet, the appearance of the mother makes the alien terrain hospitable. The fact that this incantation takes place on Easter, a Christian holiday, further reproduces the activities the day would dictate (going to church as a family, wearing clean Sunday clothes), activities impossible in this war setting.

The Christian link to the *white* female body and its domestic performance are further replicated when Peter Moor and his company come across the woman sitting with her child. Again, Christian iconography is adopted, this time Peter Moor becomes one of the Three Wise Men, implying that the woman be Maria. Although the encounter is brief, the soldiers are again revitalised and make their way to the nearby fort. Both examples create a space in which the appearance of the *white* domestic female is invested with biblical imagery, which in turn creates conditions in which the *white* male coloniser is able to continue with his mission. And yet, the two *white* women have very little influence on the further development of the either the war or the narrative. They appear only as metropolitan signs in support of the male-dominated war arena, not as influencing characters.

Heim Neuland, on the other hand, is centralised around the impact of the *white* colonial woman on the colony. As argued by Brockmann, the role of the colonial female is multitudinous. First, it is her job to replicate a certain level of homeliness in the colony (a job described by Hans Gothland in its elemental steps, 1908:34–35). Secondly, it is her job to guarantee the reproduction of *white* culture. As the word 'reproduction' suggests, this takes two forms: cultural and biological. On the cultural front, this means the reproduction of certain activities (singing, playing music, reading) as well as specific cultural products (meals, decorations, artefacts). Etta is the most active example of these forms of reproduction – further extending her cultural mission to the servants of the house. This mission includes the introduction of German as the house language as well as the reproduction of a number of domestic exercises (from cooking, to cleaning, to laying the table).

A final job of the *white* colonial female is her supportive role for her husband (or male authority[13]). Etta's running of the farm stall supports Dirich's efforts in acquiring the necessary cattle. Etta's successful organisation of the house supports Dirich's work on the farm. The same cannot necessarily be said for Ingeborg or Carola Oberländer. Neither of them is involved in housework, nor do they give birth to any children. They do, however, create their own connections to what they consider the domestic. This takes the form of their position as *white* women in their respective social circles. Carola feels it is her responsibility to create a home with aesthetic qualities and fills it with social activities such as the ball and social calls. Nonetheless, she takes no part in the activities of the house, but does oversee its running. So, contrary to Etta, Carola's connection to the domestic is on an authorial level, not on a participatory level. Ingeborg is even further removed from domestic duties as she is only considered a guest. Both women, however, do need to fulfil one aspect of their general mission: to marry a fellow German. Carola is already married, while Ingeborg will marry Herbert Klinger at the end of the novel. They complete their prescribed role on this level. Furthermore, they are invested in maintaining the 'racial' purity of the Germans in the colony – a mission Etta is successful in accomplishing.

The *white* colonial female's influence and function becomes secondary and negligible in the literature of apartheid. This is most noticeable in the lack of focus on women in general in the two narratives. *A Twist of Sand* has only one recurring female character, Dr. Anne Nielsen, and one further nominal character, namely Simon Peace's nurse. Both women are constructed around their supportive role to men, with Dr. Nielsen linked to Dr. Stein and Captain Macdonald, while the nurse is only mentioned in respect to Simon Peace. "The Narrative of Jacobus Coetzee" has no female colonisers at all, only briefly mentioning the difference between Dutch women and ~~Bushman~~ *girls*. The two groups are, unsurprisingly, only mentioned in regard to sexual domination and (lack of) property. The *white* female coloniser is thus attributed a minimal role in the male-dominated environments of appropriation, discovery, exploration, landscaping, and naming. Captain Macdonald and Jacobus Coetzee do not need the support of an 'Other' (in respect to

---

[13]   Some women came to GSWA as servants to *white* households, not as wives.

their masculinity) in their undertakings. In fact, it is the reliance on themselves and their separation from everyone else that prohibits any other/'Other' character from influencing their narratives and the narratives of themselves.

A Colonial Network of Spaces and Strategies

The spaces and places in which these strategies are made use of and reproduced differ from novel to novel. However, far from being contradictory or paradox, they actually create a web of relations. The spaces inform each other and spread the influence of these strategies. This begins with Etta and Dirich's strong cultural and industrious link to the soil. The attack on this link (in the form of the resistant Herero) is avenged by Peter Moor, who battles a number of imagined and projected "enemies" throughout the territory. This culminates in the destruction of the Herero population, creating a further entrenching *white*-Black/master-servant dialectic. Adolf Oberländer and Oskar Vollmüller profit from this dialectic on the different diamond mines, as does the national economy of GSWA and consequentially, Germany. But before Etta, Dirich, Peter Moor, or Ingeborg enter into a network of strategies, Jacobus Coetzee opens up the territory through his act of "penetration". His unwavering belief in the authority of *whiteness*, especially in comparison to an invented Blackness, lays the foundation for future characters to build upon his 'achievements'. A later character, Captain Macdonald, benefits from these strategies by acquiring his own stretch of island; replete with an entrance inaccessible to others/'Others' and containing unfathomable oil deposits.

The narratives permit a mapping of spaces of influence, tracing these from the erasure of frontiers ("The Narrative of Jacobus Coetzee"), to the establishment of a culture of cultivation (*Heim Neuland*), to the submission of space and its subjects (*Peter Moor*), to the 'internationalisation' of the territory (*Du heiliges Land!*), and finally, to the production of a personal, unlocatable territory (*A Twist of Sand*). This progression contains numerous fantasies of personal utopias, built on the endlessness of the landscape and the controllable labour offered by the Africanist characters. The 'emptiness' projected onto the landscapes as well as the host of substitute signs and symbols imported from the metropole (and its accompanying rhetoric) only serve the colonising eye. The colonising eye narrates the landscapes into being, thus personalising them and emphasising relevant elements. These are focussed on aspects such as endlessness and emptiness, but are also designed around concepts such as ownership, danger, exclusivity, and aesthetic qualities[14]. With these fantasies come the claims: claims to the aesthetic (re)production of

---

[14] Jacobus Coetzee refers to the scene just before he and his accomplices wipe out the Namaqua village as

spaces, claims to the ownership of space, and claims to the subjects within these spaces. It becomes clear that there is an observable progression of the *invention* of GSWA from a pre-colonial space of 'unexplored emptiness' ("The Narrative of Jacobus Coetzee") to it becoming an international playground for adventure (*A Twist of Sand*). What these narratives reveal is a fantasy projected onto a surface that has already been configured and defined, explored, and named.

The link between the strategies of colonialism and the succeeding apartheid regime have so far been discussed and illuminated. Ideas of *whiteness*, rooted in Christian iconography and rhetoric, labour, and 'empty spaces' inextricably string these two systems together. These ideas underline a certain continuity between the two regimes, relying on similar disciplining technologies (laws, violence) and *Selbstdarstellung*. The conviction that laws and violence benefiting *whites* were necessary in the running and organisation of the installed state also justifies the two branches of state power. However, these ideas run on the fantasy or dream of a subservient and submissive Black populace, one that can be controlled and manipulated. And, although many of the inhumane laws and punishments were realised to a large extent (most notably those concerning habitation, occupation, and mobility), these were always destined to fail because they were in the service of a very small minority.

By ostracising the majority from most forms of official spatial discourse and developments, the desired utopian spaces could only remain a *white* dream. On many levels these were resisted through counter-dreams, most prominently with Hendrik Witbooi's desire to remain autonomous. *Born of Sun* offers a similar counter-dream, a dream in which liberation from the tyrannies of *white* rule is possible. The counter-dreams designed by Witbooi and Muronga emerge from periods of strong turmoil. Power relations and previous hierarchies were violently overturned and cultural practices and communal networks were forcefully reconfigured. However, these changes awaken a dynamic creativity. This creativity is most present in the elementary act of dreaming and imagining. The dream of an alternate present and future, one that is inclusive, can therefore be deemed the best strategy with which to oppose dehumanising systems of control. The dream of independence from a foreign regime, rooted in Witbooi's desire to remain autonomous and sovereign, becomes the basis for Muronga's introduction into a national dream in which independence can potentially become a reality. This wish is projected onto a national community, spreading the dream over the whole occupied territory – and beyond. This dream is strengthened through the desire for self-improvement and extending this to the rest of the social group.

---

a tableau. This is one example of the aestheticisation of *white* violence against Black bodies.

Thus Muronga bases his personal independence on the *acquisition* of language, of knowledge, and of skills. His dream is realisable through action. The independence of SWA only becomes possible once those fighting for it have freed themselves. Freeing oneself does not have to involve physical confrontations with the system, but it begins with the realisation that the first step to freedom is dreaming, and then acting upon that dream. Personal liberation then leads to social liberation, which may culminate in national freedom. Muronga's dream is a polyphonous dream, one that includes a multitude of voices and perspectives. It is a dream uniting different and disparate people. This social dream links Muronga to the initial dreamers of independence, meaning that the community is stretched over time while the dream is kept alive within even the most extreme spaces of suffering.

The Metropole in Crisis

The colonial and apartheid narratives are revealing of certain crises in the occupying metropoles. *Peter Moor* can be seen as an attempt to bridge the perceived distance between homeland Germans and the *Auslandsdeutschen*. The war situation produces a space in which both sections are united against a common "enemy" and both do it for the advancement of the German state. The killed Germans form a blood bond between the disparate groups. Peter Moor and the fellow soldiers and colonisers have begun to reproduce the metropole without being fully integrated into the colony. The absence and scarcity of metropolitan signs is evidence of this. However, as the narrative progresses, this is changed with Peter Moor beginning to Germanise these extreme spaces. He locates images of domesticity in an Easter fire, the Holy Mother in a mother on a porch, and a German forest in the "bush". He starts with the violent occupation of a foreign territory, officially sanctioned by the metropole. It is with this act that the metropole has successfully incorporated the colony into its modes of production and reproduction. The unification of the two remote territories is achieved through the introduction and withdrawal of metropolitan resources. Examples include the soldiers, the revitalising projections, and material (capital, raw materials, commodities). This allows the dream of a mini-Germany to form, one into which the metropole can expand its influence and continue reproducing itself (narratively, spatially, historiographically, politically).

Heim Neuland's Dirich Dierksen speaks of a liminal period in "the Kaiserreich". He cites the state's transformation from a rural economy to an industrial and capital economy. (618–619). This is where the colony becomes profitable as it allows the controlled progression from the former to the latter. Argumentation like this is reflective of the fear of *Raumschwund*, the slow erasure of space in the metropole. The colony now offers an escape from this fear (realised by Etta and Dirich) through its "Freiheit" and "Größe". The uncertainty of industrialisation and its unforeseeable impact are countered through a return to the agricultural. It is also an escape form the uncertainties of capital (Dirich loses his fortune after a banker steals it), the farm life offering more stability and control. The farm further gives a high level of personal organisation, impossible in the strongly governed metropolitan spaces. Reflective of Hans Grimm's *Volk ohne Raum*, the fear of a loss of space (and subsequent loss of freedom) is theorised as a threat and can be treated with an expansion into further spaces – which are incorporated into the metropole. Like *Peter Moor*, this is achieved with the help of metropolitan resources, but in this instance these are much more concentrated. Domesticity is not imagined or inferred, it is lived. The appropriation of the soil and its spaces (the enclosed farm, the farm house, the garden) is accomplished by expelling 'Others'. The realisation of this return to an agricultural society is tested in the colonial setting. Although this desired return is interrupted through the war, the return is imagined as inevitable (1908:647). Etta and Dirich are able to escape their metropolitan spatial crisis by creating a new crisis for the people they have displaced in the colony. Their aim is to establish an imaged (rural) German-ness outside of the metropole. This would guarantee an expansion of German (cultivated) territory into an area as yet unaffected by the advances of European industrialisation.

Ingeborg Oberländer encounters a different metropolitan crisis. With the colonial agricultural economy slowly being replaced by the mining sector in respect to capital returns, questions of German-ness reappear. This was not only based on the *Mischehenverbot* (which offered a legal definition), but on a character level as well. As the turning of the soil did not constitute a current template for such an elusive term, the diamond fields of the *Sperrgebiet* offered a new laboratory. The procurement of diamonds turned Lüderitzbucht from an invisible player in the global economy to a centre of capital accumulation[15]. The flow of international capital meant the flow of an international clientele, threatening the 'purity' of the colony. Biological in its initial discourse, purity now became a question of character. Hans Gothland dies after stealing from the state. Adolf Oberländer dies as a morphine addict, leaving Carola Oberländer widowed and penniless. Oskar Vollmüller is destroyed financially and socially. Only Herbert Klinger and Ingeborg emerge from the test unscathed. The evils of greed, *Diamantenfieber*, vice, and dishonesty, amongst others, are countered through ideals of purity. This is exercised on a reproductive level in which sexual relations with non-Germans were socially despised, especially those with Black people. On a second level, this purity is reproduced through

---

[15] The stock exchange of GSWA was founded in Lüderitzbucht.

the constant negotiation of temptation. The characters who fail are punished, those who succeed are rewarded. The colony is constructed as a testing ground for the moral purity (which includes biological purity) of colonists and immigrants.

A German-ness is produced which leaves behind the Romanticism of an agricultural era and replaces it with one that is centred on navigating an ever-expanding as well as ever-contracting world. The identity-forming element for this is not fixed on soil anymore. The main element has become the idealisation of purity, creating a national identity that cuts itself off from its surroundings. Physical boundaries that were originally erected, such as borders and enclosures, are expanded to include new and abstract borders. These may include the monitoring of excessive behaviour such as drinking, drug addiction, and greed. It may include acts such as the differentiation of communities into German and non-German, with the former representing the default and the ideal. The intrusion of the international (as an outside influence) is compensated with the redefinition of the national. The metropole protects itself by erecting boundaries against external interruptions in its expansion.

This fantasy and strategy is also utilised by Captain Macdonald. His legal link to the island of Curva dos Dunas is guaranteed on a judicial level (through the signed propriety documents), on a spatial level (through the charts, as well as his ability to locate it), and most significantly, on a symbolic level. At one point he thinks to himself that Curva dos Dunas "is my island, and I'm going to protect my property" (100), only to fully tie himself to the space when he decides that "Curva dos Dunas and I must keep our secret – until death do us part" (142). He cements this link between place and history in a scene of disclosure:

> "Now see here," I said. "This particular place happens to belong to me. In that sense, it's private. And NP I is part of its *private* history. You, John can go and tell your *story* to the Admiralty — if you like. They'll want some proof. And where will you get it? Do you think the Admiralty is going to believe a sentimental, unlikely little story about a hidden anchorage from a friend who feels sorry that his former chief was kicked out of the Service years ago? They'll want proof." I turned to Anne. "John's a sailor. He couldn't find this place, let alone bring in a ship. There's only one man living who can do that, and that is me. The only other man to do it was the skipper of the U-boat, and he's roasted." (my emphasis, 198–199)

This is reflective of Förster's observation that the owners of the properties in Namibia on which anti-German colonial battles occurred saw themselves as custodians of the history that took place there[16]. Captain Macdonald wants to prevent his property from being

---

[16] "Die Familien hatten die örtlichen Kriegsgräber meist über mehrere Generationen hinweg instand- und zugänglich gehalten und fühlten sich bereits dadurch als >Hüter der Geschichte< die sich auf ihrem

discovered which in turn would make his history, his metanarrative, accessible. The control over personal history allows Captain Macdonald to set up boundaries in regard to all the other characters, manipulating them and his surroundings to that end. Not even his closest accomplice, John Garland, has any access to his captain's inner workings. These boundaries are set up around access to spaces of history (the *Etosha*, Curva dos Dunas), and access to the narrative. This is granted to the *white* characters of Dr. Stein and Dr. Nielsen, but this is mainly because they will die in one of the main spaces of his history[17], the Skeleton Coast. He is then able to insert himself into a powerful history of achievement by entering spaces that are as yet untouched by *white* men. This would include the examples of his scaling of a valley[18], as well as his discovery of Curva dos Dunas, and the subsequent acts of naming. This comes in the face of highly dangerous terrain, one that is specifically hostile towards *white* intruders:

> All of Africa's pent-up hatred of man, of his ways, of his cities he has thrown up out of steel and concrete on the veld, of his roads and railways through which her wealth and secrets have been won, stands at bay, fangs bared against the last intrusion, here in this remote corner of the continent called the Kaokoveld. Round her skirts she has gathered the last untamed remnants of her once countless herds of antelope, giraffe, zebra, lion and elephant. (46–47)

The promise of "penetration" and progress find their limits when challenged by the Skeleton Coast. The feminisation of the terrain ("her skirts", "her once countless herds"), however, constructs the landscape in such a way that the right *man* can unlock its secrets. This description emphasises Captain Macdonald's later suitability as a male explorer – especially as the Skeleton Coast rewards him with the elimination of his enemies, his escape, and the wealth that huge amounts of oil brings. Captain Macdonald can therefore be said to replicate the strategies employed by S.J. Coetzee in respect to the potency of *whiteness*, although he utilises history for a different purpose. Instead of applying it in the service of the state, for example by abdicating his island to the government, he applies it the service of self-enrichment. *White* potency is released from its nationally controlled construction via its links to the past, and replaced by a potency in which the individual is central to the progression of *whiteness*. The metropolitan fear of stagnation in its own reproduction due to a lack of spatial resources[19] is dealt with by creating new narratives

---

Grund und Boden zugetragen hatte" (2010:95).

[17] The Skeleton Coast is styled as being a keeper of history, as the examples of the Cape lion ("'It's been extinct for over a century'") and the stranded Spanish ship ("'It's like — the past coming alive'") giving the chapter "500 years of love" its title.

[18] "'I don't suppose any white man has ever been up it before'" (225).

[19] A receding frontier and a reduction in potentially 'new' space to appropriate reduces the metropole's ability to reproduce itself as well as its spheres of influence.

of discovery. The acts of discovering and naming by Jacobus Coetzee in 1760 are mirrored 200 years later by Captain Macdonald. The invention of spaces which legitimise the establishment of *whiteness* as a state system (apartheid) is central to the relationship of the protagonists vis-à-vis the perceived emptiness of their explored spaces. The main difference is the level of officialdom of their discoveries. The strong contractual relation between Jacobus Coetzee makes him an official agent of the metropole while Captain Macdonald is an unofficial agent.

The build up of "The Narrative of Jacobus Coetzee" deals with metropolitan crises on two different levels. Because of the temporal contexts between the narrative (as written by S.J. Coetzee), the deposition (by Jacobus Coetsé at the Castle of Good Hope), and the 'afterword' (by S.J. Coetzee), two different metropoles are involved. The first one is the Cape Colony. Jacobus Coetzee and the metropole are confronted by a limit, a limit to knowledge and space. This limit is the (until then) unnamed river separating the colony from its hinterland. A hunter-explorer is allowed to cross the boundary of what is known. The fear of limits and boundaries is concentrated in the character of Jacobus Coetzee. He transcends his mental limits (in respect of his rationality), his spatial limits (by becoming the landscape), and his temporal limits (by 'becoming' history through his violence and his narrative). His Second Return reflects another fear of the metropole – the possible impotence of *whiteness*. The destruction of a whole village is indicative of Jacobus Coetzee's impotence in respect to entering into the Namaqua society. This is because he can only see difference and has to rationalise this difference. His arguments concerning difference (either feverish or sober) are rooted in discourses of violence, discourses in which difference is considered an unbridgeable crevice. And it is this inaccessibility to the 'Other' that needs to be dismantled in order to be purged. For Jacobus Coetzee, this can only be realised by making the Namaqua part of *his* history (with fellow explorer Hendrik Hop as a witness) and thus at least rationalising their relationship to him[20]. Having spent the majority of the time ostracised from the Namaqua community, he inserts himself into their history, overwrites it, and creates his own version of history. He "reduce[s] the dialogic nature of history to a monologic story in which the subject of Empire acts upon and predicates docile colonial subjects" (Marais 1993:52). Metropolitan impotence is compensated through the excessive exercise of violence against Black bodies.

S.J. Coetzee replicates this line of argumentation in the afterword-introduction. His appraisal of Jacobus Coetzee's achievements with respect to his discoveries is a reflection of the periods he: a) gives his lectures in (1934–1948) and b) the publication of *Het relaas*

---

[20] Marais (1993) makes this part of his "imperial syntax", arguing that "African raw material which cannot be narrativized must be annihilated" (51).

van Jacobus Coetzee, Janszoon (1951). Both periods signal the rise of the National Party, and with it the rise of Afrikaner nationalism and its final iteration, apartheid. 1948 is the year the party came into power, while 1951 is the year in which the NP government lays the foundation for apartheid. With the great age of South African explorers a distant memory, there was a need to reproduce that era in order to legitimise state policy. The long history connecting Afrikaners to the territory and their 'achievements' concerning war victories and successful settlement are reactivated in a new era. This act of reactivating the past becomes a tactic in writing a national history from a *white* perspective. The history of an already-contested territory is reduced to a mythologisation of a certain group, namely the group in power.

The relegation of the original inhabitants of the territory to obstacles needing to overcome (a point of view shared by *Peter Moor* and *Heim Neuland*), or a resource to be controlled and exploited (*Du heiliges Land!*) elevates the coloniser's own position. With an absence of 'discoverable' matter, *whiteness* loses much of its potency. Thus, the incantation of the past at these strategic points in time are reflective of a nostalgic backward look, one in which the reproduction of *whiteness* could be said to have its roots. The achievements of colonists such as Jacobus Coetzee, "[a]mong the heroes who first ventured into the interior of Southern Africa" (1974:108), feed into the myth of *white* achievement in producing history, a myth which cannot allow ruptures from outside forces. Controlling the narratives of the state thus creates the conditions in which histories are silenced or rewritten in order to fit into the state's myth of origin. The construction of this state is the epitome of *white* achievement in an endless and boundless 'emptiness'. The apartheid state is imagined as being its perfected form, where *whiteness* is marked as *the* technology of progress. The re-emerging fear of *white* impotence on a national level is dismantled through the construction of a state history built upon annihilation, overwriting, and expansion. The fact that S.J. Coetzee links Jacobus Coetzee not only to his own lineage ("ancestor") but the 'nation' ("one of the founders of our people") exemplifies the close connection between personal and state narratives.

A Root of the Metropolitan Crisis

The crises experienced by the metropoles regulating the territory of GSWA and SWA were deepened due to a number of interruptions from the Black communities. This began in earnest in 1903[21] and ended in 1989. New technologies of oppression and state

---

[21] While resistance informed much of the interaction between Black people and the state apparatus, a full-scale war is usually the final resort as an oppositional strategy.

reproduction needed new strategies of resistance. One of the forms in which space was appropriated by the occupying nations was through narratives, whether state sponsored or literary. A language of ownership in diary entries and travelogues was replicated in fictions about the spaces beyond national borders. The linguistic and dreamt-up inclusion of foreign territories within one's own national borders became a reality. Courts, bureaucratic offices, and the military were the most intensive attempts in organising and acquiring new spaces. However, the emergence of counter-discourses and alternative histories threatened the lifespan of imperial theories and discourses. On one level, the impossible task of hiding indigenous people from *white* spaces, as well as regulating their behaviour in these spaces, made the abolition of metropolitan fears a deferred process. The reminder of a failed project and the inadequacy of an artificial superior self-image were constantly present, undermining perceived achievements. On a second level, the rejection of the state narrative as *the* overarching narrative further deepened the crisis of *white* potency, especially since it became eroded through alternative dreams. Add to these two points the loss in the ability to reproduce itself meant that the metropole was facing threats from within (loss of new spaces to incorporate), and from outside (counter-narratives).

Born of the Sun falls into the latter category, as it creates a narrative able to compete with official stories and histories. By drawing on the past, Muronga is able to negotiate present problems and challenges. The common enemy of foreign oppression in the colonial and apartheid periods link the protagonist to those before him, both on an immaterial and on a material level. The strategies offered by anti-colonial personalities (Hendrik Witbooi and Samuel Maharero being the most prominent) are reworked to fit the current context. A further influence from the past is Muronga's community's social practices. This includes kinships, mythologies, and spaces of orientation such as his village, his home, and his position within his community. Old and new relationships support his efforts in: a) orientating himself within the limits set out by the apartheid government, and b) trying to change the oppressive system from the inside. And while he is constantly faced with new horrors[22], he finds new hope and energy when locating past strategies in his various situations. The networks he forms further help his resistant strategies, above all the network he forms with people with similar dreams. The organisation of this network thus decreases the potency and power of the metropole.

An increase in state violence, in harsh laws, and the need to reproduce *white* hegemony is evidence of the loss of authority of the metropole. This impotence is revealed through the loss of control of the metropole over its disciplining spaces (the jail, the

---

[22] He is twice imprisoned, the victim of police violence, and dislocated from his family and social networks, amongst other brutalities.

mine compound) and the resistant bodies who have interrupted these disciplining spaces. Contrary to their function, the jail and the mine compound help in liberating Muronga intellectually, while simultaneously providing the fertile soil in which resistant dreams are born and formed. It is in these extreme spaces in which control is at its most concentrated that this control must be confronted. With time and space being out of flux[23], he is able to inhabit another time and another space – that of mythology. This 'escape' from his confinement becomes the engine of his socialisation and politicisation, a process in which he expands his village kinship into an international network, stretching from South Africa to Botswana. His deconstruction of *whiteness* (in respect to its tools of authority, its signs and symbols, its claims to power) becomes a further factor in his identity formation. This is because he reaffirms his Blackness in confrontations with the myth of *whiteness*. As a technology of resistance, Muronga's reactivation of his and his community's past practices starts to overwrite metropolitan influence. The crisis of the metropole in *Born of the Sun* is concentrated in the deconstruction and devaluation of the myth of *whiteness* and a simultaneous revitalisation of Blackness. Muronga's dream of independence from the Afrikaner metropole and the final achievement of autonomy is the engine of the narrative.

Lefebvre does however, not deconstruct the metropole's violent intrusions into the colony. Enlightenment rationale and the will to produce knowledge and power is only fixed in the city-countryside dialectic, the role of the colony is not included in the theorisation of imperial expansion. In a way it locates the evils of current oppression and metropolitan power within capital's global reach while silencing imperialism's function in first creating the conditions for capital expanse and, second, imperialism's maintenance of this function. Colonial and imperial destruction of societies and cultures, as well as the need for wars in the service of expansion, must be included and discussed when looking at the genealogy of European cities. The city-countryside dialectic also focusses on the relationship between relatively homogeneous societies, reflected in the city's appropriation of its own countryside. Certain social constructs such as language and cosmology are already linked in this relationship, as a German city would in essence appropriate a German countryside.

The internationalisation and globalisation of these processes during the 19th and 20th centuries do not consider the fact that European cities started to appropriate distant, non-European spaces on a large scale[24], destroying more than was able to be produced. Furthermore, the already imbalanced power relations between city and countryside were

---

[23] The fact that Muronga is not fully able to determine how long he has been incarcerated shows the strong chronotopic character of the jail.
[24] As mentioned before, colonialism did not start in 1884, but this should be considered as the most intensified period of European territorialisation outside of what is generally accepted to be Europe.

magnified due to the technological superiority of the colonising nations, especially in respect to war and disciplinary machinery. The countryside-colony's mirroring of the 'home empire', not as an ever expanding construct but as *the* point of reference, indicates that the members of the colonising nations did not see the colony as a product of the metropole, but as an extension. The violence in the colony could thus be rationalised as a residual by-product of territorial expansion, not the engine driving it.

Monologic and Dialogic Narratives

The influence and reproductive vigour of the metropole has changed from novel to novel, and from era to era. The spaces of interrogation have been multifarious, revealing the reach and influence of the metropole and its capabilities. Furthermore, the spaces produced and incorporated by the metropole affirm the numerous strategies at its disposal. As the narratives have shown, one of the most influential strategies in its own production and reproduction is its ability to narrate. By narrating the 'Other' into being, the metropole also narrates itself into being. As Lefebvre argues, the city needs the countryside to mirror itself, just as the metropole needs the colony in order to mirror itself. The authority to define and bring into being, authorised by the metropole and its extensions, exercise power over the subjects/objects that are narrated into being. Peter Moor's objective field report, as the most obvious example is reflective of the scientific products such as travelogues and official reports and are centralised in the I-narrator.

Monologic narration is highly exclusive and privileges the metropolitan agent over 'Other' subjects as well as the landscape. This singular focalisation creates a space in which the narrator is the only access to the relational spaces of the text, i.e. the relation between the world-making subject, the spaces in this world, and the objects of this world. This form of narration reproduces the myth of *whiteness* by silencing or overwriting Black narratives and voices concerning space and place. Although *Born of the Sun* is the most prominent and obvious example in my analysis, certain passages in the colonial and apartheid novels reveal the impossibility of the strategies of silencing and evasion. The continual reliance on Black characters for labour (*Heim Neuland, Du heiliges Land!*), as well as support and orientation (*Peter Moor*[25], *A Twist of Sand*, "The Narrative of Jacobus Coetzee") means that they cannot be kept invisible. It is only at strategic points where they are employed that the narratives can maintain their preservation of *whiteness*.

---

[25] The "enemy"-Herero are not the only Black characters in the novel. There are the Nama soldiers who fight with the *Schutztruppe* as well as Nama women who do domestic work in the various forts and barracks.

By attempting to eliminate Black voices from the 'master narratives' of *white* spatial production, the narrative empties the not-yet-narrated spaces from its previously established relations. The metropole can now subsume the narrated spaces into its own processes of reproduction, accumulating resources, signs, symbols, and relations for itself. The omnipresence of the I-narrator further extends the reach of the metropole by infusing him/her with god-like creative powers. This is most evident in "The Narrative of Jacobus Coetzee", in which the protagonist is stylised as a god. His narrative marks him as such, but so does the historian responsible for the exposé. He is celebrated for his naming and "bringing into existence", referring to his world-making abilities. Jacobus Coetzee, however, does not only name and bring into existence; he also defines and disseminates knowledge. His close proximity to the reader of his narrative (there are a number of passages in which a communal "we" and "us" is evoked) is revealing of his intended audience. The employed "we" includes the reader, a point again supported by S.J. Coetzee who calls Jacobus Coetzee "one of the founders of our people". The narrative is designed to reproduce achievements of *whiteness* while celebrating these achievements within a community of *whiteness*. The demeaning definitions of Black people and Africanist characters exclude them from participating in the world-making potential of the narrative.

Peter Moor and Jacobus Coetzee relegate Africanist characters to objects that help in the construction of *whiteness* while offering a legitimisation for the necessity of the narrative. Captain Macdonald is the third character to be given the ability of world-making. He is placed in the original 'empty space', namely the sea. Nonetheless, he also recounts *white* achievements, personal and communal. Missing from his narrative is a dialogical approach, just like *Peter Moor* and "The Narrative of Jacobus Coetzee". The all-powerful voice of the *white* protagonist eliminates any other dissenting voices and any interruption in the continuation of his *white* achievements. On a plot level this is realised through the physical deaths of any oppositional characters (Jim, the commander of NP I, Dr. Nielsen, Dr. Stein). On a formal level this is achieved by eliminating oppositional characters from the narrative (Jim, Hendriks). The narrative becomes the space of *white* reproduction, a reproduction with the metropole at its centre. *A Twist of Sand*'s silencing of other/'Other' voices and its elimination of threatening characters reflects the apartheid metropole's fantasy of achieving similar results.

Heim Neuland and *Du heiliges Land!* employ a different narrative strategy. The narrators in this case are not the main characters. They are omnipresent and omniscient entities that do not impact the unfolding of the story. Both narrators are necessary tools in order to create an over-arching network of relations. The characters are unable to do so because of their limited capabilities. While Peter Moor, Jacobus Coetzee, and Captain Macdonald all have the ability of world-making, the characters in the two colonial novels are placed within the worlds these three I-narrators have brought into being. The narrators in *Heim Neuland* and *Du heiliges Land!* can therefore be said to have god-like powers with the characters, for example Etta and Ingeborg, being elements of the narrative. This change in narrative strategies does not diminish *whiteness* as world-making force. Rather, it relocates the world-making potential in the narration of a *white* world being brought into being. In other words: while the I-narrators create their world as they encounter it, the heterodiegetic narrators create the world according to how the characters encounter it. The characters are relieved of their fictioning potential, the focus being on their ability to navigate the produced world. The narrator's of *Heim Neuland* and *Du heiliges Land!* can therefore be contrasted with the I-narrator's of the other three novels in three ways. Firstly, they are not as overtly marked as masculine. The possible inclusion of female voices in the production of colonial spaces is a testament to the expansion of metropolitan influence. This is because male-dominated discourses are undercut, offering other perspectives, offering different strategies in the appropriation of spaces and the reproduction of *whiteness*.

The broadening of social relations through the omnipresence of the narrators allows for a broader intrusion of *whiteness* into the landscape. This is because a network of spatial relations is created, with each space being connected to others. The network is increased in order to form a national space, or at least the space of the nation[26]. These aspects are absent in the texts with I-narrators because they are only able to produce their own space/world. A final difference between the two forms of world-making is the levels of penetration. While the I-narrators permeate all the spaces they enter into, they are unable to enter into the other characters. The inferences by Jacobus Coetzee concerning the ~~Bushmen~~, ~~Hottentot~~, and Namaqua prove his inability to perceive internal processes beyond his own. The same can be said for Captain Macdonald, who is able to read other characters, yet he too can only assume. Peter Moor is a character who shows some access to other characters. This access is, however, constructed around his own responses to certain situations. The communal "we" is used in order to link his reactions and responses to the group. The narrators in the other two novels are able to bring up past episodes, expose character's inner workings, and reveal fantasies, fears, and desires. This creates an intimate and intricate web of dreams, moving away from the individual dream to the group dream.

Both strategies of narration are nonetheless connected by two defining characteristics. The first is the focus on narrative control, i.e. excluding voices which may threaten the uniformity of the world-making. 'Other' dreams, desires, and fantasies are relegated to

---

[26] This space is not reliant on physical borders but is organised according to cultural borders. Ettenhof, for example, can be considered a space of the nation due to its focus on cultural purity and reproduction.

the sphere of the negligible, with the 'masternarrative' constructed as the only truth. The second strategy, and one which augments the first, is the reproduction of *white* hegemony. The repetition of *white* achievement and the exclusion of Black counter-narratives maintains *whiteness*' privileged position – even if only on a fictional, fictioning level. The I-narrators and the omnipresent, omniscient narrators therefore perpetually produce *white* exclusive worlds with the resources of the empty landscape and the metropole, resulting in the reproduction of the myth of *whiteness* and its justification of the metropole's intrusion into the spaces it is "bringing into being". The narrative voices of the texts are thus as complicit as the characters in the overwriting of African spatial and temporal regimes.

Born of the Sun is narrated from a similar position as *Heim Neuland* and *Du heiliges Land!*. This creates instances in which access to certain concepts is established[27], but its main function is – like its two predecessors – the connection of its main character to the other characters. The world Muronga inhabits is tiny in its initial conception (consisting of only his village), but is expanded to include a network of spaces of oppression. These include South Africa, Botswana, and Malawi. The 'home' nation itself is still a spatial concern, most prominently in the dream of an independent Namibia. However, in the case *Born of the Sun*, the destruction of *white* rule is central to the narrated world. An international community is formed in order to liberate the national community. Aspects such as translations, hearsay from the village, and the reactivation of the past are all focal points in order to establish new relationships, garner new points of view and discursive tools, and produce a new community of dreamers. The fact that Muronga only begins his journey to self-discovery and participation in the liberation struggle after his maltreatment in the Pretoria prison is evidence of the influence of others on his dream. He in turn is able to influence others, most notably as a political activist and public speaker. Instead of being a monologic narrative in which *whiteness* as a point of view is treated as the only one, *Born of the Sun* creates a dialogic (possibly even polyphonous) narrative strategy, one that is inclusive of excluded voices and dreams. By utilising the same technology, which was manipulated to invent and define, this Namibian novel uses the narrative techniques in order to reinvent and redefine. This palimpsestic approach to the production of a counter-discourse, and its resultant voicing of different imaginings and desires, creates a national space in which Muronga can reassert himself and his culture. The narrator "brings into being" a world of re-emergence buried by *white* narratives. New knowledge is produced and disseminated, new dreams can take root and replace the daily nightmares that colonialism and apartheid dreamt up. That which appeared to be overpowering and

---

[27] This includes Muronga and Makena's wedding rituals, the traditional division of labour as well as traditional roles in the village.

overwhelming is made manageable through the focus on the communal, the social. The *white* spaces of discipline are robbed of their potency and reconfigured to reveal resistant energies. *White* spaces of utopia are contested and disconnected from their exclusivity. Blackness is treated as a communal asset, as a liberating force, and removed from its *white*-defined meaning. The narrative opens up a different approach to 'colonised' spaces, whether they are physical or psychological. The landscape becomes nationalised through the introduction of resistant signs, symbols, and temporal and spatial regimes. European fantasies are replaced with liberating visions of a liveable future, rooted in the revitalisation of destroyed cultural artefacts and practices. *White* dreams of, and for, (G)SWA are contested, in turn fuelling Namibian dreams.

Bibliography

|Khaxas, Elizabeth (ed.). *Between Yesterday and Tomorrow. Writings by Namibian Women.* Women's Leadership Centre: Windhoek. 2005. Print.

Achebe, Chinua. *Things Fall Apart.* London: Heinemann, 1958. Print.

Agamben, Giorgio. *Homo Sacer: Sovereign Power and Bare Life.* Paris: Seuil, 1997. Print.

Amin, Samir and Brian Pearce. *Unequal Development: An Essay on the Social Formations of Peripheral Capitalism..* New York: Monthly Review, 1976. Print.

Anderson, Charles, John. *The Okavango River: a Narrative of Travel Exploration and Adventure.* London: Hurst and Blackett. 1861. Print.

_____. *Notes of Travel in South West Africa.* London: Hurst and Blackett. 1875. Print.

Arich-Gerz, Bruno. *Namibias Postkolonialismen: Texte Zu Gegenwart Und Vergangenheiten in Südwestafrika.* Bielefeld: Aisthesis, 2008. Print.

Arich-Gerz, Bruno, Kira Schmidt, and Antje Ziethen. *Afrika-Raum-Literatur/Africa-Space Literature: Fiktionale Geographien/Fictional Geographies.* Remscheid: Gardez! Verlag, 2014. Print.

Arndt, Susan. *Die 101 Wichtigsten Fragen – Rassismus.* München: C.H. Beck, 2012. Print.

_____. "Weißsein – zur Genese eines Konzeptes. Von der griechischen Antike zum postkolonialen ‚racial turn'. In: Standke, Jan & Thomas Düllo (eds.). *Theorie und Praxis der Kulturwissenschaften. Series: Culture. Discourse History.* Vol. 1. Berlin: Logos. 95–120. 2008. Print.

_____. "Whiteness as Category of Literary Analysis. Racializing Markers and *Race* Evasiveness in J.M. Coetzee's *Disgrace*". In: Meyer, Michael (ed.). *Word and Image in Colonial and Postcolonial Literatures.* Amsterdam: Rodopi. 167–189. 2009. Print.

_____. *Afrika Und Die Deutsche Sprache: Ein Kritisches Nachschlagewerk.* Münster: Unrast, 2004. Print.

Arndt, Susan, and Marek Spitczok Von Brisinski. *Africa, Europe and (post)colonialism: Racism, Migration and Diaspora in African Literatures.* Bayreuth: Breitinger, 2006. Print.

Ashcroft, Bill. *Post-colonial Transformation.* London: Routledge, 2001. Print.

Ashcroft, Bill, Gareth Griffiths, and Helen Tiffin. *Key Concepts in Post-colonial Studies.* London: Routledge, 1998. Print.

Atwell, David. ""The Labyrinth of My History": J. M. Coetzee's "Dusklands"" *NOVEL: A Forum on Fiction* 25.1 (1991): 7. Web. Accessed on 16.03.2015.

Bakhtin, M. M., and Michael Holquist. "Forms of Time and of the Chronotope in the Novel." *The Dialogic Imagination: Four Essays.* Austin: University of Texas, 1981. Print.

Bakhtin, M. M., and Caryl Emerson (ed.). *Problems of Dostoevsky's Poetics.* Minneapolis & London: University of Minnesota. 1972. Print.

Balslev, Anindita N., and J. N. Mohanty. *Religion and Time.* Leiden: E.J. Brill, 1993. Print.

Barnard, Rita. *Apartheid and Beyond: South African Writers and the Politics of Place.* Oxford: Oxford UP, 2007. Print.

Behn, Aphra. *Ooronoko: or, the Royal Slave.* London: William Canning. 1688. Print.

Bhabha, Homi K. *The Location of Culture.* London: Routledge, 1993. Print.

Biwa, Memory. '*Weaving the past with threads of memory': narratives and commemorations of the colonial war in southern Namibia.* Doctoral Thesis: University of Western Cape. 2012. Print.

Bley, Helmut. *Kolonialherrschaft Und Sozialstruktur in Deutsch-Südwestafrika 1894–1914.* Hamburg: Leibniz-Verlag, 1968. Print.

Bloch, Ernst. *Geist Der Utopie.* Muenchen: Duncker Und Humblot, 1918. Print.

Bradford, Robert L. "Blacks against the Walls." Ed. R. Segal and Ruth First. *South West Africa: Travesty of Trust.* London: Andre Deutsch, 1967. 87–102. Print.

Brehl, Medardus. *Vernichtung Der Herero: Diskurse Der Gewalt in Der Deutschen Kolonialliteratur.* München: Fink. 2007. Print.

_____. "'Diese Schwarzen haben vor Gott und Menschen den Tod verdient'. Der Völkermord an den Herero 1904 und seine zeitgenössische Legitimation" in:

Völkermord, Genozid und Kriegsverbrechen in der ersten Hälfte des 20. Jahrhunderts, hrsg. im Auftrag des Fritz Bauer Instituts von Irmtrud Wojak und Susanne Meinl, Frankfurt am Main: Campus 2004, S. 77–97. Print.

Brockmann, Clara. *Die Deutsche Frau in Südwestafrika; Ein Beitrag Zur Frauenfrage in Unseren Kolonien.* Berlin: Mittler, 1910. Print.

_____. *Briefe Eines Deutschen Maedchens Aus Suedwest.* Berlin: Mittler, 1912. Print.

Buys, Gerhard L., and Shekutaamba W. Nambala (eds.). *History of the Church in Namibia: An Introduction.* Windhoek: Gamsberg Macmillan. 2003. Print.

Carter, Paul. *The Road to Botany Bay: An Essay in Spatial History.* London: Faber and Faber, 1987. Print.

Chapman, Michael. "The story of the Colony. Fiction, 1880 –" in: *Southern African Literatures*. Published by University of KwaZulu Natal Press: Durban. 2003. pp. 129–133. Print.

_____. "Making a Literature: The Case of Namibia." *English in Africa* 22.2 (1995): 19–28. Web. Accessed on 26.08.2015.

Christopher, A. J. *The Atlas of Apartheid*. London: Routledge, 1994. Print.

Clegg, Brian, and Oliver Pugh. *Introducing Infinity: A Graphic Guide*. London: Icon, 2012. Print.

Coetzee, J. M., and David Attwell. *Doubling the Point: Essays and Interviews*. Cambridge, MA: Harvard University Press, 1992. Print.

Coetzee, J. M. *Dusklands*. London: Penguin, 1974. Print.

_____. *White Writing: On the Culture of Letters in South Africa*. New Haven: Yale University Press, 1988. Print.

Coleridge, Samuel Taylor. *The Poetical and Dramatic Works ... of Coleridge*. Boston: Crosby and Ainsworth, 1866. Print.

Comaroff, Jean and John L. Comaroff. "Naturing the Nation: Aliens, Apocalypse, and the Postcolonial State." *Journal of Southern African Studies* 27.3 (2001): 627–651. Print.

Colonel Neyland. Confidential report, dated 03.08.1905. In: *Correspondence re Campaigns against Natives in German South West Africa (1907)*. Box 4567, Western Cape Archives and Record Services, Cape Town. Print.

_____. Telegram, dated 28.12.1904. In: *Correspondence re Campaigns against Natives in German South West Africa (1907)*. Box 4567, Western Cape Archives and Record Services, Cape Town. Print.

Conrad, Joseph. *Heart of Darkness*. Edinburgh & London: Blackwood's Magazine, 1899. Print.

Cornevin, Robert, and Hans Jenny. *Geschichte Der Deutschen Kolonisation*. Goslar: H. Hübener, 1974. Print.

Dangarembga, Tsitsi. *Nervous Conditions: A Novel*. New York: Seal, 1989. Print.

Defoe, Daniel. *Robinson Crusoe*. London: W. Taylor. 1719. Print.

De Lange, Attie, Gail Fincham, Jeremy Hawthorn, and Jakob Lothe, eds. *Literary Landscapes: From Modernism to Postcolonialism*. Basingstoke: Palgrave Macmillan, 2008. Print.

Denison, Barbara J. *History, Time, Meaning, and Memory: Ideas for the Sociology of Religion*. Leiden: Brill, 2011. Print.

Dennerlein, Katrin. *Narratologie Des Raumes*. Berlin: De Gruyter, 2009. Print.

Diaz, Herbert Ndango. *A Definitive Edition and Analysis of the Tjakova Myth of the Vakavago*. Doctoral Thesis: University of Cape Town. 1992. Print.

Tink Diaz (Dir.). *Wir Hatten Eine Dora in Südwest*. EZEF, 1991. DVD.

Diescho, Joseph, and Celeste Wallin. *Born of the Sun: A Namibian Novel*. New York: Friendship, 2002 [1988]. Print.

Djomo, Esaïe. *Imperiale Kulturbegegnung Als Identitätsstiftungsprozess: Studien Zu Literatur, Kolonialität Und Postkolonialität*. St. Ingbert: Röhrig, 2011. Print.

Döring, Jörg, and Tristan Thielmann. *Spatial Turn: Das Raumparadigma in Den Kultur- Und Sozialwissenschaften*. Bielefeld: Transcript, 2008. Print.

Drechsler, Horst. "Die Eroberung Der Kolonien." *Drang Nach Afrika: Die Deutsche Koloniale Expansionspolitik Und Herrschaft in Afrika Von Den Anfängen Bis Zum Verlust Der Kolonien*. Ed. Eberhard Czaja and Horst Drechsler (eds.). 2nd ed. Berlin: Akademieverlag, 1991. 36–58. Print.

_____. *Südwestafrika Unter Deutscher Kolonialherrschaft. Der Kampf Der Herero Und Nama Gegen Den Deutschen Imperialismus*. Berlin: Akademie-Verlag, 1966. Print.

Dünne, Jörg, and Stephan Günzel, eds. *Raumtheorie. Grundlagentexte Aus Philosophie Und Kulturwissenschaften*. Frankfurt Am Main: Suhrkamp, 2006. Print.

Dyer, Richard. *White: Essays on Race and Culture*. Hove: Psychology Press. 1997. Print.

El-Tayeb, Fatima. *Schwarze Deutsche: Der Diskurs Um "Rasse" Und Nationale Identität 1890–1933*. Frankfurt/Main: Campus, 2001. Print.

Förster, Larissa. *Postkoloniale Erinnerungslandschaften: Wie Deutsche Und Herero in Namibia Des Kriegs Von 1904 Gedenken*. Frankfurt, M.: Campus-Verl., 2010. Print.

Förster, Larissa, Dag Henrichsen, and Michael Bollig, eds. *Namibia-Deutschland, Eine Geteilte Geschichte: Widerstand, Gewalt, Erinnerung*. Wolfratshausen: Edition Minerva, 2004. Print.

Foucault, Michel, and Jay Miskowiec. "Of Other Spaces: Utopias and Heterotopias" in: *Architecture/ Movement/ Continuité*. March 1967/October 1984. 1–11. Print.

Foucault, Michel, and Alan Sheridan. *Discipline and Punish: The Birth of the Prison*. London: Penguin, 1977. Print.

Foucault, Michel. *The History of Sexuality*. London: Allen Lane, 1978. Print.

_____. *Madness and Civilization; a History of Insanity in the Age of Reason*. New York: Pantheon, 1965. Print.

Frankenberg, Ruth. *White Women, Race Matters: The Social Constructedness of Whiteness*. Abingdon & New York: Routledge. 1993. Print.

Frenssen, Gustav. *Peter Moors Fahrt Nach Südwest, Ein Feldzugsbericht*. Berlin: G. Grote'sche Verlagsbuchhandlung, 1906. Print.

Frye, Northrop. "Introduction" in: Michael Dolzani (ed). *Collected Works of Northrop Frye*. Vol. 15. Toronto: University of Toronto, 2004. xxi–lviii. Print.

Fuhrmann, Malte. *Der Traum Vom Deutschen Orient: Zwei Deutsche Kolonien Im Osmanischen Reich 1851–1918*. Frankfurt Am Main: Campus, 2006. Print.

Gallois, William. *Time, Religion and History*. Harlow, England: Pearson Longman, 2007. Print.

Gevisser, Mark, and Edwin Cameron. *Defiant Desire: Gay and Lesbian Lives in South Africa*. New York: Routledge, 1994. Print.

Gilroy, Paul. *The Black Atlantic: Modernity and Double-Consciousness*. Massachusetts: Harvard UP, 1995. Print.

_____. *Small Acts: Thoughts on the Politics of Black Cultures*. London: Serpent's Tail, 1993. Print.

Goodman, Nelson. *Ways of Worldmaking*. Indianapolis: Hackett Publishers, 1978. Print.

Gordimer, Nadine. "Great Problems in the Street" in: Clingman, Stephen (ed.). *The Essential Gesture: Writing, Politics and Places*. Harmondsworth: Penguin Books. 1988. pp. 52–57. Print.

"Government Condemns KKK 'glorification'." *New Era*. 2 July 2015. Web. Accessed on 5.07.2015.

Grimm, Hans. *Volk Ohne Raum*. Munich: Albert Langen, 1926. Print.

Haarhoff, Dorian. *The Wild South-West: Frontier Myths and Metaphors in Literature Set in Namibia, 1760–1988*. Johannesburg: Witwatersrand UP, 1991. Print.

Hahn, Carl Hugo. *Lüderitzland und Sieben Begebemhieten*. München: Albert Langen. 1934. Print.

Haggard, H. Rider. *King Solomon's Mines*. New York: F.M. Lupton, 1885. Print.

_____. *She: A History of Adventure*. London: Longmans, Green & Co. 1887. Print.

Hamann, Ulrike. *Prekäre Koloniale Ordnung Rassistischen Konjunkturen Im Widerspruch. Deutsches Kolonialregime 1884–1914*. Bielefeld: Transcript, 2015. Print.

Hayes, Patricia. "'When You Shake a Tree'. The Precolonial and the Postcolonial in Northern Namibian History". In: *Recasting the Past. History Writing and Political Work in Modern Africa*. Peterson, Derek R., Giacomo Macola (eds.). Ohio University Press: Athens. 2009. pg. 75–94. Print

Hegel, Georg Wilhelm Friedrich, and J. Sibree. *The Philosophy of History*. New York: Dover Publications, 1956. Print.

Heinisch, Klaus Joachim., Thomas More, Tommaso Campanella, and Francis Bacon. *Der Utopische Staat*. Reinbek Bei Hamburg: Rowohlt, 1983. Print.

Henrichsen, Dag. *Herrschaft Und Alltag Im Vorkolonialen Zentralnamibia: Das Herero Und Damaraland Im 19. Jahrhundert*. Basel, Switzerland: Basler Afrika Bibliographien, 2011. Print.

Heuner, Ulf. "Introduction" in: *Klassische Texte Zum Raum*. Berlin: Parodos Verl., 2006. Print.

Hoffmann, Annette. *'Since the Germans Came It Rains Less': Landscape and Identity of Herero Communities in Namibia. PhD thesis*. University of Amsterdam, 2005. Print.

Ingold, Tim. "The Temporality of the Landscape." *World Archaeology* 25.2 (1993): 152–74. Web. Accessed on: 02.02.2016.

iconic. "Hendrik Verwoerd Defines Apartheid". Online video clip. Youtube. Youtube, Dec 10, 2010. Web. Accessed on 15.07.2016.

Jenkins, Geoffrey. *A Twist of Sand, A Novel*. Bloomington: Author's Choice Press.1959 (2009). Print.

Jureit, Ulrike. *Das Ordnen Von Räumen: Territorium Und Lebensraum Im 19. Und 20. Jahrhundert*. Hamburg: Hamburger Edition, HIS, 2012. Print.

Kachipande, Sitinga. "Ghana's Dubious Decolonization Distinction – The First Independent African Country". www.africaontheblog.com. Accessed on: 15.05.2016.

Keil, Thomas. *Die postkoloniale deutsche Literatur in Namibia (1920 – 2000)*. Dissertation (University of Stuttgart). http//dx.doi.org/10.18419/opus-5230. Web. Accessed on 01.10.1015.

Kleinau, Elke. "Das Eigene und das Fremde. Frauen und ihr Beitrag zum kolonialen Diskurs". Lohmann, Ingrid, and Ingrid Gogolin, eds. *Die Kultivierung Der Medien: Erziehungs- Und Sozialwissenschaftliche Beiträge*. Opladen: Leske Budrich, 2000. 201–218. Print.

Knapp, Adrian. *The Past Coming to Roost in the Present Historicising History in Four Post apartheid South African Novels*. Stuttgart (DE): Ibidem-Verlag, 2006. Print.

Kraze, Friede H. *Heim Neuland: Ein Roman von der Wasserkante und aus Deutsch- Südwest*. Stuttgart: Deutsche Verlagsanstalt, 1908. Print.

Kul-Want, Christopher, and Piero. *Introducing Continental Philosophy. A Graphic Guide.* London: Icon, 2013. Print.

Lefebvre, Henri, and Donnald Nicholson-Smith. *The Production of Space.* Oxford, OX, UK: Blackwell, 1991. Print.

Lem, Stanisław, and Michael Kandel. *Highcastle: A Remembrance.* New York: Harcourt, Brace. 1966/1995. Print.

Leutwein, Theodor. *Deutsch-Süd-West-Afrika: Mit Einer Karte.* Berlin: n.p., 1898. Print.

Lorde, Audre. "Litany of Survival" in: *The Black Unicorn: Poems.* London & New York: W.W. Norton. 1995. Print.

Mamozai, Martha. "Einheimische und 'koloniale' Frauen" in: Marianne Bechhaus-Gerst, Mechthild Leutner (eds). *Frauen in den deutschen Kolonien*, Ch. Links Verlag, Berlin 2009. 14–31. Print.

Maus, Derek. "Kneeling before the Fathers' Wand: Violence, Eroticism and Paternalism in Thomas Pynchon's V. and J.M. Coetzee's Dusklands". *Journal of Literary Studies* 15.12 (1999): 195–217. Web. Accessed on 16.03.2015.

Marais, M. "Looking Backward to the 'new South Africa' – J.M. Coetzee's Exploration of the Protocols of Travel Writing". *Literator* 15.1 (1994): 21–32. Web. Accessed on 12.02.2014.

_____. "'Omnipotent Fantasies' of a Solitary Self: J.M. Coetzee's 'The Narrative of Jacobus Coetzee'". *The Journal of Commonwealth Literature* 28.2 (1993): 48–65. Web. Accessed on 16.03.2014.

Mbembe, A. "Necropolitics." *Public Culture* 15.1 (2003): 11–40. Web. Accessed on 20.10.2015.

_____ "African Modes of Self-Writing". 2002. http://calternatives.org. Accessed on 26.01.2016.

McCann, Eugene J. "Race, Protest, and Public Space: Contextualizing Lefebvre in the U.S. City." *Antipode* 31.2 (1999): 163–84. Web. Accessed 05.05.2014.

McClintock, Anne. *Imperial Leather: Race, Gender, and Sexuality in the Colonial Contest.* New York: Routledge, 1995. Print.

Melville, Herman. *Moby Dick.* London: Richard Bentley, 1851. Print.

Memmi, Albert and Howard Greenfeld. *The Colonizer and the Colonized.* London & New York: Earthscan, 1965/2003. Print.

Meyn, Rolf. "Abstecher in die Kolonialliteratur. Gustav Frenssens *Peter Moors nach Südwest*" in: Donhnke, Kay und Dietrich Stein (eds.). *Gustav Frenssen in seiner Zeit. Von* der Massenliteratur im Kaiserreich zur Massenideologie im NS-Staat. Heide: Boyens. 1997. Print.

Morrison, Toni. "Black Matter" in: *Playing in the Dark: Whiteness and the Literary Imagination*. Massachusetts: Harvard UP, 1992. 1–29. Print.

Motyl, Alexander J. *Encyclopedia of Nationalism: Leaders, Movements, and Concepts*. Vol. 2. San Diego, CA: Academic, 2001. Print.

Mudimbe, V. Y. *The Invention of Africa: Gnosis, Philosophy, and the Order of Knowledge*. Bloomington: Indiana UP, 1988. Print.

Nampa. "Media Ombudsman Says Küska Photos Not Offensive." *The Namibian*. 11 July 2015. Web. Accessed on 11.07.2015.

Noyes, John K. *Colonial Space: Spatiality in the Discourse of German South West Africa 1884–1915*. Chur, Switzerland: Harwood Academic, 1992. Print.

Nujoma, Samuel D. "Speech by Sam Nujoma, President of SWAPO to the Namibian Consultation, 19–21 June, 1988, Stockholm". Namibian National Archives. 1–9. Print.

_____. "Statement By His Excellency President Sam Nujoma on the occasion of the official inauguration of Heroes' Acre 26 August 2002". http://www.namibia1on1.com/a-central/heroes-acre-2.html. Accessed on 25.05.2016. Web.

Odendaal, F. H. *Verslag Van Die Kommissie Van Ondersoek Na Aangeleenthede Van* Suid-wes-Afrika: 1962–1963 = Report of the Commission of Enquiry into South West

Africa Affairs: 1962–1963 = Report of the Commission of Enquiry into South West Africa Affairs. Pretoria: Staatsdrukker, 1964. Print.

O'Sullivan, Simon. "Art Practice as Fictioning (or myth-science). (2014). www.simonosullivan.net. Accessed on 01.07.2016. Web.

Parry, Benita. "Speech and Silence in the Fictions of J. M. Coetzee." *Critical Perspectives on J.M. Coetzee* (1996): 37–65. Web. Accessed on 15.03. 2015.

Piatti, Barbara. *Die Geographie Der Literatur: Schauplätze, Handlungsräume, Raumphantasien*. Göttingen: Wallstein, 2008. Print.

Piesche, Peggy. "Der 'Fortschritt der Aufklärung – Kants 'Race' und die Zentrierung des *weißen* Subjekts" in: Eggers, Maureen Maisha., Grada Kilomba, Peggy Piesche, and Susan Arndt. *Mythen, Masken Und Subjekte: Kritische Weißseinsforschung in Deutschland*. Münster: Unrast, 2009. Print.

Pratt, Mary Louise. *Imperial Eyes: Mary Louise Pratt*. London: New York, 1991. Print.

Pynchon, Thomas. *V., a Novel*. Philadelphia: Lippincott, 1963. Print.

_____. *Gravity's Rainbow*. New York: Viking, 1973. Print.

Quayson, Ato. *The Cambridge Companion to the Postcolonial Novel*. Cambridge: Cambridge University Press. 2016. Print.

_____. *Postcolonialism: Theory, Practice or Process?* Oxford: Blackwell. 2000. Print.

Rasmussen, Birgit Brander, Eric Klinenberg, Irene J. Nexica, and Matt Wray (eds). "Introduction" in: *The Making and Unmaking of Whiteness*. Durham, NC: Duke UP, 2001. 1–24. Print.

Reagin, Nancy. "The Imagined Hausfrau: National Identity, Domesticity, and Colonialism in Imperial Germany." *The Journal of Modern History* 73.1 (2001): 54–86. Web. Accessed on 25.11.2015.

Reeh, Günther. *Hendrik Witbooi, Ein Leben Für Die Freiheit: Zwischen Glaube Und Zweifel*. Köln: Köppe, 2000. Print.

"Report on Consultation between SWAPO and the Representatives of the White Community of Namibia" from June 19–21, 1988 in Stockholm. Namibian National Archives. 1–7. Print.

Report on the Natives of South-west Africa and Their Treatment by Germany. London: H.M. Stationery Office. 1918. Print.

Riruako, Kuaima. "Das Leiden des Hererovolkes unter den Deutschen" in: *1884–1984. Vom Schutzgebiet bis Namibia*. Klaus Becker, Jürgen Hecker (eds.). Hannover: Schäder Th. 1985. pg. 247&248. Print.

Rose, Andreas. *Deutsche Aussenpolitik in Der Ära Bismarck: (1862–1890)*. Darmstadt: Wissenschaftliche Buchgesellschaft, 2013. Print.

Said, Edward W. "Empire, Geography, and Culture." in: *Culture and Imperialism*. New York: Knopf. 1993. pp. 3–15. Print.

_____. "Introduction." in: *Orientalism*. New York: Vintage, 1979. 1–28. Print.

Salván, Paula Martín. "Topographies of Blankness in J.M. Coetzee's Fiction". Odisea 9 (2009): 145–153. Print.

Sarkin-Hughes, Jeremy. *Germany's Genocide of the Herero: Kaiser Wilhelm II, His General, His Settlers, His Soldiers*. Cape Town, South Africa: UCT, 2011. Print.

Schmidt, Sigrid. *Tricksters, Monsters and Clever Girls. African Folktales – Texts and Discussions*. Rüdiger Köppe Verlag: Köln. 2001. Print.

Schneider-Waterberg, H. R. *Der Wahrheit Eine Gasse: Beiträge Zum Hererokrieg in Deutschsüdwestafrika, 1904–1907*. Swakopmund: Wissenschaftliche Gesellschaft Swakopmund, 2012. Print.

Schönauer, Matts. "Die Einfallsreichen Ku-Klux-Karnevalisten." Web log post. *BILDblog*. VICE Digital, 10 July 2015. Web. Accessed on 12.07.2015.

Selmeci, Andreas, and Dag Henrichsen. *Das Schwarzkommando: Thomas Pynchon Und Die Geschichte Der Herero*. Bielefeld: Aisthesis Verlag, 1995. Print.

Sienaert, Marilet & Stiebel, Lindy. "Writing on the earth: Early European travellers to South Africa". In: Literator 17(1). Published by AOSIS Publishing: Durbanville. April 1996: 91–101. Print.

Simmel, Georg. *Soziologie. Untersuchungen über Die Formen Der Vergesellschaftung*. Leipzig: Duncker & Humblot, 1908. Print.

Slowik, Edward, "Descartes' Physics", *The Stanford Encyclopedia of Philosophy* (Summer 2014 Edition), Edward N. Zalta (ed.), URL = <http://plato.stanford.edu/archives/sum2014/entries/descartes-physics/>. Accessed on 15.07.1015.

Smith, David. "Lüderitz v !Nami≠nüs: Dispute over Town's Name Divides Namibia." *The Guardian*. Guardian News and Media Limited, 26 Feb. 2015. Web. Accessed on 30.06.2015

Soja, Edward W. *Postmodern Geographies: The Reassertion of Space in Critical Social Theory*. London: Verso, 1989. Print.

Soyinka, Wole. *Death and the King's Horseman*. New York: W. W. Norton, 1994. Print.

Steenkamp, Philip. "The Churches." In: *Namibia's Liberation Struggle: The Double-Edged Sword*. Ed. Colin Leys and John S. Saul. Athens: Ohio UP, 1995. 94–114 . Print.

Stiebel, Lindy. *Imagining Africa: Landscape in H. Rider Haggard's African Romances*. Westport, CT: Greenwood, 2001. Print.

Stockhammer, Robert. *Die Kartierung Der Erde: Macht Und Lust in Karten Und Literatur*. München: W. Fink, 2007. Print.

Stotesbury, John A. "The Function of Borders in the Popular Novel on South Africa." *English in Africa* 17.2 (1990): 71–89. Web. Accessed on 12.03.2014.

_____. "Passages to Nowhere? Transition in South African Popular Fiction." *Current Research on Peace and Violence* 12.1 (1989): 38–42. Web. Accessed on 12.03.2014.

Tinsley, O. N. "Black Atlantic, Queer Atlantic: Queer Imaginings of the Middle Passage." *GLQ:A Journal of Lesbian and Gay Studies* 14.2-3 (2008): 191–215. Web. Accessed on 12.05.2015.

Tjihenuna, Gerson Uaripi. "Cry The Land Between Two Deserts" in: Melber, Henning. *It Is No More a Cry: Namibian Poetry in Exile*. Basel: Basler Afrika Bibliographien, 1982. Print.

Thiel, Gudrun. "The Diamond Novels of Luderitz: Fact or Fiction?" *Literator* 9.3 (1988): 44–60. Web. Accessed on 13.02.2014.

Tröndle, Rainer. *Gewisse Ungewissheiten: Überlegungen Zum Krieg Der Herero Gegen Die Deutschen, Insbesondere Zu Den Ereignissen Am Waterberg Und Danach*. Windhoek: Namibia Wissenschaftliche Gesellschaft. 2012. Print.

Tuan, Yi-fu. *Space and Place: The Perspective of Experience*. Minneapolis: University of Minnesota, 1977. Print.

Verne, Jules. *Twenty Thousand Leagues under the Sea*. London: George Routledge, 1876. Print.

Wallace, Marion, and John Kinahan. *A History of Namibia: From the Beginning to 1990*. New York: Columbia UP, 2011. Print

Walgenbach, Katharina. "Weiße Identität und Geschlecht" in: Rehberg, Karl-Siegbert (ed.). *Soziale Ungleichheit, kulturelle Unterschiede: Verhandlungen des 32. Kongresses der Deutschen Gesellschaft für Soziologie in München. Teilbd. 1 und 2*. Frankfurt am Main: Campus Verlag. 2006. 1705–1717. Print.

Ward, Margaret May. *Peter Moor: A Narrative of the German Campaign in South-West Africa*. London: Constable & Company, 1908. Print.

Watson, Stephen. "Colonialism and the Novels of J. M. Coetzee." *Critical Perspectives on J. M. Coetzee* (1996): 13–36. Web. Accessed on 15.03.2015.

Watt, Ian. *The Rise of the Novel: Studies in Defoe, Richardson, and Fielding*. Berkeley: U of California, 1957. Print.

Weicker, Anna, and Ingrid Jokob. "Afrika" in: Arndt, Susan, and Nadja Ofuatey-Alazard. *Wie Rassismus Aus Wörtern Spricht: (K)Erben Des Kolonialismus Im Wissensarchiv Deutsche Sprache: Ein Kritisches Nachschlagewerk*. Münster: Unrast Verlag, 2011. Print.

Westerlind, Marianne. *Du Heiliges Land!: Roman Aus Den Diamantfeldern Südwestafrikas*. Hamburg: Broschek, 1914. Print.

Wildenthal, Lora. "'She is the Victor':Bourgeois Women, Nationalist Identities and the Ideal of the Independent Woman Farmer in German Southwest Africa" in: Social Analysis 33 (1993): 68–88. Web. Accessed on 07.06.2015.

Witbooi, Hendrik, Annemarie Heywood, Eben Maasdorp, and Brigitte Lau. *The Hendrik Witbooi Papers*. Windhoek: National Archives of Namibia, 1989. Print.

Wood, Denis, and John Fels. *The Power of Maps*. New York: Guilford, 1992. Print.

Yancy, George. *What White Looks Like: African-American Philosophers on the Whiteness Question*. New York: Routledge, 2004. Print.

Yekani, Elahe Haschemi. *The Privilege of Crisis: Narratives of Masculinities in Colonial and Postcolonial Literature, Photography, and Film*. Frankurt Am Main: Campus Verlag GmbH, 2011. Print.

Young, Robert J.C. *White Mythologies. Writing History and the West.* Abingdon & New-York: Routledge. 1990. Print.

_____. "Foucault on Race and Colonialism". 1995. http://robertjcyoung.com/Foucault.pdf. Web.

Index

A

Africanist 6, 18, 20, 21, 22, 25, 33, 62, 84, 95, 128, 130, 178, 198, 202, 249, 256, 267
apartheid 1, 2, 4, 5, 6, 10, 13, 14, 19, 20, 21, 22, 23, 24, 25, 29, 30, 31, 33, 34, 37, 39, 62, 67,
    68, 69, 78, 84, 86, 152, 153, 154, 155, 156, 157, 158, 159, 160, 165, 166, 167, 169,
    170, 174, 175, 179, 181, 183, 184, 186, 196, 197, 198, 199, 200, 201, 202, 204, 205,
    206, 207, 211, 212, 213, 217, 218, 221, 222, 224, 225, 227, 229, 234, 235, 237, 239,
    242, 244, 255, 257, 258, 262, 263, 264, 266, 267, 269
A Twist of Sand 12, 20, 33, 62, 75, 82, 159, 161, 162, 163, 165, 166, 173, 179, 184, 188, 191,
    250, 251, 252, 255, 256, 266, 267

B

Born of the Sun 6, 33, 69, 79, 82, 84, 197, 198, 200, 202, 239, 264, 265, 266, 269
Brockmann 15, 18, 96, 97, 136, 138, 143, 145, 254

C

chronotope 13, 14, 26, 39, 40, 73, 78, 79, 203
Coetzee 12, 13, 21, 30, 33, 37, 40, 46, 47, 56, 69, 70, 77, 79, 82, 105, 111, 118, 122, 123,
    124, 126, 130, 136, 151, 159, 160, 161, 162, 163, 164, 166, 168, 169, 170, 171, 172,
    173, 175, 177, 178, 184, 185, 186, 187, 190, 191, 192, 193, 194, 195, 209, 235, 247,
    248, 249, 250, 251, 252, 255, 256, 261, 262, 263, 266, 267, 268
colonialism 4, 5, 7, 8, 12, 22, 25, 49, 51, 54, 70, 74, 85, 90, 137, 152, 153, 154, 156, 160,
    185, 198, 203, 205, 230, 233, 257, 265, 269

D

Du heiliges Land! 18, 32, 50, 68, 82, 83, 92, 94, 96, 97, 98, 116, 119, 120, 131, 143, 145,
    151, 251, 256, 263, 266, 267, 269
Du heiliges Land! Roman aus den Diamantfeldern Südwestafrikas... 18

E

Europe 7, 8, 18, 20, 30, 48, 51, 55, 59, 71, 72, 89, 90, 118, 123, 125, 183, 192, 202, 219,
    221, 265
European 1, 4, 5, 6, 7, 8, 16, 18, 20, 21, 22, 23, 26, 31, 32, 33, 38, 40, 45, 48, 55, 60, 62, 67,
    68, 70, 71, 72, 77, 84, 86, 89, 90, 99, 101, 109, 113, 114, 115, 118, 122, 123, 125,
    131, 132, 137, 138, 139, 141, 149, 150, 152, 153, 166, 167, 171, 172, 174, 181, 183,
    190, 192, 197, 200, 202, 210, 212, 217, 218, 219, 222, 228, 229, 233, 237, 243, 259,
    265, 270

F

fictioning 4, 6, 10, 14, 15, 79, 132, 158, 268, 269

G

garden 33, 54, 91, 92, 95, 96, 97, 98, 109, 110, 111, 122, 123, 124, 125, 126, 127, 128, 129, 130, 131, 132, 133, 134, 135, 136, 137, 138, 139, 140, 142, 144, 151, 249, 259
genocide 1, 8, 17, 48, 86, 88, 89, 119, 138, 230, 231, 233, 234, 240
German 1, 2, 3, 7, 8, 10, 14, 16, 17, 18, 19, 20, 21, 23, 27, 45, 50, 54, 56, 67, 85, 86, 87, 88, 89, 90, 91, 92, 93, 94, 95, 96, 97, 99, 100, 101, 102, 103, 104, 105, 106, 109, 111, 113, 115, 118, 119, 120, 121, 122, 123, 124, 125, 127, 128, 130, 131, 132, 135, 137, 138, 139, 140, 141, 142, 143, 144, 145, 146, 147, 148, 149, 150, 151, 152, 155, 156, 158, 161, 166, 170, 196, 219, 220, 223, 224, 226, 227, 228, 229, 232, 233, 240, 243, 250, 255, 258, 259, 260, 265
German South West Africa 3, 152
Germany 3, 4, 5, 8, 9, 10, 17, 18, 25, 39, 68, 69, 85, 86, 87, 88, 93, 95, 97, 102, 103, 106, 113, 117, 119, 121, 131, 133, 136, 137, 138, 142, 143, 144, 148, 150, 151, 152, 155, 163, 196, 230, 231, 251, 256, 258
GSWA 3, 7, 8, 10, 15, 16, 17, 18, 20, 21, 34, 44, 51, 75, 83, 85, 86, 87, 89, 90, 92, 93, 94, 96, 97, 100, 101, 102, 103, 104, 105, 106, 108, 117, 119, 120, 125, 127, 132, 133, 134, 135, 136, 140, 144, 145, 150, 151, 152, 153, 156, 159, 166, 172, 201, 219, 223, 224, 226, 228, 231, 245, 247, 250, 251, 255, 256, 257, 259, 263

H

Heim Neuland 8, 14, 17, 19, 20, 32, 54, 62, 68, 69, 75, 82, 83, 90, 92, 93, 96, 97, 105, 106, 108, 109, 110, 113, 120, 124, 126, 137, 142, 143, 146, 151, 178, 209, 249, 251, 252, 254, 256, 258, 263, 266, 267, 269
Heim Neuland. Ein Roman von der Wasserkante und aus Deutsch-Südwest 17
Herero 1, 2, 3, 8, 16, 17, 23, 30, 45, 60, 86, 87, 88, 89, 93, 94, 97, 98, 101, 102, 103, 105, 106, 114, 119, 120, 148, 196, 204, 210, 218, 219, 220, 221, 222, 223, 226, 227, 228, 229, 230, 231, 232, 233, 234, 235, 239, 240, 241, 242, 243, 244, 246, 252, 256, 266

I

imagination 5, 11, 12, 14, 25, 28, 33, 80, 81, 104, 130, 132, 134, 147, 199
imagine 6, 104, 141, 171, 177, 211, 221

L

landscape 3, 6, 13, 14, 15, 16, 17, 20, 21, 26, 27, 28, 29, 32, 33, 40, 44, 45, 48, 51, 69, 83, 90, 92, 95, 96, 98, 99, 101, 102, 103, 104, 105, 106, 108, 109, 110, 116, 117, 118, 125, 126, 131, 132, 133, 135, 136, 137, 141, 146, 147, 151, 158, 159, 160, 164, 165, 170, 171, 172, 173, 174, 175, 177, 178, 179, 185, 187, 188, 190, 192, 194, 197, 223, 228, 247, 249, 256, 261, 262, 266, 268, 269, 270
Liberation Struggle 154
literature 3, 4, 6, 7, 10, 11, 12, 13, 14, 15, 19, 20, 22, 23, 24, 26, 30, 31, 32, 33, 36, 37, 38, 39, 40, 55, 62, 67, 68, 73, 74, 75, 76, 78, 80, 82, 86, 89, 90, 92, 94, 105, 109, 112, 137, 145, 147, 151, 156, 158, 159, 160, 161, 165, 166, 168, 171, 178, 197, 198, 199, 202, 225, 255

M

metropole 5, 6, 9, 10, 14, 16, 25, 34, 45, 49, 50, 62, 69, 73, 74, 80, 91, 95, 96, 100, 103, 109, 116, 118, 121, 125, 128, 131, 132, 134, 136, 140, 141, 142, 143, 146, 164, 172, 178, 185, 186, 187, 188, 195, 204, 205, 213, 251, 256, 258, 259, 260, 261, 262, 264, 265, 266, 267, 269
myth 15, 21, 29, 30, 67, 68, 80, 92, 116, 135, 156, 180, 188, 195, 224, 225, 249, 250, 263, 265, 266, 269

N

Nama 1, 2, 3, 8, 17, 21, 24, 86, 88, 89, 98, 114, 120, 168, 172, 192, 204, 218, 219, 221, 224, 225, 226, 230, 231, 232, 234, 239, 241, 245, 246, 266
Namibia 2, 3, 4, 5, 9, 16, 23, 24, 33, 34, 37, 70, 75, 82, 85, 86, 87, 88, 89, 120, 131, 154, 160, 168, 170, 179, 190, 196, 197, 198, 199, 200, 201, 212, 218, 219, 220, 223, 226, 230, 231, 233, 241, 242, 245, 260, 269
narrative 2, 5, 6, 12, 13, 15, 16, 17, 18, 19, 20, 21, 28, 37, 39, 40, 44, 45, 47, 49, 56, 74, 77, 78, 79, 80, 81, 82, 83, 84, 91, 93, 96, 97, 98, 99, 101, 105, 107, 112, 113, 126, 128, 141, 145, 161, 162, 163, 164, 165, 166, 168, 169, 171, 172, 173, 175, 176, 178, 180, 183, 185, 188, 189, 191, 192, 194, 195, 198, 199, 201, 202, 222, 237, 248, 250, 254, 258, 261, 262, 264, 265, 267, 268, 269

O

Owambo 1, 23, 105, 149, 154, 200, 204, 234

P

Peter Moor 8, 12, 14, 16, 17, 19, 20, 30, 32, 44, 45, 56, 62, 69, 82, 86, 87, 90, 92, 93, 95, 96, 97, 98, 99, 100, 101, 102, 103, 104, 105, 106, 107, 108, 114, 117, 119, 120, 123, 124, 125, 135, 138, 139, 140, 141, 143, 144, 146, 151, 159, 163, 165, 170, 178, 179, 189, 209, 247, 249, 250, 251, 252, 254, 256, 258, 259, 263, 266, 267, 268
Peter Moors Fahrt nach Südwest 16, 62
postcolonial 1, 4, 78, 86, 87, 244

R

race 22, 29, 35, 55, 61, 66, 67, 70, 79, 89, 113, 114, 116, 138, 139, 148, 150, 151, 152, 159, 216, 242, 243, 247
resistance 2, 3, 4, 5, 6, 34, 69, 151, 192, 197, 198, 199, 202, 204, 212, 214, 215, 219, 220, 227, 229, 230, 231, 234, 236, 240, 241, 243, 246, 249, 263, 264, 265
  immaterial 219

S

South Africa 2, 4, 5, 10, 11, 19, 20, 21, 23, 24, 25, 33, 37, 67, 68, 85, 103, 104, 151, 152, 153, 154, 155, 156, 157, 159, 160, 161, 164, 165, 166, 168, 169, 170, 171, 175, 182, 183, 196, 198, 199, 202, 203, 212, 213, 215, 230, 236, 239, 242, 263, 265, 269
South West Africa 3, 11, 54, 69, 86, 161, 196, 199, 200, 203, 212, 241

SWA 3, 10, 11, 16, 19, 20, 33, 39, 70, 75, 85, 86, 152, 153, 154, 155, 156, 158, 163, 165, 170, 172, 201, 202, 211, 232, 242, 258, 263, 270

T

The Production of Space 9, 35, 58

W

war 16, 17, 45, 52, 54, 82, 88, 91, 92, 93, 94, 95, 96, 97, 99, 101, 102, 103, 104, 105, 106, 107, 110, 113, 114, 115, 116, 117, 119, 120, 121, 124, 126, 128, 133, 134, 135, 141, 142, 146, 147, 148, 160, 161, 181, 196, 200, 219, 220, 221, 222, 225, 226, 228, 229, 230, 231, 232, 233, 234, 239, 241, 249, 250, 253, 254, 258, 259, 263, 266

whiteness 14, 18, 22, 29, 30, 32, 33, 41, 67, 80, 82, 83, 90, 91, 92, 97, 113, 114, 115, 116, 129, 142, 143, 145, 147, 148, 150, 151, 160, 163, 164, 170, 178, 183, 188, 190, 208, 248, 249, 256, 257, 261, 262, 263, 265, 266, 267, 268, 269

www.ingramcontent.com/pod-product-compliance
Lightning Source LLC
Chambersburg PA
CBHW060418300426
44111CB00018B/2898